ANNUAL EDITIONS

W9-BWS-900

Human Development

07/08

Thirty-fifth Edition

EDITOR

Karen L. Freiberg

University of Maryland, Baltimore County

Dr. Karen Freiberg has an interdisciplinary educational and employment background in nursing, education, and developmental psychology. She received her B.S. from the State University of New York at Plattsburgh, her M.S. from Cornell University, and her Ph.D. from Syracuse University. Dr. Freiberg has worked as a school nurse, a pediatric nurse, a public health nurse for the Navajo Indians, an associate project director for a child development clinic, a researcher in several areas of child development, and a university professor. She is the author of an award-winning textbook, *Human Development: A Life-Span Approach*, which is now in its fourth edition. Dr. Freiberg is currently on the faculty at the University of Maryland, Baltimore County.

McGraw Hill **Contemporary Learning Series**

2460 Kerper Blvd., Dubuque, IA 52001

Visit us on the Internet
http://www.mhcls.com

Credits

1. **Genetic and Prenatal Influences on Development**
   Unit photo—Brand X Pictures/PunchStock
2. **Development During Infancy and Early Childhood**
   Unit photo—Skip Nall/Getty Images
3. **Development During Childhood: Cognition and Schooling**
   Unit photo—Dynamic Graphics/Jupiter Images
4. **Development During Childhood: Family and Culture**
   Unit photo—Royalty Free/CORBIS
5. **Development During Adolescence and Young Adulthood**
   Unit photo—Digital Vision
6. **Development During Middle and Late Adulthood**
   Unit photo—Royalty Free/CORBIS

Copyright

ing in Publication Data
ry under title: Annual Editions: Human Development. 2007/2008.
Development—Periodicals. I. Freiberg, Karen L., *comp*. II. Title: Human Development.
)78-0-07-351615-8   ISBN-10: 0-07-351615-5   658'.05   ISSN 0278-4661

cGraw-Hill Contemporary Learning Series, Dubuque, IA 52001, A Division of The McGraw-Hill Companies.

/Jupiterimages and IT Stock/Punch Stock.
of America   1234567890QPDQPD9876   Printed on Recycled Paper

Editors/Advisory Board

Members of the Advisory Board are instrumental in the final selection of articles for each edition of ANNUAL EDITIONS. Their review of articles for content, level, currentness, and appropriateness provides critical direction to the editor and staff. We think that you will find their careful consideration well reflected in this volume.

Preface

In publishing ANNUAL EDITIONS we recognize the enormous role played by the magazines, newspapers, and journals of the public press in providing current, first-rate educational information in a broad spectrum of interest areas. Many of these articles are appropriate for students, researchers, and professionals seeking accurate, current material to help bridge the gap between principles and theories and the real world. These articles, however, become more useful for study when those of lasting value are carefully collected, organized, indexed, and reproduced in a low-cost format, which provides easy and permanent access when the material is needed. That is the role played by ANNUAL EDITIONS.

The development of the human species has had dramatic help from scientific research and technology in the last decade. Nevertheless, humans still struggle with the effects of stress, overeating, and underexercising on physical processes. Stress, peer conformity, and unchallenging work, among other things, stifle much human cognitive expansion. Human social and emotional advancements are stymied by the primordial quest for power, carrying in its wake the complementary quests for material possessions and sexual prominence. How far can scientific advances and technological progress go toward improving life-span human growth and change? Many people around the globe give lip service to downsizing, seeking inner peace, and living more fulfilling, environmentally friendly, loving lives. Do you see it happening around you? How has the development of the human species been impacted by the 21st millennium?

This compendium of articles about human development covers the life span, considering physical, cognitive, and psychosocial components. Development should be viewed as a circle of life. Conception begins each new human being, but each unique individual carries genetic materials from biological relatives alive and dead.

Development through infancy proceeds from sensory and motor responses to verbal communication, thinking, conceptualizing, and learning from others. Childhood brings rapid physical growth, improved cognition, and social learning. Adolescence is when the individual begins to test out sexual maturity. Values and identity are questioned. Separation from parents begins. Under the influence of sex hormones the brain undergoes multiple changes. Emotions may fluctuate rapidly.

Early adulthood usually establishes the individual as an independent person. Employment, further education, the beginning of one's own family are all aspects of setting up a distinct life, with both its own characteristics and the characteristics and customs of previous generations.

During middle adulthood persons have new situations to face, new transitions with which to cope. Children grow up and leave home. Signs of aging become apparent. Relationships change, roles shift. New abilities may be found and opportunities created.

Finally, during late adulthood, people assess what they've accomplished. Some are pleased. Some feel they could have done more or lived differently. In the best of instances, individuals accept who they are and are comfortable with themselves.

As you explore this anthology, you will discover that many articles ask questions that have no answers. As a student, I felt frustrated by such writing. I wanted answers, right answers, right away. However, over time I learned that lessons that are necessary to acquire maturity include accepting relativity and acknowledging extenuating circumstances. Life frequently has no right or wrong answers, but rather various alternatives with multiple consequences. Instead of right versus wrong, a more helpful consideration is "What will bring about the greater good for the greater number?" Controversies, whether about terrorism or war, good or evil, stem cells or organ transplants, body-soul separated or unified, can promote healthy discussions. Different viewpoints should be weighed against societal standards. Different philosophies should be celebrated for what they offer in creativity of intellect and human beings' ability to adapt to changing circumstances.

The Greek sophists were philosophers who specialized in argumentation, rhetoric (using language persuasively), and dialectics (finding synthesis or common ground between contradictory ideas). From their skilled thinking came the derogatory term "sophism," suggesting that some argumentation was deceptive or fallacious rather than wise. The term sophomore, which now means second-year student, comes from this variation of sophism, combining "sophos" (wise) with "moros" (dull or foolish). "Sophomoric" translates to exhibiting immaturity and lack of judgment, while "sophisticated" translates to having acquired knowledge. Educators strive to have their students move from knowing all the answers (sophomoric) to asking intelligent questions (sophisticated).

This anthology is dedicated to seekers of knowledge and searchers for what is true, right, or lasting. To this end, articles have been selected to provide you with information that will stimulate discussion and that will give your thoughts direction, but not articles that tell you what to think. May you be "seeking" learners all through your own years of human development. May each suggestive answer you discover open your mind to more erudite (instructive) learning, questioning, and sophistication.

Karen Freiberg

Karen Freiberg, Ph.D.
Editor

Contents

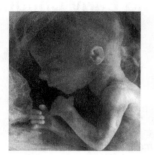

UNIT 1
Genetic and Prenatal Influences on Development

Part A.   Genetic Influences

Part B.   Prenatal Influences

The concepts in bold italics are developed in the article. For further expansion, please refer to the Topic Guide and the Index.

UNIT 2
Development During Infancy and Early Childhood

The concepts in bold italics are developed in the article. For further expansion, please refer to the Topic Guide and the Index.

UNIT 3
Development During Childhood: Cognition and Schooling

The concepts in bold italics are developed in the article. For further expansion, please refer to the Topic Guide and the Index.

UNIT 4
Development During Childhood: Family and Culture

The concepts in bold italics are developed in the article. For further expansion, please refer to the Topic Guide and the Index.

UNIT 5
Development During Adolescence and Young Adulthood

The concepts in bold italics are developed in the article. For further expansion, please refer to the Topic Guide and the Index.

UNIT 6
Development During Middle and Late Adulthood

The concepts in bold italics are developed in the article. For further expansion, please refer to the Topic Guide and the Index.

The concepts in bold italics are developed in the article. For further expansion, please refer to the Topic Guide and the Index.

Topic Guide

This topic guide suggests how the selections in this book relate to the subjects covered in your course. You may want to use the topics listed on these pages to search the Web more easily.

On the following pages a number of Web sites have been gathered specifically for this book. They are arranged to reflect the units of this *Annual Edition.* You can link to these sites by going to the student online support site at *http://www.mhcls.com/online/.*

ALL THE ARTICLES THAT RELATE TO EACH TOPIC ARE LISTED BELOW THE BOLD-FACED TERM.

Adolescence
23. The Power of No
27. *Brown v. Board*: A Dream Deferred
28. What Makes Teens Tick
29. A Peaceful Adolescence
30. Jail Time Is Learning Time
31. Hello to College Joys: Keep Stress Off Campus

Adulthood
29. A Peaceful Adolescence
32. How Spirit Blooms
34. Grow Up? Not So Fast
36. Alcohol's Deadly Triple Threat
37. How AIDS Changed America
38. The Myth of the Midlife Crisis

Aggression
14. Raising a Moral Child
21. Raising Happy Achieving Children in the New Millennium
30. Jail Time Is Learning Time
38. The Myth of the Midlife Crisis

Aging
38. The Myth of the Midlife Crisis
39. Aging Naturally
40. When Your Paycheck Stops
41. Secrets of the Centenarians
42. Lost & Found
43. Navigating Practical Dilemmas in Terminal Care

Anxiety
7. The Smallest Patients
13. Guilt Free TV
27. *Brown v. Board*: A Dream Deferred
28. What Makes Teens Tick
31. Hello to College Joys: Keep Stress Off Campus
36. Alcohol's Deadly Triple Threat
37. How AIDS Changed America
38. The Myth of the Midlife Crisis
40. When Your Paycheck Stops

Attachment
8. Four Things You Need to Know About Raising Baby
12. Long-Term Studies of Preschool: Lasting Benefits Far Outweigh Costs

Birth and birth defects
5. Inside the Womb
36. Alcohol's Deadly Triple Threat

Brain development
5. Inside the Womb
10. Reading Your Baby's Mind
11. 20 Ways to Boost Your Baby's Brain Power
17. The Trouble with Boys
18. Why We Need "The Year of Languages"
19. Failing Our Children: No Child Left Behind Undermines Quality and Equity in Education
28. What Makes Teens Tick

33. The Battle for Your Brain
35. Emotions and the Brain: Laughter
36. Alcohol's Deadly Triple Threat
38. The Myth of the Midlife Crisis
39. Aging Naturally

Career
30. Jail Time Is Learning Time
32. How Spirit Blooms
34. Grow Up? Not So Fast
40. When Your Paycheck Stops

Children
8. Four Things You Need to Know About Raising Baby
12. Long-Term Studies of Preschool: Lasting Benefits Far Outweigh Costs
16. The New Science of Dyslexia
17. The Trouble with Boys
22. The Blank Slate
23. The Power of No
24. Parents Behaving Badly
25. Where Personality Goes Awry
26. When Cultures Clash
27. *Brown v. Board*: A Dream Deferred
34. Grow Up? Not So Fast
35. Emotions and the Brain: Laughter
36. Alcohol's Deadly Triple Threat

Cognition
6. The Mystery of Fetal Life: Secrets of the Womb
8. Four Things You Need to Know About Raising Baby
10. Reading Your Baby's Mind
13. Guilt Free TV
15. A Time and a Place for Authentic Learning
16. The New Science of Dyslexia
21. Raising Happy Achieving Children in the New Millennium
28. What Makes Teens Tick
30. Jail Time Is Learning Time
32. How Spirit Blooms
33. The Battle for Your Brain
38. The Myth of the Midlife Crisis
41. Secrets of the Centenarians

Creativity
17. The Trouble with Boys
20. The Power of Teaching Students Using Strengths
21. Raising Happy Achieving Children in the New Millennium
38. The Myth of the Midlife Crisis

Culture
14. Raising a Moral Child
18. Why We Need "The Year of Languages"
19. Failing Our Children: No Child Left Behind Undermines Quality and Equity in Education
21. Raising Happy Achieving Children in the New Millennium
22. The Blank Slate
24. Parents Behaving Badly
26. When Cultures Clash
27. *Brown v. Board*: A Dream Deferred
29. A Peaceful Adolescence

Internet References

The following Internet sites have been carefully researched and selected to support the articles found in this reader. The easiest way to access these selected sites is to go to our student online support site at *http://www.mhcls.com/online/*.

AE: Human Development 07/08

The following sites were available at the time of publication. Visit our Web site—we update our student online support site regularly to reflect any changes.

General Sources

Association for Moral Education
http://www.amenetwork.org/
This association is dedicated to fostering communication, cooperation, training, curriculum development, and research that links moral theory to educational practices.

Behavior Analysis Resources
http://www.coedu.usf.edu/behavior/bares.htm
Dedicated to promoting the experimental, theoretical, and applied analysis of behavior, this site encompasses contemporary scientific and social issues, theoretical advances, and the dissemination of professional and public information.

Healthfinder
http://www.healthfinder.gov
Healthfinder is a consumer health site that contains the latest health news, prevention and care choices, and information about every phase of human development.

UNIT 1: Genetic and Prenatal Influences on Development

American Academy of Pediatrics (AAP)
http://www.aap.org
AAP provides data on optimal physical, mental, and social health for all children. The site links to professional educational sources and current research.

Basic Neural Processes
http://psych.hanover.edu/Krantz/neurotut.html
An extensive tutorial on brain structures is provided here.

Evolutionary Psychology: A Primer
http://www.psych.ucsb.edu/research/cep/
A link to an evolutionary psychology primer is available on this site. Extensive background information is included.

Genetics Education Center
http://www.kumc.edu/gec/
The University of Kansas Medical Center provides information on human genetics and the human genome project at this site. Included are a number of links to research areas.

MedlinePlus Health Information/Prenatal Care
http://www.nlm.nih.gov/medlineplus/prenatalcare.html
On this site of the National Library of Medicine and the National Institutes of Health, you'll find prenatal-related sections such as General Information, Diagnosis/Symptoms, Nutrition, Organizations, and more.

UNIT 2: Development During Infancy and Early Childhood

BabyCenter
http://www.babycenter.com
This well-organized site offers quick access to practical information on a variety of baby-related topics that span the period from preconception to toddlerhood.

Children's Nutrition Research Center (CNRC)
http://www.bcm.tmc.edu/cnrc/
CNRC is dedicated to defining the nutrient needs of healthy children, from conception through adolescence, and of pregnant and nursing mothers.

Early Childhood Care and Development
http://www.ecdgroup.com
Child development theory, programming and parenting data, and research can be found on this site of the Consultative Group. It is dedicated to the improvement of conditions of young children at risk.

Zero to Three: National Center for Infants, Toddlers, and Families
http://www.zerotothree.org
Zero to Three is dedicated solely to infants, toddlers, and their families. Organized by recognized experts in the field, it provides technical assistance to communities, states, and the federal government.

UNIT 3: Development During Childhood: Cognition and Schooling

Children Now
http://www.childrennow.org
Children Now focuses on improving conditions for children who are poor or at risk. Articles include information on education, the influence of media, health, and security.

Council for Exceptional Children
http://www.cec.sped.org
This is the home page of the Council for Exceptional Children, which is dedicated to improving education for exceptional children and the gifted child.

Educational Resources Information Center (ERIC)
http://www.eric.ed.gov/
Sponsored by the U.S. Department of Education, this site will lead to numerous documents related to elementary and early childhood education.

Federation of Behavioral, Psychological, and Cognitive Science
http://federation.apa.org
The federation's mission is fulfilled through legislative and regulatory advocacy, education, and information dissemination to

the scientific community. Hotlink to the National Institutes of Health's Project on the Decade of the Brain.

The National Association for the Education of Young Children (NAEYC)

http://www.naeyc.org

NAEYC is the nation's largest organization of early childhood professionals. It is devoted to improving the quality of early childhood education programs for children from birth through the age of eight.

Project Zero

http://pzweb.harvard.edu

Following 30 years of research on the development of learning processes in children and adults, Project Zero is now helping to create communities of reflective, independent learners; to enhance deep understanding within disciplines; and to promote critical and creative thinking.

UNIT 4: Development During Childhood: Family and Culture

Childhood Injury Prevention Interventions

http://depts.washington.edu/hiprc/

Systematic reviews of childhood injury prevention and interventions on such diverse subjects as adolescent suicide, child abuse, accidental injuries, and youth violence are offered on this site.

Families and Work Institute

http://www.familiesandwork.org/index.html

The Families and Work Institute conducts policy research on issues related to the changing workforce, and it operates a national clearinghouse on work and family life.

Parentsplace.com: Single Parenting

http://www.parentsplace.com/

This resource focuses on issues concerning single parents and their children. The articles range from parenting children from infancy through adolescence.

UNIT 5: Development During Adolescence and Young Adulthood

ADOL: Adolescent Directory On-Line

http://education.indiana.edu/cas/adol/adol.html

The ADOL site contains a wide array of Web documents that address adolescent development. Specific content ranges from mental health issues to counselor resources.

Adolescence: Change and Continuity

http://inside.bard.edu/academic/specialproj/darling/adolesce.htm

This site offers a discussion of puberty, sexuality, biological changes, cross-cultural differences, and nutrition for adolescents, including a look at obesity.

AMA—Adolescent Health On-Line

http://www.ama-assn.org/ama/pub/category/1947.html

This AMA adolescent health initiative describes clinical preventive services that primary care physicians and other health professionals can provide to young people.

American Academy of Child and Adolescent Psychiatry

http://www.aacap.org/

Up-to-date data on a host of topics that include facts for families, public health, and clinical practice may be found here.

UNIT 6: Development During Middle and Late Adulthood

Alzheimer's Disease Research Center

http://alzheimer.wustl.edu/adrc2//

ADRC facilitates advanced research on clinical, genetic, neuropathological, neuroanatomical, biomedical, neuropsychological, and psychosocial aspects of Alzheimer's disease and related brain disorders.

Lifestyle Factors Affecting Late Adulthood

http://www.school-for-champions.com/health/lifestyle_elderly.htm

The way a person lives his or her life in the later years can affect the quality of life. Find here information to improve a senior's lifestyle plus a few relevant links.

National Aging Information Center (NAIC)

http://www.aoa.dhhs.gov/naic/

This service by the Administration on Aging is a central source of data on demographic, health, economic, and social status of older Americans.

We highly recommend that you review our Web site for expanded information and our other product lines. We are continually updating and adding links to our Web site in order to offer you the most usable and useful information that will support and expand the value of your Annual Editions. You can reach us at: *http://www.mhcls.com/annualeditions/*.

UNIT 1

Genetic and Prenatal Influences on Development

Unit Selections

Key Points to Consider

- Will genetic technology result in more attempts to alter genes than environment in the 21st century? Will life experiences still conspire to switch new DNA sequences on or off?

- Will the United States become a laggard in body-part replacement research using stem cells? Why do many people oppose this life-saving technology?

- Will sex selection of babies at conception become widespread? Will this result in a world overpopulated by males?

- Why should embryonic development become a political priority in the 21st century?

- Describe the long-term effects of health status during pregnancy on the development of mental abilities in infants and children.

- Is it possible for surgeons to correct heart defects before a fetus is born? Is such an operating procedure safe?

Student Website

www.mhcls.com/online

Internet References

Further information regarding these websites may be found in this book's preface or online.

American Academy of Pediatrics (AAP)
http://www.aap.org

Basic Neural Processes
http://psych.hanover.edu/Krantz/neurotut.html

Evolutionary Psychology: A Primer
http://www.psych.ucsb.edu/research/cep/

Genetics Education Center
http://www.kumc.edu/gec/

MedlinePlus Health Information/Prenatal Care
http://www.nlm.nih.gov/medlineplus/prenatalcare.html

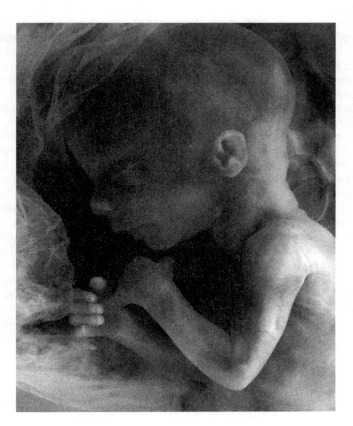

The total human genome was fully mapped in 2003. This knowledge of the human complement of twenty-three pairs of chromosomes with their associated genes in the nucleus of every cell has the potential for allowing genetic manipulation. The use of stem cells (undifferentiated embryonic cells) in animal research has documented the possibility of morphing stem cells into any kind of human cells. Stem cells will turn into desired tissue cells when the gene sequences of cytosine, adenine, thymine, and guanine (CATG) of the desired tissues are expressed. Scientists may eventually use their knowledge of the human genome, plus embryonic stem cells, to alter behavior or cure diseases. Cloning (complete reproduction) of a human already exists when one egg fertilized by one sperm separates into identical twins. Monozygotic twin research suggests that one's genetic CATG sequencing does not determine human behaviors, diseases, and traits without environmental input. Nature versus nurture is better phrased nature plus nurture. Genes appear to have mechanisms by which environmental factors can turn them on or leave them dormant.

Genetic precursors of human development and the use of stem cells, morphing, and cloning will be hot topics of the next several years as genetic manipulation becomes feasible. As DNA sequences associated with particular human traits (genetic markers) are uncovered, pressure will appear to alter these traits. Will the focus be on altering the CATG sequencing, or altering the environmental factors that will "operate" on the genes?

Human embryology (the study of the first through seventh weeks after conception) and human fetology (the study of the eighth week of pregnancy through birth) have given verification to the idea that behavior precedes birth. The genetic hardwiring of CATG directs much of this behavior. However, the developing embryo/fetus reacts to the internal and external environments provided by the mother as well. Substances diffuse through the placental barrier from the mother's body. The embryo reacts to toxins (viruses, antigens) that pass through the umbilical cord. The fetus reacts to an enormous number of other stimuli, such as the sounds from the mother's body (digestive rumblings, heartbeat) and the mother's movements, moods, and medicines. How the embryo/fetus reacts (weakly to strongly, positively to negatively) depends, in large part, on his or her genetic preprogramming. Genes and environment are so inextricably intertwined that the effect of each cannot be studied separately. Prenatal development always has strong environmental influences and vice versa.

The two articles in the genetic influences section of this unit are state-of-the-science expositions on how decoding of the human genome will affect our future views about human development. The information in them is central to many ongoing discussions of human development. The potentialities for altering structures and behaviors, by altering the CATG messages of DNA on chromosomes within cells or by cloning humans, are massive. We all need to understand what is happening. We need to make knowledgeable and well-thought-out choices for our futures.

The first article, "The Identity Dance," addresses the interplay of genes and environment. It presents research on identical twins suggesting that life factors conspire to switch genetic sequences of CATG on, or off, to create personality traits, diseases, and other human behaviors. What will we, the human race, choose to do with the technology in our hands: alter gene sequences or alter environment? The author poses several questions about human twins that should stimulate lively debates.

The second article, "The Power to Divide," explains how stem cell research could launch an era of body-part replacement. Tissues and organs can be custom-made for recipients. Will the political/moral movers of different countries allow this to take place? What are the objections to, and dangers of, creating new body parts for individuals with diseased tissues and/or organs? Which countries are moving ahead with this technology? Will the United States continue to be a cell replacement laggard?

"Brave New Babies," discusses the use of genetic technology to choose the sex of a child at the time of conception. The price tag approaches $20,000, but many parents are willing to pay this price for a boy or for a girl. The science behind this sex selection is illustrated and described. More parents choose boys than girls. If gender selection becomes widespread, will we have a world overpopulated with males?

The first article in the prenatal section of this unit discusses what scientists have learned about the nine months from conception through birth. Sophisticated ultrasound technology and computer-enhanced images reveal in exquisite detail what goes on "Inside the Womb." Parents viewing their unborn child(ren) in this way find it difficult not to believe in life before birth. The human race may give more priority to embryonic and fetal development as this knowledge is disseminated. Concern for maternal and prenatal health care may move from a low-order to highest priority.

The next article, "The Mystery of Fetal Life: Secrets of the Womb," answers questions on fetal psychological development. Human behaviors such as intelligence and personality may be profoundly influenced by the environment of the mother's uterus. Nurture occurs before and after birth. John Pekkanen addresses issues such as over-the-counter drugs, caffeine, infections, pets, and environmental pollutants. He reviews what is known about fetal memory, including the much-misunderstood "Mozart effect."

The final article, "The Smallest Patients," discusses the ability to surgically correct heart defects in unborn fetuses. The success rate is about 75%. A few decades ago most babies with heart defects died in infancy. What other prenatally diagnosed defects will be repaired before birth in the future? Will prenatal surgery become a highly skilled specialty?

The Identity Dance

The battle between genes and the environment is over. As the dust settles, scientists piece together how DNA and life experience conspire to create personality.

GUNJAN SINHA

In recent years, we've, come to believe that genes influence character and personality more than anything else does. It's not just about height and hair color—DNA seems to have its clutches on our very souls. But spend a few hours with identical twins, who have exactly the same set of genes, and you'll find that this simplistic belief crumbles before your eyes. If DNA dictates all, how can two people with identical genes—who are living, breathing clones of each other—be so different?

To answer such questions, scientists have begun to think more broadly about how genes and life experience combine to shape us. The rigid idea that genes determine identity has been replaced with a more flexible and complex view in which DNA and life experience conspire to mold our personalities. We now know that certain genes make people susceptible to traits like aggression and depression. But susceptibility is not inevitability. Gene expression is like putty: Genes are turned on and off, dialed up or down both by other genes and by the ups and downs of everyday life. A seminal study last year found that the ideal breeding ground for depression is a combination of specific genes *and* stressful triggers—simply having the gene will not send most people into despair. Such research promises to end the binary debate about nature vs. nurture—and usher in a revolution in understanding who we are.

We've come to believe genes influence character more than anything else—DNA seems to have its clutches on our souls.

"While scientists have been trying to tease apart environmental from genetic influences on diseases like cancer, this is the first study to show this effect [for a mental disorder]," says Thomas Insel, director of the National Institute of Mental Health. "This is really the science of the moment."

About ten years ago, technological advances made it possible to quickly identify human genes. That breakthrough launched a revolution in human biology—and in psychiatry.

Not only were scientists rapidly discovering genes linked to illnesses such as cancer and birth defects like dwarfism, they also found genes associated with such traits as sexual preference and aggression as well as mental illnesses such as schizophrenia.

Genetic discoveries transformed the intellectual zeitgeist as well, marking a decisive shift from the idea that environment alone shapes human personality. Nurture-heavy theories about behavior dominated in the 1960s and 1970s, a reaction in part to the legacy of Nazi eugenics. By the 1990s, the genome was exalted as "the human blueprint," the ultimate dictator of our attributes. Behavioral geneticists offered refreshingly simple explanations for human identity—and for social problems. Bad parenting, poor neighborhoods or amoral television didn't cause bad behavior; genes did. No wonder all those welfare programs weren't working.

"People really believed that there must be something exclusively genetically wrong with people who are not successful. They were exhausted with these broken-hearted liberals saying that it's all social," says Andreas Heinz, professor of psychiatry at Humboldt and Freie University in Berlin, who has been studying the influence of genes and environment on behavior for years. The idea that violent behavior in particular might be genetically "set" was so accepted that in 1992, the director of the agency overseeing the National Institute of Mental Health compared urban African-American youth with "hyperaggressive" and "hypersexual" monkeys in a jungle.

Behavioral genetics had a simple argument: Bad parenting, poor neighborhoods or TV didn't cause bad behavior. Genes did.

Genetic explanations for behavior gained ground in part through great leaps in our understanding of mood disorders. In the early 1990s, research at the federal labs of Stephen Suomi and Dee Higley found that monkeys with low levels of serotonin—now known to be a major player in human anxiety and depression—were prone to alcoholism, anxiety and aggression. Around the same time, Klaus-Peter Lesch at the University of Würtzburg in Germany identified the serotonin transporter gene, which produces a protein that ferries serotonin between brain cells. Prozac and other drugs work by boosting levels of serotonin in the brain, so this gene seemed like an obvious target in the search for the genetic roots of depression.

Lesch, who was working on the connection between this gene and psychiatric disorders, later found that people who had at least one copy of the short version of this gene were much more likely to have an anxiety disorder. Short and long versions of genes function much like synonymous words: Different lengths, or "spellings," generate subtle but critical differences in biology.

Genetics couldn't explain why some people bounce back from terrible trauma that shatters others, or why some people are ruthlessly ambitious and others laid-back.

Despite these groundbreaking insights, it quickly became clear that complex human behaviors couldn't be reduced to pure genetics. Apart from a few exceptions, scientists couldn't find a gene that directly caused depression or schizophrenia or any other major mental of mood disorder. The new research also failed to answer a lot of common-sense questions: If identical twins are genetically indistinguishable, how could just one end up schizophrenic or homosexual? And it couldn't address subtler questions about character and behavior. Why do some people bounce back from terrible trauma that shatters others? Why are some people ruthlessly ambitious and others laid-back?

Thanks to misfit monkeys like George, a rhesus macaque living in a lab in Maryland, researchers have clues to the missing element. In most ways, George is a typical male monkey. He's covered in sandy fur and has a rubbery, almost maniacal grin. But a couple of things set George apart. After he was born, Higley and Suomi's team separated George from his mother, raising him instead in a nursery with other macaque infants his own age. George has another strike against him: a short version of the serotonin transporter gene (monkeys, like people, can have either a short form or a long form of the gene).

But the most notable thing about George is that he is an alcoholic. Each day, George and his simian chums have happy hour, with alcohol freely available in their cage for one hour. Unlike his buddies, George drinks like the resident barroom lush—he sways and wobbles and can't walk a straight line.

And his problems go beyond the bottle. He's reluctant to explore new objects, and he is shy around strangers. He always seems to be on edge and tends to get aggressive and impulsive quickly. In short, he's a completely different animal from his cousin Jim, who also has the short version of the transporter gene but was raised by his biological mom. Jim's "normal" up-

bringing seems to have protected him from the gene: This monkey is laid-back and prefers sugar water to booze.

After studying 36 family-raised monkeys and 79 nursery-raised animals, the team found that the long version of the gene seems to help the animals shrug off stress. The short form of the gene, by contrast, doesn't directly *cause* alcoholism: Monkeys with the short gene and a normal family upbringing have few personality problems. But the short version of the gene definitely puts the animals at a disadvantage when life gets tough. Raised without the care and support of their mothers, their predisposition toward anxiety and alcoholism comes to the fore.

"Maternal nurturing and discipline seem to buffer the effect of the serotonin gene," says Suomi. "If they don't have good mothers, then the [troubled] behavior comes out loud and clear."

The implications of this research are tantalizing, since people also carry long and short versions of the transporter gene. These variants, unlike those that have been identified as making people susceptible to diseases like breast cancer or Alzheimer's, are very common: Among Caucasians, about one-fifth of the population has two copies of the short gene (everyone gets one copy from Mom and the other from Dad), and another third have two copies of the long gene. The rest have one of each. (The gene has not yet been studied in other populations.) The evidence indicated that this gene was related to resilience and depression in humans. Why, then, had researchers thus far failed to find a convincing correlation between the gene and the risk of depression?

Terrie Moffitt and Avshalom Caspi, a husband-and-wife team of psychologists at King's College in London, had the insight that environmental influences might be the missing part of the puzzle. Moffitt and Caspi turned to a long-term study of almost 900 New Zealanders, identified these subjects' transporter genes and interviewed the subjects about traumatic experiences in early adulthood—like a major breakup, death in the family or serious injury—to see if the difficulties brought out an underlying genetic tendency toward depression.

The results were striking: 43 percent of subjects who had the short genes and who had experienced four or more tumultuous events became clinically depressed. By contrast, only 17 percent of the long-gene people who had endured four or more stressful events wound up depressed—no more than the rate of depression in the general population. People with the short gene who experienced no stressful events fared pretty well too—they also became depressed at the average rate. Clearly, it was the combination of hard knocks and short genes that more than doubled the risk of depression.

Caspi and Moffitt's study, published last summer, was one of the first to examine the combined effects of genetic predisposition and experience on a specific trait. Psychiatrists were delighted. "It's just a wonderful story," says Insel. "It changed the way we think about genes and psychiatric disorders."

Moffitt and Caspi have found a similar relationship between another gene and antisocial behavior. Abused and neglected children with a gene responsible for low levels of monoamine oxidase in the brain were nine times more likely to engage in violent of other antisocial behavior as adults than

to engage in violent of other antisocial behavior as adults than were people with the same gene who were not mistreated. Finnish scientists have since found similar effects on genes for novelty seeking—a trait associated with attention deficit hyperactivity disorder. Children who had the genes and who were also raised by strict, emotionally distant parents were much more likely to engage in risky behavior and make impulsive decisions as adults than children with the same genes who were raised in more tolerant and accepting environments.

While scientists don't exactly know how genes are influenced by environment at the molecular level, there are clues that genes have the equivalent of molecular "switches" and can be programmed—turned on or off, up or down—very early. Both Lesch and Suomi have shown that the level of biochemicals such as the serotonin transporter molecule can be "set" as early as in the womb, at least in mice and monkeys.

Mothers of multiples will tell you their babies were distinct the moment they were born.

The prenatal environment also has a major influence on differences between identical twins. Mothers of multiples will tell you that their babies were distinct the moment they were born, and research backs them up. Twins experience different environments even in the womb, as they compete with each other for nutrients. One can beat out the other, which is why they often have different birth weights: Marisa Pena is a bit taller and heavier than her sister.

Prenatal experiences are just the first in a lifetime of differentiating factors. Only about 50 percent of the characteristics twins have in common are due to genes alone. Researchers now believe that an illness suffered by only one twin, or different amounts of attention from peers or parents, can set the stage for personality differences. This makes it easier to understand why the Pena sisters reacted as they did: By the time their parents died, "these twins had had a lifetime of experiences which might have made them react differently," says Moffitt. "In addition, some pairs of identical twins individuate themselves in early childhood. They seem to take on the roles of 'the shy one' and 'the outgoing one' and then live up to those roles." in other words, they customize their environment, and the world treats them accordingly.

The new science of nature *and* nurture isn't as straightforward as the DNA-is-destiny mantra, but it is more accurate. "People have a really hard time understanding the probabilistic nature of how genes impact traits like depression," says Kenneth Kendler, director of the Virginia Institute for Psychiatric and Behavioral Genetics at Virginia Commonwealth University, who heads a major twin registry. "They think that if something is heritable, then it can't be modified by the environment." The knowledge that the traits we inherit are also contingent on what the world does to us promises more insight into why people act and feel differently—even when they look exactly the same.

GUNJAN SINHA is an award-winning science writer based in Frankfurt, Germany.

Additional reporting by Jeff Grossman.

The Power to Divide

Stem cells could launch a new era of medicine, curing deadly diseases with custom-made tissues and organs. But science may take a backseat to politics in deciding if—and where—that hope will be realized.

RICK WEISS

In the beginning, one cell becomes two, and two become four. Being fruitful, they multiply into a ball of many cells, a shimmering sphere of human potential. Scientists have long dreamed of plucking those naive cells from a young human embryo and coaxing them to perform, in sterile isolation, the everyday miracle they perform in wombs: transforming into all the 200 or so kinds of cells that constitute a human body. Liver cells. Brain cells. Skin, bone, and nerve.

The dream is to launch a medical revolution in which ailing organs and tissues might be repaired—not with crude mechanical devices like insulin pumps and titanium joints but with living, homegrown replacements. It would be the dawn of a new era of regenerative medicine, one of the holy grails of modern biology.

Revolutions, alas, are almost always messy. So when James Thomson, a soft-spoken scientist at the University of Wisconsin in Madison, reported in November 1998 that he had succeeded in removing cells from spare embryos at fertility clinics and establishing the world's first human embryonic stem cell line, he and other scientists got a lot more than they bargained for. It was the kind of discovery that under most circumstances would have blossomed into a major federal research enterprise. Instead the discovery was quickly engulfed in the turbulent waters of religion and politics. In church pews, congressional hearing rooms, and finally the Oval Office, people wanted to know: Where were the needed embryos going to come from, and how many would have to be destroyed to treat the millions of patients who might be helped? Before long, countries around the world were embroiled in the debate.

Most alarmed have been people who see embryos as fully vested, vulnerable members of society, and who decry the harvesting of cells from embryos as akin to cannibalism. They warn of a brave new world of "embryo farms" and "cloning mills" for the cultivation of human spare parts. And they argue that scientists can achieve the same results using adult stem cells—immature cells found in bone marrow and other organs in adult human beings, as well as in umbilical cords normally discarded at birth.

Immature and full of potential, stem cells haven't yet differentiated into the specialized cells that form body parts, like the museum specimens stacked in the Berlin lab of pathologist Rudolf Virchow. He pioneered the idea, in the 1800s, that disease begins at the cellular level.

Advocates counter that adult stem cells, useful as they may be for some diseases, have thus far proved incapable of producing the full range of cell types that embryonic stem cells can. They point out that fertility clinic freezers worldwide are bulging with thousands of unwanted embryos slated for disposal. Those embryos are each smaller than the period at the end of this sentence. They have no identifying features or hints of a nervous system. If parents agree to donate them, supporters say, it would be unethical not to do so in the quest to cure people of disease.

Few question the medical promise of embryonic stem cells. Consider the biggest United States killer of all: heart disease. Embryonic stem cells can be trained to grow into heart muscle cells that, even in a laboratory dish, clump together and pulse in spooky unison. And when those heart cells have been injected into mice and pigs with heart disease, they've filled in for injured or dead cells and sped recovery. Similar studies have suggested stem cells' potential for conditions such as diabetes and spinal cord injury.

Critics point to worrisome animal research showing that embryonic stem cells sometimes grow into tumors or morph into unwanted kinds of tissues—possibly forming, for example, dangerous bits of bone in those hearts they are supposedly repairing. But supporters respond that such problems are rare and a lot has recently been learned about how to prevent them.

The arguments go back and forth, but policymakers and governments aren't waiting for answers. Some countries, such as Germany, worried about a slippery slope toward unethical human experimentation, have already prohibited some types of stem cell research. Others, like the U.S., have imposed severe limits on government funding but have left the private sector to do what it wants. Still others, such as the U.K., China, Korea, and Singapore, have set out to become the epicenters of stem cell research, providing money as well as ethical oversight to encourage the field within carefully drawn bounds.

In such varied political climates, scientists around the globe are racing to see which techniques will produce treatments soonest. Their approaches vary, but on one point, all seem to agree: How humanity handles its control over the mysteries of embryo development will say a lot about who we are and what we're becoming.

For more than half of his seven years, Cedric Seldon has been fighting leukemia. Now having run out of options, he is about to become a biomedical pioneer—one of about 600 Americans last year to be treated with an umbilical cord blood transplant.

Cord blood transplants—considered an adult stem cell therapy because the cells come from infants, not embryos—have been performed since 1988. Like bone marrow, which doctors have been transplanting since 1968, cord blood is richly endowed with a kind of stem cell that gives rise to oxygen-carrying red blood cells, disease-fighting white blood cells, and other parts of the blood and immune systems. Unlike a simple blood transfusion, which provides a batch of cells destined to die in a few months, the stem cells found in bone marrow and cord blood can—if all goes well—burrow into a person's bones, settle there for good, and generate fresh blood and immune cells for a lifetime.

Propped on a hospital bed at Duke University Medical Center, Cedric works his thumbs furiously against a pair of joysticks that control a careening vehicle in a Starsky and Hutch video game. "Hang on, Hutch!" older brother Daniel shouts from the bedside, as a nurse, ignoring the screeching tires and gunshots, sorts through a jumble of tubes and hangs a bag of cord blood cells from a chrome pole. Just an hour ago I watched those cells being thawed and spun in a centrifuge—awakening them for the first time since 2001, when they were extracted from the umbilical cord of a newborn and donated by her parents to a cell bank at Duke. The time has come for those cells to prove their reputed mettle.

For days Cedric has endured walloping doses of chemotherapy and radiation in a last-ditch effort to kill every cancer cell in his body. Such powerful therapy has the dangerous side-effect of destroying patients' blood-making stem cells, and so is never applied unless replacement stem cells are available. A search of every bone marrow bank in the country had found no match for Cedric's genetic profile, and it was beginning to look as if he'd run out of time. Then a computer search turned up the frozen cord blood cells at Duke—not a perfect match, but close enough to justify trying.

"Ready?" the nurse asks. Mom and dad, who have spent hours in prayer, nod yes, and a line of crimson wends its way down the tube, bringing the first of about 600 million cells into the boy's body. The video game's sound effects seem to fade

behind a muffling curtain of suspense. Although Cedric's balloon-laden room is buoyant with optimism, success is far from certain.

"Grow, cells, grow," Cedric's dad whispers.

His mom's eyes are misty. I ask what she sees when she looks at the cells trickling into her son.

"Life," she says. "It's his rebirth."

It will be a month before tests reveal whether Cedric's new cells have taken root, but in a way he's lucky. All he needs is a new blood supply and immune system, which are relatively easy to re-create. Countless other patients are desperate to regenerate more than that. Diabetics need new insulin-producing cells. Heart attack victims could benefit from new cardiac cells. Paraplegics might even walk again if the nerves in their spinal cords could regrow.

In a brightly lit laboratory halfway across the country from Cedric's hospital room, three teams of scientists at the University of Wisconsin in Madison are learning how to grow the embryonic stem cells that might make such cures possible. Unlike adult stem cells, which appear to have limited repertoires, embryonic stem cells are pluripotent—they can become virtually every kind of human cell. The cells being nurtured here are direct descendants of the ones James Thomson isolated seven years ago.

For years Thomson and his colleagues have been expanding some of those original stem cells into what are called stem cell lines—colonies of millions of pluripotent cells that keep proliferating without differentiating into specific cell types. The scientists have repeatedly moved each cell's offspring to less crowded laboratory dishes, allowing them to divide again and again. And while they worked, the nation struggled to get a handle on the morality of what they were doing.

It took almost two years for President Bill Clinton's administration to devise ethics guidelines and a system for funding the new field. George W. Bush's ascension prevented that plan from going into effect, and all eyes turned to the conservative Texan to see what he would do. On August 9, 2001, Bush announced that federal funds could be used to study embryonic stem cells. But to prevent taxpayers from becoming complicit in the destruction of human embryos, that money could be used only to study the stem cell lines already in the works as of that date—a number that, for practical reasons, has resulted in about two dozen usable lines. Those wishing to work with any of the more than a hundred stem cell lines created after that date can do so only with private funding.

Every month scientists from around the world arrive in Madison to take a three-day course in how to grow those approved cells. To watch what they must go through to keep the cells happy is to appreciate why many feel hobbled by the Bush doctrine. For one thing—and for reasons not fully understood—the surest way to keep these cells alive is to place them on a layer of other cells taken from mouse embryos, a time-consuming requirement. Hunched over lab benches, deftly handling forceps and pipettes with blue latex gloves, each scientist in Madison spends the better half of a day dissecting a pregnant mouse, removing its uterus, and prying loose a string of embryos that look like little red peas in a pod. They then wash them, mash them, tease apart their cells, and get them growing in lab dishes. The result is a hormone-rich carpet of mouse cells upon which a few human embryonic stem cells are finally placed. There they live like pampered pashas.

If their scientist-servants don't feed them fresh liquid nutrients at least once a day, the cells die of starvation. If each colony is not split in half each week, it dies from overcrowding. And if a new layer of mouse cells is not prepared and provided every two weeks, the stem cells grow into weird and useless masses that finally die. By contrast, scientists working with private money have been developing embryonic stem cell lines that are hardier, less demanding, and not dependent on mouse cells. Bypassing the use of mouse cells is not only easier, but it also eliminates the risk that therapeutic stem cells might carry rodent viruses, thereby potentially speeding their approval for testing in humans.

Here in the Madison lab, scientists grumble about how fragile the precious colonies are. "They're hard to get to know," concedes Leann Crandall, one of the course's instructors and a co-author of the 85-page manual on their care and feeding. "But once you get to know them, you love them. You can't help it. They're so great. I see so many good things coming from them."

A few american scientists are finding it is easier to indulge their enthusiasm for stem cells overseas. Scores of new embryonic stem cell lines have now been created outside the U.S., and many countries are aggressively seeking to spur the development of therapies using these cells, raising a delicate question: Can the nation in which embryonic stem cells were discovered maintain its initial research lead?

"I know a lot of people back in the U.S. who would like to move into embryonic stem cell work but who won't because of the political uncertainties" says Stephen Minger, director of the Stem Cell Biology Laboratory at King's College in London, speaking to me in his cramped and cluttered office. "I think the United States is in real danger of being left behind."

Minger could be right. He is one of at least two high-profile stem cell scientists to move from the U.S. to England in the past few years, something less than a brain drain but a signal, perhaps, of bubbling discontent.

The research climate is good here, says Minger. In 2003 his team became the first in the U.K. to grow colonies of human embryonic stem cells, and his nine-person staff is poised to nearly double. He's developing new growth culture systems that won't rely on potentially infectious mouse cells. He's also figuring out how to make stem cells morph into cardiac, neural, pancreatic, and retinal cells and preparing to test those cells in animals. And in stark contrast to how things are done in the U.S., Minger says, he's doing all this with government support—and oversight.

The Human Fertilisation and Embryology Authority (HFEA), the government agency that has long overseen U.K. fertility clinics, is now also regulating the country's embryonic stem cell research. In closed-door meetings a committee of 18 people appointed by the National Health Service considers all requests to conduct research using embryos. The committee includes scientists, ethicists, lawyers, and clergy, but the majority are lay people representing the public.

To an American accustomed to high security and protesters at venues dealing regularly with embryo research, the most striking thing about the HFEA's headquarters in downtown London is its ordinariness. The office, a standard-issue warren of cubicles and metal filing cabinets, is on the second floor of a building that also houses the agency that deals with bankruptcy. I ask Ross Thacker, a research officer at the authority, whether the HFEA is regularly in need of yellow police tape to keep protesters at bay.

"Now that you mention it,' he says, "there was a placard holder outside this morning ..."

Aha!

"... but he was protesting something about the insolvency office."

Thacker politely refrains from criticizing U.S. policy on embryo research, but he clearly takes pride in the orderliness of the British system. The committee has approved about a dozen requests to create stem cell lines in the past 18 months, increasing the number of projects to 35. Most were relatively routine—until a strong-willed fertility doctor named Alison Murdoch decided to ask for permission to do something nobody had done before: create cloned human embryos as sources of stem cells.

As controversial as embryonic stem cell research can be, cloning embryos to produce those stem cells is even thornier. Much of the world became familiar with cloning in 1997, when

how many lines exist?

Since President Bush banned U.S. government funding for the study of embryonic stem cell lines created after August 9, 2001, the number of lines worldwide has doubled, though reliable data are hard to come by. Biologist Douglas Melton of Harvard says many lines approved for federal dollars "are old fuddy-duddies that have lost potential" because of how they were cultured. "That's why we need new lines," he says.

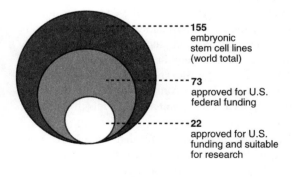

155 embryonic stem cell lines (world total)

73 approved for U.S. federal funding

22 approved for U.S. funding and suitable for research

International Society for Stem Cell Research (published data only)

scientists announced they'd cloned a sheep named Dolly. The process involves creating an animal not from egg and sperm but by placing the nucleus of a cell inside an egg that's had its nucleus removed. It's since been used to replicate mice, rabbits, cats, and cattle, among others.

As in many other countries and a few U.S. states, it's illegal in the U.K. to create cloned human babies (called reproductive cloning), because of concerns that clones may be biologically abnormal and because of ethical issues surrounding the creation of children who would be genetic replicas of their one-and-only "parent."

In 2001 the British Parliament made it legal to create cloned human embryos—as opposed to babies—for use in medical research (called therapeutic cloning). Still, no one on the HFEA was completely comfortable with the idea. The fear was that some rogue scientist would take the work a step further, gestate the embryo in a woman's womb, and make the birth announcement that no one wanted to hear.

But Murdoch, of the University of Newcastle upon Tyne, made a compelling case. If replacement tissues grown from stem cells bore the patient's exact genetic fingerprint, they would be less likely to be rejected by a patient's immune system, she told the committee. And what better way to get such a match than to derive the cells from an embryo cloned from the patient's own DNA? Disease research could also benefit, she said. Imagine an embryo—and its stem cells—cloned from a person with Lou Gehrig's disease, a fatal genetic disorder that affects nerves and muscles. Scientists might learn quite a bit, she argued, by watching how the disease damages nerve and muscle cells grown from those stem cells, and then testing various drugs on them. It's the kind of experiment that could never be done in a person with the disease.

The HFEA deliberated for five months before giving Murdoch permission to make human embryo clones in her lab at the Centre for Life in Newcastle, a sprawling neon-illuminated complex of buildings that strikes a decidedly modern note in the aging industrial hub. But there was a catch: It takes an egg to make a clone. And under the terms of HFEA approval, Murdoch is allowed to use only those eggs being disposed of by the center's fertility clinic after they failed to fertilize when mixed with sperm.

It's not a perfect arrangement, Murdoch says. After all, eggs that have failed to fertilize are almost by definition of poor quality. "They're not brilliant," she says of the eggs. "But the U.K. has decided at the moment that these are the most ethical sort to use. So that's really all we can work with." As of April the group hadn't managed to clone any embryos, despite numerous attempts.

No such obstacle faced Woo-Suk Hwang and his colleagues at Seoul National University in February 2004 when they became the world's first to clone human embryos and extract stem cells from them. The South Korean government allows research on human embryos made from healthy eggs—in this case, donated by 16 women who took egg-ripening hormones.

Cloning is an arduous process that requires great patience and almost always ends in failure as cells burst, tear, or suffer damage to their DNA, but the Koreans are expert cloners, their skills sharpened in the country's state-funded livestock-cloning enterprise. In Hwang's lab alone, technicians produce more than 700 cloned pig or cattle embryos every day, seven days a week, in a quest to produce livestock with precise genetic traits. "There is no holiday in our lab," Hwang told me with a smile.

But there is something else that gives Koreans an edge over other would-be cloners, Hwang says. "As you know, Asian countries use chopsticks, but only the Koreans use steel chopsticks," he explains. "The steel ones are the most difficult to use. Very slippery." I look at him, trying to tell if he's kidding. A lifetime of using steel chop sticks makes Koreans better at manipulating tiny eggs? "This is not simply a joke," he says.

Time will tell whether such skill will be enough to keep Korea in the lead as other countries turn to cloning as a source of stem cells. The competition will be tough. China has pioneered a potentially groundbreaking technique that produces cloned human embryos by mixing human skin cells with the eggs of rabbits, which are more easily obtained than human eggs. A few privately funded researchers in the U.S. are also pursuing therapeutic cloning.

Yet the biggest competition in the international race to develop stem cell therapies may ultimately come from one of the smallest of countries—a tiny nation committed to becoming a stem cell superpower. To find that place, one need only track the migration patterns of top scientists who've been wooed there from the U.S., Australia, even the U.K. Where they've been landing, it turns out, is Singapore.

Amid the scores of small, botanically rich but barely inhabited islands in the South China Sea, Singapore stands out like a post-modern mirage. The towering laboratory buildings of its Biopolis were created in 2001 to jump-start Singapore's biotechnology industry. Like a scene from a science fiction story, it features futuristic glass-and-metal buildings with names like Matrix, Proteos, and Chromos, connected by skywalks that facilitate exchanges among researchers.

Academic grants, corporate development money, laws that ban reproductive cloning but allow therapeutic cloning, and a science-savvy workforce are among the lures attracting stem cell researchers and entrepreneurs. Even Alan Colman—the renowned cloning expert who was part of the team that created Dolly, the cloned sheep—has taken leave of his home in the U.K. and become the chief executive of ES Cell International, one of a handful of major stem cell research companies blossoming in Singapore's fertile environs.

"You don't have to fly from New York to San Diego to see what's going on in other labs," says Robert Klupacs, the firm's previous CEO. "You just walk across the street. Because Singapore is small, things can happen quickly. And you don't have to go to Congress at every turn."

The company's team of 36, with 15 nationalities represented, has taken advantage of that milieu. It already owns six stem cell lines made from conventional, noncloned embryos that are approved for U.S. federal funding. Now it is perfecting methods of turning those cells into the kind of pancreatic islet cells that

where are they?

The U.S. still leads in the number of embryonic stem cell lines, despite the restrictions on federal funding; states such as California are investing in research to create new and better lines. But the U.K. and rising Asian economies, such as South Korea and Singapore, are pouring funds into their research labs in an effort to catch up—with government oversight and financial support.

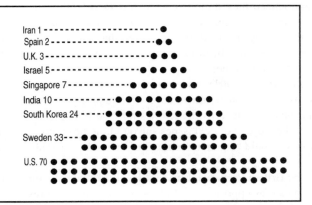

International Society for Stem Cell Research (published data only)

diabetics need, as well as into heart muscle cells that could help heart attack patients. The company is developing new, mouse-free culture systems and sterile production facilities to satisfy regulators such as the U.S. Food and Drug Administration. It hopes to begin clinical tests in humans by 2007.

Despite its research-friendly ethos—and its emphasis on entrepreneurial aspects of stem cell science—Singapore doesn't want to be known as the world's "Wild West" of stem cell research. A panel of scientific and humanitarian representatives spent two years devising ethical guidelines, stresses Hwai-Loong Kong, executive director of Singapore's Biomedical Research Council. Even the public was invited to participate, Kong says—an unusual degree of democratic input for the authoritarian island nation. The country's policies represent a "judicious balance," he says, that has earned widespread public support.

Widespread, perhaps, but not universal. After my conversation with Kong, a government official offered me a ride to my next destination. As we approached her parked car, she saw the surprise on my face as I read the bumper sticker on her left rear window: "Embryos—Let Them Live. You Were Once an Embryo Too!"

"I guess this is not completely settled," I said. "No," she replied, choosing not to elaborate.

That bumper sticker made me feel strangely at home. I am an American, after all. And no country has struggled more with the moral implications of embryonic stem cell research than the U.S., with its high church attendance rates and pockets of skepticism for many things scientific. That struggle promises to grow in the months and years ahead. Many in Congress want to ban the cloning of human embryos, even in those states where it is currently legal and being pursued with private funding. Some states have already passed legislation banning various kinds of embryo research. And federally backed scientists are sure to become increasingly frustrated as the handful of cell colonies they're allowed to work with becomes an ever smaller fraction of what's available.

Yet one thing I've noticed while talking to stem cell experts around the world: Whenever I ask who is the best in the field, the answers are inevitably weighted with the names of Ameri-

cans. The work of U.S. researchers still fills the pages of the best scientific journals. And while federal policy continues to frustrate them, they are finding some support. Following the lead of California, which has committed 300 million dollars a year for embryonic stem cell research for the next decade, several states are pushing initiatives to fund research, bypassing the federal restrictions in hopes of generating well-paying jobs to boost their economies. Moves like those prompt some observers to predict that when all is said and done, it will be an American team that wins the race to create the first FDA-approved embryonic stem cell therapy.

Tom Okarma certainly believes so, and he intends to be that winner. Okarma is president of Geron, the company in Menlo Park, California, that has been at the center of the embryonic stem cell revolution from the beginning. Geron financed James Thomson's discovery of the cells in Wisconsin and has since developed more than a dozen new colonies. It holds key patents on stem cell processes and products. And now it's laying the groundwork for what the company hopes will be the first controlled clinical trials of treatments derived from embryonic stem cells. Moreover, while others look to stem cells from cloned embryos or newer colonies that haven't come into contact with mouse cells, Okarma is looking no further than the very first colonies of human embryonic stem cells ever grown: the ones Thomson nurtured back in 1998. That may seem surprising, he acknowledges, but after all these years, he knows those cells inside out.

"We've shown they're free of human, pig, cow, and mouse viruses, so they're qualified for use in humans," Okarma says at the company's headquarters. Most important, Geron has perfected a system for growing uniform batches of daughter cells from a master batch that resides, like a precious gem, in a locked freezer. The ability to produce a consistent product, batch after batch, just as drug companies do with their pills is what the FDA wants—and it will be the key to success in the emerging marketplace of stem cell therapies, Okarma says. "Why do you think San Francisco sourdough bread is so successful?" he asks. "They've got a reliable sourdough culture, and they stick with it."

Geron scientists can now make eight different cell types from their embryonic lines, Okarma says, including nerve cells, heart cells, pancreatic islet cells, liver cells, and the kind of brain cells that are lost in Parkinson's disease. But what Geron wants most at this point is to develop a treatment for spinal cord injuries.

Okarma clicks on a laptop and shows me a movie of white rats in a cage. "Pay attention to the tail and the two hind legs," he says. Two months before, the rats were subjected to spinal cord procedures that left their rear legs unable to support their weight and their tails dragging along the floor. "That's a permanent injury," he says. He flips to a different movie: white rats again, also two months after injury. But these rats received injections of a specialized nervous system cell grown from human embryonic stem cells. They have only the slightest shuffle in their gait. They hold their tails high. One even stands upright on its rear legs for a few moments.

"It's not perfect," Okarma says. "It's not like we've made a brand new spinal cord." But tests show the nerves are regrowing, he says. He hopes to get FDA permission to start testing the cells in people with spinal cord injuries in 2006.

Those experiments will surely be followed by many others around the world, as teams in China, the U.K., Singapore, and other nations gain greater control over the remarkable energy of stem cells. With any luck the political and ethical issues may even settle down. Many suspect that with a little more looking, new kinds of stem cells may be found in adults that are as versatile as those in embryos.

At least two candidates have already emerged. Catherine Verfaillie, a blood disease specialist at the University of Minnesota, has discovered a strange new kind of bone marrow cell that seems able to do many, and perhaps even all, the same things human embryonic stem cells can do. Researchers at Tufts University announced in February that they had found similar cells. While some scientists have expressed doubts that either kind of cell will prove as useful as embryonic ones, the discoveries have given birth to new hopes that scientists may yet find the perfect adult stem cell hiding in plain sight.

Maybe Cedric Seldon himself will discover them. The stem cells he got in his cord blood transplant did the trick, it turns out. They took root in his marrow faster than in anyone his doctors have seen. "Everyone's saying, 'Oh my God, you're doing so well'" his mother says.

That makes Cedric part of the world's first generation of regenerated people, a seamless blend of old and new—and, oddly enough, of male and female. His stem cells, remember, came from a girl, and they've been diligently churning out blood cells with two X chromosomes ever since. It's a detail that will not affect his sexual development, which is under the control of his hormones, not his blood. But it's a quirk that could save him, his mother jokes, if he ever commits a crime and leaves a bit of blood behind. The DNA results would be unambiguous, she notes correctly. "They'll be looking for a girl."

The Age of Genetic Technology Arrives

Leon R. Kass

As one contemplates the current and projected state of genetic knowledge and technology, one is astonished by how far we have come in the less than fifty years since Watson and Crick first announced the structure of DNA. True, soon after that discovery, scientists began seriously to discuss the futuristic prospects of gene therapy for genetic disease and of genetic engineering more generally. But no one then imagined how rapidly genetic technology would emerge. The Human Genome Project, disclosing the DNA sequences of all thirty thousand human genes, is all but completed. And even without comprehensive genomic knowledge, biotech business is booming. According to a recent report by the research director for GlaxoSmithKline, enough sequencing data are available to keep his researchers busy for the next twenty years, developing early-detection screening techniques, rationally designed vaccines, genetically engineered changes in malignant tumors leading to enhanced immune response, and, ultimately, precise gene therapy for specific genetic diseases. The age of genetic technology has arrived.

Genetic technology comes into existence as part of the large humanitarian project to cure disease, prolong life, and alleviate suffering. As such, it occupies the moral high ground of compassionate healing. Who would not welcome personal genetic profiling that would enable doctors to customize the most effective and safest drug treatments for individuals with hypertension or rheumatoid arthritis? Who would not welcome genetic therapy to correct the defects that lead to sickle cell anemia, Huntington's disease, and breast cancer, or to protect against the immune deficiency caused by the AIDS virus?

And yet genetic technology has also aroused considerable public concern, for it strikes most people as different from other biomedical technologies. Even people duly impressed by the astonishing genetic achievements of the last decades and eager for the medical benefits are nonetheless ambivalent about these new developments. For they sense that genetic technology, while in some respects continuous with the traditional medical project of compassionate healing, also represents something radically new and disquieting. Often hard-pressed to articulate the precise basis of their disquiet, they talk rather in general terms about the dangers of eugenics or the fear of "tampering with human genes" or, for that matter, "playing God."

Enthusiasts for genetic technology, made confident by their expertise and by their growing prestige and power, are often impatient with the public's disquiet. Much of it they attribute to ignorance of science: "If the public only knew what we know, it would see things our way and give up its irrational fears." For the rest, they blame outmoded moral and religious notions, ideas that scientists insist no longer hold water and only serve to obstruct scientific progress.

In my own view, the scientists' attempt to cast the debate as a battle of beneficial and knowledgeable cleverness versus ignorant and superstitious anxiety should be resisted. For the public is right to be ambivalent about genetic technology, and no amount of instruction in molecular biology and genetics should allay its—our—legitimate human concerns. Rightly understood, these worries are, in fact, in touch with the deepest matters of our humanity and dignity, and we ignore them at our peril.

I will not dispute here which of the prophesied technologies will in fact prove feasible or how soon.[1] To be sure, as a practical matter we must address the particular ethical issues raised by each new technical power as it comes into existence. But the moral meaning of the entire enterprise does not depend on the precise details regarding what and when. I shall proceed by raising a series of questions, the first of which is an attempt to say how genetic technology is different.

Is Genetic Technology Special?

What is different about genetic technology? At first glance, not much. Isolating a disease-inducing aberrant gene looks fairly continuous with isolating a disease-inducing intracellular virus. Supplying diabetics with normal genes for producing insulin has the same medical goal as supplying them with insulin for injection.

Nevertheless, despite these obvious similarities, genetic technology is also decisively different. When fully developed, it will wield two powers not shared by ordinary medical practice. Medicine treats only existing individuals, and it treats them only remedially, seeking to correct deviations from a more or less stable norm of health. By contrast, genetic engineering will, first of all, deliberately make changes that are transmissible into succeeding generations and may even alter in advance specific *future* individuals through direct "germ-line" or embryo interventions. Secondly, genetic engineering may be able, through so-called genetic enhancement, to create new human capacities and, hence, new norms of health and fitness.[2]

For the present, it is true, genetic technology is hailed primarily for its ability better to diagnose and treat *disease* in *existing* individuals. Confined to such practices, it would raise few questions (beyond the usual ones of safety and efficacy). Even intrauterine gene therapy for existing fetuses with diagnosable genetic disease could be seen as an extension of the growing field of fetal medicine.

But there is no reason to believe that the use of gene-altering powers can be so confined, either in logic or in practice. For one thing, "germ-line" gene therapy and manipulation, affecting not merely the unborn but also the unconceived,[3] is surely in our future. The practice has numerous justifications, beginning with the desire to reverse the unintended dysgenic effects of modern medical success. Thanks to medicine, for example, individuals who would have died from diabetes now live long enough to transmit their disease-producing genes. Why, it has been argued, should we not reverse these unfortunate changes by deliberate intervention? More generally, why should we not effect precise genetic alteration in disease-carrying sperm or eggs or early embryos, in order to prevent in advance the emergence of disease that otherwise will later require expensive and burdensome treatment? In short, even before we have had more than trivial experience with gene therapy for existing individuals—none of it successful—sober people have called for overturning the current (self-imposed) taboo on germ-line modification. The line between somatic and germ-line modification cannot hold.

Despite the naive hopes of many, neither will we be able to defend the boundary between therapy and genetic enhancement. Will we reject novel additions to the human genome that enable us to produce, internally, vitamins or amino acids we now must get in our diet? Will we decline to make alterations in the immune system that will increase its efficacy or make it impervious to HIV? When genetic profiling becomes able to disclose the genetic contributions to height or memory or intelligence, will we deny prospective parents the right to enhance the potential of their children?[4] Finally, should we discover—as no doubt we will—the genetic switches that control our biological clock and that very likely influence also the maximum human life expectancy, will we opt to keep our hands off the rate of aging or our natural human life span? Not a chance.

We thus face a paradox. On the one hand, genetic technology really *is* different. It can and will go to work directly and deliberately on our basic, heritable, life-shaping capacities at their biological roots. It can take us beyond existing norms of health and healing—perhaps even alter fundamental features of human nature. On the other hand, precisely because the goals it will serve, at least to begin with, will be continuous with those of modern high-interventionist medicine, we will find its promise familiar and irresistible.

This paradox itself contributes to public disquiet: rightly perceiving a powerful difference in genetic technology, we also sense that we are powerless to establish, on the basis of that dif-

ference, clear limits to its use. The genetic genie, first unbottled to treat disease, will go its own way, whether we like it or not.

How Much Genetic Self-Knowledge Is Good For Us?

Quite apart from worries about genetic engineering, gaining genetic knowledge is itself a legitimate cause of anxiety, not least because of one of its most touted benefits—the genetic profiling of individuals. There has been much discussion about how knowledge of someone's genetic defects, if leaked to outsiders, could be damaging in terms of landing a job or gaining health or life insurance, and legislative measures have been enacted to guard against such hazards. Little attention has been paid, however, to the implications of genetic knowledge for the person himself. Yet the deepest problem connected with learning your own genetic sins and unhealthy predispositions is neither the threat to confidentiality nor the risk of "genetic discrimination" in employment or insurance, important though these practical problems may be.[5] It is, rather, the various hazards and deformations in living your life that will attach to knowing in advance your likely or possible medical future. To be sure, in some cases such foreknowledge will be welcome, if it can lead to easy measures to prevent or treat the impending disorder, and if the disorder in question does not powerfully affect self-image or self-command. But will and should we welcome knowledge that we carry a predisposition to Alzheimer's disease or schizophrenia, or genes that will definitely produce, at an unknown future time, a serious but untreatable disease?

Still harder will it be for most people to live easily and wisely with less certain information—say, where multigenic traits are involved. The recent case of a father who insisted that ovariectomy and mastectomy be performed on his ten-year-old daughter because she happened to carry the BRCA-1 gene for breast cancer dramatically shows the toxic effective of genetic knowledge.

Less dramatic but more profound is the threat to human freedom and spontaneity, a subject explored twenty-five years ago by the philosopher Hans Jonas, one of our wisest commentators on technology and the human prospect. As Jonas observed, "Knowledge of the future, especially one's own, has always been excepted [from the injunction to 'Know thyself'] and the attempt to gain it by whatever means (astrology is one) disparaged—as futile superstition by the enlightened, but as sin by theologians." Everyone remembers that Prometheus was the philanthropic god who gave fire and the arts to humans. But it is often forgotten that he gave them also the greater gift of "blind hopes"—"to cease seeing doom before their eyes"—precisely because he knew that ignorance of one's own future fate was indispensable to aspiration and achievement. I suspect that many people, taking their bearings from life lived open-endedly rather than from preventive medicine practiced rationally, would prefer ignorance of the future to the scientific astrology of knowing their genetic profile. In a free society, that would be their right.

Or would it? This leads us to the third question.

What About Freedom?

Even people who might otherwise welcome the growth of genetic knowledge and technology are worried about the coming power of geneticists, genetic engineers and, in particular, governmental authorities armed with genetic technology.[6] Precisely because we have been taught by these very scientists that genes hold the secret of life, and that our genotype is our essence if not quite our destiny, we are made nervous by those whose expert knowledge and technique touch our very being. Even apart from any particular abuses and misuses of power, friends of human freedom have deep cause for concern.

C. S. Lewis, no friend of ignorance, put the matter sharply in *The Abolition of Man*:

> If any one age really attains, by eugenics and scientific education, the power to make its descendants what it pleases, all men who live after it are the patients of that power.... But even within this master generation (itself an infinitesimal minority of the species) the power will be exercised by a minority smaller still. Man's conquest of Nature, if the dreams of some scientific planners are realized, means the rule of a few hundreds of men over billions upon billions of men.

Most genetic technologists will hardly recognize themselves in this portrait. Though they concede that abuses or misuses of power may occur, especially in tyrannical regimes, they see themselves not as predestinators but as facilitators, merely providing increased knowledge and technique that people can freely choose to use in making decisions about their health or reproductive choices. Genetic power, they tell us, serves not to limit freedom, but to increase it.

But as we can see from the already existing practices of genetic screening and prenatal diagnosis, this claim is at best self-deceptive, at worst disingenuous. The choice to develop and practice genetic screening and the choices of which genes to target for testing have been made not by the public but by scientists—and not on liberty-enhancing but on eugenic grounds. In many cases, practitioners of prenatal diagnosis refuse to do fetal genetic screening in the absence of a prior commitment from the pregnant woman to abort any afflicted fetus. In other situations, pregnant women who still wish *not* to know prenatal facts must withstand strong medical pressures for testing.

In addition, economic pressures to contain health-care costs will almost certainly constrain free choice. Refusal to provide insurance coverage for this or that genetic disease may eventually work to compel genetic abortion or intervention. State-mandated screening already occurs for PKU (phenylketonuria) and other diseases, and full-blown genetic screening programs loom large on the horizon. Once these arrive, there will likely be an upsurge of economic pressure to limit reproductive freedom. All this will be done, of course, in the name of the well-being of children.

Already in 1971, geneticist Bentley Glass, in his presidential address to the American Association for the Advancement of Science, enunciated "the right of every child to be born with a sound physical and mental constitution, based on a sound genotype." Looking ahead to the reproductive and genetic technologies that are today rapidly arriving, Glass proclaimed: "No parents will in that future time have a right to burden society with a malformed or a mentally incompetent child." It remains to be seen to what extent such prophecies will be realized. But they surely provide sufficient and reasonable grounds for being concerned about restrictions on human freedoms, even in the absence of overt coercion, and even in liberal polities like our own.

What About Human Dignity?

Here, rather than in the more-discussed fears about freedom, lie our deepest concerns, and rightly so. For threats to human dignity can—and probably will—arise even with the free, humane, and "enlightened" use of these technologies. Genetic technology, the practices it will engender, and above all the scientific teachings about human life on which it rests are not, as many would have it, morally and humanly neutral. Regardless of how they are practiced or taught, they are pregnant with their own moral meanings and will necessarily bring with them changes in our practices, our institutions, our norms, our beliefs, and our self-conception. It is, I submit, these challenges to our dignity and humanity that are at the bottom of our anxiety over genetic science and technology. Let me touch briefly on four aspects of this most serious matter.

"Playing God"

Paradoxically, worries about dehumanization are sometimes expressed in the fear of superhumanization, that is, that man will be "playing God." This complaint is too facilely dismissed by scientists and nonbelievers. The concern has meaning, God or no God.

Never mind the exaggeration that lurks in this conceit of man's playing God. (Even at his most powerful, after all, man is capable only of *playing* God.) Never mind the implicit innuendo that nobody has given to others this creative and judgmental authority, or the implicit retort that there is theological warrant for acting as God's co-creator in overcoming the ills and suffering of the world. Consider only that if scientists are seen in this godlike role of creator, judge, and savior, the rest of us must stand before them as supplicating, tainted creatures. Despite the hyperbolic speech, that is worry enough.

Practitioners of prenatal diagnosis, working today with but a fraction of the information soon to be available from the Human Genome Project, already screen for a long list of genetic diseases and abnormalities, from Down syndrome to dwarfism. Possession of any one of these defects, they believe, renders a prospective child unworthy of life. Persons who happen still to be born with these conditions, having somehow escaped the spreading net of detection and eugenic abortion, are increasingly regarded as "mistakes," as inferior human beings who should not have been born.[7] Not long ago, at my own university, a physician making rounds with medical students stood over the bed of an intelligent, otherwise normal ten-year-old boy with spina bifida. "Were he to have been conceived today," the physician casually informed his entourage, "he would have been aborted." Determining who shall live and who shall die—on the basis of genetic merit—is a godlike power already wielded by genetic medicine. This power will only grow.

Manufacture & Commodification

But, one might reply, genetic technology also holds out the premise of redemption, of a *cure* for these life-crippling and life-forfeiting disorders. Very well. But in order truly to practice their salvific power, genetic technologists will have to increase greatly their manipulations and interventions, well beyond merely screening and weeding out. True, in some cases genetic testing and risk management aimed at prevention may actually cut down on the need for high-tech interventions aimed at cure. But in many other cases, ever-greater genetic scrutiny will lead necessarily to ever more extensive manipulation. And, to produce Bentley Glass's healthy and well-endowed babies, let alone babies with the benefits of genetic enhancement, a new scientific obstetrics will be necessary, one that will come very close to turning human procreation into manufacture.

This process was already crudely begun with in vitro fertilization. It is now taking giant steps forward with the ability to screen in vitro embryos before implantation (so-called pre-implantation genetic diagnosis). And it will come to maturity with interventions such as cloning and, eventually, with precise genetic engineering. Just follow the logic and the aspirations of current practice: the road we are traveling leads all the way to the world of designer babies—reached not by dictatorial fiat, but by the march of benevolent humanitarianism, and cheered on by an ambivalent citizenry that also dreads becoming merely the last of man's manmade things.

Make no mistake: the price to be paid for producing optimum or even only genetically sound babies will be the transfer of procreation from the home to the laboratory. Such an arrangement will be profoundly dehumanizing, no matter how genetically good or healthy the resultant children. And let us not forget the powerful economic interests that will surely operate in this area; with their advent, the commodification of nascent human life will be unstoppable.

Standards, Norms, & Goals

According to Genesis, God, in His creating, looked at His creatures and saw that there were *good*—intact, complete, well-working wholes, true to the spoken idea that guided their creation. What standards will guide the genetic engineers?

For the time being, one might answer, the norm of health. But even before the genetic enhancers join the party, the standard of health is being deconstructed. Are you healthy if, although you show no symptoms, you carry genes that will definitely produce Huntington's disease? What if you carry, say, 40 percent of the genetic markers thought to be linked to the appearance of Alzheimer's disease? And what will "healthy" and "normal" mean when we discover your genetic propensities for alcoholism, drug abuse, pederasty, or violence?[8] The idea of health progressively becomes at once both imperial and vague: medicalization of what have hitherto

been mental or moral matters paradoxically brings with it the disappearance of any clear standard of health itself.

Once genetic *enhancement* comes on the scene, standards of health, wholeness, or fitness will be needed more than ever, but just then is when all pretense of standards will go out the window. "Enhancement" is, of course, a euphemism for "improvement," and the idea of improvement necessarily implies a good, a better, and perhaps even a best. If, however, we can no longer look to our previously unalterable human nature for a standard or norm of what is good or better, how will anyone know what constitutes an improvement? It will not do to assert that we can extrapolate from what we like about ourselves. Because memory is good, can we say how much more memory would be better? If sexual desire is good, how much more would be better? Life is good, but how much extension of the life span would be good for us? Only simplistic thinkers believe they can easily answer such questions.[9]

More modest enhancers, like more modest genetic therapists and technologists, eschew grandiose goals. They are valetudinarians, not eugenicists. They pursue not some faraway positive good, but the positive elimination of evils: diseases, pain, suffering, the likelihood of death. But let us not be deceived. Hidden in all this avoidance of evil is nothing less than the quasi-messianic goal of a painless, suffering-free and, finally, immortal existence. Only the presence of such a goal justifies the sweeping-aside of any opposition to the relentless march of medical science. Only such a goal gives trumping moral power to the principle "cure disease, relieve suffering."

"Cloning human beings is unethical and dehumanizing, you say? Never mind: it will help us treat infertility, avoid genetic disease, and provide perfect materials for organ replacement." Such, indeed, was the tenor of the June 1997 report of the National Bioethics Advisory Commission, *Cloning Human Beings*. Notwithstanding its call for a temporary ban on the practice, the only moral objection the commission could agree upon was that cloning "is not safe to use in humans at this time," because the technique has yet to be perfected.[10] Even this elite ethical body, in other words, was unable to muster any other moral argument sufficient to cause us to forgo the possible health benefits of cloning.[11]

The same argument will also justify creating and growing human embryos for experimentation, revising the definition of death to increase the supply of organs for transplantation, growing human body parts in the peritoneal cavities of animals, perfusing newly dead bodies as factories for useful biological substances, or reprogramming the human body and mind with genetic or neurobiological engineering. Who can sustain an objection if these practices will help us live longer and with less overt suffering?

It turns out that even the more modest biogenetic engineers, whether they know it or not, are in the immortality business, proceeding on the basis of a quasi-religious faith that all innovation is by definition progress, no matter what is sacrificed to attain it.

The Tragedy Of Success

What the enthusiasts do not see is that their utopian project will not eliminate suffering but merely shift it around. Forgetting that contentment requires that our desires do not outpace our powers, they have not noticed that the enormous medical progress of the last half-century has not left the present generation satisfied. Indeed, we are already witnessing a certain measure of public discontent as a paradoxical result of rising expectations in the health care field: although their actual health has improved substantially in recent decades, people's *satisfaction* with their current health status has remained the same or declined. But that is hardly the highest cost of success in the medical/humanitarian project.

As Aldous Huxley made clear in his prophetic. *Brave New World,* the road chosen and driven by compassionate humaneness paved by biotechnology, if traveled to the end, leads not to human fulfillment but to human debasement. Perfected bodies are achieved at the price of flattened souls. What Tolstoy called "real life"—life in its immediacy, vividness, and rootedness—has been replaced by an utterly mediated, sterile, and disconnected existence. In one word: dehumanization, the inevitable result of making the essence of human nature the final object of the conquest of nature for the relief of man's estate. Like Midas, bioengineered man will be cursed to acquire precisely what he wished for, only to discover—painfully and too late—that what he wished for is not exactly what he wanted. Or, worse than Midas, he may be so dehumanized he will not even recognize that in aspiring to be perfect, he is no longer even truly human. To paraphrase Bertrand Russell, technological humanitarianism is like a warm bath that heats up so imperceptibly you don't know when to scream.

The main point here is not the rightness or wrongness of this or that imagined scenario; all this is, admittedly, highly speculative. I surely have no way of knowing whether my worst fears will be realized, but you surely have no way of knowing they will not. The point is rather the plausibility, even the wisdom, of thinking about genetic technology like the entire technological venture, under the ancient and profound idea of tragedy in which success and failure are inseparably grown together like the concave and the convex. What I am suggesting is that genetic technology's way of approaching human life, a way spurred on by the utopian promises and perfectionist aims of modern thought and its scientific crusaders, may well turn out to be inevitable, heroic, and doomed. If this suggestion holds water, then the question regarding genetic technology is not "triumph OR tragedy," because the answer is "both together."

In the nineteenth and early twentieth century, the challenge came in the form of Darwinism and its seeming opposition to biblical religion, a battle initiated not so much by the scientists as by the beleaguered defenders of orthodoxy. In our own time, the challenge comes from molecular biology, behavioral genetics, and evolutionary psychology, fueled by their practitioners' overconfident belief in the sufficiency of their reductionist explanations of all vital and human phenomena. Never mind "created in the image of God"; what elevated *humanistic* view of human life or human goodness is defensible against the belief, asserted by most public and prophetic voices of biology, that man is just a collection of molecules, an accident on the stage of evolution, a freakish speck of mind in a mindless universe, fundamentally no different from other living—or even nonliving—things? What chance have our treasured ideas of freedom and dignity against the reductive notion of "the selfish gene" (or, for that matter, of "genes for altruism"), the belief that DNA is the essence of life, or the teaching that all human behavior and our rich inner life are rendered intelligible only in terms of their contributions to species survival and reproductive success?

These transformations are, in fact, welcomed by many of our leading scientists and intellectuals. In 1997 the luminaries of the International Academy of Humanism—including biologists Crick, Dawkins, and Wilson, and humanists Isaiah Berlin, W. V. Quine, and Kurt Vonnegut—issued a statement in defense of cloning research in higher mammals and human beings. Their reasons were revealing:

> Views of human nature rooted in humanity's tribal past ought not to be our primary criterion for making moral decisions about cloning.... The potential benefits of cloning may be so immense that it would be a tragedy if ancient theological scruples should lead to a Luddite rejection of cloning.

In order to justify ongoing research, these intellectuals were willing to shed not only traditional religious views, but any view of human distinctiveness and special dignity, their own included. They failed to see that the scientific view of man they celebrated does more than insult our vanity. It undermines our self-conception as free, thoughtful, and responsible beings, worthy of respect because we alone among the animals have minds and hearts that aim far higher than the mere perpetuation of our genes.

The problem may lie not so much with scientific findings themselves, but with the shallow philosophy that recognizes no other truths but these and with the arrogant pronouncements of the bioprophets. For example, in a letter to the editor complaining about a review of his book *How the Mind Works,* the well-known evolutionary psychologist and popularizer Stephen Pinker rails against any appeal to the human soul:

> Unfortunately for that theory, brain science has shown that the mind is what the brain does. The supposedly immaterial soul can be bisected with a knife, altered by chemicals, turned on or off by electricity, and extinguished by a sharp blow or a lack of oxygen. Centuries ago it was unwise to ground morality on the dogma that the earth sat at the center of the universe. It is just as unwise today to ground it on dogmas about souls endowed by God.

One hardly knows whether to be more impressed by the height of Pinker's arrogance or by the depth of his shallowness. But he speaks with the authority of science, and few are able and willing to dispute him on his own grounds.

There is, of course, nothing novel about reductionism, materialism, and determinism of the kind displayed here; these are doctrines with which Socrates contended long ago. What is new is that, as philosophies, they seem (to many people) to be vindicated by scientific advance. Here, in consequence, is perhaps the most pernicious result of our technological progress, more dehumanizing than any actual manipulation or technique, present or future: the erosion, perhaps the final erosion, of the idea of man as noble, dignified, precious, or godlike, and its re-placement with a view of man, no less than of nature, as mere raw material for manipulation and homogenization.

Hence our peculiar moral crisis. We are in turbulent seas without a landmark precisely because we adhere more and more to a view of human life that both gives us enormous power and, *at the same time,* denies every possibility of nonarbitrary stan-dards for guiding its use. Though well equipped, we know not who we are or where we are going. We triumph over nature's unpredictability only to subject ourselves, tragically, to the still greater unpredictability of our capricious wills and our fickle opinions. Engineering the engineer as well as the engine, we race our train we know not where. That we do not recognize our predicament is itself a tribute to the depth of our infatuation with scientific progress and our naive faith in the sufficiency of our humanitarian impulses.

Does this mean that I am therefore in favor of ignorance, suf-fering, and death? Of killing the goose of genetic technology even before she lays her golden eggs? Surely not. But unless we mobilize the courage to look foursquare at the full human mean-ing of our new enterprise in biogenetic technology and engi-neering, we are doomed to become its creatures if not its slaves. Important though it is to set a moral boundary here, devise a regulation there, hoping to decrease the damage caused by this or that little rivulet, it is even more important to be sober about the true nature and meaning of the flood itself.

That our exuberant new biologists and their technological minions might be persuaded of this is, to say the least, highly unlikely. For all their ingenuity, they do not even seek the wis-dom that just might yield the kind of knowledge that keeps hu-man life human. But it is not too late for the rest of us to become aware of the dangers—not just to privacy or insurability, but to our very humanity. So aware, we might be better able to defend the increasingly beleaguered vestiges and principles of our hu-man dignity, even as we continue to reap the considerable ben-efits that genetic technology will inevitably provide.

Notes

1. I will also not dispute here the scientists' reductive understanding of life and their treatment of rich vital activities solely in terms of the in-teractions of genes. I do, however, touch on the moral significance of such reductionism toward the end of this essay.

2. Some commentators, in disagreement with these arguments, insist that genetic technology differs only in degree from previous human practices that have existed for millennia. For example, they see no difference between the "social engineering" of education, which works on the next generation through speech or symbolic deed, and biological engineering, which inscribes its effects, directly and irre-versibly, into the human constitution. Or they claim to see no differ-ence between the indirect genetic effects of human mate selection and deliberate, direct genetic engineering to produce offspring with pre-cise biological capacities. Such critics, I fear, have already bought into a reductionist view of human life and the relation between the

generations. And they ignore the fact that most people choose their mates for reasons different from stud farming.

3. Correction of a genetically abnormal egg or sperm (that is, of the "germ cells"), however, worthy an activity, stretches the meaning of "therapy" beyond all normal uses. Just who is the "patient" being "treated"? The potential child-to-be that might be formed out of such egg or sperm is, at the time of the treatment, at best no more than a hope and a hypothesis. There is no medical analogue for treatment of nonexistent patients.

4. To be sure, not all attempts at enhancement will require genetic alter-ations. We have already witnessed efforts to boost height with sup-plementary growth hormone or athletic performance with steroids or "blood doping." Nevertheless, the largest possible changes in what is "normally" human are likely to come about only with the help of ge-netic alterations or the joining of machines (for example, computers) to human beings.

5. I find it odd that it is these issues that have been put forward as the special ethical problems associated with genetic technology and the Human Genome Project. Issues of privacy and risks of discrimination related to medical conditions are entirely independent of whether the medical condition is genetic in origin. Only if a special stigma were attached to having an inherited disease—for example, only if having thalassemia or sickle cell anemia were more shameful than having gonorrhea or lung cancer—would the genetic character of a disease create special or additional reasons for protecting against breaches of confidentiality or discrimination in the workplace.

6. Until the events of September 11 and the anthrax scare that followed, they did not worry enough. It is remarkable that most bioethical dis-cussions of genetic technology had naively neglected its potential usefulness in creating biological weapons, such as, to begin with, an-tibiotic-resistant plague bacteria, or later, aerosols containing cancer-inducing or mind-scrambling viral vectors. The most outstanding molecular geneticists were especially naive in this area. When Amer-ican molecular biologists convened the 1975 Asilomar Conference on recombinant DNA research, which called for a voluntary morato-rium on experiments until the biohazards could be evaluated, they in-vited Soviet biologists to the meeting who said virtually nothing but who photographed every slide that was shown.

7. One of the most worrisome but least appreciated aspects of the god-like power of the new genetics is its tendency to "redefine" a human being in terms of his genes. Once a person is decisively characterized by his genotype, it is but a short step to justifying death solely for ge-netic sins.

8. Many scientists suspect that we have different inherited propensities for these and other behavioral troubles, though it is almost certain that there is no single "gene for x" that is responsible.

9. This strikes me as the deepest problem with positive eugenics: less the threat of coercion, more the presumption of thinking we are wise enough to engineer "improvements" in the human species.

10. This is, of course, not an objection to cloning itself but only to hazards tied to the technique used to produce the replicated children.

11. I forbear mentioning what is rapidly becoming another trumping ar-gument: increasing the profits of my biotech company and its share-holders, an argument often presented in more public-spirited dress: if we don't do it, other countries will, and we will lose our competitive edge in biotechnology.

LEON R. KASS, M.D. is professor in social thought at the University of Chicago, Hertog fellow at the American Enterprise Institute, and chairman of the President's Council on Bioethics. Excerpted from Life, Liberty and the Defense of Dignity. Published by Encounter Books, San Francisco, October 2002. Reprinted with permission.

Brave New Babies

Parents now have the power to choose the sex of their children. But as technology answers prayers, it also raises some troubling questions.

CLAUDIA KALB

Sharla Miller of Gillette, Wyo., always wanted a baby girl, but the odds seemed stacked against her. Her husband, Shane, is one of three brothers, and Sharla and her five siblings (four girls, two boys) have produced twice as many males as females. After the Millers' first son, Anthony, was born in 1991, along came Ashton, now 8, and Alec, 4. Each one was a gift, says Sharla, but the desire for a girl never waned. "I'm best friends with my mother;' she says. "I couldn't get it out of my mind that I wanted a daughter." Two years ago Sharla, who had her fallopian tubes tied after Alec's birth, began looking into adopting a baby girl. In the course of her Internet research, she stumbled upon a Web site for the Fertility Institutes in Los Angeles, headed by Dr. Jeffrey Steinberg, where she learned about an in vitro fertilization technique called pre-implantation genetic diagnosis. By creating embryos outside the womb, then testing them for gender, PGD could guarantee with almost 100 percent certainty—the sex of her baby. Price tag: $18,480, plus travel. Last November Sharla's eggs and Shane's sperm were mixed in a lab dish, producing 14 healthy embryos, seven male and seven female. Steinberg transferred three of the females into Sharla's uterus, where two implanted successfully. If all goes well, the run of Miller boys will end in July with the arrival of twin baby girls. "I have three wonderful boys," says Sharla, "but since there was a chance I could have a daughter, why not?"

The brave new world is definitely here. After 25 years of staggering advances in reproductive medicine—first test-tube babies, then donor eggs and surrogate mothers—technology is changing babymaking in a whole new way. No longer can science simply help couples have babies, it can help them have the kind of babies they want. Choosing gender may obliterate one of the fundamental mysteries of procreation, but for people who have grown accustomed to taking 3-D ultrasounds of fetuses, learning a baby's sex within weeks of conception and scheduling convenient delivery dates, it's simply the next logical step. That gleeful exclamation, "It's a boy!" or "It's a girl!" may soon just be a quaint reminder of how random births used to be.

Throughout history, humans have wished for a child of one sex or the other and have been willing to do just about anything to get it. Now that gender selection is scientifically feasible, in-terest in the controversial practice (banned, except for medical reasons, in the United Kingdom) is exploding. Despite considerable moral murkiness, Americans are talking to their doctors and visiting catchy Web sites like www.choosethesexofyourbaby.com and myboyorgirl.com—many of them offering money-back guarantees. In just the last six months, Steinberg's site has had 85,000 hits. At the Genetics and IVF Institute (GIVF) in Fairfax, Va., an FDA clinical trial of a sophisticated sperm-sorting technology called MicroSort is more than half-way to completion. Through radio, newspaper and magazine ads ("Do you want to choose the gender of your next baby?"), the clinic has recruited hundreds of eager couples, and more than 400 babies out of 750 needed for the trial have been born. Other couples continue to flock to older, more low-tech and questionable sperm-sorting techniques like the Ericsson method, which is offered at about two dozen clinics nationwide. By far, the most provocative gender-selection technique is PGD. Some clinics offer the procedure as a bonus for couples already going through fertility treatments, but a small number are beginning to provide the option for otherwise healthy couples. Once Steinberg decided to offer PGD gender selection to all comers, he says, "word spread like wildfire."

The ability to create baby Jack or baby Jill opens a high-tech can of worms. While the advances have received kudos from grateful families, they also raise loaded ethical questions about whether science is finally crossing a line that shouldn't be crossed. Even fertility specialists are divided over whether choosing a male or female embryo is acceptable. If couples can request a baby boy or girl, what's next on the slippery slope of modern reproductive medicine? Eye color? Height? Intelligence? Could picking one gender over the other become the 21st century's form of sex discrimination? Or, as in China, up-set the ratio of males to females? Many European countries already forbid sex selection; should there be similar regulations in the United States? These explosive issues are being debated in medical journals, on university ethics boards and at the highest levels in Washington. Just last week the President's Council on Bioethics discussed proposals for possible legislation that would ban the buying and selling of human embryos and far-out reproductive experimentation, like creating human-animal hybrids. While the recommendations—part of a report due out this spring—do not suggest limiting IVF or gender selection, the goals are clear: the government should clamp down before technology goes too far. "Even though people have strong differences of opinion on some issues," says council chair and leading bioethieist Leon Kass, "all of us have a stake in keeping human reproduction human."

After their first son, Jesse, was born in 1988, Mary and Sam Toedtman tried all sorts of folksy remedies to boost their chances of having a girl. When Jesse was followed by Jacob, now 10, and Lucas, 7, it seemed clear that boys would be boys in the Toedtman family. Sam has two brothers and comes from a line of boys 70 years long. So, after a lot of serious thinking, the Toedtmans decided to enroll in GIVF's clinical trial of MicroSort for "family balancing." That's the popular new term for gender selection by couples who already have at least one child and want to control their family mix. Since MicroSort's family balance trial began in 1995, more than 1,300 couples have signed on—almost 10 times more than joined a companion trial aimed at avoiding genetic illnesses that strike boys. GIVF is actively recruiting new candidates for both trials. In 2003 a second MicroSort clinic was opened near Los Angeles, and a third is planned for Florida this year. GIVF hopes MicroSort will become the first sperm-sorting device to receive the FDA's stamp of approval for safety and effectiveness. "This will completely change reproductive choices for women, and that's very exciting," says MicroSort's medical director, Dr. Keith Blauer. "We hope to make it available to as many couples as possible."

The MicroSort technology—created originally by the Department of Agriculture to sort livestock sperm—works by mixing sperm with a DNA-specific dye that helps separate X's from Y's (graphic).The majority of couples who use MicroSort for gender selection have no fertility problems and use standard artificial insemination to conceive. The technique is far from perfect: most participants have to make more than one attempt, each costing at least $2,500, to get pregnant. And not all end up with the gender of choice. At last count, 91 percent of couples who requested an "X sort" gave birth to a baby girl and 76 percent who chose a "Y sort" produced a boy. It worked for the Stock family. Six-month-old Amberlyn was spared the debilitating neuromuscular disorder that plagues her brother, Chancellor, 7. The Toedtmans were lucky, too. Though it took three tries to get pregnant, Mary finally delivered a girl, Natalie, last April. "She's a total joy," she says.

Determined as she was, Toedtman says she would not have felt comfortable creating embryos to ensure that Natalie was Natalie and not Nathaniel. But a small number of others, knowing that their chance of success with PGD is exponentially better, are becoming pioneers in the newest form of family planning. Available at a limited number of clinics nationwide, PGD was designed and originally intended to diagnose serious genetic diseases in embryos, like Tay-Sachs and cystic fibrosis, before implantation. Over the last decade the technology has allowed hundreds of couples, many of whom have endured the death of sick children, to have healthy babies. Today, some doctors are using PGD to increase the odds of successful IVF pregnancies by screening out chromosomally abnormal embryos.

Some of those patients are asking about gender—and it's their right to do so, many doctors say. After an embryo screening, "I tell them it's normal and I tell them it's male or female," says PGD expert Yury Verlinsky of the Reproductive Genetics Institute in Chicago. "It's their embryo. I can't tell them which one to transfer."

It's one thing to allow infertile couples to choose gender after PGD. Creating embryos solely to sort boys from girls sets off ethical and moral alarm bells. In the last year or so, several clinics have begun to offer the procedure for gender balance without restrictions. Steinberg, of Fertility Institutes, says his team methodically debated the pros and cons before doing so. The logic, he says, is simple: "We've been offering sperm sorting for 20 years without any stipulations. Now, in 2004, I can offer almost 100 percent success with PGD. Why would I make it less available?" Steinberg.'s clinic, which also has offices in Las Vegas and Mexico, will soon perform its 100th PGD sex-selection procedure. So far, about 40 babies have been born, every one of them the desired sex. It's unclear how many couples will actually want to endure the hefty cost, time commitment and physical burden of fertility drugs and IVF just to ensure gender. But the idea is intriguing for a lot of couples. "I've had friends and neighbors discreetly inquire," says Dr. David Hill, head of ART Reproductive Center in Beverly Hills, Calif., where about 5 to 10 percent of patients are requesting PGD solely for sex selection. Hill has no problem offering it, but he respects colleagues who say no. "This is a really new area," he says. "It's pretty divided right now as to those who think it's acceptable and those who don't."

Dr. Mark Hughes, a leading PGD authority at Wayne State University School of Medicine in Detroit, is one of the latter. "The last time I checked, your gender wasn't a disease," he says. "There is no illness, no suffering and no reason for a physician to be involved. Besides, we're too busy helping desperate couples with serious disease build healthy families." At Columbia University, Dr. Mark Sauer balks at the idea of family balance. "What are you balancing? It discredits the value of an individual life." For those few patients who ask for it, "I look them straight in the face and say, 'We're not going to do that'." And at Northwestern, Dr. Ralph Kazer says bluntly: " 'Gattaca' was a wonderful movie. That's not what I want to do for a living."

One of the most vexing concerns is what some consider gender selection's implicit sexism. When you choose one sex, the argument goes, you reject the other. In Asia girls have been aborted or killed, and populations skewed, because of favoritism toward boys. Could the same thing happen here? GIVF's Blauer says the vast majority of MicroSort couples want girls, not boys, though that could change if Y-sort statistics improve. At Hill's clinic, about 65 percent request boys; at Steinberg's, 55 percent. "It's not going to tip the balance one way or the other," he says. But what if a couple doesn't get the boy or girl they desire? PGD comes as close as it gets to guaranteeing outcome, but there remains the thorny question of what to do with "wrong sex" embryos. Opponents worry that they'll be destroyed simply because they're male or female, but the options are identical for everyone going through IVF: discard the extras, freeze them for later use, donate them or offer them up for scientific research. As for MicroSort, of the more than 500 pregnancies achieved so far, four have been terminated at other facilities (GIVF won't perform abortions) because of "non-desired gender," says Blauer. "It's important to realize that couples have reproductive choice in this country," he says, but "the vast majority of patients want another healthy child and are happy with either gender."

Just beyond these clinical worries lies a vast swamp of ethical quandaries and inherent contradictions. People who support a woman's right to choose find themselves cringing at the idea of terminating a fetus based on sex. Those who believe that embryos deserve the status of personhood decry their destruction, but gender selection could result in fewer abortions. Choosing sex can skew male-female ratios, but it might also reduce overpopulation. Requesting a girl could mean she will be more desired by her parents, but it's also possible she'll grow up and decide she'd rather have been a boy. "Children are going to hold their parents responsible for having made them this way," says bioethicist Kass, "and that may not be as innocent as it sounds."

And then there is the most fundamental conflict of all: science versus religion. One Korean-American couple, with two daughters has been on both sides. Feeling an intense cultural pressure to produce a son, the woman, 31, attended a MicroSort information session, where Blauer reviewed the technique. Intrigued, she went back for a second session and convinced her husband to come along. When it was time to move forward, though, a greater power took over. "I don't think God intended us to do that," she says. "We decided we should just pray about it and leave it up to God."

There are no laws against performing gender selection in the United States. Many people believe that the safety and effectiveness of reproductive technologies like PGD should be regulated, says Kathy Hudson, of the Genetics and Public Policy Center at Johns Hopkins, which recently polled 1,200 Americans on the topic. But, she says, many Americans "are uncomfortable with the government being the arbiter of how to use these technologies." Meanwhile, fertility doctors look to the American Society for Reproductive Medicine for professional standards. John Robertson, head of ASRM's ethics committee, says preconception techniques like MicroSort "would be fine once safety is established." So far, MicroSort reports, 2.4 percent of its babies have been born with major malformations, like Down syndrome, compared with 3 to 4 percent in the general population. But until the trial is completed, there are no definitive data. As for PGD, the ASRM currently discourages its use for sex selection, but Robertson says he wouldn't rule out the possibility that it might become acceptable in the future.

So what, in the end, should we make of gender selection? Will programming of human DNA before birth become inevitable? "I learned a long time ago never to say never," says Rick Myers, chief of Stanford's genetics department. Still, he says, traits we're all worried about, like height, personality and intelligence, aren't the products of single genes. They're cooked in a complex stew of DNA and environment—a stew that boggles scientists, even those with IQs so high you'd swear they were bioengineered. And even if we could create designer Uma Thurmans, would we want to? Sharla Miller and Mary Toedtman say absolutely not. "That's taking it too far," says Miller.

We wouldn't be human if we didn't fantasize about the sci-fi universe around the corner. Steinberg, who has worked in IVF since its conception in the 1970s, remembers finding notes on his windshield in the early days that said, TEST-TUBE BABIES HAVE NO SOUL. The very idea of creating life outside the womb "was unthinkable," he says. And yet, some 1 million test-tube babies later, the practice has become routine. The same will likely be true of gender selection, says Robin Marantz Henig, author of the new book "Pandora's Baby," a history of IVF "The more it's done," she says, "the less you're going to see concerns."

Lizette Frielingsdorf doesn't have any. She and her husband have three boys—Jordan, 8, Justin, 6, and Jake, 5—and one MicroSort girl, Jessica, who just turned 2. "I call her my $15,000 baby. We felt like we won the lottery," says Frielingsdorf "Probably once a week someone will say, 'You got your girl. How did you do that?' and I'll say, 'Here's the number.' I want others to experience the same joy we have." No doubt, many will.

Inside the Womb

What scientists have learned about those amazing first nine months—and what it means for mothers

J. Madeleine Nash

As the crystal probe slides across her belly, Hilda Manzo, 33, stares wide-eyed at the video monitor mounted on the wall. She can make out a head with a mouth and two eyes. She can see pairs of arms and legs that end in tiny hands and feet. She can see the curve of a backbone, the bridge of a nose. And best of all, she can see movement. The mouth of her child-to-be yawns. Its feet kick. Its hands wave.

Dr. Jacques Abramowicz, director of the University of Chicago's ultrasound unit, turns up the audio so Manzo can hear the gush of blood through the umbilical cord and the fast thump, thump, thump of a miniature heart. "Oh, my!" she exclaims as he adjusts the sonic scanner to peer under her fetus' skin. "The heart is on the left side, as it should be," he says, "and it has four chambers. Look—one, two, three, four!"

Such images of life stirring in the womb—in this case, of a 17-week-old fetus no bigger than a newborn kitten—are at the forefront of a biomedical revolution that is rapidly transforming the way we think about the prenatal world. For although it takes nine months to make a baby, we now know that the most important developmental steps—including laying the foundation for such major organs as the heart, lungs and brain—occur before the end of the first three. We also know that long before a child is born its genes engage the environment of the womb in an elaborate conversation, a two-way dialogue that involves not only the air its mother breathes and the water she drinks but also what drugs she takes, what diseases she contracts and what hardships she suffers.

One reason we know this is a series of remarkable advances in MRIs, sonograms and other imaging technologies that allow us to peer into the developmental process at virtually every stage—from the fusion of sperm and egg to the emergence, some 40 weeks later, of a miniature human being. The extraordinary pictures on these pages come from a new book that captures some of the color and excitement of this research: *From Conception to Birth: A Life Unfolds* (Doubleday), by photographer Alexander Tsiaras and writer Barry Werth. Their computer-enhanced images are reminiscent of the remarkable fetal portraits taken by medical photographer Lennart Nilsson, which appeared in Life magazine in 1965. Like Nilsson's work, these images will probably spark controversy. Antiabortion activists may interpret them

as evidence that a fetus is a viable human being earlier than generally believed, while pro-choice advocates may argue that the new technology allows doctors to detect serious fetal defects at a stage when abortion is a reasonable option.

The other reason we know so much about what goes on inside the womb is the remarkable progress researchers have made in teasing apart the sequence of chemical signals and switches that drive fetal development. Scientists can now describe at the level of individual genes and molecules many of the steps involved in building a human, from the establishment of a head-to-tail growth axis and the budding of limbs to the sculpting of a four-chambered heart and the weaving together of trillions of neural connections. Scientists are beginning to unroll the genetic blueprint of life and identify the precise molecular tools required for assembly. Human development no longer seems impossibly complex, says Stanford University biologist Matthew Scott. "It just seems marvelous."

How is it, we are invited to wonder, that a fertilized egg—a mere speck of protoplasm and DNA encased in a spherical shell—can generate such complexity? The answers, while elusive and incomplete, are beginning to come into focus.

Only 20 years ago, most developmental biologists thought that different organisms grew according to different sets of rules, so that understanding how a fly or a worm develops—or even a vertebrate like a chicken or a fish—would do little to illuminate the process in humans. Then, in the 1980s, researchers found remarkable similarities in the molecular tool kit used by organisms that span the breadth of the animal kingdom, and those similarities have proved serendipitous beyond imagining. No matter what the species, nature uses virtually the same nails and screws, the same hammers and power tools to put an embryo together.

Among the by-products of the torrent of information pouring out of the laboratory are new prospects for treating a broad range of late-in-life diseases. Just last month, for example, three biologists won the Nobel Prize for Medicine for their work on the nematode *Caenorhabditis elegans*, which has a few more than 1,000 cells, compared with a human's 50 trillion. The three winners helped establish that a fundamental mechanism that *C. elegans* embryos employ to get rid of redundant or abnormal

How They Did It

With just a few keystrokes, Alexander Tsiaras does the impossible. He takes the image of a 56-day-old human embryo and peers through its skin, revealing liver, lungs, a bulblike brain and the tiny, exquisite vertebrae of a developing spine.

These are no ordinary baby pictures. What Tsiaras and his colleagues are manipulating are layers of data gathered by CT scans, micro magnetic resonance imaging (MRI) and other visualization techniques. When Lennart Nilsson took his groundbreaking photographs in the 1960s, he was limited to what he could innovatively capture with a flash camera. Since then, says Tsiaras, "there's been a revolution in imaging."

What's changed is that development can now be viewed through a wide variety of prisms, using different forms of energy to illuminate different aspects of the fetus. CT scans, for example, are especially good at showing bone, and MRI is excellent for soft tissue. These two-dimensional layers of information are assembled, using sophisticated computer software, into a three-dimensional whole.

The results are painstakingly accurate and aesthetically stunning. Tsiaras, who trained as a painter and sculptor, used medical specimens from the Carnegie Human Embryology Collection at the National Museum of Health and Medicine in Washington as models for all but a few images. The specimens came from a variety of sources, according to museum director Adrianne Noe, including miscarriages and medically necessary procedures. None were acquired from elective abortions.

—By David Bjerklie

cells also exists in humans and may play a role in AIDS, heart disease and cancer. Even more exciting, if considerably more controversial, is the understanding that embryonic cells harbor untapped therapeutic potential. These cells, of course, are stem cells, and they are the progenitors of more specialized cells that make up organs and tissues. By harnessing their generative powers, medical researchers believe, it may one day be possible to repair the damage wrought by injury and disease. (That prospect suffered a political setback last week when a federal advisory committee recommended that embryos be considered the same as human subjects in clinical trials.)

To be sure, the marvel of an embryo transcends the collection of genes and cells that compose it. For unlike strands of DNA floating in a test tube or stem cells dividing in a Petri dish, an embryo is capable of building not just a protein or a patch of tissue but a living entity in which every cell functions as an integrated part of the whole. "Imagine yourself as the world's tallest skyscraper, built in nine months and germinating from a single brick," suggest Tsiaras and Werth in the opening of their book. "As that brick divides, it gives rise to every other type of material needed to construct and operate the finished tower—a million tons of steel, concrete, mortar, insulation, tile, wood, granite, solvents, carpet, cable, pipe and glass as well as all furniture, phone systems, heating and cooling units, plumbing, electrical wiring, artwork and computer networks, including software."

Given the number of steps in the process, it will perhaps forever seem miraculous that life ever comes into being without a major hitch. "Whenever you look from one embryo to another," observes Columbia University developmental neurobiologist Thomas Jessell, "what strikes you is the fidelity of the process."

Sometimes, though, that fidelity is compromised, and the reasons why this happens are coming under intense scrutiny. In laboratory organisms, birth defects occur for purely genetic reasons when scientists purposely mutate or knock out specific sequences of DNA to establish their function. But when development goes off track in real life, the cause can often be traced to a lengthening list of external factors that disrupt some aspect of the genetic program. For an embryo does not develop in a vacuum but depends on the environment that surrounds it. When a human embryo is deprived of essential nutrients or exposed to a toxin, such as alcohol, tobacco or crack cocaine, the consequences can range from readily apparent abnormalities—spina bifida, fetal alcohol syndrome—to subtler metabolic defects that may not become apparent until much later.

Ironically, even as society at large continues to worry almost obsessively about the genetic origins of disease, the biologists and medical researchers who study development are mounting an impressive case for the role played by the prenatal environment. A growing body of evidence suggests that a number of serious maladies—among them, atherosclerosis, hypertension and diabetes—trace their origins to detrimental prenatal conditions. As New York University Medical School's Dr. Peter Nathanielsz puts it, "What goes on in the womb before you are born is just as important to who you are as your genes."

Most adults, not to mention most teenagers, are by now thoroughly familiar with the mechanics of how the sperm in a man's semen and the egg in a woman's oviduct connect, and it is at this point that the story of development begins. For the sperm and the egg each contain only 23 chromosomes, half the amount of DNA needed to make a human. Only when the sperm and the egg fuse their chromosomes does the tiny zygote, as a fertilized egg is called, receive its instructions to grow. And grow it does, replicating its DNA each time it divides—into two cells, then four, then eight and so on.

If cell division continued in this fashion, then nine months later the hapless mother would give birth to a tumorous ball of literally astronomical proportions. But instead of endlessly dividing, the zygote's cells progressively take form. The first striking change is apparent four days after conception, when a 32-cell clump called the morula (which means "mulberry" in Latin) gives rise to two distinct layers wrapped around a fluid-filled core. Now known as a blastocyst, this spherical mass will proceed to burrow into the wall of the uterus. A short time later, the outer layer of cells will begin turning into the placenta and amniotic sac, while the inner layer will become the embryo.

The formation of the blastocyst signals the start of a sequence of changes that are as precisely choreographed as a ballet. At the end of Week One, the inner cell layer of the blastocyst balloons into two more layers. From the first layer, known as

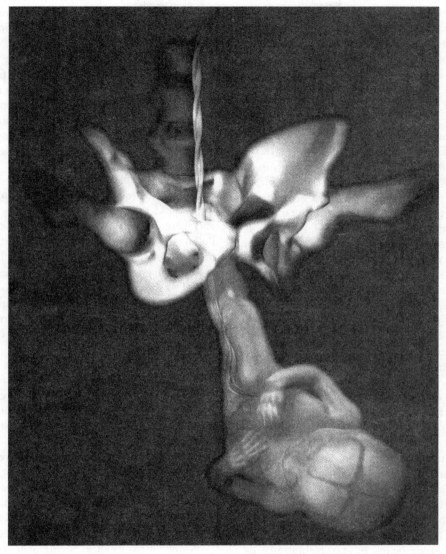

Photo © Alexander Tsiaras/SPL/Photo Researchers, Inc.

9 months—shows how a baby emerges from the birth canal began with an unusual delivery that required doctors to place the mother in a spiral CT scanner. The image was merged with CT and ultrasound data from other babies to create this re-enacted birth.

the endoderm, will come the cells that line the gastrointestinal tract. From the second, the ectoderm, will arise the neurons that make up the brain and spinal cord along with the epithelial cells that make up the skin. At the end of Week Two, the ectoderm spins off a thin line of cells known as the primitive streak, which forms a new cell layer called the mesoderm. From it will come the cells destined to make the heart, the lungs and all the other internal organs.

At this point, the embryo resembles a stack of Lilliputian pancakes—circular, flat and horizontal. But as the mesoderm forms, it interacts with cells in the ectoderm to trigger yet another transformation. Very soon these cells will roll up to become the neural tube, a rudimentary precursor of the spinal cord and brain. Already the embryo has a distinct cluster of cells at each end, one destined to become the mouth and the other the anus. The em-

bryo, no larger at this point than a grain of rice, has determined the head-to-tail axis along which all its body parts will be arrayed.

How on earth does this little, barely animate cluster of cells "know" what to do? The answer is as simple as it is startling. A human embryo knows how to lay out its body axis in the same way that fruit-fly embryos know and *C. elegans* embryos and the embryos of myriad other creatures large and small know. In all cases, scientists have found, in charge of establishing this axis is a special set of genes, especially the so-called homeotic homeobox, or HOX, genes.

HOX genes were first discovered in fruit flies in the early 1980s when scientists noticed that their absence caused striking mutations. Heads, for example, grew feet instead of antennae, and thoraxes grew an extra pair of wings. HOX genes have been found in virtually every type of animal, and while their number varies—fruit flies have nine, humans have 39—they are invariably arrayed along chromosomes in the order along the body in which they are supposed to turn on.

Many other genes interact with the HOX system, including the aptly named Hedgehog and Tinman genes, without which fruit flies grow a dense covering of bristles or fail to make a heart. And scientists are learning in exquisite detail what each does at various stages of the developmental process. Thus one of the three Hedgehog genes—Sonic Hedgehog, named in honor of the cartoon and video-game character—has been shown to play a role in making at least half a dozen types of spinal-cord neurons. As it happens, cells in different places in the neural tube are exposed to different levels of the protein encoded by this gene; cells drenched in significant quantities of protein mature into one type of neuron, and those that receive the barest sprinkling mature into another. Indeed, it was by using a particular concentration of Sonic Hedgehog that neurobiologist Jessell and his research team at Columbia recently coaxed stem cells from a mouse embryo to mature into seemingly functional motor neurons.

At the University of California, San Francisco, a team led by biologist Didier Stainier is working on genes important in cardiovascular formation. Removing one of them, called Miles Apart, from zebra-fish embryos results in a mutant with two nonviable hearts. Why? In all vertebrate embryos, including humans, the heart forms as twin buds. In order to function, these buds must join. The way the Miles Apart gene appears to work, says Stainier, is by detecting a chemical attractant that, like the smell of dinner cooking in the kitchen, entices the pieces to move toward each other.

The crafting of a human from a single fertilized egg is a vastly complicated affair, and at any step, something can go wrong. When the heart fails to develop properly, a baby can be born with a hole in the heart or even missing valves and chambers. When the neural tube fails to develop properly, a baby can be born with a brain not fully developed (anencephaly) or with an incompletely formed spine (spina bifida). Neural-tube defects, it has been firmly established, are often due to insufficient levels of the water-soluble B vitamin folic acid. Reason: folic acid is essential to a dividing cell's ability to replicate its DNA.

Vitamin A, which a developing embryo turns into retinoids, is another nutrient that is critical to the nervous system. But watch out, because too much vitamin A can be toxic. In another newly released book, *Before Your Pregnancy* (Ballantine Books), nutritionist Amy Ogle and obstetrician Dr. Lisa Mazzullo caution would-be mothers to limit foods that are overly rich in vitamin A, especially liver and food products that contain lots of it, like foie gras and cod-liver oil. An excess of vitamin A, they note, can cause damage to the skull, eyes, brain and spinal cord of a developing fetus, probably because retinoids directly interact with DNA, affecting the activity of critical genes.

Folic acid, vitamin A and other nutrients reach developing embryos and fetuses by crossing the placenta, the remarkable temporary organ produced by the blastocyst that develops from the fertilized egg. The outer ring of cells that compose the placenta are extremely aggressive, behaving very much like tumor cells as they invade the uterine wall and tap into the pregnant woman's blood vessels. In fact, these cells actually go in and replace the maternal cells that form the lining of the uterine arteries, says Susan Fisher, a developmental biologist at the University of California, San Francisco. They trick the pregnant woman's immune system into tolerating the embryo's presence rather than rejecting it like the lump of foreign tissue it is.

In essence, says Fisher, "the placenta is a traffic cop," and its main job is to let good things in and keep bad things out. To this end, the placenta marshals platoons of natural killer cells to patrol its perimeters and engages millions of tiny molecular pumps that expel poisons before they can damage the vulnerable embryo.

Alas, the placenta's defenses are sometimes breached—by microbes like rubella and cytomegalovirus, by drugs like thalidomide and alcohol, by heavy metals like lead and mercury, and by organic pollutants like dioxin and PCBs. Pathogens and poisons contained in certain foods are also able to cross the placenta, which may explain why placental tissues secrete a nausea-inducing hormone that has been tentatively linked to morning sickness. One provocative if unproved hypothesis says morning sickness may simply be nature's crude way of making sure that potentially harmful substances do not reach the womb, particularly during the critical first trimester of development.

Timing is decisive where toxins are concerned. Air pollutants like carbon monoxide and ozone, for example, have been linked to heart defects when exposure coincided with the second month of pregnancy, the window of time during which the heart forms. Similarly, the nervous system is particularly vulnerable to damage while neurons are migrating from the part of the brain where they are made to the area where they will ultimately reside. "A tiny, tiny exposure at a key moment when a certain process is beginning to unfold can have an effect that is not only quantitatively larger but qualitatively different than it would be on an adult whose body has finished forming," observes Sandra Steingraber, an ecologist at Cornell University.

Among the substances Steingraber is most worried about are environmentally persistent neurotoxins like mercury and lead (which directly interfere with the migration of neurons formed during the first trimester) and PCBs (which, some evidence suggests, block the activity of thyroid hormone). "Thyroid hormone plays a noble role in the fetus," says Steingraber. "It actually goes into the fetal brain and serves as kind of a conductor of the orchestra."

PCBs are no longer manufactured in the U.S., but other chemicals potentially harmful to developing embryos and fetuses are. Theo Colborn, director of the World Wildlife Fund's contaminants program, says at least 150 chemicals pose possible risks for fetal development, and some of them can interfere with the naturally occurring sex hormones critical to the development of a fetus. Antiandrogens, for example, are widely found in fungicides and plastics. One in particular—DDE, a breakdown product of DDT—has been shown to cause hypospadias in laboratory mice, a birth defect in which the urethra fails to extend to the end of the penis. In humans, however, notes Dr. Allen Wilcox, editor of the journal *Epidemiology*, the link between hormone-like chemicals and birth defects remains elusive.

The list of potential threats to embryonic life is long. It includes not only what the mother eats, drinks or inhales, explains N.Y.U.'s Nathanielsz, but also the hormones that surge through her body. Pregnant rats with high blood-glucose levels (chemically induced by wiping out their insulin) give birth to female offspring that are unusually susceptible to developing gestational diabetes. These daughter rats are able to produce enough insulin to keep their blood glucose in check, says Nathanielsz, but only until they become pregnant. At that point, their glucose level soars, because their pancreases were damaged by prenatal exposure to their mother's sugar-spiked blood. The next generation of daughters is, in turn, more susceptible to gestational diabetes, and the transgenerational chain goes on.

In similar fashion, atherosclerosis may sometimes develop because of prenatal exposure to chronically high cholesterol levels. According to Dr. Wulf Palinski, an endocrinologist at the University of California at San Diego, there appears to be a kind of metabolic memory of prenatal life that is permanently retained. In genetically similar groups of rabbits and kittens, at least, those born to mothers on fatty diets were far more likely to develop arterial plaques than those whose mothers ate lean.

But of all the long-term health threats, maternal undernourishment—which stunts growth even when babies are born full term—may top the list. "People who are small at birth have, for life, fewer kidney cells, and so they are more likely to go into renal failure when they get sick," observes Dr. David Barker, director of the environmental epidemiology unit at England's University of Southampton. The same is true of insulin-producing cells in the pancreas, so that low-birth-weight babies stand a higher chance of developing diabetes later in life because their pancreases—where insulin is produced—have to work that much harder. Barker, whose research has linked low birth weight to heart disease, points out that undernourishment can trigger life-long metabolic changes. In adulthood, for example, obesity may become a problem because food scarcity in prenatal life causes the body to shift the rate at which calories are turned into glucose for immediate use or stored as reservoirs of fat.

But just how does undernourishment reprogram metabolism? Does it perhaps prevent certain genes from turning on, or does it turn on those that should stay silent? Scientists are racing to answer those questions, along with a host of others. If they succeed, many more infants will find safe passage through the critical first months of prenatal development. Indeed, our expanding knowledge about the interplay between genes and the prenatal environment is cause for both concern and hope. Concern because maternal and prenatal health care often ranks last on the political agenda. Hope because by changing our priorities, we might be able to reduce the incidence of both birth defects and serious adult diseases.

—***With reporting by David Bjerklie and Alice Park/New York and Dan Cray/Los Angeles***

The Mystery of Fetal Life: Secrets of The Womb

JOHN PEKKANEN

I n the dim light of an ultrasound room, a wand slides over the abdomen of a young woman. As it emits sound waves, it allows us to see into her womb. The video screen brightens with a grainy image of a 20-week-old fetus. It floats in its amniotic sac, like an astronaut free of gravity.

The fetal face stares upward, then turns toward us, as if to mug for the camera. The sound waves strike different tissues with different densities, and their echoes form different images. These images are computer-enhanced, so although the fetus weights only 14 ounces and is no longer than my hand, we can see its elfin features.

Close up, we peek into the fetal brain. In the seconds we observe, a quarter million new brain cells are born. This happens constantly. By the end of the nine months, the baby's brain will hold 100 billion brain cells.

The sound waves focus on the chest, rendering images of a vibrating four-chambered heart no bigger than the tip of my little finger. The monitor tells us it is moving at 163 beats a minute. It sounds like a frightened bird fluttering in its cage.

We watch the rib cage move. Although the fetus lives in an airless environment, it "breathes" intermittently inside the womb by swallowing amniotic fluid. Some researchers speculate that the fetus is exercising its chest and diaphragm as its way of preparing for life outside the womb.

The clarity of ultrasound pictures is now so good that subtle abnormalities can be detected. The shape of the skull, brain, and spinal cord, along with the heart and other vital organs, can be seen in breathtaking detail.

In this ultrasound exam, there are no hints to suggest that anything is abnormal. The husband squeezes his wife's hand. They both smile.

The fetus we have just watched is at the midpoint of its 40-week gestation. At conception 20 weeks earlier, it began as a single cell that carried in its nucleus the genetic code for the human it will become.

After dividing and redividing for a week, it grew to 32 cells. Like the initial cell, these offspring cells carry 40,000 or so genes, located on 23 pairs of chromosomes inherited from the mother and father. Smaller than the head of a pin, this clump of cells began a slow journey down the fallopian tube and attached itself to the spongy wall of the uterus.

Once settled, some embryonic cells began to form a placenta to supply the embryo with food, water, and nutrients from the mother's bloodstream. The placenta also filtered out harmful substances in the mother's bloodstream. The embryo and mother exchange chemical information to ensure that they work together toward their common goal.

Instructed by their genes, the cells continued to divide but didn't always produce exact replicas. In a process still not well understood, the cells began to differentiate to seek out their own destinies. Some helped build internal organs, others bones, muscles, and brain.

At 19 days postconception, the earliest brain tissues began to form. They developed at the top end of the neural tube, a sheath of cells that ran nearly the entire length of the embryo.

The human brain requires virtually the entire pregnancy to emerge fully, longer than the other organ systems. Even in the earliest stage of development, the fetus knows to protect its brain. The brain gets the most highly oxygenated blood, and should there be any shortage, the fetus will send the available blood to the brain.

Extending downward from the brain, the neural tube began to form the spinal cord. At four weeks, a rudimentary heart started to beat, and four limbs began sprouting. By eight weeks, the two-inch-long embryo took human form and was more properly called a fetus. At 10 to 12 weeks, it began moving its arms and legs, opened its jaws, swallowed, and yawned, Mostly it slept.

"We are never more clever than we are as a fetus," says Dr. Peter Nathanielsz, a fetal researcher, obstetrician, and professor of reproductive medicine at Cornell University. "We pass far more biological milestones before we are born than we'll ever pass after we're born."

Not long ago, the process of fetal development was shrouded in mystery. But through the power of scanning techniques, biotechnology, and fetal and animal studies, much of the mystery of fetal life has been unveiled.

We now know that as the fetus matures it experiences a broad range of sensory stimulation. It hears, sees, tastes, smells, feels, and has rapid eye movement (REM) sleep, the sleep stage we associate with dreaming. From observation of its sleep and wake cycles, the fetus appears to know night from day. It learns and remembers, and it may cry. It seems to do everything in utero that it will do after it is born. In the words of one researcher, "Fetal life is us."

Studies now show that it's the fetus, not the mother, who sends the hormonal signals that determine when a baby will be born. And we've found out that its health in the womb depends in part on its mother's health when she was in the womb.

Finally, we've discovered that the prenatal environment is not as benign, or as neutral, as once thought. It is sensitive to the mother's health, emotions, and behavior.

The fetus is strongly affected by the mother's eating habits. If the mother exercises more than usual, the fetus may become temporarily short of oxygen. If she takes a hot bath, the fetus feels the heat. If she smokes, so does the fetus. One study has found that pregnant women exposed to more sunlight had more-outgoing children.

We now know that our genes do not encode a complete design for us, that our "genetic destiny" is not hard-wired at the time of conception. Instead, our development involves an interplay between genes and the environment, including that of the uterus. Because genes take "cues" from their environment, an expectant mother's physical and psychological health influences her unborn child's genetic well-being.

Factors such as low prenatal oxygen levels, stress, infections, and poor maternal nutrition may determine whether certain genes are switched on or off. Some researchers believe that our time in the womb is the single most important period of our life.

"Because of genetics, we once thought that we would unfold in the womb like a blueprint, but now we know it's not that simple," says Janet DiPietro, an associate professor of maternal and child health at the Johns Hopkins School of Public Health and one of a handful of fetal-behavior specialists. "The mother and the uterine environment she creates have a major impact on many aspects of fetal development, and a number of things laid down during that time remain with you throughout your life."

The impact of the womb on our intelligence, personality, and emotional and physical health is beginning to be understood. There's also an emerging understanding of something called fetal programming, which says that the effects of our life in the womb may be not felt until decades after we're born, and in ways that are more powerful than previously imagined.

Says Dr. Nathanielsz, whose book *Life in the Womb* details the emerging science of fetal development: "It's an area of great scientific importance that until recently remained largely unknown."

"I'm pregnant. Is it okay to have a glass of wine? Can I take my Prozac? What about a Diet Coke?"

Years ago, before she knew she was pregnant, a friend of mine had a glass of wine with dinner. When she discovered she was pregnant, she worried all through her pregnancy and beyond. She feels some guilt to this day, even though the son she bore turned out very well.

Many mothers have experienced the same tangled emotions. "There's no evidence that a glass of wine a day during pregnancy has a negative impact on the developing fetus," says Dr. John Larsen, professor and chair of obstetrics and gynecology at George Washington University. Larsen says that at one time doctors gave alcohol by IV to pregnant women who were experiencing preterm labor; it relaxed the muscles and quelled contractions.

Larsen now sometimes recommends a little wine to women who experience mild contractions after a puncture from an amniocentesis needle, and some studies suggest that moderate alcohol intake in pregnancy may prevent preterm delivery in some women.

Even though most experts agree with Larsen, the alcohol message that most women hear calls for total abstinence. Experts worry that declaring moderate alcohol intake to be safe in pregnancy may encourage some pregnant women to drink immoderately. They say that pregnant women who have an occasional drink should not think they've placed their baby at risk.

What is safe? Some studies show children born to mothers who consumed three drinks a day in pregnancy averaged seven points lower on IQ tests than unexposed children. There is evidence that six drinks a day during pregnancy puts babies at risk of fetal alcohol syndrome (FAS), a constellation of serious birth defects that includes mental retardation. The higher the alcohol intake, the higher the FAS risk.

Are there drugs and drug combinations that women should avoid or take with caution during pregnancy? Accutane (isotretinoin), a prescription drug for acne and psoriasis, is known to cause birth defects. So too are some anticonvulsant drugs, including Epitol, Tegretol, and Valproate. Tetracycline, a widely prescribed antibiotic, can cause bone-growth delays and permanent teeth problems for a baby if a mother takes it during pregnancy.

Most over-the-counter drugs are considered safe in pregnancy, but some of them carry risks. Heavy doses of aspirin and other nonsteroidal anti-inflammatory drugs such as ibuprofen can delay the start of labor. They are also linked to a life-threatening disorder of newborns called persistent pulmonary hypertension (PPHN), which diverts airflow away from the baby's lungs, causing oxygen depletion. The March issue of the journal *Pediatrics* published a study linking these nonprescription painkillers to PPHN, which results in the death of 15 percent of the infants who have it.

OTC DRUGS

In 1998, researchers at the University of Nebraska Medical Center reported dextromethorphan, a cough suppressant found in 40 or more OTC drugs including Nyquil, Tylenol Cold, Dayquil, Robitussin Maximum Strength, and Dimetapp DM, caused congenital malformations in chick embryos. The research was published in *Pediatric Research* and supported by the National Institutes of Health.

Although no connection between dextromethorphan and human birth defects has been shown, the Nebraska researchers noted that similar genes regulate early development in virtually all species. For this reason, the researchers predicted that dextromethorphan, which acts on the brain to suppress coughing, would have the same harmful effect on a human fetus.

Many women worry about antidepressants. Some need them during pregnancy or took them before they knew they were pregnant. A study published in the *New England Journal of Medicine* found no association between fetal exposure to antidepressants and brain damage. The study compared the IQ, temperament, activity level, and distractibility of more than 125 children whose mothers took antidepressants in pregnancy with 84 children whose mothers took no drugs known to harm the fetus.

The two groups of children, between 16 months and eight years old when tested, were comparable in every way. The antidepressants taken by the mothers included both tricyclates such as Elavil and Tofranil and selective serotonin reuptake inhibitors such as Prozac.

Not all mood-altering drugs may be safe. There is some evidence that minor tranquilizers taken for anxiety may cause developmental problems if taken in the first trimester, but there is no hard proof of this. Evidence of fetal damage caused by illegal drugs such as cocaine is widely accepted, as is the case against cigarette smoking. A 1998 survey found that 13 percent of all mothers who gave birth smoked. Evidence is striking that cigarette smoking in pregnancy lowers birth weight and increases the risks of premature birth, attention deficit hyperactive disorder, and diminished IQ.

A long-running study based on information from the National Collaborative Perinatal Project found that years after they were born, children were more apt to become addicted to certain drugs if their mother took them during delivery.

"We found drug-dependent individuals were five times more likely to have exposure to high doses of painkillers and anesthesia during their delivery than their nonaddicted siblings," says Stephen Buka of the Harvard School of Public Health. Buka suspects this is caused by a modification in the infant's brain receptors as the drugs pass from mother to child during an especially sensitive time.

CAFFEINE

Coffee consumption has worried mothers because there have been hints that caffeine may be harmful to the fetus. Like most things in life, moderation is the key. There's no evidence that 300 milligrams of caffeine a day (about three cups of coffee, or four or five cups of most regular teas, or five to six cola drinks) harms a developing baby. Higher caffeine consumption has been weakly linked to miscarriage and difficulty in conceiving.

Expectant mothers concerned about weight gain should be careful of how much of the artificial sweetener aspartame they consume. Marketed under brand names such as NutraSweet and Equal, it's found in diet soft drinks and foods.

The concern is this: In the body, aspartame converts into phenylalanine, a naturally occurring amino acid we ingest when we eat protein. At high levels, phenylalanine can be toxic to brain cells.

When we consume phenylalanine in protein, we also consume a number of other amino acids that neutralize any ill effects. When we consume it in aspartame, we get none of the neutralizing amino acids to dampen phenylalanine's impact. And as it crosses the placenta, phenylalanine's concentrations are magnified in the fetal brain.

If a fetal brain is exposed to high levels of phenylalanine because its mother consumes a lot of aspartame, will it be harmed? One study found average IQ declines of ten points in children born to mothers with a fivefold increase of phenylalanine blood levels in pregnancy. That's a lot of aspartame, and it doesn't mean an expectant mother who drinks moderate amounts of diet soda need worry.

Researchers say consuming up to three servings of aspartame a day—in either diet soda or low-calorie foods—appears to be safe for the fetus. However, a pregnant woman of average weight who eats ten or more servings a day may put her unborn baby at risk. In testimony before Congress, Dr. William Pardridge, a neuroscience researcher at UCLA, said it's likely that the effect of high phenylalanine levels in the fetal brain "will be very subtle" and many not manifest until years later.

One wild card concerns the 10 to 20 million Americans who unknowingly carry a gene linked to a genetic disease called phenylketonuria (PKU), which can lead to severe mental retardation. Most carriers don't know it, because PKU is a recessive genetic disorder, and both mother and father must carry the defective gene to pass PKU on to their child. A carrier feels no ill effects. According to researchers, a pregnant woman who unknowingly carries the PKU gene might place her unborn child at risk if she consumes even relatively moderate amounts of aspartame. There is no hard evidence that this will happen, but it remains a serious concern. PKU can be detected in the fetus by amniocentesis; a restrictive diet can prevent the worst effects of PKU on the child.

How does a mother's getting an infection affect her unborn baby? And should she be careful of cats?

Many experts think pregnant women should be more concerned about infections and household pets than a glass of wine or can of diet drink. There's overwhelming evidence of the potential harm of infections during pregnancy. We've known for a long time that rubella (German measles), a viral infection, can cause devastating birth defects.

More worrisome are recent studies showing that exposure to one of the most common of winter's ills—influenza—may put an unborn child at risk of cognitive and emotional problems. If flu strikes in the second trimester, it may increase the unborn baby's risk of developing schizophrenia later in life. While the flu may be a trigger, it's likely that a genetic susceptibility is also needed for schizophrenia to develop.

Some evidence exists that maternal flu may also lead to dyslexia, and suspicions persist that a first-trimester flu may cause fetal neural-tube defects resulting in spina bifida. The common cold, sometimes confused with the flu, has not been linked to any adverse outcomes for the baby.

"Infections are probably the most important thing for a pregnant woman to protect herself against," says Lise Eliot, a developmental neurobiologist at the Chicago Medical School. "She should always practice good hygiene, like washing her hands frequently, avoiding crowds, and never drinking from someone else's cup." She adds that the flu vaccine has been approved for use during pregnancy.

Some researchers recommend that pregnant women avoid close contact with cats. Toxoplasmosis, a parasitic infection, can travel from a cat to a woman to her unborn child.

Most humans become infected through cat litter boxes. An infected woman might experience only mild symptoms, if any, so the illness usually goes undetected. If she is diagnosed with the infection, antiparasitic drugs are helpful, but they don't completely eliminate the disease. The infection is relatively rare, and the odds of passing it from mother to child are only one in five during the first two trimesters, when the fetal harm is most serious. The bad news is that a fetus infected by toxoplasmosis can suffer severe brain damage, including mental retardation and epilepsy. Some researchers also suspect it may be a latent trigger for serious mental illness as the child grows older.

CEREBRAL PALSY

An expectant mother may not realize she has potentially harmful infections. The prime suspects are infections in the reproductive tract. Researchers suspect most cerebral-palsy cases are not caused by delivery problems, as has been widely assumed. There's strong evidence that some cases of cerebral-palsy may be linked to placental infections that occur during uterine life. Other cerebral-palsy cases may be triggered by oxygen deprivation in early development, but very few appear to be caused by oxygen deprivation during delivery. It's now estimated that only 10 percent of cerebral-palsy cases are related to delivery problems.

Maternal urinary-tract infections have been linked to lower IQs in children. Another infection, cytomegalovirus (CMV), has been linked to congenital deafness. Sexually transmitted diseases such as chlamydia are suspected to be a trigger for preterm birth. Despite the serious threat posed to developing babies, infections during pregnancy remain poorly understood.

"We just don't know right now when or how the uterine infections that really make a difference to the fetus are transmitted in pregnancy," says Dr. Karin Nelson, a child neurologist and acting chief of the neuro-epidemiology branch of the National Institute of Neurologic Disorders and Stroke at NIH. "Nor do we know all the potential problems they may cause."

Because of this, researchers offer little in the way of recommendations other than clean living and careful sex. They recommend that any woman contemplating pregnancy get in her best physical condition, because a number of studies have found that a woman's general health before she becomes pregnant is vital to fetal health. They also recommend a thorough gynecological exam because it may detect a treatable infection that could harm the fetus.

Rachel Carson was right about pesticides. So if you're pregnant, how careful should you be about what you eat?

In her book *Silent Spring,* author Rachel Carson noted that when pregnant mammals were exposed to synthetic pesticides, including DDT and methoxychlor, the pesticides caused developmental abnormalities in offspring. Carson, a scientist, noted that some pesticides mimicked the female hormone estrogen and caused the male offspring to be feminized.

About the time of Carson's 1962 book, another story was emerging about diethylstilbestrol (DES), a man-made female hormone administered in the 1940s and '50s to prevent miscarriages. In the 1960s it became clear that many young daughters of DES mothers were turning up reproductive malformations and vaginal cancers. Sons born to DES mothers suffered reproductive problems, including undescended testicles and abnormal sperm counts.

ENDOCRINE DISRUPTERS

Over the years, suspicion grew from both animal and human studies that something in the environment was disrupting fetal development. In the 1990s it was given a name—endocrine disruption. The theory was that DES and the pesticides cited by Carson caused defects in offspring because they disrupted the normal endocrine process. They did this by mimicking hormones inside the human body.

It's now clear that DDT and DES are the tip of the iceberg. Today more than 90,000 synthetic chemicals are used, most made after World War II. New chemicals are produced every week. They are used in everything from pesticides to plastics.

How many of these man-made chemicals might act as endocrine disrupters? More than 50 have been identified, and hundreds more are suspects.

To understand the threat from endocrine disrupters, it helps to understand what human hormones do. Secreted by endocrine glands, these tiny molecules circulate through the bloodstream to the organs. They include estrogen, adrenalin, thyroid, melatonin, and testosterone. Each is designed to fit only into a specific receptor on a cell, like a key that fits only one lock. When a hormone connects with the cell receptor, it enters the cell's nucleus. Once there, the hormone acts as a signaling agent to direct the cell's DNA to produce specific proteins.

During fetal life, the right type and concentration of hormones must be available at the right time for normal fetal development to occur. Produced by both mother and fetus, hormones are involved in cell division and differentiation, the development of the brain and reproductive organs, and virtually everything else needed to produce a baby.

"We know from animal experiments and wildlife observations that periods in development are very sensitive to alterations in the hormone levels," says Robert Kavlock, director of reproductive toxicology for the Environmental Protection Agency.

The damage is done when chemical mimickers get into cells at the wrong time, or at the wrong strength, or both. When this happens, something in the fetus will not develop as it should.

After years of witnessing the harmful impact on wildlife, we now know that humans are not immune to endocrine disrupters. More troubling, because of the pervasiveness of these chemicals, is that we can't escape them. We get them in the food we eat, the water we drink, the products we buy.

One of the most dramatic examples came to light in the 1970s when researchers wanted to find out why so many babies born in the Great Lakes region suffered serious neurological defects. They found the answer in polychlorinated biphenyls (PCBs), organic chemicals once used in electrical insulation and adhesives. Heavy PCB contamination of Great Lakes fish eaten by the mothers turned out to be the cause.

It is not clear how PCBs cause fetal brain damage, but it's believed to happen when they disrupt thyroid hormones. Severe thyroid deficiency in pregnancy is known to cause mental retardation. Another study found reduced penis size in boys born to mothers exposed to high levels of PCBs.

The U.S. manufacture of PCBs ended in 1977. PCB levels found in the mothers and the fish they ate suggested at the time that only very high exposure caused a problem for developing babies. Now we know this isn't true.

Because PCBs don't break down, they've remained a toxin that continues to enter our bodies through the food we eat. They have leached into soil and water and are found in shellfish and freshwater fish and to a smaller degree in ocean fish. Bottom-feeding freshwater fish, such as catfish and carp, have the highest PCB concentrations.

PCBs store in fat tissue and are found in dairy products and meats. Fatty meats, especially processed meats like cold cuts, sausages, and hot dogs, are usually heaviest in PCBs. They get into these products because farm animals graze on PCB-contaminated land. However, eating fish from PCB-contaminated water remains the primary way we get these chemicals into our systems. In pregnant women, PCBs easily cross the placenta and circulate in the fetus.

PCBs are ubiquitous. They've been detected in the Antarctic snow. If you had detection equipment sensitive enough, you'd find them in the milk at the supermarket.

What concerns experts are findings from studies in the Netherlands and upstate New York that found even low maternal PCB exposures pose risk to a fetus.

The Dutch study followed 418 children from birth into early childhood. In the final month of pregnancy, researchers measured the maternal PCB blood levels, and at birth they measured PCB levels in the umbilical cord. None of the mothers was a heavy fish eater or had any history of high PCB exposure, and none of their PCB levels was considered high by safety standards.

At 3 1/2 years of age, the children's cognitive abilities were assessed with tests. After adjusting for other variables, the researchers found that maternal and cord blood PCB levels correlated with the children's cognitive abilities. As the PCB blood levels went up, the children suffered more attention problems and their cognitive abilities went down. It should be noted that the brain damage in these Dutch children was not devastating. They were not retarded or autistic. But on a relative scale, they had suffered measurable harm.

The Dutch researchers concluded that the in utero PCB exposure, and not any postnatal exposure, caused the children's brain damage. The study also revealed that these children had depressed immune function.

"All we can say now," says Deborah Rice, a toxicologist at the EPA's National Center for Environmental Assessment in Washington, "is we have strong evidence that PCB levels commonly found among women living in industrialized society can cause subtle neurological damage in their offspring." But one of the difficulties, according to Rice, is that we really don't yet know what an unsafe maternal PCB level might be.

"I think the bottom line is that women should be aware of PCBs and aware of what they're putting in their mouth," adds Rice.

The Dutch study is a warning not only about the potential impact of low levels of PCBs but about the potential harm from low levels of other endocrine disrupters.

More news arrived in March when the results from the federal government's on-going Fourth National Health and Nutrition Examination Survey (NHANES) became public. The survey of 38,000 people revealed that most of us have at least trace levels of pesticides, heavy metals, and plastics in our body tissues. In all, NHANES tested for 27 elements.

The survey found widespread exposure to phthalates, synthetic chemicals used as softeners in plastics and other products. Phthalates are one of the most heavily produced chemicals and have been linked in animal studies to endocrine disruption and birth defects. The likely sources of human exposure are foods and personal-care products such as shampoos, lotions, soaps, and perfumes; phthalates are absorbed through the skin.

Dr. Ted Schettler, a member of the Greater Boston Physicians for Social Responsibility, suspects endocrine disrupters may be linked to increases in the three hormone-driven cancers—breast, prostate, and testicular. The rate of testicular cancer among young men has nearly doubled in recent years, and the rates of learning disabilities and infertility also have increased.

"We can't blame all that is happening on toxic chemicals," says Schettler, who coauthored *In Harm's Way,* a report on how chemical contaminants affect human health. "But we need to ask ourselves if we're seeing patterns that suggest these chemicals are having a major impact on fetal development and human populations. We also need to ask what level of evidence we're going to need before we take public-health measures. That's a political question."

The EPA's Kavlock says, "We don't know the safe or unsafe levels for many of these chemicals." Nor do we know how many of the thousands of man-made chemicals in the environment will turn out to be endocrine disrupters or cause human harm. The EPA received a mandate from Congress in 1996 to find the answers, but it will be a long wait.

"If we devoted all the toxicology testing capacity in the entire world to look for endocrine-disrupting chemicals, we couldn't do all the chemicals. There's just not enough capacity," Kavlock says. "So we are focusing on 500 to 1,000 chemicals that are the major suspects. It will take many years and a lot of money just to understand how they interact with hormonal-system and fetal development."

What is all this bad stuff we can get from eating fish or from microwaving food in plastics? Do vitamins help?

Methylmercury is a heavy metal that can cause fetal brain damage. NHANES revealed that 10 percent of American women of child-bearing age—a representative sample of all American women—had methylmercury blood and hair levels close to "potentially hazardous levels." The EPA and some nongovernment experts consider these existing methylmercury levels already above what is safe.

Dr. Jill Stein, an adolescent-medicine specialist and instructor at Harvard Medical School, has studied methylmercury's toxicity. She says the acceptable levels of methyl- mercury in the NHANES report were too high and that many more women are in the danger zone. "The NHANES data tells me that more than 10 percent of American women today are carrying around enough mercury to put their future children at risk for learning and behavior problems," she says.

Like PCBs and other toxic chemicals, mercury is hard to avoid because it is abundant in our environment. It comes from natural and man-made sources, chiefly coal-fired power plants and municipal waste treatment. Each year an estimated 160 tons of mercury is released into the nation's environment. In water, mercury combines with natural bacteria to form methylmercury, a toxic form of the metal. It is easily absorbed by fish. When a pregnant woman consumes the contaminated fish, methylmercury crosses the placenta and the fetal blood-brain barrier.

The world became aware of methylmercury's potential for harm more than 40 years ago in the fishing village of Minamata in Japan. People there were exposed to high levels of the heavy metal from industrial dumping of mercury compounds into Minamata Bay. The villagers, who ate a diet heavy in fish caught in the bay, experienced devastating effects. The hardest hit were the unborn. Women gave birth to babies with cerebral-palsy-like symptoms. Many were retarded.

MERCURY

Fish are the major source of mercury for humans. The Food and Drug Administration recommends that pregnant women not eat swordfish, king mackerel, shark, and tilefish. These fish are singled out because large oceangoing fish contain more methylmercury. Smaller ocean fish, especially cod, haddock, and pollock, generally have low methylmercury levels. A whitefish found off the coast of Alaska, pollock is commonly found in fish sticks and fast-food fish. Salmon have low methylmercury levels, but they are a fatty fish and apt to carry higher levels of PCBs.

Like the Dutch PCB studies, recent studies of maternal methylmercury exposure have turned up trouble. They've shown that the so-called "safe" maternal levels of the metal can cause brain damage during fetal development.

One study was carried out in the 1990s by a Danish research team that studied 917 children in the Faroe Islands, where seafood is a big part of the diet. Children were grouped into categories depending on their level of maternal methylmercury exposure; they were assessed up to age seven by neurological tests. None of the children's methylmercury exposure levels was considered high, yet many of the children had evidence of brain damage, including memory, attention, and learning problems.

"Subtle effects on brain function therefore seem to be detectable at prenatal methylmercury exposure levels currently considered safe," the study concluded. In a follow-up report published in a 1999 issue of the *Journal of the American Medical Association,* the authors said the blood concentrations of methylmercury found in the umbilical cord corresponded with the severity of the neurological damage suffered by the children.

In a study of 237 children, New Zealand researchers found similar neurological harm, including IQ impairment and attention problems, in children whose mothers' exposure to methylmercury came from fish they ate during pregnancy.

"The children in these studies were not bathed in methylmercury," notes Rita Schoeny, a toxicologist in the EPA's Office of Water. "Can people in the U.S. be exposed to the same levels of mercury in the course of their dietary practice? We think so."

Jill Stein and other experts worry that the more scientific studies we do, the more we'll realize that in fetal development there may be no such thing as a "safe" maternal level for methylmercury, PCBs, and scores of other synthetic chemicals.

"We keep learning from studies that these chemicals are harmful to fetal development at lower and lower doses," Stein says. "It's what we call the declining threshold of harm."

What about canned tuna? It has been assumed to contain low methylmercury levels because most of it comes from smaller fish. The FDA offers no advisories about it. But according to EPA researchers, a recent State of Florida survey of more than 100 samples of canned tuna found high levels of methylmercury. The more-expensive canned tuna, such as albacore and solid white tuna, usually carried higher methylmercury levels, according to the survey. This apparently is because more expensive canned tuna comes from larger tuna. In some of the canned tuna, the methylmercury levels were high enough to prevent their export to several countries, including Canada.

Some of the methylmercury levels were "worrisomely high," according to Kathryn Mahaffey, a toxicologist and director of the division of exposure assessment at the EPA. They were high enough to cause concern for pregnant women.

"A big problem is the tremendous variability out there in the tuna supply," adds Stein. "You have no idea when you're eating a can of tuna how much methylmercury you're getting."

"Even if you ate just a small serving of some of these canned tunas each day," says Mahaffey, "you'd be substantially above a level we would consider safe."

Mahaffey and Stein agree that an expectant mother who ate even a few servings a week with methylmercury levels found in some of the canned tuna would put her developing baby at risk of brain and other neurological damage.

Now that we know a developing fetus is sensitive to even low levels of toxic chemicals, women can exercise some basic precautions to help protect their developing babies.

Don't microwave food that is wrapped in plastic or is still in plastic containers. "There are endocrine-disrupting chemicals in these plastics," Schettler says, "that leach right into the food when it's microwaved. This has been well documented and measured." Studies suggest that even at very low levels these chemicals can have an adverse effect on the fetus's hormonal system.

The EPA's Kavlock considers the fruits and vegetables you buy at the supermarket to be safe in pregnancy, but Schettler says you should try to eat organic foods to avoid even trace amounts of pesticides. Wash fruits and vegetables before eating them. Avoid pesticides or insecticide use around the house during pregnancy as well as the use of chemical solvents for painting or remodeling.

Herbicides and pesticides have leached into reservoirs that supply home drinking water, and filtration plants can't remove them all. Some are known to be endocrine disrupters. Home water filters can reduce contaminants; the best ones use active charcoal as a filtering agent.

Experts agree that a pregnant woman, or a woman who may get pregnant, can eat fish but should be careful about the kind she eats and how much of it. EPA's Rice cautions any woman who is pregnant or thinking of becoming pregnant to avoid eating any sport fish caught in a lake or river.

VEGETABLE FATS

Rice adds that the PCB risk with fish can be reduced. "Trim the fish of fat and skin, and broil or grill it," see says. "That way you cook off fat and minimize your PCB exposure." There is not much you can do to reduce the methylmercury levels in fish because it binds to protein.

"Fat is important for a baby's neurological development before and after birth, so pregnant women should consider vegetable fats like olive oil and flaxseed oil as a source," Rice adds. She says low fat dairy and meat products carry fewer PCBs than higher-fat ones.

The EPA has issued a PCB advisory for the Potomac River in the District, Virginia, and Maryland, citing in particular catfish and carp. You can go to *www.epa.gov/ost/fish/epafish.pdf*

for EPA advisories on PCB and methylmercury environmental contamination. From there you can connect to state Web sites for advisories on local waters and specific fish.

Women can help prevent neurological and other birth defects by taking vitamin supplements before pregnancy. A daily dose of 400 micrograms of folic acid can reduce the risk of such problems as spina bifida by more than 70 percent as well as prevent brain defects and cleft lip and palate. Indirect evidence from a study published last year in the *New England Journal of Medicine* suggests that folic acid may also help prevent congenital heart defects.

To be effective, folic acid should be taken before pregnancy to prevent developmental defects. Folic acid comes in multivitamins and prenatal vitamins and is found naturally in legumes, whole-wheat bread, citrus fruits, fortified breakfast cereal, and leafy green vegetables. Despite the proven value of folic acid, a recent March of Dimes survey found that only 32 percent of American women of childbearing age—including pregnant women—took folic-acid supplements.

What can a fetus learn in the womb? And does playing Mozart make a baby lots smarter?

Developmental psychologist Anthony DeCasper wanted to answer two questions: What does a fetus know, and when does it know it?

DeCasper's aim was to find out if a fetus could learn in utero and remember what it learned after it was born. He enlisted the help of 33 healthy expectant mothers and asked each to tape-record herself reading passages from Dr. Seuss's *The Cat in the Hat* or from another children's book, *The King, the Mice, and the Cheese.* The mothers were randomly assigned to play one of these readings, each of which lasted two or three minutes, to their unborn children three times a day during the final three weeks of their pregnancies.

DeCasper, a professor of developmental psychology at the University of North Carolina at Greensboro, could do the experiment because it was known that fetuses could hear by the third trimester and probably earlier. DeCasper had shown earlier that at birth, babies preferred their mother's voice to all other voices. Studies in the early 1990s found that fetuses could be soothed by lullabies and sometimes moved in rhythm to their mother's voice. Fetuses hear their mother's voice from the outside, just as they can hear any other voice, but they hear the mother's voice clearer and stronger through bone conduction as it resonates inside her.

A little more than two days after birth, each of the newborns in DeCasper's study was given a specially devised nipple. The device worked by utilizing the baby's sucking reflex. When the baby sucked on the nipple, it would hear its mother's voice. But if it paused for too long a time between sucks, it would hear another woman's voice. This gave the baby control over whose voice it would hear by controlling the length of its pause between sucks.

DeCasper also placed small earphones over the infant's ears through which it could hear its mother's voice read from the books.

"Now two days or so after it was born, the baby gets to choose between two stories read by its own mother," DeCasper said. "One was the story she'd recited three times a day for the last three weeks of pregnancy, and the other is one the baby's never heard before, except for the one day his mother recorded it. So the big question was: Would the babies prefer the story they'd heard in the womb, or wouldn't they? The answer was a clear yes—the babies preferred to hear the familiar story."

DeCasper did a second experiment by having women who were not the baby's mothers recite the same two stories. The babies again showed a strong preference for the story they'd heard in the womb.

"These studies not only tell us something about the fidelity with which the fetal ear can hear," DeCasper says, "but they also show that during those two or three weeks in the womb, fetal learning and memory are occurring."

British researchers observed expectant mothers who watched a TV soap opera. The researchers placed monitors on the mother's abdomens to listen in on fetal movements when the program aired. By the 37th week of pregnancy, the babies responded to the show's theme music by increasing their movements, an indication they remembered it.

Soon after the babies were born, the researchers replayed the theme music to them. This time, instead of moving more, the babies appeared to calm down and pay attention to the music. The researchers considered this a response to familiar music.

FETAL MEMORY

"The fact that we find evidence of fetal memory doesn't mean fetuses carry conscious memories, like we remember what we ate for breakfast," explains Lise Eliot, author of *What's Going On in There?*, a book on early brain development. "But we now know there is a tremendous continuity from prenatal to postnatal life, and the prenatal experience begins to shape a child's interaction with the world it will confront after birth. Babies go through the same activity patterns and behavioral states before and after birth. Well before it is born, the baby is primed to gravitate to its mother and its mother's voice."

Some researchers speculate a baby's ability to remember in the womb may be a way of easing its transition from prenatal life to postnatal life. A baby already accustomed to and comforted by its mother's voice may be reassured as it enters a new world of bright lights, needle pricks, curious faces, and loud noises.

The question arises: Can the uterine environment affect a baby's intelligence? Twins studies have shown that genes exert an all-powerful influence on IQ. The role of environment in IQ has traditionally meant the nurturance and stimulation the baby receives after birth.

Bernie Devlin, a biostatistician and assistant professor of psychiatry at the University of Pittsburgh, did an analysis of 212 twins studies on intelligence. In a paper published in *Nature,* he concluded that the accepted figure of 60 to 80 percent for IQ heritability is too high. It should be closer to 50 percent, he says, which leaves more room for environmental factors. Devlin says the one environmental factor that's been missing in understanding human intelligence is time in the womb.

"I'm surprised that the impact of fetal life on a child's intelligence had not been accounted for in these IQ studies," Devlin says. "I know it's very complicated, but it's surprising that people who study the heritability of intelligence really haven't considered this factor."

What is the impact of life in the womb on intelligence? Devlin thinks it's equal to if not greater than the impact of a child's upbringing. In other words, it's possible a mother may have more influence over her child's intelligence before birth than after.

As the brain develops in utero, we know it undergoes changes that affect its ultimate capacity. Nutritional and hormonal influences from the mother have a big impact. And twins studies show that the heavier twin at birth most often has the higher IQ.

A number of studies from the United States and Latin America also found that a range of vitamins, as well as sufficient protein in the mother's prenatal diet, had an impact on the child's intelligence.

Links between specific vitamins and intelligence have been borne out in two studies. An animal study conducted at the University of North Carolina and published in the March issue of *Developmental Brain Research* found that rats with a choline deficiency during pregnancy gave birth to offspring with severe brain impairments. Choline, a B-complex vitamin involved in nerve transmission, is found in eggs, meat, peanuts, and dietary supplements.

The August 1999 issue of the *New England Journal of Medicine* reported that expectant mothers with low thyroid function gave birth to children with markedly diminished IQs as well as motor and attention deficits. The study said one cause of hypothyroidism—present in 2 to 3 percent of American women—is a lack of iodine in the American diet. Women whose hypothyroidism was detected and treated before pregnancy had children with normal test scores. Hypothyroidism can be detected with a blood test, but expectant mothers who receive little or late prenatal care often go undiagnosed or are diagnosed too late to help their child.

Although most American women get the nutrition they need through diet and prenatal vitamins, not all do. According to a National Center for Health Statistics survey, more than one in four expectant mothers in the U.S. received inadequate prenatal care.

Devlin's *Nature* article took a parting shot at the conclusions reached in the 1994 book *The Bell Curve,* in which Richard J. Herrnstein and Charles Murray argued that different social classes are a result of genetically determined, and therefore unalterable, IQ levels. The lower the IQ, the argument goes, the lower the social class.

Not only does the data show IQ to be far less heritable than that book alleges, Devlin says, but he suspects improvements in the health status of mostly poor expectant mothers would see measurable increases in the IQs of their offspring.

Devlin's argument is supported by Randy Thornhill, a biologist at the University of New Mexico. Thornhill's research suggests that IQ differences are due in part to what he calls "heritable vulnerabilities to environmental sources of developmental stress." In other words, vulnerable genes interact with environmental insults in utero resulting in gene mutations that affect fetal development. Thornhill says environmental insults may include viruses, maternal drug abuse, or poor nutrition.

"The developmental instability that results," Thornhill says, "is most readily seen in the body's asymmetry when one side of the body differs from the other. For example, on average an individual's index fingers will differ in length by about two millimeters. Some people have much more asymmetries than others."

But the asymmetries we see on the outside also occur in the nervous system. When this happens, neurons are harmed and memory and intelligence are impaired. Thornhill says the more physical asymmetries you have, the more neurological impairment you have. He calculates that these factors can account for as much as 50 percent of the differences we find in IQ.

Thornhill adds that a fetus that carries these genetic vulnerabilities, but develops in an ideal uterine environment, will not experience any serious problems because the worrisome mutations will not occur.

"The practical implications for this are tremendous," Thornhill says. "If we can understand what environmental factors most disrupt fetal development of the nervous system, then we'll be in a position to remove them and have many more intelligent people born."

Studies on fetal IQ development suggest that the current emphasis on nurturance and stimulation for young children be rethought. The philosophy behind initiatives such as Zero to Three and Early Head Start makes sense. The programs are based on evidence that the first three years are very important for brain development and that early stimulation can effect positive changes in a child's life. But Devlin and Thornhill's research suggests a stronger public-health emphasis on a baby's prenatal life if we are to equalize the opportunities for children.

Does that mean unborn babies need to hear more Mozart? Companies are offering kits so expectant mothers can play music or different sounds to their developing babies—the prenatal "Mozart effect." One kit promises this stimulation will lead to "longer new-born attention span, better sleep patterns, accelerated development, expanded cognitive powers, enhanced social awareness and extraordinary language abilities." Will acceptance to Harvard come next?

"The number of bogus and dangerous devices available to expectant parents to make their babies smarter constantly shocks me," says DiPietro. "All these claims are made without a shred of evidence to support them."

Adds DeCasper: "I think it is dangerous to stimulate the baby in the womb. If you play Mozart and it remembers Mozart, is it going to be a smarter baby? I haven't got a clue. Could it hurt the baby? Yes, I think it could. If you started this stimulation too early and played it too loud, there is evidence from animal studies that you can destroy the ear's ability to hear sounds in a particular range. That's an established fact. Would I take a risk with my fetus? No!"

DeCasper and other researches emphasize that no devices or tricks can enhance the brainpower of a developing baby. Their advice to the expectant mother: Take the best possible care of yourself.

"The womb is a quiet, protective place for a reason," DiPietro concludes. "Nature didn't design megaphones to be placed on the abdomen. The fetus gets all the stimulation it needs for its brain to develop."

MR. PEKKANEN is a contributing editor to The Washingtonian. From "Secrets of the Womb," by John Pekkanen, The Washingtonian, August 2001, pages 44–51, 126–135.

The Smallest Patients

To help babies with heart defects, doctors can now operate in the womb.

CLAUDIA KALB

Melissa Paske was 29 weeks pregnant with a girl when she asked her doctor for a second ultrasound. Her belly had been scanned at 24 weeks, and there was no medical reason to take additional images. But, says Paske, "something in me felt that I needed to see her again." That something turned out to be a devastating diagnosis for her baby: a badly clogged aortic valve, which doctors feared could lead to a massively underdeveloped left side of the heart, a condition called hypoplastic left heart syndrome (HLHS). The news, says Paske, "was like a truck backing up over me."

Babies with HLHS typically undergo a complex series of surgeries after birth to compensate for the defect. But a team of doctors at Children's Hospital Boston and neighboring Brigham and Women's Hospital offered Melissa Paske and her husband, Travis, of Spokane, Wash., something new: a revolutionary procedure performed while their baby was still floating in Melissa's womb. Within days the Paskes were flying across the country. In her 30th week of pregnancy, doctors inserted a needle through Melissa's uterus into her fetus's heart, where they dilated a balloon and opened the blocked valve. Six weeks later the Paskes' daughter, Camryn, was born HLHS-free. Last week the slender little girl with eight tiny teeth and a mop of light brown hair celebrated her 1st birthday. "She's just beautiful," says Melissa.

She's also a medical pioneer. Thirty years ago, babies diagnosed with HLHS were doomed to die within the first days to weeks of life. Today, thanks to earlier detection through ultrasound and postnatal surgery, the majority of the 1,500-plus HLHS babies born every year now survive; the oldest are in their early 20s. The medical journey, however, is far from easy. Ten to 25 percent of infants die during or after their first operation, and those who do make it require lifelong care; some will need pacemakers or even heart transplants. The condition is so severe that

many couples choose to terminate their pregnancies. The Boston team is now trying to change all that by waging a pre-emptive strike through fetal intervention. The procedure is experimental, but the potential payoff is huge: warding off HLHS before it even develops. It's way too early to claim victory, but Dr. Jim Lock, Children's cardiologist in chief, is optimistic: "This is clearly the wave of the future."

Development of the human heart is nothing short of anatomical wizardry. The organ starts out as a narrow tube, then twists and turns during the first eight weeks of gestation to create its elegant final design: four chambers, four valves, two walls or septums and an assortment of veins and arteries. The two lower chambers of the heart operate as pumping stations: the right ventricle squeezes blood out to the lungs, and the left—responsible for the lion's share of the work—pumps to the rest of the body. Nobody knows precisely what causes HLHS, but one key factor is the plumbing problem that Camryn suffered early on in development: a narrowing of the aortic valve. The malfunction causes blood to back up in the left ventricle, forcing the developing heart muscle to squeeze extra hard. Eventually the muscle tires, stops pumping and growing, and withers. The outcome is dire: babies with HLHS have one working ventricle instead of two, making their hearts incapable of sustaining life.

As of now, the best treatment for HLHS is a three-stage open-heart surgery—performed at birth, at 6 months and around the age of 2 or 3—which re-engineers the heart's plumbing, making the right side take on the pumping job of the left side as well. (A complete heart transplant is also an option, but few infant hearts are available for donation.) "We don't fix the heart," says Dr. Jack Rychik, director of the Fetal Heart Program at Children's Hospital of Philadelphia (CHOP). "We cheat nature by redirecting the blood." Since it was first attempted in the early 1980s, the procedure has been a godsend, saving the lives of thousands. But it's not a cure. The goal among fetal experts is to redirect the heart toward normal development and get rid of HLHS altogether.

Operating in the womb raises the surgical stakes. For starters, there are two patients—mother and fetus—and one of them is floating in fluid. A team of doctors, including anesthesiologists (both mother and fetus are given medication to relieve pain), echocardiographers, obstetricians, radiologists and cardiologists, must work together, using snowy ultrasound images as their only road map. A needle must be carefully guided through the mother's abdomen and uterine wall into the grape-size fetal heart and then on to the aortic valve, about the diameter of spaghetti, where doctors dilate a balloon to stretch the opening. Along with the technical challenges come operational dangers. Both mother and fetus are susceptible to complications from anesthesia. The mother could develop blood clots or an infection or go into premature labor. Her fetus could be injured by the needle, suffer cardiac distress, even die in utero. "There are risks with no guarantee that the intervention will work," says Lock's colleague Dr. Wayne Tworetzky, who counsels prospective parents. "We have to be very straightforward with families."

A needle is guided into the grape-size fetal heart.

Since 2000, the Boston team has performed just over 50 procedures. Most have been aortic-valve dilations, but the team is using a similar approach to try to fix blocked pulmonary valves, which can lead to a mirror image of HLHS called hypoplastic right heart syndrome. And the team is intervening in an even more dangerous problem that strikes some fetuses who have already developed HLHS: a blockage in the atrial septum, which divides the two upper chambers of the heart. In addition to withered left hearts, these babies are susceptible to lung damage. Not all the procedures have been technically successful—the needle hasn't gone in properly or the balloon hasn't dilated. Some of the sickest babies have died despite the intervention; others have developed HLHS. But seven babies who had successful aortic-valve dilations have been spared the syndrome, a home run in congenital heart disease. "We now have significant evidence that we can remodel hearts before birth," says Lock. "This represents a major potential breakthrough in the field."

There are still challenges ahead. The womb is new territory, the learning curve is steep and the parents, desperate to help their babies, are vulnerable. Doctors can't predict with certainty which babies will benefit from the procedure, making patient selection tricky. And even if a procedure does seem warranted, there's no guarantee that the

baby's outcome will be better than what standard surgery now offers. CHOP's Rychik believes more research is needed on the evolution of congenital heart disease before those dilemmas can be solved. "I'm encouraged by the Boston experience, and I applaud it," says Rychik, who is launching a nationwide study to document fetal heart development, but "we're still very early in all of this." Other clinics are taking the plunge, albeit in very small numbers. Doctors at the University of California, San Francisco, have performed one fetal procedure; the Cleveland Clinic has completed two. "We're seeing the fetus as a patient, and we're prepared to do everything in our power to make things better," says Cleveland's Dr. Stephen Emery.

Fetal intervention is still in its infancy. The number of affected babies is small, and the technique requires highly skilled doctors at topnotch clinics. But the odds for sick babies could improve immediately simply through better detection of abnormalities during pregnancy. Alex Osborne of Lebanon, Pa., is proof of that. His heart defect was identified during a routine 19-week ultrasound, allowing his parents, Julie and David, to seek out cardiac experts at CHOP well before their baby's due date. Doctors were able to counsel the couple about Alex's condition—he had HLHS complicated by a blocked atrial septum—and prepare them for surgical intervention. And a team of experts, including obstetricians, pediatric cardiologists and cardiac surgeons, could be assembled for Julie's delivery, ready to provide immediate care. "We delivered him and rushed him to the OR," says Rychik. Just two hours after birth, Alex had his first surgery. Today he's 7 years old and a four-foot-tall, 50-pound budding paleontologist. "It's unlikely he would have survived if we hadn't known about his condition ahead of time," says Rychik.

Alex, however, is in the minority. Today more than 90 percent of women receive midtrimester ultrasounds, and yet only 20 to 30 percent of congenital heart defects are picked up, says Dr. Lisa Hornberger, director of UCSF's Fetal Cardiovascular Program. That means doctors are delivering babies with ticking time bombs inside: they look perfectly healthy at birth, then suddenly crash, gasping for air. Ultrasound works, says Hornberger; "the problem is, people don't know what to look for." Today Hornberger is conducting seminars for obstetricians and other diagnosticians, teaching them to identify the earliest signs of trouble. Once they do, babies can be scheduled for surgery after birth, or perhaps even referred for fetal intervention. "We're at the tip of the iceberg," she says. "We need to be improving detection, or we're not going to be making a difference."

Camryn Paske is making a difference in her own little 1-year-old way. "She's crawling and getting into everything," says Melissa. "I call her my 'terror on knees'." She's also laughing and playing around with pet beagles Copper and Bagel. Camryn's heart isn't perfect. She takes three medications a day to make sure it pumps efficiently, and one day she may need her damaged aortic valve repaired or replaced. But she's been spared the worst. "I feel so fortunate and indebted to the doctors," says Melissa. Her family may live in Spokane, but "we're Red Sox fans now," she says. Rooting not just for baseball—but for every fragile little heart that makes its way to Boston.

UNIT 2

Development During Infancy and Early Childhood

Unit Selections

Key Points to Consider

- What are the four new ways of thinking about infant development that all parents and caregivers should know?

- What purposes are served by involving babies in hectic activity schedules and introducing them to academics as early as possible?

- How much do babies understand at birth? What emotions do they feel? Are there social and emotional "milestones" to help caregivers watch progress?

- Are there inexpensive and easy ways to boost a baby's brain power? Can any caregiver incorporate them into daily activities?

- Should the United States provide free preschool to every child? What would be the advantages of this expensive undertaking?

- How much television should infants and preschoolers be allowed to watch? What shows are good for them? What aspects of television viewing are bad for them?

- When should children know right from wrong? How is it learned?

Student Website

www.mhcls.com/online

Internet References

Further information regarding these websites may be found in this book's preface or online.

BabyCenter
http://www.babycenter.com

Children's Nutrition Research Center (CNRC)
http://www.bcm.tmc.edu/cnrc/

Early Childhood Care and Development
http://www.ecdgroup.com

Zero to Three: National Center for Infants, Toddlers, and Families
http://www.zerotothree.org

Developmental researchers go back and forth between demonstrating environmental causes of behavior, genetic influences on behavior, and the interactions of both. The articles selected for inclusion in this unit reflect both the known influences of nurture (environment) and nature (biology) and the relationships and interactions of multiple variables, and child outcomes about which we hope to know more in the new millennium.

Newborns are quite well developed in some areas, and incredibly deficient in others. Babies' cerebral hemispheres already have their full complement of neurons (worker cells). The neuroglia (supportive cells) are almost completely developed and will reach their final numbers by age one. In contrast, babies' legs and feet are tiny, weak, and barely functional. Look at newborns from another perspective, however, and their brains seem somewhat less superior. The neurons and neuroglia present at birth must be protected. We may discover ways to make more cerebral neurons in the future, but such knowledge now is in its infancy and does not go very far. By contrast, the cells of the baby's legs and feet (skin, fat, muscles, bones, blood vessels) are able to replace themselves by mitosis indefinitely. Their numbers will continue to grow through early adulthood; then their quantity and quality can be regenerated through advanced old age.

The developing brain in infancy is a truly fascinating organ. At birth it is poorly organized. The lower (primitive) brain parts (brain stem, pons, medulla, cerebellum) are well enough developed to allow the infant to live. The lower brain directs vital organ systems (heart, lungs, kidneys, etc.). The higher (advanced) brain parts (cerebral hemispheres) have allocated neurons, but the nerve cells and cell processes (axons, dendrites) are small, underdeveloped, and unorganized. During infancy, these higher (cerebral) nerve cells (that allow the baby to think, reason, and remember) grow at astronomical rates. They migrate to permanent locations in the hemispheres, develop myelin sheathing (insulation), and conduct messages. Many twentieth-century researchers, including Jean Piaget, the father of cognitive psychology, believed that all brain activity in the newborn was reflexive, based on instincts for survival. They were wrong. New research has documented that fetuses can learn and newborns can think as well as learn.

The role played by electrical and chemical activity of neurons in actively shaping the physical structure of the brain is particularly awe inspiring. The neurons are produced prenatally. After birth, the flood of sensory inputs from the environment (sights, sounds, smells, tastes, touch, balance, and kinesthetic sensations) drives the neurons to form circuits and become wired to each other. Trillions of connections are established in a baby's brain. During childhood the connections that are seldom or never used are eliminated or pruned. The first 3 years are critical for establishing these connections. Environments that provide both good nutrition and lots of sensory stimulation really do produce richer, more connected brains.

The first article in this section on infancy explains what mothers, fathers, and all other infant caregivers need to know immediately upon birth of their precious baby. The Human Genome Project gives new life to attempts to integrate all the separate pieces of knowledge about infant development from biology and psychology. Joanna Lipari articulates the old thinking with its counterpoint new thinking.

The next selection on infancy asks and partially answers the question, "Who's Raising Baby?" Anne Pierce discusses the challenges to modern day parenting from a mother's-eye view. Contemporary parents seem to be on a competitive merry-go-round to have their offspring involved in as many "enriching" activities as their neighbors, friends, coworkers, etc. What is the purpose of all this activity? The article cites the opinions of renowned child psychologists such as David Elkind and Stanley Greenspan that this race for supremacy is not healthy. In infancy, emotional learning and the ability to relate to others are more important than literacy. Home life is valuable. The author believes lessons learned at home supercede those obtained in day care.

The third selection on infancy, "Reading Your Baby's Mind," addresses a concern of many parents: How much does this baby understand? With electroencephalography and laser eye tracking, scientists are providing surprising answers. In short, a lot! They feel empathy when others are stressed, as well as fear and contentment from birth onwards. This article explains how infant minds develop, the role of environment, and gives it milestones of progress in the first 18 months of life.

To complete the infancy section, Alice Honig suggests "20 Ways to Boost Your Baby's Brain Power." These ideas are easily put into practice without a great deal of time or money. They really work, too!

The first early childhood article addresses "Long-Term Studies of Preschool: Lasting Benefits Far Outweigh Costs." Many industrialized nations subsidize high-quality early childhood education. The United States does not. Long-term studies of three excellent preschool programs in the United States have documented long-lasting benefits. While national preschool funding would be an expensive investment, the authors argue that it would be worth the costs.

Daniel McGinn, in the next early childhood selection, praises what has happened to children's television programming in recent years. Nickelodeon, Fox, and the Disney Channel now compete with the public broadcasting station in the United States (PBS) for early childhood education excellence. Despite more and better programs, parents need to monitor what, and how much, is consumed by toddlers. Play is still the best brain enhancer, and interaction with live humans vastly outweighs the possible benefits of television.

The last article in this unit discusses how parents can instill and nurture moral values and behaviors in young children. Although states vary in the ages that they hold children legally accountable for knowing right from wrong, child developmentalists believe that preschoolers can grasp, and should be taught, moral values.

Four Things You Need to Know About Raising Baby

New thinking about the newborn's brain, feelings and behavior are changing the way we look at parenting

JOANNA LIPARI, M.A.

Bookstore shelves are crammed with titles purporting to help you make your baby smarter, happier, healthier, stronger, better-behaved and everything else you can imagine, in what I call a shopping-cart approach to infant development. But experts are now beginning to look more broadly, in an integrated fashion, at the first few months of a baby's life. And so should you.

Psychological theorists are moving away from focusing on single areas such as physical development, genetic inheritance, cognitive skills or emotional attachment, which give at best a limited view of how babies develop. Instead, they are attempting to synthesize and integrate all the separate pieces of the infant-development puzzle. The results so far have been enlightening, and are beginning to suggest new ways of parenting.

The most important of the emerging revelations is that the key to stimulating emotional and intellectual growth in your child is your own behavior—what you do, what you don't do, how you scold, how you reward and how you show affection. If the baby's brain is the hardware, then you, the parents, provide the software. When you understand the hardware (your baby's brain), you will be better able to design the software (your own behavior) to promote baby's well-being.

The first two years of life are critical in this regard because that's when your baby is building the mental foundation that will dictate his or her behavior through adulthood. In the first year alone, your baby's brain grows from about 400g to a stupendous 1000g. While this growth and development is in part predetermined by genetic force, exactly how the brain grows is dependent upon emotional interaction, and that involves you. "The human cerebral cortex adds about 70% of its final DNA content after birth," reports Allan N. Schore, Ph.D., assistant clinical professor of psychiatry and biobehavioral sciences at UCLA Medical School, "and this expanding brain is directly influenced by early environmental enrichment and social experiences."

Failure to provide this enrichment during the first two years can lead to a lifetime of emotional disability, according to attachment theorists. We are talking about the need to create a relationship and environment that allows your child to grow up with an openness to learning and the ability to process, understand and experience emotion with compassion, intelligence and resilience. These are the basic building blocks of emotional success.

Following are comparisons of researchers' "old thinking" and "new thinking." They highlight the four new insights changing the way we view infant development. The sections on "What To Do" then explain how to apply that new information.

1 **FEELINGS TRUMP THOUGHTS** It is the emotional quality of the relationship you have with your baby that will stimulate his or her brain for optimum emotional and intellectual growth.

OLD THINKING: In this country, far too much emphasis is placed on developing babies' cognitive abilities. Some of this push came out of the promising results of the Head Start program. Middle-class families reasoned that if a little stimulation in an underendowed home environment is beneficial, wouldn't "more" be better? And the race to create the "superbaby" was on.

Gone are the days when parents just wished their child were "normal" and could "fit in" with other kids. Competition for selective schools and the social pressure it generates has made parents feel their child needs to be "gifted." Learning exercises, videos and educational toys are pushed on parents to use in play with their children. "Make it fun," the experts say. The emphasis is on developing baby's cognitive skills by using the emotional reward of parental attention as a behavior-training tool.

THE NEW THINKING: Flying in the face of all those "smarter" baby books are studies suggesting that pushing baby to learn words, numbers, colors and shapes too early forces the child to use lower-level thinking processes, rather than develop his or her learning ability. It's like a pony trick at the circus: When the pony paws the ground to "count" to three, it's really not counting; it's simply performing a stunt. Such "tricks" are not only not helpful to baby's learning process, they are potentially harmful. Tufts University child psychologist David Elkind, Ph.D., makes it clear that putting pressure on a child to learn information sends the message that he or she needs to "perform" to gain the parents' acceptance, and it can dampen natural curiosity.

Instead, focus on building baby's emotional skills. "Emotional development is not just the foundation for important capacities such as intimacy and trust," says Stanley Greenspan, M.D., clinical professor of psychiatry and pediatrics at George Washington University Medical School and author of the new comprehensive book *Building Healthy Minds*. "It is also the foundation of intelligence and a wide variety of cognitive skills. At each stage of development, emotions lead the way, and learning facts and skills follow. Even math skills, which appear [to be] strictly an impersonal cognition, are initially learned through the emotions: 'A lot' to a 2-year-old, for example, is more than he would expect, whereas 'a little' is less than he wants."

It makes sense: Consider how well you learn when you are passionate about a subject, compared to when you are simply required to learn it. That passion is the emotional fuel driving the cognitive process. So the question then becomes not "what toys and games should I use to make my baby smarter?" but "how should I interact with my baby to make him 'passionate' about the world around him?"

WHAT TO DO: When you read the baby "milestone" books or cognitive development guides, keep in mind that the central issue is your baby's *emotional* development. As Greenspan advises, "Synthesize this information about milestones and see them with emotional development as the central issue. This is like a basketball team, with the coach being our old friend, emotions. Because emotions tell the child what he wants to do—move his arm, make a sound, smile or frown. As you look at the various 'milestone components'—motor, social and cognitive skills—look to see how the whole mental team is working together."

Not only will this give you more concrete clues as to how to strengthen your emotional relationship, but it will also serve to alert you to any "players" on the team that are weak or injured, i.e., a muscle problem in the legs, or a sight and hearing difficulty.

2 NOT JUST A SCREAMING MEATLOAF: BIRTH TO TWO MONTHS

It's still largely unknown how well infants understand their world at birth, but new theories are challenging the traditional perspectives.

OLD THINKING: Until now, development experts thought infants occupied some kind of presocial, precognitive, preorganized life phase that stretched from birth to two months. They viewed newborns' needs as mainly physiological—with sleep-wake, day-night and hunger-satiation cycles, even calling the first month of life "the normal autism" phase, or as a friend calls it, the "screaming meatloaf" phase. Certainly, the newborn has emotional needs, but researchers thought they were only in response to basic sensory drives like taste, touch, etc.

THE NEW THINKING: In his revolutionary book, *The Interpersonal World of the Infant*, psychiatrist Daniel Stern, Ph.D.,

challenged the conventional wisdom on infant development by proposing that babies come into this world as social beings. In research experiments, newborns consistently demonstrate that they actively seek sensory stimulation, have distinct preferences and, from birth, tend to form hypotheses about what is occurring in the world around them. Their preferences are emotional ones. In fact, parents would be unable to establish the physiological cycles like wake-sleep without the aid of such sensory, emotional activities as rocking, touching, soothing, talking and singing. In turn, these interactions stimulate the child's brain to make the neuronal connections she needs in order to process the sensory information provided.

WHAT TO DO: "Take note of your baby's own special biological makeup and interactive style," Greenspan advises. You need to see your baby for the special individual he is at birth. Then, "you can deliberately introduce the world to him in a way that maximizes his delight and minimizes his frustrations." This is also the time to learn how to help your baby regulate his emotions, for example, by offering an emotionally overloaded baby some soothing sounds or rocking to help him calm down.

3 THE LOVE LOOP: BEGINNING AT TWO MONTHS

At approximately eight weeks, a miraculous thing occurs—your baby's vision improves and for the first time, she can fully see you and can make direct eye contact. These beginning visual experiences of your baby play an important role in social and emotional development. "In particular, the mother's emotionally expressive face is, by far, the most potent visual stimulus in the infant's environment," points out UCLA's Alan Schore, "and the child's intense interest in her face, especially in her eyes, leads him/her to track it in space to engage in periods of intense mutual gaze." The result: Endorphin levels rise in the baby's brain, causing pleasurable feelings of joy and excitement. But the key is for this joy to be interactive.

OLD THINKING: The mother pumps information and affection into the child, who participates only as an empty receptacle.

THE NEW THINKING: We now know that the baby's participation is crucial to creating a solid attachment bond. The loving gaze of parents to child is reciprocated by the baby with a loving gaze back to the parents, causing their endorphin levels to rise, thus completing a closed emotional circuit, a sort of "love loop." Now, mother (or father) and baby are truly in a dynamic, interactive system. "In essence, we are talking less about what the mother is doing to the baby and more about how the mother is being with the baby and how the baby is learning to be with the mother," says Schore.

The final aspect of this developing interactive system between mother and child is the mother's development of an "emotional synchronization" with her child. Schore defines this as the mother's ability to tune into the baby's internal states and respond accordingly. For example: Your baby is quietly lying on the floor, happy to take in the sights and sounds of the environment. As you notice the baby looking for stimulation, you respond with a game of "peek-a-boo." As you play with your child and she responds with shrieks of glee, you escalate the emotion with bigger and bigger gestures and facial expressions.

Shortly thereafter, you notice the baby turns away. The input has reached its maximum and you sense your child needs you to back off for awhile as she goes back to a state of calm and restful inactivity. "The synchronization between the two is more than between their behavior and thoughts; the synchronization is on a biological level—their brains and nervous systems are linked together," points out Schore. "In this process, the mother is teaching and learning at the same time. As a result of this moment-by-moment matching of emotion, both partners increase their emotional connection to one another. In addition, the more the mother fine-tunes her activity level to the infant during periods of play and interaction, the more she allows the baby to disengage and recover quietly during periods of nonplay, before initiating actively arousing play again."

Neuropsychological research now indicates that this attuned interaction—engaged play, disengagement and restful nonplay, followed by a return to play behavior—is especially helpful for brain growth and the development of cerebral circuits. This makes sense in light of the revelation that future cognitive development depends not on the cognitive stimulation of flashcards and videos, but on the attuned, dynamic and emotional interactions between parent and child. The play periods stimulate baby's central nervous system to excitation, followed by a restful period of alert inactivity in which the developing brain is able to process the stimulation and the interaction.

In this way, you, the parents, are the safety net under your baby's emotional highwire; the act of calming her down, or giving her the opportunity to calm down, will help her learn to handle ever-increasing intensity of stimulation and thus build emotional tolerance and resilience.

WHAT TO DO: There are two steps to maximizing your attunement ability: spontaneity and reflection. When in sync, you and baby will both experience positive emotion; when out of sync, you will see negative emotions. If much of your interactions seem to result in negative emotion, then it is time to reflect on your contribution to the equation.

In these instances, parents need to help one another discover what may be impeding the attunement process. Sometimes, on an unconscious level, it may be memories of our own childhood. For example, my friend sings nursery rhymes with a Boston accent, even though she grew up in New York, because her native Bostonian father sang them to her that way. While the "Fah-mah in the Dell" will probably not throw baby into a temper tantrum, it's a good example of how our actions or parenting style may be problematic without our realizing it.

But all parents have days when they are out of sync with baby, and the new perspective is that it's not such a bad thing. In fact, it's quite valuable. "Misattunement" is not a bioneurological disaster if you can become attuned again. The process of falling out of sync and then repairing the bond actually teaches children resilience, and a sense of confidence that the world will respond to them and repair any potential hurt.

Finally, let your baby take the lead. Schore suggests we "follow baby's own spontaneous expression of himself," which lets the child know that another person, i.e., mom or dad, can understand what he is feeling, doing, and even thinking. Such experiences, says Schore, assist in the development of the prefrontal area, which controls "empathy, and therefore that which makes us most 'human.'"

4 THE SHAME TRANSACTION Toward the end of the first year, as crawling turns to walking, a shift occurs in the communication between child and parents. "Observational studies show that 12-month-olds receive more positive responses from mothers, while 18-month-olds receive more instructions and directions," says Schore. In one study, mothers of toddlers expressed a prohibition—basically telling the child "no"—approximately every nine minutes! That's likely because a mobile toddler has an uncanny knack for finding the most dangerous things to explore!

Yesterday, for example, I walked into the living room to find my daughter scribbling on the wall with a purple marker. "NO!" shot out of my mouth. She looked up at me with stunned shock, then realized what she had done. Immediately, she hung her head, about to cry. I babbled on a bit about how markers are only for paper, yada-yada and then thought, "Heck, it's washable." As I put my arm around my daughter, I segued into a suggestion for another activity: washing the wall! She brightened and raced to get the sponge. We had just concluded a "shame transaction."

OLD THINKING: Researchers considered all these "no's" a necessary byproduct of child safety or the socialization process. After all, we must teach children to use the potty rather than wet the bed, not to hit another child when mad, to behave properly in public. Researchers did not consider the function of shame vis-à-vis brain development. Instead, they advised trying to limit situations in which the child would feel shame.

NEW THINKING: It's true that you want to limit the shame situations, but they are not simply a necessary evil in order to civilize your baby. Neurobiological studies indicate that episodes of shame like the one I described can actually stimulate the development of the right hemisphere, the brain's source of creativity, emotion and sensitivity, as long as the shame period is short and followed by a recovery. In essence, it's not the experience of shame that can be damaging, but rather the inability of the parent to help the child recover from that shame.

WHAT TO DO: It's important to understand "the growth-facilitating importance of small doses of shame in the socialization process of the infant," says Schore. Embarrassment (a component of shame) first emerges around 14 months, when mom's "no" results in the child lowering his head and looking down in obvious sadness. The child goes from excited (my daughter scribbling on the wall) to sudden deflation (my "NO!") back to excitement ("It's okay, let's wash the wall together"). During this rapid process, various parts of the brain get quite a workout and experience heightened connectivity, which strengthens these systems. The result is development of the orbitofrontal cortex (cognitive area) and limbic system (emotional area) and the ability for the two systems to interrelate emotional resiliency in the child and the ability to self-regulate emotions and impulse control.

What is important to remember about productive shame reactions is that there must be a quick recovery. Extended periods of shame result in a child learning to shut down, or worse, become hyperirritable, perhaps even violent. It's common sense: Just think how you feel when someone embarrasses you. If that embarrassment goes on without relief, don't you tend to either flee the situation or rail against it?

From these new research findings, it's clear that successful parenting isn't just about intuition, instinct and doing what your mother did. It's also not about pushing the alphabet, multiplication tables or violin lessons. We now believe that by seeing the newborn as a whole person—as a thinking, feeling creature who can and should participate in his own emotional and cognitive development—we can maximize the nurturing and stimulating potential of our relationship with a newborn baby.

JOANNA LIPARI is pursuing a Psy.D. at Pepperdine University in Los Angeles..

Reprinted with permission from *Psychology Today*, July/August 2000, pp. 38–43. © 2000 by Sussex Publishers, Inc.

Who's Raising Baby?

Challenges to Modern-Day Parenting

Anne R. Pierce

Drive through the empty streets of our neighborhoods and ask yourself not merely where the children have gone but where childhood has gone. It is most unlikely you will see such once-familiar scenes as these: a child sitting under a tree with a book, toddlers engaged in collecting leaves and sticks, friends riding bikes or playing tag, parents and their offspring working together in the yard, families (in no hurry to get anywhere) strolling casually along. Today's children are too busy with other things to enjoy the simple pleasures children used to take for granted. Preoccupied with endless "activities" and diversions, they have little time for simply going outside.

Where are the children and what are they doing? They are in day-care centers, now dubbed "learning centers." They are in "early childhood programs" and all-day kindergarten. They are acquiring new skills, attending extracurricular classes, and participating in organized sports. They are sitting in front of the computer, the TV, and the Play Station. They are not experiencing the comfortable ease of unconditional love, nor the pleasant feeling of familiarity. They are not enjoying a casual conversation, nor are they playing. They are working—at improving their talents, at competing with their peers, at "beating the enemy" in a video game, at just getting by, at adapting to the new baby-sitter or coach, at not missing Mom or Dad. They, like their computers, are "on." Being, for them, is doing, adjusting, coping. Parenting, for us, is providing them with things to do.

Young children expend their energy on long days in group situations, in preschool and after-school programs, in music and athletic lessons. For much-needed relaxation, they collapse in front of the TV or computer, the now-defining features of "homelife." Relaxation no longer signifies quiet or repose. The hyperactive pace of children's television shows and video games, always accompanied by driving music, exacerbates and surpasses the fast pace of modern life. Children stare at the screen, though the inanity, violence, and doomsday sociopolitical messages of the programming are anything but reassuring.

From doing to staring, from staring to doing. There is little room in this scenario for idle contentment, playful creativity, and the passionate pursuit of interests. Alternatives to this framework for living are provided neither in thought nor in deed by busy parents who, themselves, end their rushed days with television and escapism.

Before nursery school starts, most children who can afford it have attended "classes," from gymnastics to ballet, piano, or swimming. Infant "swim lessons," in which an instructor in diving gear repeatedly forces screaming babies underwater so that they are forced to swim, are now commonplace. Day-care centers claim to give toddlers a head start in academic advancement and socialization. Increasing numbers of bright young children spend time with tutors or at the learning center to attain that ever-elusive "edge."

Children in elementary school now "train" and lift weights in preparation for their sports. Football and track are new options for first-graders. A recent trend in elementary athletic programs is to recruit professional coaches, due to the supposed competitive disadvantage of amateur coaching done by parents. It is more common for young children to "double up," participating in two team sports at a time. A constantly increasing selection of stimulating activities lures modern families, making downtime more elusive.

What used to be "time for dinner" (together) is, more often than not, time for family members to rush and scatter in different directions. A typical first-grade soccer team practices two evenings a week, from 6:00 to 7:30. The stress involved in getting six-year-olds fed and in gear by practice time and, after practice, bathed and in bed at an appropriate hour is obvious. And yet, if you attend a first-grade soccer game, you'll likely find parents eager to discover the activities of other people's children and anxious to sign their children up for—whatever it might be. Some parents appear to be jealous of the activities others have discovered.

The New Conformism—Afraid of Missing Out

In asking scores of parents about the purpose of all this activity, I have never received a clear or, to my mind, satisfactory answer. The end, apparently, is unclear apart from the idea, often expressed, that if one's child starts activities later than other children, he (or she) will be "left behind." Some of the more cohesive explanations I have received are these: A mother described herself as being "swept along by the inevitable"; she didn't want her young daughter to be "the only one missing out." A couple explained their determination to expose their toddler to a wide variety of opportunities so that he would know which sports he excelled in "by the time things get competitive." A father said, simply, that he saw his role in terms of making sure his children were "the best at something," and with all the other kids starting activities at such an early age, this meant that his kids "had to start even earlier."

In effect, this is the "do what everyone else does, only sooner and more intensely" theory of child rearing. This theory creates a constant downward pressure upon children of a younger and younger age. This was evident to me when my youngest son entered kindergarten and I discovered he was within a small minority of boys who had not *already* participated in team sports. Only five years earlier, my oldest son was within the sizable majority of kindergartners whose parents had decided kindergarten was a little too early for such endeavors. (First grade was then the preferred starting point.)

The more families subscribe to this "lifestyle," the more there is another reason for pushing kids off to the races: If no children are around to play with, then, especially for only children, organized activities become their only opportunity to "play" with other kids. Playing is thus thoroughly redefined.

The philosophy of child rearing as a race and of homelife as oppressive for women compels families toward incessant action. Love, nurture, and, concomitantly, innocence have been demoted as compared to experience and exposure. The family is viewed as a closedness to experience, the nurturing role within the family as the most confining of all. Indeed, busyness supplants togetherness in many modern families.

One legacy of Freud, Piaget, Pavlov, and the behaviorists, neodevelopmentalists, and social scientists who followed them has been the decreasing respect for the child's being and the increasing emphasis upon his "becoming." The child is seen as "socializable" and is studied as a clinical object whose observable response to this or that "environmental stimulus" becomes more important than his deeper, more complicated features. With the clinical interpretation of childhood, social engineering projects and "activities" that make the child's world more stimulating gain momentum.

Conformism, convenience, and new interpretations of childhood are, then, contributing factors in the hectic existence and the premature introduction to academics that parents prescribe for their children.

In addition to the advantage that all this activity supposedly gives children, there is also the element of convenience. If parents are too busy to supervise their children, it behooves them to keep the kids so busy and under the auspices of so many (other) adults that they are likely to "stay out of trouble." Such is the basis of many modern choices. Children spend much of their time exhausted by activities, the purposes of which are ill construed.

Conformism, convenience, and new interpretations of childhood are, then, contributing factors in the hectic existence and the premature introduction to academics that parents prescribe for their children. For example, before the 1960s, it was generally believed that placing young children in out-of-home learning programs was harmful. The concern for the harmfulness of such experiences was abandoned when these learning programs became convenient and popular.

Education As 'Socialization'

In *Miseducation: Preschoolers at Risk*, David Elkind expressed dismay at the fact that age-inappropriate approaches to early education have gained such momentum despite the undeniable evidence that pushing children into formal academics and organized activities before they are ready does more harm than good. He lamented, "In a society that prides itself on its preference for facts over hearsay, on its openness to research, and on its respect for 'expert' opinion, parents, educators, administrators, and legislators are ignoring the facts, the research and the expert opinion about how young children learn and how best to teach them.... When we instruct children in academic subjects, or in swimming, gymnastics, or ballet, at too early an age, we miseducate them; we put them at risk for short-term stress and long-term personality damage for no useful purpose."

Elkind pointed to the consistent result of reputable studies (such as that conducted by Benjamin Bloom) that a love of learning, not the inculcation of skills, is the key to the kind of early childhood development that can lead to great things. These findings, warned Elkind, point to the fallacy of early instruction as a way of producing children who will attain eminence. He noted that with gifted and talented individuals, as with children in general, the most important thing is an excitement about learning: "Miseducation, by focusing on skills to the detriment of motivation, pays an enormous price for teaching infants and young children what amounts to a few tricks."

He further observed that those advocating early instruction in skills and early out-of-home education rely upon youngsters who are very disadvantaged to tout early education's advantages. "Accordingly, the image of the competent child introduced to remedy the understimulation of low-income children now serves as the rationale for the overstimulation of middle-class children."

Dr. Jack Westman of the Rockford Institute, renowned child psychiatrist Dr. Stanley Greenspan, and brain researcher Jane Healy are among the many unheeded others who warn of the implications of forcing the "childhood as a race" approach upon young children. Laments Westman, "The result is what is now referred to as the 'hothousing movement' for infants and toddlers devoted to expediting their development. This is occurring in spite of the evidence that the long-term outcomes of early didactic, authoritarian approaches with younger children relate negatively to intellectual development."

In an interview for "Parent and Child" magazine, Dr. Greenspan insisted that young children suffer greatly if there is inadequate "emotional learning" in their daily lives.

In an interview for *"Parent and Child"* magazine, Dr. Greenspan insisted that young children suffer greatly if there is inadequate "emotional learning" in their daily lives. Such learning, he explained, is both a requisite for their ability to relate well with others and the foundation of cognitive learning. "Emotional development and interactions form the foundation for all children's learning— especially in the first five years of life. During these years, children abstract from their emotional experiences constantly to learn even the most basic concepts. Take, for example, something like saying hello or learning when you can be aggressive and when you have to be nice—and all of these are cues by emotions."

In *Endangered Minds: Why Children Don't Think and What We Can Do About It*, Healy states the case for allowing young children to play with those who love them before requiring them to learn academic skills. She intones, "Driving the cold spikes of inappropriate pressure into the malleable heart of a child's learning may seriously distort the unfolding of both intellect and motivation. This self-serving intellectual assault, increasingly condemned by teachers who see its warped products, reflects a more general ignorance of the growing brain.... Explaining things to children won't do the job; they must have the chance to experience, wonder, experiment, and act it out for themselves. It is this process, throughout life, that enables the growth of intelligence."

Healy goes so far as to describe the damaging effect on the "functional organization of the plastic brain" in pushing too hard too soon: "Before brain regions are myelinated, they do not operate efficiently. For this reason, trying to 'make' children master academic skills for which they do not have the requisite maturation may result in mixed-up patterns of learning.... It is possible to force skills by intensive instruction, but this may cause a child to use immature, inappropriate neural networks and distort the natural growth process."

Play is a way for children to relish childhood, prepare for adulthood, and discover their inner passions.

Play is important for intellectual growth, the exploration of individuality, and the growth of a conscience. Play is a way for children to relish childhood, prepare for adulthood, and discover their inner passions. Legendary psychoanalyst D.W. Winnicott warned us not to underestimate the importance of play. In *The Work and Play of Winnicott*, Simon A. Grolnick elucidates Winnicott's concept of play.

Play in childhood and throughout the life cycle helps to relieve the tension of living, helps to prepare for the serious, and sometimes for the deadly (e.g., war games), helps define and redefine the boundaries between ourselves and others, helps give us a fuller sense of our own personal and bodily being. Playing provides a trying-out ground for proceeding onward, and it enhances drive satisfaction.... Winnicott repeatedly stressed that when playing becomes too drive-infested and excited, it loses its creative growth-building capability and begins to move toward loss of control or a fetishistic rigidity.... Civilization's demands for controlled, socialized behavior gradually, and sometimes insidiously, supersedes the psychosomatic and aesthetic pleasures of open system play.

When we discard playtime, we jeopardize the child's fresh, creative approach to the world. The minuscule amount of peace that children are permitted means that thinking and introspection are demoted as well. Thought requires being, not always doing. Children who are not allowed to retreat once in a while into themselves are not allowed to find out what is there. Our busy lives become ways of hiding from the recesses of the mind. Teaching children to be tough and prepared for the world, making them into achieving doers instead of capable thinkers, has its consequences. Children's innate curiosity is intense. When that natural curiosity has no room to fulfill itself, it burns out like a smothered flame.

In an age when "socialization" into society's ideals and mores is accepted even for babies and toddlers, we should remember that institutionalized schooling even for older children is a relatively new phenomenon. Mass education was a post-Industrial Revolution invention, one that served the dual purposes of preparing children for work and freeing parents to contribute fully to the industrial structure. No longer was work something that families did together, as a unit.

The separation of children from the family's work paved the way for schools and social reformers to assume the task of preparing children for life. This is a lofty role. As parents, we need to inform ourselves as to what our children are being prepared *for* and *how* they are being prepared.

Although our children's days are filled with instruction, allowing them little time of their own, we seem frequently inattentive as to just what they are learning. As William Bennett, Allan Bloom, and others have pointed out, recent years have been characterized by the reformulation of our schools, universities, and information sources according to a relativist, left-leaning ideology saturated with cynicism. This ideology leaves students with little moral-intellectual ground to stand on, as they are taught disrespect not only for past ideas and literary works but for the American political system and Judeo-Christian ethics. Such works as *The Five Little Peppers and How They Grew* and *Little Women* are windows into the soul of a much less cynical (and much less hectic) time.

Teaching children about the great thinkers, writers, and statesmen of the past is neglected as the very idea of greatness and heroism is disputed. Thus, the respect for greatness that might have caused children to glance upward from their TV show or activity and the stories about their country's early history that might have given them respect for a time when computer games didn't exist are not a factor in their lives. The word *preoccupied* acquires new significance, for children's minds are stuffed with the here and now.

The Devaluation Of Homelife

The busyness of modern child rearing and the myopia of the modern outlook reinforce each other. The very ideas that education is a race and that preschool-age children's participation in beneficial experience is more important than playing or being with the family are modern ones that continually reinforce themselves for lack of alternatives. Our busy lives leave insufficient time to question whether all this busyness is necessary and whether the content of our childrens' education is good.

The possibility that children might regard their activities less than fondly when they are older because these activities were forced upon them is not addressed. The possibility that they may never find their own passionate interests is not considered. (I came across an interesting television show that discussed the problem middle-school coaches are having with burned-out and unenthusiastic participants in a wide range of sports. The coaches attributed this to the fact that children had already been doing these sports for years and were tired of the pressure.)

One needs time to be a thinker, freedom to be creative, and some level of choice to be enthusiastic. Families can bestow upon children opportunities for autonomy while at the same time giving them a stable base to fall back upon and moral and behavioral guidelines. Having a competitive edge is neither as important nor as lasting as the ability to lead a genuine, intelligently thought-out, and considerate life.

Some of the best learning experiences happen not in an institution, not with a teacher, but in a child's independent "research" of the world at hand.

Some of the best learning experiences happen not in an institution, not with a teacher, but in a child's independent "research" of the world at hand. As the child interprets the world around her, creates new things with the materials available to her, and extracts new ideas from the recesses of her mind, she is learning to be an active, contributing participant in the world. She occupies her physical, temporal, and intellectual space in a positive, resourceful way. Conversely, if she is constantly stuffed with edifying "opportunities," resentment and lack of autonomy are the likely results.

In *The Erosion of Childhood*, Valerie Polakow insists upon the child's ability to "make history" as opposed to simply receiving it. Lamenting the overinstitutionalization of children in day care and school, she warns, "Children as young as a year old now enter childhood institutions to be formally schooled in the ways

of the social system and emerge eighteen years later to enter the world of adulthood having been deprived of their own history-making power, their ability to act upon the world in significant and meaningful ways." She adds, "The world in which children live—the institutional world that babies, toddlers and the very young have increasingly come to inhabit and confront—is a world in which they become the objects, not the subjects of history, a world in which history is being made of them."

Day care provides both too much stimulation of the chaotic, disorganized kind, which comes inevitably from the cohabitation of large numbers of babies and toddlers, and too much of the organized kind that comes, of necessity, from group-centered living. It provides too little calm, quiet, space, or comfort and too little opportunity to converse and relate to a loving other.

Imagine, for example, a parent sitting down with her child for a "tea party." As she pours real tea into her own cup and milk into her child's, the "how to do things" is taken seriously. The child is encouraged to say "thank you" and to offer cookies to his mother, and their chat begins. Although they are pretending to be two adults, the ritual is real; it occurs in a real home setting; it provides the child with real food and a real opportunity for "mature" conversation. The mother says, "I'm so glad to be here for tea. How have you been?" The child, enjoying the chance to play the part of his mother's host, answers, "Fine! Would you like another cookie?" "Oh yes, thank you," answers his mother. "These cookies are delicious!" The child is learning about civilized behavior.

Children living in the new millennium need a refuge from the impersonal, the mechanical, and the programmed. We must provide them with more than opportunities for skill learning, socialization, and competition.

Then, picture the toy tea set at the learning center. Two children decide "to have tea." They fight over who has asked whom over. When one child asks, "How have you been?" the other loses interest and walks away. Too much of this peer-centered learning and not enough of adult-based learning clearly has negative implications for social development. The child simply cannot learn right from wrong, proper from improper, from other children who themselves have trouble making these distinctions.

Homelife that provides a break from group action has innumerable advantages for older children as well. Think of the different learning experiences a child receives from sitting down at the dinner table with his family and from gulping down a hamburger on the way to a nighttime game. In one case, the child has the opportunity to learn about manners and conversation. In the other, he is given another opportunity to compete with peers. (This is not to deny the benefits of being part of a team but simply to state that homelife itself is beneficial.) I hear many parents of high-school students complain about the competitive, selfish manner of today's students. And, yet, most of these students have not a moment in their day that is not competitive.

How can we expect children to value kindness and cooperation when their free time has been totally usurped by activities wherein winning is everything? At home, winning is not everything (unless the child expends all his time trying to "beat the enemy" in a video game). At home, a child is much more likely to be reprimanded for not compromising with his siblings than for not "defeating" them. If homelife provides children with time to define their individuality and interact with family members (and all the give-and-take implied), then it is certainly an invaluable aspect of a child's advancement.

Children living in the new millennium need a refuge from the impersonal, the mechanical, and the programmed. We must provide them with more than opportunities for skill learning, socialization, and competition. Otherwise, something will be missing in their humanness. For to be human is to have the capacity for intimate attachments based upon love (which can grow more intimate because of the closeness that family life provides); it is to reason and to have a moral sense of things; it is to be capable of a spontaneity that stems from original thought or from some passion within.

We must set our children free from our frenetic, goal-oriented pace. We must create for them a private realm wherein no child-rearing "professional" can tread. Within this secure space, the possibilities are endless. With this stable base to fall back upon, children will dare to dream, think, and explore. They will compete, learn, and socialize as the blossoming individuals that they are, not as automatons engineered for results.

ANNE R. PIERCE is an author and political philosopher who lives in Cincinnati with her husband and three children. As a writer, she finds that bringing up children in the modern world gives her much food for thought.

From *The World & I*, February 2002, pp. 306-317. © 2002 by The World & I online. **www.WorldandIJournal.com**. Reprinted by permission.

Reading Your Baby's Mind

New research on infants finally begins to answer the question: what's going on in there?

Pat Wingert and Martha Brant

Little Victoria Bateman is blond and blue-eyed and as cute a baby as there ever was. At 6 months, she is also trusting and unsuspecting, which is a good thing, because otherwise she'd never go along with what's about to happen. It's a blistering June afternoon in Lubbock, Texas, and inside the Human Sciences lab at Texas Tech University, Victoria's mother is settling her daughter into a high chair, where she is the latest subject in an ongoing experiment aimed at understanding the way babies think. Sybil Hart, an associate professor of human development and leader of the study, trains video cameras on mother and daughter. Everything is set. Hart hands Cheryl Bateman a children's book, "Elmo Pops In," and instructs her to engross herself in its pages. "Just have a conversation with me about the book," Hart tells her. "The most important thing is, do not look at [Victoria.]" As the two women chat, Victoria looks around the room, impassive and a little bored.

After a few minutes, Hart leaves the room and returns cradling a lifelike baby doll. Dramatically, Hart places it in Cheryl Bateman's arms, and tells her to cuddle the doll while continuing to ignore Victoria. "That's OK, little baby," Bateman coos, hugging and rocking the doll. Victoria is not bored anymore. At first, she cracks her best smile, showcasing a lone stubby tooth. When that doesn't work, she begins kicking. But her mom pays her no mind. That's when Victoria loses it. Soon she's beet red and crying so hard it looks like she might spit up. Hart rushes in. "OK, we're done," she says, and takes back the doll. Cheryl Bateman goes to comfort her daughter. "I've never seen her react like that to anything," she says. Over the last 10 months, Hart has repeated the scenario hundreds of times. It's the same in nearly every case: tiny babies, overwhelmed with jealousy. Even Hart was stunned to find that infants could experience an emotion, which, until recently, was thought to be way beyond their grasp.

And that's just for starters. The helpless, seemingly clueless infant staring up at you from his crib, limbs flailing, drool oozing, has a lot more going on inside his head than you ever imagined. A wealth of new research is leading pediatricians and child psychologists to rethink their long-held beliefs about the emotional and intellectual abilities of even very young babies. In 1890, psychologist William James famously described an infant's view of the world as "one great blooming, buzzing confusion." It was a notion that held for nearly a century: infants were simple-minded creatures who merely mimicked those around them and grasped only the most basic emotions—happy, sad, angry. Science is now giving us a much different picture of what goes on inside their hearts and heads. Long before they form their first words or attempt the feat of sitting up, they are already mastering complex emotions—jealousy, empathy, frustration—that were once thought to be learned much later in toddlerhood.

They are also far more sophisticated intellectually than we once believed. Babies as young as 4 months have advanced powers of deduction and an ability to decipher intricate patterns. They have a strikingly nuanced visual palette, which enables them to notice small differences, especially in faces, that adults and older children lose the ability to see. Until a baby is 3 months old, he can recognize a scrambled photograph of his mother just as quickly as a photo in which everything is in the right place. And big brothers and sisters beware: your sib has a long memory—and she can hold a grudge.

> **Babies yet to utter an INTELLIGENT SYLLABLE are now known to feel a range of COMPLEX EMOTIONS like envy and empathy.**

The new research is sure to enthrall new parents—See, Junior *is* a genius!—but it's more than just an academic exercise. Armed with the new information, pediatricians are starting to change the way they evaluate their youngest patients. In addition to tracking physical development, they are now focusing much more deeply on emotional advancement. The research shows how powerful emotional well-being is to a child's future health. A baby who fails to meet certain key "emotional milestones" may have trouble learning to speak, read and, later, do well in school. By reading emotional responses, doctors have begun to discover ways to tell if a baby as young as 3 months is showing early signs of possible psychological disorders, including depression, anxiety, learning disabilities and perhaps autism. "Instead of just asking if they're crawling or sitting, we're asking more questions about how they share their world with their caregivers," says Dr. Chet Johnson, chairman of the American Academy of Pediatrics' early-childhood committee. "Do they point to things? When they see a new person, how do they react? How children do on social and emotional and language skills are better predictors of success in adulthood than motor skills are." The goal: in the not-too-distant future, researchers hope doctors will routinely identify at-risk kids years earlier than they do now—giving parents crucial extra time to turn things around.

One of the earliest emotions that even tiny babies display is, admirably enough, empathy. In fact, concern for others may be hard-wired into babies' brains. Plop a newborn down next to another crying infant, and chances are, both babies will soon be wailing away. "People have always known that babies cry when they hear other babies cry," says Martin Hoffman, a psychology professor at New York University who did the first studies on infant empathy in the 1970s. "The question was, why are they crying?" Does it mean that the baby is truly concerned for his fellow human, or just annoyed by the racket? A recent study conducted in Italy, which built on Hoffman's own work, has largely settled the question. Researchers played for infants tapes of other babies crying. As predicted, that was enough to start the tears flowing. But when researchers played babies recordings of their own cries, they rarely began crying themselves. The verdict: "There is some rudimentary empathy in place, right from birth," Hoffman says. The intensity of the emotion tends to fade over time. Babies older than 6 months no longer cry but grimace at the discomfort of others. By 13 to 15 months, babies tend to take matters into their own hands. They'll try to comfort a crying playmate. "What I find most charming is when, even if the two mothers are present, they'll bring their own mother over to help," Hoffman says.

Part of that empathy may come from another early-baby skill that's now better understood, the ability to discern emotions from the facial expressions of the people around them. "Most textbooks still say that babies younger than 6 months don't recognize emotions," says Diane Montague, assistant professor of psychology at LaSalle University in Philadelphia. To put that belief to the test, Montague came up with a twist on every infant's favorite game, peekaboo, and recruited dozens of 4-month-olds to play along. She began by peeking around a cloth with a big smile on her face. Predictably, the babies were delighted, and stared at her intently—the time-tested way to tell if a baby is interested. On the fourth peek, though, Montague emerged with a sad look on her face. This time, the response was much different. "They not only looked away," she says, "but wouldn't look back even when she began smiling again. Refusing to make eye contact is a classic baby sign of distress. An angry face got their attention once again, but their faces showed no pleasure. "They seemed primed to be alert, even vigilant," Montague says. "I realize that's speculative in regard to infants ... I think it shows that babies younger than 6 months find meaning in expressions."

This might be a good place to pause for a word about the challenges and perils of baby research. Since the subjects can't speak for themselves, figuring out what's going on inside their heads is often a matter of reading their faces and body language. If this seems speculative, it's not. Over decades of trial and error, researchers have fine-tuned their observation skills and zeroed in on numerous consistent baby responses to various stimuli: how long they stare at an object, what they reach out for and what makes them recoil in fear or disgust can often tell experienced researchers everything they need to know. More recently, scientists have added EEGs and laser eye tracking, which allow more precise readings. Coming soon: advanced MRI scans that will allow a deeper view inside the brain.

When infants near their first birthdays, they become increasingly sophisticated social learners. They begin to infer what others are thinking by following the gaze of those around them. "By understanding others' gaze, babies come to understand others' minds," says Andrew Meltzoff, a professor of psychology at the University of Washington who has studied the "gaze following" of thousands of babies. "You can tell a lot about people, what they're interested in and what they intend to do next, by watching their eyes. It appears that even babies know that . . . This is how they learn to become expert members of our culture."

Meltzoff and colleague Rechele Brooks have found that this skill first appears at 10 to 11 months, and is not only an important marker of a baby's emotional and social growth, but can predict later language development. In their study, babies who weren't proficient at gaze-following by their first birthday had much less advanced-language skills at 2. Meltzoff says this helps explain why language occurs more slowly in blind children, as well as children of depressed mothers, who tend not to interact as much with their babies.

In fact, at just a few months, infants begin to develop superpowers when it comes to observation. Infants can easily tell the difference between human faces. But at the University of Minnesota, neuroscientist Charles Nelson (now of Harvard) wanted to test how discerning infants really are. He showed a group of 6-month-old babies a photo of a chimpanzee, and gave them time to stare at it until they lost interest. They were then shown another chimp. The babies perked up and stared at the new photo. The infants easily recognized each chimp as an individual—they were fascinated by each new face. Now unless you spend a good chunk of your day hanging around the local zoo, chances are you couldn't tell the difference between a roomful of chimps at a glance. As it turned out, neither could babies just a few months older. By 9 months, those kids had lost the ability to tell chimps apart; but at the same time, they had increased their powers of observation when it came to human faces.

Nelson has now taken his experiment a step further, to see how early babies can detect subtle differences in facial expressions, a key building block of social development. He designed a new study that is attempting to get deep inside babies' heads by measuring brain-wave activity. Nelson sent out letters to the parents of nearly every newborn in the area, inviting them to participate. Earlier this summer it was Dagny Winberg's turn. The 7-month-old was all smiles as her mother, Armaiti, carried her into the lab, where she was fitted with a snug cap wired with 64 sponge sensors. Nelson's assistant, grad student Meg Moulson, began flashing photographs on a screen of a woman. In each photo, the woman had a slightly different expression—many different shades of happiness and fear. Dagny was given time to look at each photo until she became bored and looked away. The whole time, a computer was closely tracking her brain activity, measuring her mind's minutest responses to the different photos. Eventually, after she'd run through 60 photos, Dagny had had enough of the game and began whimpering and fidgeting. That ended the session. The point of the experiment is to see if baby brain scans look like those of adults. "We want to see if babies categorize emotions in the ways that adults do," Moulson says. "An adult can see a slight smile and categorize it as happy. We want to know if babies can do the same." They don't have the answer yet, but Nelson believes that infants who display early signs of emotional disorders, such as autism, may be helped if they can develop these critical powers of observation and emotional engagement.

Halfway across the country, researchers are working to dispel another baby cliché: out of sight, out of mind. It was long believed that babies under 9 months didn't grasp the idea of "object permanence"—the ability to know, for instance, that when Mom leaves the room, she isn't gone forever. New research by psychologist Su-hua Wang at the University of California, Santa Cruz, is showing that babies understand the concept as early as 10 weeks. Working with 2- and 3-month-olds, she performs a little puppet show. Each baby sees a duck on a stage. Wang covers the duck, moves it across the stage and lifts the cover. Sometimes the duck is there. Other times, the duck disappears beneath a trapdoor. When they see the duck has gone missing, the babies stare intently at the empty stage, searching for it. "At 2½ months," she says, "they already have the idea that the object continues to exist."

A strong, well-developed ability to connect with the world—and with parents in particular—is especially important when babies begin making their first efforts at learning to speak. Baby talk is much more than mimickry. Michael Goldstein, a psychologist at Cornell University, gathered two groups of 8-month-olds and decked them out in overalls rigged up with wireless microphones and transmitters. One group of mothers was told to react immediately when their babies cooed or babbled, giving them big smiles and loving pats. The other group of parents was also told to smile at their kids, but randomly, unconnected to the babies' sounds. It came as no surprise that the babies who received immediate feedback babbled more and advanced quicker than those who didn't. But what interested Goldstein was the way in which the parents, without realizing it, raised the "babble bar" with their kids. "The kinds of simple sounds that get parents' attention at 4 months don't get the same reaction at 8 months," he says. "That motivates babies to experiment with different sound combinations until they find new ones that get noticed."

A decade ago Patricia Kuhl, a professor of speech and hearing at the University of Washington and a leading authority on early language, proved that tiny babies have a unique ability to learn a foreign language. As a result of her well-publicized findings, parents ran out to buy foreign-language tapes, hoping their little Einsteins would pick up Russian or French before they left their cribs. It didn't work, and Kuhl's new research shows why. Kuhl put American 9-month-olds in a room with Mandarin-speaking adults, who showed them toys while talking to them. After 12 sessions, the babies had learned to detect subtle Mandarin phonetic sounds that couldn't be heard by a separate group of babies who were exposed only to English. Kuhl then repeated the experiment, but this time played the identical Mandarin lessons to babies on video- and audiotape. That group of babies failed to learn any Mandarin. Kuhl says that without the emotional connection, the babies considered the tape recording just another background noise, like a vacuum cleaner. "We were genuinely surprised by the outcome," she says. "We all assumed that when infants stare at a television, and look engaged, that they are learning from it." Kuhl says there's plenty of work to be done to explain why that isn't true. "But at first blush one thinks that people—at least babies—need people to learn."

So there you have it. That kid over there with one sock missing and smashed peas all over his face is actually a formidable presence, in possession of keen powers of observation, acute emotional sensitivity and an impressive arsenal of deductive powers. "For the last 15 years, we've been focused on babies' abilities—what they know and when they knew it," says the University of Washington's Meltzoff. "But now we want to know what all this predicts about later development. What does all this mean for the child?"

Some of these questions are now finding answers. Take shyness, for instance. It's long been known that 15 to 20 percent of children are shy and anxious by nature. But doctors didn't know why some seemed simply to grow out of it, while for others it became a debilitating condition. Recent studies conducted by Nathan Fox of the University of Maryland show that shyness is initially driven by biology. He proved it by wiring dozens of 9-month-olds to EEG machines and conducting a simple experiment. When greeted by a stranger, "behaviorally inhibited" infants tensed up, and showed more activity in the parts of the brain associated with anxiety and fear. Babies with outgoing personalities reached out to the stranger. Their EEG scans showed heightened activity in the parts of the brain that govern positive emotions like pleasure.

Just because your baby is MORE PERCEPTIVE than you thought doesn't mean she'll be DAMAGED if she cries for a minute.

But Fox, who has followed some of these children for 15 years, says that parenting style has a big impact on which kind of adult a child will turn out to be. Children of overprotective parents, or those whose parents didn't encourage them to overcome shyness and childhood anxiety, often remain shy and anxious as adults. But kids born to confident and sensitive parents who gently help them to take emotional risks and coax them out of their shells can often overcome early awkwardness. That's an important finding, since behaviorally inhibited kids are also at higher risk for other problems.

Stanley Greenspan, clinical professor of psychiatry and pediatrics at George Washington University Medical School, is one of the leaders in developing diagnostic tools to help doctors identify babies who may be at risk for language and learning problems, autism and a whole range of other problems. He recently completed a checklist of social and emotional "milestones" that babies should reach by specific ages (graphic). "I'd like to see doctors screen babies for these milestones and tell parents exactly what to do if their babies are not mastering them. One of our biggest problems now is that parents may sense intuitively that something is not right," but by the time they are able to get their child evaluated, "that family has missed a critical time to, maybe, get that baby back on track."

So what should parents do with all this new information? First thing: relax. Just because your baby is more perceptive than you might have thought doesn't mean she's going to be damaged for life if she cries in her crib for a minute while you answer the phone. Or that he'll wind up quitting school and stealing cars if he witnesses an occasional argument between his parents. Children crave—and thrive on—interaction, one-on-one time and lots of eye contact. That doesn't mean filling the baby's room with "educational" toys and posters. A child's social, emotional and academic life begins with the earliest conversations between parent and child: the first time the baby locks eyes with you; the quiet smile you give your infant and the smile she gives you back. Your child is speaking to you all the time. It's just a matter of knowing how to listen.

With T. Trent Gegax, Margaret Nelson, Karen Breslau, Nadine Joseph and Ben Whitford

20 Ways to Boost Your Baby's Brain Power

ALICE STERLING HONIG, PH.D.

At birth, your baby's brain contains 100 billion neurons (as many as there are stars in the Milky Way)! During his first years, he will grow trillions of brain-cell connections, called neural synapses.

The rule for brain wiring is "use it or lose it." Synapses that are not "wired together" through stimulation are pruned and lost during a child's school years. Although an infant's brain does have some neurological hard wiring (such as the ability to learn any language), it is more pliable and more vulnerable than an adult's brain. And, amazingly, a toddler's brain has twice as many neural connections as an adult's.

When you provide loving, language-enriched experiences for your baby, you are giving his brain's neural connections and pathways more chances to become wired together. In turn, he will acquire rich language, reasoning, and planning skills.

1. **Give your baby a physically healthy start before he is born.** Stay healthy while you are pregnant, and be aware that certain drugs can be destructive to your baby's brain in utero. Many children who were drug-abused in the womb struggle with severe learning problems and suddenly act with unprovoked aggressive behaviors. Studies have also revealed that cigarette smoking during pregnancy causes lower fourth-grade reading scores.

2. **Have meaningful conversations.** Respond to infant coos with delighted vocalizations. Slowly draw out your syllables in a high-pitched voice as you exclaim, "Pretty baby!" This talk is called "parentese." The areas in the brain for understanding speech and producing language need your rich input.

3. **Play games that involve the hands** (Patty-cake, Peekaboo, This Little Piggy). Babies respond well to learning simple sequential games.

4. **Be attentive.** When your baby points, be sure to follow with your gaze and remark on items or events of interest to her. This "joint attention" confirms for your baby how important her interests and observations are to you.

5. **Foster an early passion for books.** Choose books with large and colorful pictures, and share your baby's delight in pointing and making noises—say, the animal sounds to go along with farm pictures. Modulate the tone of your voice; simplify or elaborate on story lines; encourage toddlers to talk about books. Remember that building your baby's "receptive" language (understanding spoken words) is more important than developing his "expressive" language (speaking) in infancy.

6. **Use diaper time to build your baby's emotional feelings** of having a "lovable body." Stroke your baby's tummy and hair. Studies have shown that babies who are not often touched have brains that are smaller than normal for their age. Also, when diapering your baby, you are at the ideal 12 to 18 inches from her eyes to attract attention to your speech.

7. **Choose developmentally appropriate toys** that allow babies to explore and interact. Toys such as a windup jack-in-the-box or stackable blocks help your baby learn cause-and-effect relationships and "if-then" reasoning. If a baby stacks a big block on a smaller one, the top block falls off. If he successfully stacks a small block on a bigger one, he "wires in" the information.

8. **Respond promptly when your baby cries.** Soothe, nurture, cuddle, and reassure him so that you build positive brain circuitry in the limbic area of the brain, which relates to emotions. Your calm holding and cuddling, and your day-to-day intimate engagement with your baby, signal emotional security to the brain.

9. **Build trust by being attentive and focused.** Babies who are securely attached to you emotionally will be able to invest more life energy in the pleasures of exploration, learning, and discovery.

10. **Use body massage** to decrease your infant's stress and enhance her feelings of well-being and emotional security. Loving touches promote growth in young babies. Research has shown that premature babies who are massaged three times daily are ready to leave the hospital days earlier than babies who do not receive massages.

11. **Enlist help from your toddler at clean-up times**—a good way to practice categorization. Toddlers learn that stuffed animals have one place to go for "night-night" time; cars, trucks, and other vehicles also have their special storage place. Children need to learn about sorting into categories and seriation (placing things in order; for example, from littlest to biggest) as part of their cognitive advancement in preschool.

12. **Set up a safe environment** for your crawling baby or toddler. Spatial learning is important, and your mobile child will begin to understand parameters such as under,

over, near, and far. He will be able to establish mental maps of his environment and a comfortable relationship with the world in which he lives.

13. **Sing songs** such as "Itsy Bitsy Spider" and "Ring-Around-the-Rosy." The body motions and finger play will help your baby integrate sounds with large and small motor actions. Songs also enhance your child's learning of rhythms, rhymes, and language patterns.

14. **Match your tempo to your child's temperament.** Some children adjust easily to strange situations, some are bold and impulsive, and some are quite shy. Go with the flow as you try to increase a shy child's courage and comfort level. Help a highly active child safely use his wonderful energy while learning impulse control. Your acceptance will give him the comfort he needs to experiment and learn freely.

15. **Make meals and rest times positive.** Say the names of foods out loud as your baby eats. Express pleasure as she learns to feed herself, no matter how messy the initial attempts may be. This will wire in good associations with mealtime and eating. Battles and nagging about food can lead to negative emotional brain patterns.

16. **Provide clear responses to your baby's actions.** A young, developing brain learns to make sense of the world if you respond to your child's behavior in predictable, reassuring, and appropriate ways. Be consistent.

17. **Use positive discipline.** Create clear consequences without frightening or causing shame to your child. If your toddler acts inappropriately, such as by hitting another child, get down to his eye level, use a low, serious tone of voice, and clearly restate the rule. Keep rules simple, consistent, and reasonable for your child's age. Expecting a toddling baby not to touch a glass vase on a coffee table is not reasonable. Expecting a toddler to keep sand in the sandbox and not throw it is reasonable!

18. **Model empathic feelings** for others. Use "teachable moments" when someone seems sad or upset to help your toddler learn about feelings, caring, sharing, and kindness. The more brain connections you create for empathic responses and gentle courtesies, the more these brain circuits will be wired in. This helps not only with language and cognitive learning, but with positive emotional skills, too!

19. **Arrange supervised play** with messy materials, such as water, sand, and even mud. This will teach your toddler about the physics and properties of mixtures and textures, liquids and solids. During bath time, the brain wires in knowledge about water, slippery soap, and terry towel textures. Sensory experiences are grist for the learning brain.

20. **Express joy and interest in your baby.** Let your body language, your shining eyes, your attentiveness to babbling and baby activities, and your gentle caresses and smiles validate the deeply lovable nature of your little one.

ALICE STERLING HONIG, Ph.D., professor emerita at Syracuse University, is the author, with **H. BROPHY**, of *Talking With Your Baby: Family as the First School.*

Long-Term Studies of Preschool:

Lasting Benefits Far Outweigh Costs

Mr. Bracey and Mr. Stellar summarize the findings of three studies that provide strong evidence of long-term positive outcomes for high-quality preschool programs. All that remains now, they argue, is for the U.S. to make a commitment to universal, free preschool.

GERALD W. BRACEY AND ARTHUR STELLAR

The November 2001 issue of the *Kappan* contained a special section offering a cross-national perspective on early childhood education and day care. Day-care programs in England, Italy, and Sweden were described and contrasted with day care in the U.S. The other countries, especially Sweden, have coherent, comprehensive programs based on a set of assumptions about the positive outcomes of early education. In the U.S., by contrast, there is a "nonsystem." Sharon Lynn Kagan and Linda Hallmark wrote that, in the U.S., "not only has early childhood never been a national priority, but decades of episodic, on-again, off-again efforts have yielded a set of uncoordinated programs and insufficient investment in the infrastructure. Often, the most important components of high-quality education and care—financing, curriculum development, and teacher education—are neglected."[1]

According to Kagan and Hallmark, the U.S. has historically resisted major government intrusions into the early years of education because such intervention would signal a failure on the part of the family. This resistance has produced a vicious circle: parents resist government intervention in the education of young children on ideological grounds; the government, for its part, doesn't produce high-quality day care; parental resistance to government day care solidifies because of the low quality of the care. Today, the ideology that seeks to keep government out of family matters is still very much alive. David Salisbury of the Cato Institute put it this way: "The key to producing intelligent, healthy children does not lie in putting more of them in taxpayer-funded preschools.... Instead of forcing mothers into the workplace through heavy taxation, the government should reduce the tax burden on families and, thereby, allow child care to remain in the capable hands of parents."[2]

This view of day care is most unfortunate, as evidence is now strong that high-quality day care produces long-term positive outcomes. Three studies of specific programs provide the evidence.

The "granddaddy" of these three studies is known as the High/Scope Perry Preschool Project.[3] In the mid-1960s, African American children whose parents had applied to a preschool program in Ypsilanti, Michigan, were randomly assigned to receive the program or not. Those who tested the children, interviewed the parents, or were the children's teachers once they reached school age did not know to which group the children had been assigned. Random assignment eliminates any systematic bias between the groups, although it cannot *guarantee* that they will be the same. By keeping the information on group assignment confidential, the experimenters sought to minimize any kind of Pygmalion effects stemming from expectations about the children who had been in preschool and those who had not. Few preschool programs existed at the time, and children in the control group remained at home.

Parents of the preschool children had completed an average of 9.4 years of school. Only 20% of the parents had high school diplomas, compared to 33% of all African American adults at the time of the study. The children attended preschool for a half day for eight months. The first group of children, entering in 1962, received one year of the preschool program; later groups received two. The program also included weekly, 90-minute home visits by members of the project staff.

The vision of childhood underlying the High/Scope Program was shaped by Piaget and other theorists who viewed children as active learners. Teachers asked questions that allowed children to generate conversations with them. Those who developed the program isolated 10 categories of preschool experience that they deemed important for developing children: creative representation, language and literacy, social relations and personal initiative, movement, music, classification, seriation (creating series and patterns), number, space, and time. Children participated in individual, small-and large-group activities. The curriculum and instruction flowed from both constructivist and cognitive/developmental approaches.[4]

Teachers rarely assessed the children's specific knowledge. This approach stood in marked contrast to another preschool curriculum, Direct Instruction (DI). DI attempts to impart specific bits of knowledge through rapid-fire drill and highly programmed scripts.

A study of the Perry preschoolers and controls at age 40 is in progress. Other studies took place when the subjects reached ages 19 and 27. At age 19, the preschoolers had higher graduation rates and were less likely to have been in special education. The graduation rate effect, though, was limited to females. The preschoolers also had higher scores on the Adult Performance Level Survey, a test from the American College Testing Program that simulates real-life problem situations.

By the time the two groups turned 27, 71% of the preschool group had earned high school diplomas or GEDs, compared to 54% of the control group. The preschoolers also earned more, were more likely to own their own homes, and had longer and more stable marriages. Members of the control group were arrested twice as often, and five times as many members of the control group (35%) had been arrested five or more times.

The second study is called the Abecedarian Project and has been run out of the University of North Carolina, Chapel Hill, since 1972.[5] The study identified children at birth and provided them full-day care, 50 weeks a year, from birth until they entered school. Adults would talk to the children, show them toys or pictures, and offer them opportunities to react to sights and sounds in the environment. As the children grew, these adult/child interactions became more concept and skill oriented. For older preschoolers, they also became more group oriented. Some children continued in the program until age 8, while another group of children began to receive an enrichment program after they started school.

Although the children were randomly assigned, it is important to note that children in the "control" group were not without assistance. To reduce the chances that any differences might come from nutritional deficiencies affecting brain growth, the researchers supplied an enriched baby formula. Social work and crisis intervention services were also available to families in the control group. If the researchers' assessments indicated that the children were lagging developmentally, the families were referred to a relevant social agency. As a consequence of these policies and services, four of the children in the control group were moved to the head of the waiting list for what the researchers called "scarce slots in other quality community child centers."

In the decade following the start of the Perry Project, early childhood education became more prevalent, especially in university areas like Chapel Hill. Thus some of the families in the control group sent their children to other preschool programs. It seems likely, therefore, that some children in the control group received benefits similar to those provided to the children in the experimental group. These benefits would tend to reduce the differences seen between experimental and control groups.

A 1988 follow-up study of the subjects at age 21 found that young adults who had taken part in the Abecedarian Project completed more years of schooling than the controls (12.2 ver-

sus 11.6). As with the Perry Project, this difference was most evident among the females in the study. More members of the experimental group were still in school (42% versus 20%), and more had enrolled in four-year colleges (35.9% versus 13.7%). Forty-seven percent of the experimental group worked at skilled jobs, such as electrician, compared to just 27% of the control group. The subjects who had attended the Abecedarian preschool were less likely to smoke or to use marijuana, but they were no less likely to use alcohol or to indulge in binge drinking.

The researchers administered reading and math tests at ages 8, 12, 15, and 21. Subjects who had been in the program for eight years showed much better reading skills than those in the control group. The "effect sizes" obtained for reading ranged from 1.04 at age 8 to .79 at age 21. Effect sizes for math ranged from .64 at age 8 to .42 at age 21. Judgment must be used in interpreting effect sizes, but all researchers would consider these to be large, with the possible exception of the .42 for math at age 21, which might be considered "medium."

For subjects who had terminated the program when they entered school, the reading effect sizes ran from .75 at age 8 to .28 at age 21. The impact of math for the same group actually grew over time, from .27 at age 8 to .73 at age 21. In general, it appears that participants who continued with the Abecedarian program into the elementary grades were affected more than those who stopped at the end of preschool.

Subjects who received the school-only program showed smaller effect sizes. For reading, the effect size was .28 at age 8 and dwindled to just .11 at age 21. Once again, math showed increased impact over time, from .11 at age 8 to .26 at age 21.

The third major long-term study of preschool outcomes is known as the Chicago Child-Parent Center Program (CPC).[6] It was a much larger study than the Perry or Abecedarian project, but the children were not randomly assigned to experimental and control groups. The CPC was also much more diffuse than the other projects, taking place in some 20 centers, and initially teachers had more latitude over what kinds of materials were incorporated. Later, all centers adopted a program developed through the Chicago Board of Education that emphasized three major areas: body image and gross motor skills, perceptual/motor and arithmetic skills, and language.

As with the other projects, extensive parent involvement was emphasized. Project staff members visited the homes of participants, and parents often accompanied children on field trips. In a 2000 follow-up study, subjects at age 21 who had taken part in the project had lower crime rates, higher high school completion rates, and fewer retentions in grade.

Quality Concerns

There is now some evidence to suggest that even diffuse programs that are broad in scope, such as Head Start, produce increases in high school graduation rates and in college attendance.[7] It seems clear, though, that high-quality programs are more effective. As laid out by Steven Barnett of Rutgers University, to be high quality, programs should have the following characteristics:

- low child/teacher ratios,
- highly qualified and well-paid teachers,
- intellectually rich and broad curricula,
- parents engaged as active partners with the program, and
- starting dates at or before the child reaches age 3.[8]

According to Kagan and Hallmark, many programs in the U.S. do not meet these criteria. Samuel Meisels of the Erikson Institute posits that the proposed "national reporting system" for Head Start will not bring such qualities to Head Start, either.[9] Indeed, Meisels worries that the system might reduce the quality of Head Start and psychologically damage children.

Costs and Benefits

The three preschool programs discussed here cost money, substantially more money than Head Start and even more than most preschools provided by private companies. The question arises as to whether the benefits from the programs are worth these costs. Cost-benefit analyses on all three conclude that they are.

A recent analysis of the Abecedarian Project by Leonard Masse and Steven Barnett of Rutgers University concluded that the benefit/cost ratio for the program was 4 to 1.[10] That is, society received four dollars in return for every dollar invested. This is not as high as analyses suggested for the Perry and Chicago projects. These yielded benefit/cost ratios on the order of 7 to 1. As we noted, though, a number of children in the Abecedarian project control groups attended some other preschools, and this could have reduced the differences between the groups.

Masse and Barnett estimated that children who took part in the program would earn $143,000 more over their lifetimes than those who did not. Their mothers would earn $133,000 more. The latter figure might surprise readers at first, but Masse and Barnett cite other studies finding that given stable, continuous child care, mothers are able to effectively reallocate their time to allow them to establish better, longer-term, and more productive relationships with employers.

Masse and Barnett also infer that the children of the children who participated in high-quality preschool programs will earn more as a consequence. Although it is difficult to quantify such projected earnings increases, they estimate a lifetime increase of $48,000 for the children of the participants. Although clearly conjectural, the logic is straightforward: the children who participated will experience outcomes, such as higher educational attainment, that are associated with higher earnings for future generations.

The cost-benefit analysts warn that these programs can be expensive. They estimated the cost of the Perry Project at $9,200 per child, per year, while the Abecedarian cost figure comes in at $13,900 (both estimates in constant 2002 dollars). This compares to $7,000 for Head Start. They worry that governments might experience "sticker shock" if they try to replicate these projects on a large-scale basis, but they caution that "costs alone offer little guidance. The costs of a program must be compared against the benefits that the program generates. Benefit/cost ratios that are greater than one indicate that a program is worthy of consideration regardless of the absolute level of program costs."[11]

The programs described in this article all involved children living in poverty. Little if any research exists on long-term benefits for middle-class children. Masse and Barnett argue that, if we limit the programs to children under age 5 and assume that 20% of those children live in poverty, the annual cost for high-quality preschool for those 20% would be $53 billion per year.

Governments, however, appear to be looking at absolute costs. The Education Commission of the States reports that eight states have cut back on funds available for preschool in 2002–03. Moreover, today, in early 2003, state government budgets are in their worst shape since World War II. Still, sentiment for universal preschool is growing. After reviewing the evidence on the impact of early childhood education, the Committee for Economic Development led off a monograph as follows:

> The Committee for Economic Development (CED) calls on the federal and state governments to undertake a new national compact to make early education available to all children age 3 and over. To ensure that all children have the opportunity to enter school ready to learn, the nation needs to reform its current, haphazard, piecemeal, and underfunded approach to early learning by linking programs and providers to coherent state-based systems. The goal should be universal access to free, high-quality prekindergarten classes, offered by a variety of providers for all children whose parents want them to participate.[12]

Such a program makes much more sense to us than a program that tests all children in reading, math, and science in grades 3 through 8. Alas, Chris Dreibelbis of the CED reports that, while the CED monograph has been well received in both the education and business communities, there is little movement that might make its proposal a reality.[13]

Notes

1. Sharon L. Kagan and Linda G. Hallmark, "Early Care and Education Policies in Sweden: Implications for the United States," *Phi Delta Kappan*, November 2001, p. 241.
2. David Salisbury, "Preschool Is Overhyped," *USA Today*, 18 September 2002.
3. John R. Berrueta-Clement et al., *Changed Lives: The Effects of the Perry Preschool Program on Youths Through Age 19* (Ypsilanti, Mich.: High/ Scope Press, 1984); and Lawrence J. Schweinhart, Helen V. Barnes, and David P. Weikart, *Significant Benefits: The High/Scope Perry Preschool Study Through Age 27* (Ypsilanti, Mich.: High/Scope Press, 1993).
4. Mary Hohmann and David P. Weikart, *Educating Young Children: Active Learning Practices for Preschool and Child Care Programs* (Ypsilanti, Mich.: High/Scope Press, 1995).
5. Frances A. Campbell et al., "Early Childhood Education: Young Adult Outcomes for the Abecedarian Project," *Applied Developmental Science*, vol. 6, 2002, pp. 42-57; and Frances A. Campbell, "The Development of Cognitive and Academic Abilities: Growth Curves from an Early Childhood Experiment," *Developmental Psychology*, vol. 37, 2001, pp. 231–42.
6. Arthur J. Reynolds et al., "Age 21 Benefit-Cost Analysis of the Chicago Child-Parent Center Program," paper presented to the

Society for Prevention Research, Madison, Wis., 21 May–2 June 2001; and idem, "Long-Term Effects of an Early Childhood Intervention on Educational Achievement and Juvenile Arrest," *Journal of the American Medical Association*, 9 May 2001.

7. Eliana Garces, Duncan Thomas, and Janet Currie, "Longer Term Effects of Head Start," Working Paper No. 8054, National Bureau of Economic Research, December 2000, available at **www.nber.org/papers/w8054**; and Janet Currie and Duncan Thomas, "School Quality and the Longer-Term Effects of Head Start," *Journal of Human Resources*, Fall 2000, pp. 755–74.

8. W. Steven Barnett, "Early Childhood Education," in Alex Molnar, ed., S*chool Reform Proposals: The Research Evidence* (Greenwich, Conn.: Information Age Publishing, 2002), available at **www.asu.edu/educ/epsl**. Click on Education Policy Research Unit, then, under "archives," click on "research and writing."

9. Samuel J. Meisels, "Can Head Start Pass the Test?," *Education Week*, 19 March 2003, p. 44.

10. Leonard N. Masse and W. Steven Barnett, *Benefit Cost Analysis of the Abecedarian Early Childhood Intervention Project* (New Brunswick, N.J.: National Institute for Early Childhood Research, Rutgers University, 2002).

11. Ibid., p. 14.

12. *Preschool for All: Investing in a Productive and Just Society* (New York: Committee for Economic Development, 2002), p. 1.

13. Personal communication, 3 February 2003.

GERALD W. BRACEY is an associate for the High/Scope Educational Research Foundation, Ypsilanti, Mich., and an associate professor at George Mason University, Fairfax, Va. He lives in the Washington, D.C., area. **ARTHUR STELLAR** is president and CEO, High/Scope Educational Research Foundation, Ypsilanti, Mich.

Guilt Free TV

In the beginning, there was Big Bird. Now, thanks to intense competition from Disney and Nick, there are more quality shows for preschoolers than ever.

Daniel McGinn

When Alicia Large was growing up, her parents rarely let her watch television. Even the Muppets were off-limits, she says, because her parents disliked the sexual tension between Kermit and Miss Piggy. Now 31 and raising her own sons—ages 2 and 3—Large views TV more benevolently. Her boys love "Dora the Explorer," so when she takes them on errands, she draws a map—the bank, the grocery store—so they can track their progress as Dora does. Among Large's friends, kids' TV—what and how much are yours watching?—is a constant conversation. Yes, many parents still use TV as a babysitter. But increasingly, she says, parents are looking to TV to help them do a better job of raising kids. "Our generation is using it completely differently," she says.

Parents have felt conflicted about television since its earliest days. Even Philo T. Farnsworth, TV's inventor, fretted over letting his son watch cowboy shows, according to biographer Evan I. Schwartz. That anxiety continues. In a survey released last week by Public Agenda, 22 percent of parents said they'd "seriously considered getting rid of [their TV] altogether" because it airs too much sex and bad language. But at the same time, for parents of the youngest viewers—ages 2 to 5—there are new reasons for optimism. Now that PBS, which invented the good-for-kids genre, has new competition from Nickelodeon and Disney, there are more quality choices for preschoolers than ever.

Inside those networks, a growing number of Ph.D.s are injecting the latest in child-development theory into new programs. In Disney's "Stanley," meet a freckle-faced kid who's fascinated with animals; in one episode, he and his pals explore the life and habitat of a platypus. Nickelodeon now airs 4.5 hours of quality preschool shows daily (in addition to learning-free fare like "SpongeBob" for older kids). Shows like "Dora" and "Blue's Clues" goad kids into interacting with the television set; studies show this improves problem-solving skills. Even the granddaddy of this genre, "Sesame Street," has undergone a makeover to better serve today's precocious viewers. The newcomers provide stiff competition to Mister Rogers, whose show stopped production in 2000 (it still airs on PBS). But he welcomes his new TV neighbors. "I'm just glad that more producers —and purveyors of television have signed the pledge to protect childhood," says Fred Rogers, who now writes parenting books.

That's the good news. The bad news is that working these shows into kids' lives in a healthy way remains a challenge. Much of what kids watch remains banal or harmful. Many kids watch too much. There are also troubling socioeconomic factors at work. In lower-income homes, for instance, kids watch more and are more likely to have TV in their bedrooms, a practice pediatricians discourage. But even as some families choose to go TV-free, more parents are recognizing that television can be beneficial. In the Public Agenda survey, 93 percent of parents agree that "TV is fine for kids as long as he or she is watching the right shows and watching in moderation."

When it comes to the right shows, "Sesame Street" remains the gold standard. Last week, as the crew taped an episode for its 34th season, the set looked comfortably familiar: while Telly and Baby Bear worked on a skit near Hooper's Store, Snuffleupagus hung from the rafters, sleeping under a sheet. The show's longevity is a testament to the research-driven process founder Joan Ganz Cooney invented in the late 1960s. Then, as now, each season begins with Ph.D.s working alongside writers to set goals and review scripts. Any time there's a question—will kids understand Slimey the Worm's mission to the moon?—they head to day-care centers to test the material.

When "Sesame" began reinventing kids' TV in the early '70s, Daniel Anderson was a newly minted professor of psychology at the University of Massachusetts, Amherst. Like most child-development pros at that time, he assumed TV was bad for kids. Then one day Anderson taught his class that young children have very short attention spans. One student challenged him: "So why do kids sit still for an hour to watch 'Sesame Street'?" "I genuinely didn't know the answer," Anderson recalls. So he went to a lab and placed kids in front of TVs to find it.

What he found surprised him. Like most researchers, he assumed that fast-moving images and sounds mesmerized young viewers. But videotapes of kids' viewing showed that their attention wandered most during transitions between segments and when dialogue or plotlines became too complex. He hypothesized that even young children watch TV for the same reason adults do: to enjoy good stories. To test that theory, he sliced up

Puppets to Muppets: A Hit Parade

Children's television has been evolving for more than half a century. A time line of highs and lows.

1947

Howdy Doody and pal Buffalo Bob were the first superstars of kids' TV. Puppet power!

1949

The first-made-for-TV animated show was **Crusader Rabbit**, created by Jay Ward, who later gave us "Rocky and His Friends."

1949

Bozo the Clown debuts. The red-haired funny man also made hit records and generated millions in merchandise sales.

1953

The first interactive kids' show was **Winky Dink and You**. Viewers put a sheet of acetate over the screen and used crayons to help Winky Dink solve problems.

1955

For 30 years, **Captain Kangaroo** and his cast of gentle characters offered simple lessons in morality.

1955

The Mickey Mouse Club. Who needs friends when the Mouseketeers are in your living room every afternoon?

1961

Say what? The FCC's **Newton Minow** dubs TV "a vast wasteland."

1961

Brilliant writing and sharp satire make **The Bullwinkle Show** a draw for kids and parents alike.

1963

Mister Rogers moves in. Three years later, the mayhem of **The Road Runner Show** arrives.

1969

The big one. Designed by experts to help children learn, **Sesame Street** set new standards for the medium and established PBS as the home of good kids' TV.

1971

Children raised on "Sesame Street" moved on to **The Electric Company**'s more mature lessons.

1979

The launch of **Nickelodeon**. The network, initially, was commercial-free.

1981

The Smurfs, a marketing juggernaut, was seen as sexist at first. It evolved into a message-heavy show by 1987.

1984

One of many shows based on boys' toys, **The Transformers** was inherently violent.

1987

It had plenty of action, but **Teenage Mutant Ninja Turtles** felt less dangerous because of an emphasis on character. Teen turtles named for Italian artists can't be *that* violent.

1990

Thanks to the **Children's Television Act**, networks must broadcast three hours of educational programming per week. Saturday's superheroes become an endangered species.

1992

Kids love **Barney**, but the purple dinosaur annoys anyone over the age of 5.

1993

Mighty Morphin Power Rangers. Finally, a girl superhero, the Pink Ranger.

1996

Blue's Clues. Detective work with an adorable pup. A fresh idea.

2002

Meet **Rolie Polie Olie**, the 6-year-old robot boy.

Users' Guide

Doctors advocate "media literacy," which includes making wise TV choices. Some tips:

Set limits. Pediatricians discourage TV for kids under 2, ration older kids to two hours of daily "screen time" (TV, computer and videogames).

Pull up a chair. When parents co-view with kids, they watch for bad shows, encourage interaction with good ones and talk together after turning off the tube.

No TV in bedrooms. More than half of kids have one, but it leads to unsupervised viewing and a potential for overdose. Make TV a family-room activity.

Use TV-book synergy. Kids' programming, from "Arthur" to "The Book of Pooh," often comes from books. After watching, children are frequently wild about reading. To exploit this, try hitting the library after a favorite show.

"Sesame Street" skits so the plot no longer made sense. Even 2-year-olds quickly realized the story was amiss and stopped watching. Some knocked on the TV screen. Others called out: "Mommy, can you fix this?" Over years of research, Anderson reached a startling conclusion: "Television viewing is a much more intellectual activity for kids than anybody had previously supposed."

This research might have stayed hidden in psych journals if it hadn't been for the work of two equally powerful forces: the U.S. Congress and a purple dinosaur named Barney. In 1990 Congress passed the Children's Television Act, increasing demand for quality kids' shows. Then "Barney & Friends" was launched as a PBS series in 1992. Kids went wild, and merchandise flew off shelves. Until then, Nickelodeon and Disney had been content to leave preschool shows to the do-gooders at PBS. Now they saw gold. "The success of 'Barney' just changed everybody's feeling—it became 'OK, we should be able to do that, too'," says Marjorie Kalins, a former "Sesame" executive.

It was a profitable move. By 2001 Nick and Disney's TV businesses had generated a combined $1.68 billion in revenue, according to Paul Kagan Associates. Everyone admits that licensing money influences programming decisions. (Ironically, merchandisers at Nickelodeon lobbied *against* "Dora" because they believed that another show would generate more sales.) Ads and toys can detract from many parents' enthusiasm for the shows; no matter how much your kid may learn from "Sagwa" or "Rolie Polie Olie," the characters are hard to love when you can't get through Wal-Mart without a giant case of "I-WANT-itis."

Until there's a way to make shows free, that overcommercialization will continue. But for parents, there's some comfort from knowing that more TV producers are applying the latest research to make their shows better. This happened partly because researchers of Anderson's generation helped grow a new crop of Ph.D.s, who began graduating into jobs at "Sesame" and Nickelodeon. And like seeds from a dandelion blown at by a

child, folks who'd trained at "Sesame" began taking root inside other networks. Anne Sweeney, who'd studied at Harvard with "Sesame" cofounder Gerald Lesser, interned with television activist Peggy Charren and spent 12 years at Nickelodeon, took over the Disney Channel in 1996. She hired a team (led by ex-Nick programmer Rich Ross) to design pre-school shows. By 1999 Disney had a full block of little-kid programming it branded Playhouse Disney. Today it uses a 28-page "Whole Child Curriculum" detailing what shows should teach.

To see how research can drive these new-generation shows, come along, neighbor, as we visit a day-care center on Manhattan's Upper West Side. Dr. Christine Ricci sits in a child-size chair, holding a script and tapping a red pen against her lip. Ricci, who holds a psychology Ph.D. from UMass, is research director for "Dora the Explorer," which airs on Nick Jr., Nickelodeon's preschool block. In each episode Dora, an animated Latina girl, goes on a journey with a monkey named Boots. Using a map to guide them (which helps kids' spatial skills), they visit three locations ("Waterfall, mountain, forest!" kids yell) and solve problems. As in "Blue's Clues," Nick Jr.'s groundbreaking hit in which a dog named Blue and the host Joe help kids solve puzzles, "Dora" encourages kids to yell back at the screen (often in Spanish) or do physical movements (like rowing a boat).

Today Ricci shows 4-year-olds a crudely animated "Dora" episode slated for next season. As they watch, Ricci's team charts, moment by moment, whether the kids are paying attention and interacting with the screen. At first the kids sit transfixed, but during a pivotal scene (in which Swiper the fox, Dora's nemesis, throws a boot down a hole) their attention wanders. One child picks up a Magic Marker, and suddenly every child is seeking out toys. All the while the researchers scribble furiously. When the episode ends, an adult asks the children questions: "What color button on the fix-it machine matched the tire?" Their recall is astonishing. "Sesame Street" has done this kind of testing off and on since the '70s. Ricci's team, however, is relentless, testing and revising every "Dora" episode repeatedly.

The following afternoon, Ricci, "Dora" creator Chris Gifford and their team study a bar graph showing how kids interacted with the episode minute by minute. To boost the numbers, sometimes they suggest better animation. Sometimes they call for a better "money shot": a big close-up of Dora. Fixing one segment—"Only 15 out of 26 kids were still watching," Ricci informs them gravely—requires more drastic measures. Gifford stands up, motioning like a cheerleader, to suggest livelier movements to get kids moving along with Dora during a song. "So often when you work on a TV show for kids, you forget about your audience," Gifford says. "We've set up a system where we can't ignore them." Similar work goes on at "Blue's Clues." Says Nick Jr. chief Brown Johnson: "It's science meets story."

For a parent, it's natural to get excited when kids shout back at the TV during "Dora" or dance to "The Wiggles," a music-and-dance show that airs on Disney. That leads some parents to look at their TVs the way a previous generation looked to Dr. Spock. Colleen Breitbord of Framingham, Mass., sees these programs as so vital to the development of her children, 7 and

2, that she installed a TV in the kitchen so they can watch "Arthur" and "Clifford" while they eat. "They learn so much," Breitbord says. "I think children who don't have the opportunity to watch some of this excellent programming miss out." In Ansonia, Conn., Patti Sarandrea uses Playhouse Disney, Nick Jr. and PBS "to reinforce what I teach the kids: colors, shapes, counting." At 3 1/2, her daughter can count to 25. Thanks to "Dora," her 18-month-old says "Hola."

As kids that young start tuning in, even "Sesame" is rethinking its approach. The show was originally designed for kids 3 to 5, but by the mid-1990s, many viewers were 2 or younger. The tykes seemed to tire of 60 minutes of fast-paced Muppet skits (the pacing was originally modeled after "Laugh-In" and TV commercials). So in 1999 "Sesame" introduced "Elmo's World," a 15-minute segment that ended every show. Even after that change, "Sesame" VP Lewis Bernstein noticed how today's little kids would sit still to watch 90-minute videotaped movies. So last February "Sesame" unveiled more longer segments. In "Journey to Ernie," Big Bird and Ernie play hide-and-seek against an animated background. Today ratings are up. The cast likes the new format, too. Before, stories were constantly cut short. "It was a little discombobulating," says Kevin Clash, the muscular, deep-voiced Muppet captain who brings Elmo to life. Now Elmo l-o-o-o-ves the longer stories.

So just how much good do these shows do? On a recent afternoon five undergrads sit around a table in the Yale University psychology department, playing a bizarre variation of bingo to try to find out. Together they watch three episodes of "Barney & Friends," each filling in hash marks on six sheets of paper. After each screening, they tally how many "teaching elements" they've counted. "I've got 9 vocabulary, 6 numbers… 11 sharing," says one student. Afterward Yale researcher Dorothy Singer will crunch the data and compare them with past seasons'. Her work has shown that the higher an episode's score, the more accurately children will be able to recount the plot and use the vocabulary words.

PBS does more of this postproduction "summative" research than other networks. Study after study shows "Sesame" viewers are better prepared for school. "Dragon Tales," a "Sesame"-produced animated show, helps kids become more goal-oriented, and "Between the Lions," a puppet show produced by Boston's WGBH, helps kids' reading. Nick research offers proof of the effectiveness of "Dora" and "Blue's Clues." Disney doesn't do summative research; Disney execs say for now they'd rather devote resources to creating more shows for new viewers. Competitors suggest another reason: Disney's shows may not measure up. "It's scary to test," says "Sesame" research chief Rosemarie Truglio. "Maybe that's a piece of it—they're afraid."

Network-funded research won't change the minds of folks who say kids are better off with no television at all. That view gained strength in 1999, when the American Academy of Pediatrics began discouraging any television for kids under 2. But when you parse the pro- and anti-TV rhetoric, the two sides don't sound as far apart as you'd suspect. The pro-TV crowd, for instance, quickly concedes that violent TV is damaging to kids, and that too many kids watch too many lousy shows. The

---

What's Right for My Kid?

We asked a panel of experts what kinds of shows are good for kids of various ages. In general, they said, trust your gut, avoid violent programs and stay tuned in to what they're watching.

Ages 2–5

The best shows for this age group—like **Dora the Explorer** and **Clifford the Big Red Dog**—are slow-moving and repetitive.

Ages 5–8

Kids begin to understand the vocabulary of TV: good and bad guys, for example. Try **Sagwa, the Chinese Siamese Cat**, based on a book by novelist Amy Tan.

Ages 9–11

At this age, kids, like adults, want TV that entertains. Shows like **Doug**, **Lizzie McGuire** and **The Wild Thornberrys** are appropriate. Characters have inner lives and complex motives.

Adolescents

Each family—and teenager—is different; TV-watching guidelines vary. Experts recommend **Gilmore Girls** and **Nick News** for "tweens" and younger teens. It's difficult to monitor older teens.

---

anti-TV crowd objects mostly to TV's widespread overuse. Like Häagen-Dazs, TV seems to defy attempts at moderation, they suggest, so it's safer to abstain entirely. They believe overviewing especially affects children because of what Marie Winn, author of "The Plug-In Drug," calls the "displacement factor." That's when kids watch so much TV that they don't engage in enough brain-enhancing free play as toddlers or read enough during elementary school. Although pro-TV researchers say there are no data to support those fears, they agree it could be true. In fact, Anderson is currently conducting an experiment to measure whether having adult shows (like "Jeopardy!") playing in the background interferes with children's play. Bad news, soap-opera fans: the early data suggest it might.

Even shows the academics applaud could be better. In his UMass office, Anderson pops in a videotape of "Dora." It's one of the handful of shows that he advised during their conception. In this episode, Dora and Boots paddle a canoe down a river, around some rocks, toward a waterfall. *Toward* a waterfall? "If I'd read this script I'd have completely blocked this," he says, because it models unsafe behavior. Anderson has his arms crossed, his eyebrows scrunched; occasionally he talks to the screen, like an NFL fan disputing a bad call. "Oh, God, another dangerous thing," he says as Dora and Boots canoe under downed tree limbs. He still likes "Dora," but not this episode.

"The education is a little thinner than I would wish, and it's a little dubious sending them on such a dumb journey." Then he watches "Bear" and "Blue's Clues," still nitpicking but happier.

Even as the kids' TV environment improves, shortcomings remain. Only PBS airs educational shows for older elementary kids (examples: "Zoom" and "Cyberchase"). In focus groups, says Nickelodeon president Herb Scannell, older kids say they get enough learning in school; what commercial broadcaster is going to argue with the audience? Producers have other worries. Mitchell Kriegman, creator of "Bear in the Big Blue House," says parents could grow too enamored of obviously educational, A-B-C/1-2-3-type shows. One of the most successful episodes of "Bear" involves potty training. "The [network's] reaction was 'Oh, my God, you can't say poop and pee on TV,'" Krieg-man says. "Bear" did, and families loved it. Tighter curricula could dampen that creativity.

But those are worries for the future. For now, it's worth celebrating the improvements—however incremental—in shows for TV's youngest audience. Not everyone will want to raise a glass: like alcohol or guns, TV will be used sensibly in some homes and wreak havoc in others. Debating its net societal value will remain a never-ending pursuit. In the meantime parents live through these trade-offs daily. A recent issue of Parenting magazine offered the following question to help assess parenting skills: "I let my child watch TV only when… A) There's an educational show on public television, B) I have time to narrate the action for him… or C) I want to take a shower." The scoring code rates the answers: "A) Liar, B) Big fat liar, and C) You may not be perfect, but at least you're honest." As kids' TV raises the bar, parents who choose a different answer—D) All of the above—have a little less reason to feel guilty.

Raising a Moral Child

For many parents, nothing is more important than teaching kids to know right from wrong. But when does a sense of morality begin?

KAREN SPRINGEN

Nancy Rotering beams as she recalls how her 3-year-old son Jack recently whacked his head against a drawer hard enough to draw blood. It's not that she found the injury amusing. But it did have a silver lining: Jack's wails prompted his 2-year-old brother, Andy, to offer him spontaneous consolation in the form of a cup of water and a favorite book, "Jamberry." "Want 'Berry' book, Jack?" he asked. Nancy loved Andy's "quick-thinking act of sympathy." "I was thrilled that such a tiny person could come up with such a big thought," she says. "He stepped up and offered Jack refreshment—and entertainment—to take his mind off the pain."

All parents have goals for their children, whether they center on graduating from high school or winning the Nobel Prize. But for a great many, nothing is more important than raising a "good" child— one who knows right from wrong, who is empathetic and who, like Andy, tries to live by the Golden Rule, even if he doesn't know yet what it is. Still, morality is an elusive—and highly subjective— character trait. Most parents know it when they see it. But how can they instill and nurture it in their children? Parents must lead by example. "The way to raise a moral child is to be a moral person," says Tufts University psychologist David Elkind. "If you're honest and straightforward and decent and caring, that's what children learn." Humans seem innately inclined to behave empathetically; doctors talk about "contagious crying" among newborns in the hospital nursery. And not all children of murderers or even tax cheats follow in their parents' footsteps. "What's surprising is how many kids raised in immoral homes grow up moral," says New York psychiatrist Alvin Rosenfeld.

81% of mothers and 78% of fathers say they plan eventually to send their young child to Sunday school or some other kind of religious training

Parents have always been preoccupied with instilling moral values in their children. But in today's fast-paced world, where reliable role models are few and acts of violence by children are increasingly common, the quest to raise a moral child has taken on new urgency. Child criminals grow ever younger; in August, a 6-year-old California girl (with help from a 5-year-old friend) smothered her 3-year-old brother with a pillow. Such horrific crimes awaken a dark, unspoken fear in many parents: Is my child capable of committing such an act? And can I do anything to make sure that she won't?

There are no guarantees. But parents are increasingly aware that even very young children can grasp and exhibit moral behaviors— even if the age at which they become "morally accountable" remains under debate. According to the Roman Catholic Church, a child reaches "the age of reason" by 7. Legally, each state determines how old a child must be to be held responsible for his acts, ranging from 7 to 15. Child experts are reluctant to offer a definitive age for accountability. But they agree that in order to be held morally responsible, children must have both an emotional and a cognitive awareness of right and wrong—in other words, to know in their heads as well as feel in their hearts that what they did was wrong. Such morality doesn't appear overnight but emerges slowly, over time. And according to the latest research, the roots of morality first appear in the earliest months of an infant's life. "It begins the day they're born, and it's not complete until the day they die," says child psychiatrist Elizabeth Berger, author of "Raising Children with Character."

It's never too early to start. Parents who respond instantly to a newborn's cries lay an important moral groundwork. "You work to understand what the baby's feeling," says Barbara Howard, a specialist in developmental behavioral pediatrics at the Johns Hopkins University School of Medicine. "Then the baby will work to understand what other people are feeling." Indeed, empathy is among the first moral emotions to develop. Even before the age of 2, children will try to comfort an upset child—though usually in an "egocentric" way, says Marvin Berkowitz, professor of character education at the University of Missouri-St. Louis: "I might give them *my* teddy even though your teddy is right there." To wit: Andy Rotering brought his brother his own favorite book.

Morality consists of not only caring for others but also following basic rules of conduct. Hurting another child, for instance, is never OK. But how you handle it depends on your child's age. If a 1-year-old is hitting or biting, "you simply say 'no' firmly, and you remove the child from the situation," says Craig Ramey, author of "Right From Birth." But once a child acquires language skills, parents can provide more detail. "You can say, 'We don't hit in this family'," says David Fassler, chairman of the American Psychiatric Association's council on children, adolescents and their families. "You can say, 'Everyone feels like hitting and biting from time to time. My job is to help you figure out what to do with those kinds of feelings'." Suggest alternatives—punching a pillow, drawing a sad picture or lying quietly on a bed.

Children grow more moral with time. As Lawrence Kohlberg of Harvard University has said, kids go through progressive stages of moral development. Between 1 and 2, children understand that there are rules—but usually follow them only if an adult is watching, says Barbara Howard. After 2, they start obeying rules—inconsistently—even if an adult isn't there. And as any adult who has ever driven faster than 65mph knows, people continue "circumstantial" morality throughout life, says Howard. "People aren't perfect, even when they know what the right thing to do is."

Though all children are born with the capacity to act morally, that ability can be lost. Children who are abused or neglected often fail to acquire a basic sense of trust and belonging that influences how people behave when they're older. "They may be callous because no one has ever shown them enough of the caring to put that into their system," says Howard. Ramey argues that "we come to expect the world to be the way we've experienced it"—whether that means cold and forbidding or warm and loving. According to Stanford developmental psychologist William Damon, morality can also be hampered by the practice of "bounding"—limiting children's contact with the world only to people who are like them—as opposed to "bridging," or exposing them to people of different backgrounds. "You can empathize with everyone who looks just like you and learn to exclude everyone who doesn't," says Damon. A juvenile delinquent may treat his sister gently—but beat up an old woman of another race. "The bridging approach ends up with a more moral child," says Damon.

No matter how hard you try, you can't force your child to be moral. But there are things you can do to send him in the right direction:

If you're honest, straightforward, decent and caring, that's what children learn

• Decide what values—such as honesty and hard work—are most important to you. Then do what you want your children to do. "If you volunteer in your community, and you take your child, they will do that themselves," says Joseph Hagan, chairman of the American Academy of Pediatrics' committee on the psychosocial aspects of child and family health. "If you stub your toe, and all you can say is the F word, guess what your child is going to say when they stub their toe?"

Always help your child see things from the other person's point of view

• Praise children liberally. "You have to ignore the behaviors you don't want and highlight the behaviors you do want," says Kori Skidmore, a staff psychologist at Children's Memorial Hospital in Chicago. Rather than criticizing a toddler for his messy room, compliment him on the neat corner, recommends Darien, Ill., pediatrician Garry Gardner. Use "no" judiciously, otherwise "a child starts to feel like 'I'm always doing something wrong'," says the APA's Fassler. "If you're trying to teach a child to share, then praise them when they share. Don't just scold them when they're reluctant to."

• Take advantage of teachable moments. When Gardner's kids were 3 and 4, they found a $10 bill in front of a store. Gardner talked to them about the value of the money—and they agreed to give it to the shopkeeper in case someone returned for it. They mutually decided "finders keepers" shouldn't apply to anything worth more than a quarter. "Certainly you wouldn't go back and say, 'I found a penny'," says Gardner. Parents can also use famous parables, like "The Boy Who Cried Wolf," or Bible stories to illustrate their point.

• Watch what your child watches. TV and computer games can glorify immoral behavior. "If children are unsupervised, watching violence or promiscuity on TV, they're going to have misguided views about how to treat other people," says Karen Bohlin, director of Boston University's Center for the Advancement of Ethics and Character. "Children by nature are impulsive and desperately need guidance to form good habits. That can come only from a loving caregiver who's by their side, teaching them how to play nicely, safely, fairly, how to take turns, how to put things back where they belong, how to speak respectfully."

• Discuss consequences. Say, "'Look how sad Mary is because you broke her favorite doll'," explains Berkowitz. Parents can also ask their children to help them pick fair punishments—for example, no TV. "They're learning that their voice is valued," says Berkowitz. Allowing kids to make choices—even about something as trivial as what to have for lunch—will enable them to make moral ones later. "If they don't learn peanut butter and jelly at 2, how are they going to decide about drinking when they're 14?" asks family physician Nancy Dickey, editor in chief of Medem, an online patient-information center.

• Always help them see things from the other person's point of view. If a child bops his new sibling, try to reflect the newborn's outlook. Say, "'Oh, my, that must hurt. How would you feel if someone did that to you?'" says Howard. Gardner encourages parents whose kids find stray teddy bears to ask their children how sad they would feel if they lost their favorite stuffed animal—and how happy they would be if someone returned it. "It's one thing to hear about it at Sunday school," he says. And another to live the "do unto others" rule in real life.

In the end, the truest test of whether a parent has raised a moral child is how that young person acts when Mom or Dad is not around. With a lot of love and luck, your child will grow up to feel happy and blessed—and to want to help others who aren't as fortunate. Now, *that's* something to be proud of.

UNIT 3

Development During Childhood: Cognition and Schooling

Unit Selections

Key Points to Consider

- What is authentic learning? Why is it vanishing in contemporary classrooms? Should it be restored?

- If dyslexia is a biologically based brain glitch, can instruction repair the short circuitry?

- Why should foreign language instruction be emphasized in American education before high school?

- Does the No Child Left Behind (NCLB) legislation in the United States need revision? What are its weaknesses? How can it be improved?

- Should school teachers emphasize students' strengths instead of weaknesses? What might be the consequences of such practice?

- What is the trouble with boys? Why are they so active? Would schooling that respected and worked with their high-energy levels be more efficacious in educating boys?

Student Website

www.mhcls.com/online

Internet References

Further information regarding these websites may be found in this book's preface or online.

Children Now
http://www.childrennow.org

Council for Exceptional Children
http://www.cec.sped.org

Educational Resources Information Center (ERIC)
http://www.eric.ed.gov/

Federation of Behavioral, Psychological, and Cognitive Science
http://federation.apa.org

The National Association for the Education of Young Children (NAEYC)
http://www.naeyc.org

Project Zero
http://pzweb.harvard.edu

In January of 2005, the President of Harvard University started a media firestorm by suggesting that males' brains are better organized for knowing math and science than are females' brains. Researchers in genetics answered back that female brains, guided by two X chromosomes rather than one, are probably better equipped for higher cognitive functions.

The mental process of knowing—cognition—includes aspects such as sensing, understanding, associating, and discriminating. Cognitive research has been hampered by the limitations of trying to understand what is happening inside the minds of living persons without doing harm. It has also been challenged by problems with defining concepts such as intuition, unconsciousness, unawareness, implicit learning, incomprehension, and all the aspects of knowing situated behind our mental perceptions (metacognition). Many kinds of achievement that require cognitive processes (awareness, perception, reasoning, judgment) cannot be measured with intelligence tests or with achievement tests. Intelligence is the capacity to acquire and apply knowledge. It is usually assumed that intelligence can be measured. The ratio of tested mental age to chronological age is expressed as an intelligence quotient (IQ). For years, school children have been classified by IQ scores. The links between IQ scores and school achievement are positive, but no significant correlations exist between IQ scores and life success. Consider, for example, the motor coordination and kinesthetic abilities of former baseball player Cal Ripken, Jr. He had a use of his body that surpassed the capacity of most other athletes and nonathletes. Is knowledge of kinesthetics a form of intelligence?

Some psychologists have suggested that uncovering more about how the brain processes various types of intelligences will soon be translated into new educational practices. Today's tests of intelligence only measure abilities in the logical/mathematical, spatial, and linguistic areas of intelligence, which is what schools now teach. Jean Piaget, the Swiss founder of cognitive psychology, was involved in the creation of the world's first intelligence test, the Binet-Simon Scale. He became disillusioned with trying to quantify how much children knew at different chronological ages. He was much more intrigued with what they did not know, what they knew incorrectly, and how they came to know the world in the ways in which they knew it. He started the Centre for Genetic Epistemology in Geneva, Switzerland, where he began to study the nature, extent, and validity of children's knowledge. He discovered qualitative, rather than quantitative, differences in cognitive processes over the life span. Infants know the world through their senses and their motor responses. After language develops, toddlers and preschoolers know the world through their language/symbolic perspectives. Piaget likened early childhood cognitive processes to bad thought, or thought akin to daydreams. By school age, children know things in concrete terms, which allows them to number, seriate, classify, conserve, think backwards and forwards, and think about their own thinking (metacognition). However, Piaget believed that children do not acquire the cognitive processes necessary to think abstractly and to use clear, consistent, logical patterns of thought until early adolescence. Their moral sense and personal philosophies of behavior are not completed until adulthood.

The first article in this unit, "A Time and a Place for Authentic Learning," considers the difficulties in contemporary educational processes. The current focus on test preparation leaves little time for the application of knowledge, or for learning by doing. The authors state the fears that the creativity and innovative ideas (that have long characterized Americans) will decrease as teachers are required to teach for the test. Authentic learning changes the focus of the student from lesson-learner to inquirer, and the role of the teacher from fact-giver to mentor and resource person. Authentic learning offers the chance to make both teachers and students excited about education in engaging, enjoyable, enriching classrooms. It is worth our efforts to find more time and places for it.

The second selection gives the reader a glimpse of the world of children with dyslexia (reading difficulties). One in five children, both girls and boys, struggles to learn to read. Neuroscientific research, using functional magnetic resonance imaging (fMRI), has new evidence that the causes of dyslexia are biological. The brain experiences glitches getting information from the sound producer to areas that analyze and detect words. Each child with dyslexia is different. Early appropriate instruction can give amazing results.

In the first school-related article, Peg Tyre explains, "The Trouble with Boys." They're kinetic and falling further behind in school, compared with girls, with every passing year. Many people are financing research to discover why and what can be done to reverse this trend. As we learn more about brain chemistry, we may educate boys in different ways and present topics in different sequences than we do with girls to maximize the learning abilities of both.

The second school-related article, "Why We Need 'The Year of Languages,'" opens the door for discussing early emphasis on second-language learning in contemporary schooling. Are American children linguistically ignorant? What effect will this have in the future global economy? Why are languages acquired more rapidly before puberty? Why do females acquire languages more rapidly than males? Should our American school children be taught languages important in global economy: Chinese? Arabic?

The third article addresses the No Child Left Behind (NCLB) Education Program introduced by President George W. Bush in 2001. What are the effects of state-mandated testing programs on teaching and learning? There have been unanticipated and unintended negative consequences of the program. The article recommends ways in which the NCLB could be changed. These suggestions should stimulate rich discussions about students.

The fourth article in the schooling section of this unit addresses the power of teaching students using strengths. Gloria Henderson discusses her conscious efforts to change her teaching style from remediation to abilities guidance. Students achieved at higher levels when they were led to improve their preexisting skills.

A Time and a Place for Authentic Learning

Challenge students to solve everyday problems in meaningful contexts, and the learning will take care of itself.

JOSEPH S. RENZULLI, MARCIA GENTRY, AND SALLY M. REIS

Each week, all the students at the Bret Harte Middle School in Oakland, California, leave their classrooms to participate in interest-based enrichment clusters. Under a teacher's guidance, one group of students is identifying, archiving, and preserving documents from the 1800s that were found in a suitcase belonging to the first pharmacist in Deadwood, South Dakota. Another group with strong interests in media, technology, and graphic arts is converting the archives into digital format and making the students' research available on a Web site.

These crossgrade clusters are scheduled on a rotating basis during the fall months. They usually last for eight weeks, generally meeting weekly for a double-period time block, with a new series scheduled in the spring. A medium-sized school might typically offer 15 to 20 clusters. The number of students in each cluster varies depending on student interest in the topic and teacher requirements for effective student participation. Teachers develop the clusters around their own strengths and interests, sometimes working in teams that include parents and community members.

Numerous schools across the United States have developed the enrichment cluster concept to deal with what many education leaders believe is a crisis in our schools. The focus on test preparation has squeezed more authentic kinds of learning out of the curriculum, thereby minimizing the one aspect of U.S. education that contributes to the innovativeness and creative productivity of the nation's culture, economy, and leadership role in the world. Improved test scores are important, but it's the *application* of knowledge in authentic learning situations—not perpetual memorization and testing—that characterizes a progressive education system.

What Is Authentic Learning?

All learning exists on a continuum that ranges from deductive and prescriptive learning on one end to inductive, self-selected, and investigative learning on the other. The essence of inductive or high-end learning is applying relevant knowledge and skills to solving real problems. Such learning involves finding and focusing on a problem; identifying relevant information; categorizing, critically analyzing, and synthesizing that information; and effectively communicating the results.

Real-life problems share four criteria. First, a real-life problem has a personal frame of reference. In other words, the problem must involve an emotional or internal commitment on the part of those involved in addition to a cognitive interest. Second, no agreed-on solutions or prescribed strategies for solving the problem exist. If they do, the process would more appropriately be classified as a training exercise because its main purpose would be to teach predetermined content or thinking skills.

Third, real-life problems motivate people to find solutions that change actions, attitudes, or beliefs. A group of students might gather, analyze, and report on data about the community's television-watching habits, causing people in that community to think critically about the television-viewing habits of young people. Last, real-life problems target a real audience. For example, students working on a local oral history project—a biographical study of Connecticut residents who died in Vietnam—initially presented their findings to their classmates, mainly to rehearse presentation skills. Their authentic audience consisted of members of a local historical society, members of veterans groups, family members of servicemen and servicewomen, attendees at a local commemoration of Vietnam veterans, and community members who had read about the research in the local newspaper.

Enrichment clusters are *not* mini-courses. There are no predetermined content or process objectives. The nature of the problem guides students toward using just-in-time knowledge, appropriate investigative techniques or creative production skills, and professional methods for communicating results. In this type of learning, students assume roles as investigators, writers, artists, or other types of practicing professionals.

Authentic learning is the vehicle through which everything from basic skills to advanced content and processes come together in the form of student-developed products and services. The student's role changes from lesson-learner to firsthand inquirer, and the role of the teacher changes from instructor and disseminator of knowledge to coach, resource procurer, and mentor. Although products play an important role in creating authentic learning, students learn principally from the cognitive, affective, and motivational processes involved.

A Different Approach

Developing an authentic enrichment cluster draws on skills that most teachers already possess, especially if they have been involved in clubs or other extracurricular activities. As you begin the process of developing your own cluster, keep in mind the following:

- *Reverse the teaching equation.* Your role in planning and facilitating an enrichment cluster differs from the teacher's traditional role. Too much preplanning on your part may push the cluster toward deductive rather than inductive teaching and learning. Enrichment clusters develop just-in-time knowledge that has immediate relevance in resolving the problem. Students typically move to higher levels of knowledge than grade-level textbooks support.

- *Reverse the role of students.* Young people working on an original piece of historical research, creative writing, or play production become young historians, authors, scenery designers, and stage managers. Instead of teaching lessons, you will begin to think about how to help a young poet get work published, how to get the shopping mall manager to provide space for a display of models of historically significant town buildings, and how to engineer a presentation by young environmentalists to the state wildlife commission.

- *Create a unique enrichment cluster.* As long as you follow the guidelines for inductive teaching, there is no wrong way to plan and facilitate an enrichment cluster. Differences in interests, personalities, and styles among cluster facilitators contribute to the uniqueness of this type of learning. Experience in an inductive learning environment will help you hone the skills that will become a natural part of your teaching repertoire both in clusters and in your classroom.

- *When in doubt, look outward.* To mirror real-world situations, examine conditions outside the classroom for

models of planning, teaching, and organizing. Athletic coaches, advisors for the drama club or the school newspaper, and 4-H Club leaders make excellent enrichment cluster facilitators. Similarly, tasks and organizational patterns should resemble the activities that take place in a small business, a social service agency, a theater production company, or a laboratory.

Guidelines for Developing an Enrichment Cluster

Select a Topic

Base enrichment clusters on topics in which you have a strong interest. Make a list of topics that fascinate you. Reflect on your choices, discuss your list with colleagues—there may be possibilities for collaboration—and prioritize the topics to help you decide on the focus of your first enrichment cluster.

Focus on Key Questions

Develop enrichment clusters around the following six key questions:

- What do people with an interest in this topic or area of study do?
- What products do they create, and what services do they provide?
- What methods do they use to carry out their work?
- What resources and materials are needed to produce high-quality products and services?
- How and with whom do they communicate the results of their work?
- What steps do cluster participants need to take to have an impact on an intended audience?

These questions do not need to be answered immediately, sequentially, or comprehensively at this stage. As your cluster develops, have students discuss the questions and allow them to reach their own conclusions about the activities, resources, and products that professionals pursue in particular areas of study. If you have all the answers ready before the cluster begins, the excitement of pure inquiry will be lost.

Students assume roles as investigators, writers, artisits, or other types of practicing professionals.

Explore the Topic

The most obvious way to learn about the work of a professional is to discuss the key questions with someone working in the field. A cartoonist, landscape architect, or fashion designer will give you the lay of the land and offer some recommended resources. When talking with professionals, keep in mind that you want to learn what they routinely do in their jobs, how they do it, and what they produce. This background material will help you plan the cluster, but students should also pursue the same questions with professionals after the cluster commences. Such interaction dramatically increases motivation and engagement.

Almost all professionals belong to professional associations. A quick Internet search turns up approximately 3,500 professional organizations. To learn about the work that genealogists do, one teacher went to the Association of Professional Genealogists Web site (**www.apgen.org**) and found a treasure trove of resources on careers in the field, conferences, publications, places where family records can be found, and local chapters. She also located a directory of members by state. Association membership lists can suggest speakers, mentors, or enrichment cluster cofacilitators. By clicking on *Connecticut*, the teacher found the names, addresses, and phone numbers of 13 professional genealogists in the state, one of whom lived in close proximity to the school.

Another way to explore the key questions as you develop cluster content is to obtain resource books on the methodology of a particular field. A visit to the Genealogical Publishing Company Web site yielded an extensive list of potential resources: 423 titles, to be exact. Librarians and college bookstores can also help locate methodological resource books.

In the real world, almost all work is intended to have an impact on at least one targeted audience. In finding target audiences, you will be serving as a referral agent, promoter, or marketing manager of student work. In school, fellow students and parents are obvious audiences for whom students can practice and perfect performances and presentations, but young people will begin to view themselves in a much more professional role when you help them seek audiences outside the school. The students themselves should make the contacts and be prepared to answer questions.

Local newspapers, city or state magazines, and literary reviews—especially those that target young authors—are excellent places to submit written work. Public buildings and business offices are often receptive to requests to display student artwork. Local or state organizations—such as historical societies, writers clubs, civic groups, environmental preservation organizations, and advocacy groups—also provide opportunities for young entrepreneurs to present their work. Young dramatists can take their performances on the road to senior citizen centers, day-care centers, religious groups, or professional organizations. One group of students who wrote and produced a legal thriller presented a synopsis of the plot at a county bar association meeting.

The essence of inductive or high-end learning is applying relevant knowledge and skills to solving real problems.

Contests and competitions are also great outlets. Most teachers are familiar with science fairs, National History Day, and Math League, but thousands of other competitions take place in such areas as photography, fashion design, inventions, drama,

and Web design. Searching for outlets and audiences; writing query letters and submitting work for possible publication, presentation, or display; and receiving replies—both positive and negative—are all part of the creative process and motivate aspiring writers, scientists, and artists.

Write Your Enrichment Cluster Description

The enrichment cluster description should convey, in no more than 100 words, the essence of the experience. Use verbs that emphasize the explorative nature of the cluster by conveying action and illustrating tasks. For example, in a cluster that involves building and marketing compost bins, you might use such verbs as *design, field-test, construct, advertise, market, contact, display,* and *sell.*

You might also pose questions about potential student interests and possible types of involvement: Do you like to express your feelings by writing poetry or short stories? Are you concerned about finding better ways to protect wildlife? Would you like to try your hand at designing fashions for teens? Each of these questions relates to a topic around which a cluster might be developed, yet they are all open-ended enough to encompass a broad range of activities in specific interest areas.

Launch Your Enrichment Cluster

Although students who have signed up for your cluster have expressed an interest in the topic, it may take them some time to understand the cluster's approach to learning. Displaying products or tools that professionals in your topic area typically use is always a good way to begin. In a cluster on archaeology, entitled *The Trash Heaps of Mankind*, the facilitator showed slides of famous and local archaeological discoveries. She opened a Mystery Box in the front of the room to reveal a trowel, a sieve, a pair of gloves, a dust brush, pegs and string, a marking pen, and a camera. She pointed out that these were the main tools of the archaeologist and that an examination of material found in garbage dumps was one of the ways in which archaeologists analyzed past and present cultures. A short videotape of a dig in the students' own state heightened student interest in the work of practicing archaeologists.

Escalate Content and Process

One of the problems we encountered in our research on enrichment clusters was a failure on the part of some facilitators to escalate the level of content and methodology pursued within a cluster. Indeed, critics may point out that clusters are nothing more than fun and games or that students carry out their work using existing skills rather than acquiring more advanced ones. You can guard against these criticisms by examining each cluster with an eye toward providing authentic and rigorous content within the topic area.

In a cluster on research about political opinion, for example, students evaluated archived news articles and editorials from the World War II and Vietnam War eras to analyze and compare public support for these wars. Students in an ecology and evolutionary biology cluster studied the survival prospects of tropical plants grown in the school's greenhouse and conducted experiments to explore optimal conditions for propagation. Content and process objectives evolve as a result of the investigations that students conduct, and this is one factor that highly differentiates the clusters from regular instruction.

Gathering Original Data

During many years of working with students in authentic learning situations, we have discovered that there is a certain magic associated with gathering original data and using that information to create new knowledge. This knowledge may not be new for all humankind, but it may be original to students and their local audiences. A group of elementary students spent an entire school year gathering and analyzing samples of rainwater for sulfur and nitrogen oxide emissions, the main pollutants responsible for acid rain. The students then prepared a report concerning the extent of acid rainfall in their region of the country. Their teacher helped them obtain a standard rain gauge and a kit for testing acidity.

Additional resources enabled these students to prepare statistical and graphic summaries of their data; compare their findings with data from national and regional reports that were easily accessed on the Internet; and design maps showing acid rain trends over time and across geographic regions. The data provided participants with the excitement and motivation to study environmental and health problems associated with various types of pollution. The students found receptive audiences for their work among state environmental protection groups, the U.S. Environmental Protection Agency, and the National Weather Bureau.

Putting It All Together

Most teachers have had a vision, at one time or another, about what they thought teaching would entail. They pictured themselves in classrooms with interested and excited students dramatizing dangerous midnight journeys on the Underground Railroad, conducting science experiments to find out how things work, or experiencing the exhilaration that occurs when a student-developed board game unlocks the relationships between a set of numbers and everyday experiences.

Real-life problems target a real audience.

Many teachers, however, experience a disconnect between their vision of a challenging and rewarding career and the day-to-day grind of test preparation. What is most ironic about the separation between the ideal and the reality of today's classrooms is that most teachers actually have the skills and motivation to do the kinds of teaching they dream of. Unfortunately, lists, regulations, and other people's requirements have resulted in both a prescriptive approach to teaching and a barrier to creating a challenging and exciting classroom. Overprescribing the work of teachers has, in some cases, lobotomized good teachers and denied them the creative teaching opportunities that attracted them to the profession in the first place.

Freedom to teach still exists, as does the possibility of making learning enjoyable, engaging, and enriching. You can find both in enrichment clusters, where authentic learning is in the driver's seat.

JOSEPH S. RENZULLI is Director of the National Research Center on the Gifted and Talented at the University of Connecticut, Storrs, Connecticut; joseph.renzulli@uconn.edu. **MARCIA GENTRY** is Associate Professor of Education Studies at Purdue University, West Lafayette, Indiana. **SALLY M. REIS** is Professor and Chair of the Educational Psychology Department at the University of Connecticut, Storrs, Connecticut.

The New Science of DYSLEXIA

Why some children struggle so much with reading used to be a mystery. Now researchers know what's wrong—and what to do about it

CHRISTINE GORMAN

When Sean Slattery, 17, looks at a page of text, he can see the letters. He can tell you the letters' names. He can even tell you what sounds those letters make. But it often takes a while for the articulate high school student from Simi Valley, Calif., to tell you what words those letters form. "I see a wall," he says. "I see a hurdle I have to get over." Some words are easier for Sean to figure out than others. "I can get longer words, like *electricity*," he says. "But I have trouble with shorter words, like *four* or *year*."

Slattery has dyslexia, a reading disorder that persists despite good schooling and normal or even above-average intelligence. It's a handicap that affects up to 1 in 5 schoolchildren. Yet the exact nature of the problem has eluded doctors, teachers, parents and dyslexics themselves since it was first described more than a century ago. Indeed, it is so hard for skilled readers to imagine what it's like not to be able to effortlessly absorb the printed word that they often suspect the real problem is laziness or obstinacy or a proud parent's inability to recognize that his or her child isn't that smart after all.

The mystery—and perhaps some of the stigma—may finally be starting to lift. The more researchers learn about dyslexia, the more they realize it's a flaw not of character but of biology— specifically, the biology of the brain. No, people with dyslexia are not brain damaged. Brain scans show their cerebrums are perfectly normal, if not extraordinary. Dyslexics, in fact, seem to have a distinct advantage when it comes to thinking outside the box.

But a growing body of scientific evidence suggests there is a glitch in the neurological wiring of dyslexics that makes reading extremely difficult for them. Fortunately, the science also points to new strategies for overcoming the glitch. The most successful programs focus on strengthening the brain's aptitude for linking letters to the sounds they represent. (More later on why that matters.) Some studies suggest that the right kinds of instruction provided early enough may rewire the brain so thoroughly that the neurological glitch disappears entirely.

The new science may even be starting to change public policy. When the U.S. government launched an education initiative in 2001 called No Child Left Behind, its administrators made clear that their funding would go only to reading programs that are based on solid evidence of the sort that has been uncovered in dyslexia research. "In education, the whole idea that there is evidence that some programs are more effective than others is new," says Dr. Sally Shaywitz, a Yale neuroscientist who has written a fascinating new book, *Overcoming Dyslexia* (Alfred A. Knopf; April 2003), that details the latest brain-scan research—much of it done in her lab. "The good news is we really understand the steps of how you become a reader and how you become a skilled reader," she says.

Along the way, a number of myths about dyslexia have been exploded. You may have heard, for example, that it's all about flipping letters, writing them backward, Toys "R" Us style. Wrong. Practically all children make mirror copies of letters as they learn to write, although dyslexics do it more. You may believe that more boys than girls are dyslexic. Wrong again. Boys are just more likely to get noticed because they often vent their frustration by acting out. You may think that dyslexia can be outgrown. This is perhaps the most damaging myth, because it leads parents to delay seeking the extra instruction needed to keep their children from falling further behind. "The majority of students who get identified with learning disorders get identified between the ages of 11 and 17," says Robert Pasternack, U.S. assistant secretary for Special Education and Rehabilitative Services. "And that's too late." They can still learn to read, but it will always be a struggle.

This is not to say that dyslexics can't succeed despite their disability. In fact, dyslexics are overrepresented in the top ranks of artists, scientists and business executives. Perhaps because their brains are wired differently, dyslexics are often skilled problem solvers, coming at solutions from novel or surprising angles and making conceptual leaps that leave tunnel-visioned, step-by-step sequential thinkers in the dust. They talk about being able to see things in 3-D Technicolor or as a multidimensional chess game. It may also be that their early struggle with reading better prepares them for dealing with adversity in a volatile, fast-changing world.

But that struggle can cut both ways. Dyslexics are also over-represented in the prison population. According to Frank Wood, a professor of neurology at Wake Forest University in Winston-Salem, N.C., new research shows that children with dyslexia are more likely than nondyslexics to drop out of school, withdraw from friends and family or attempt suicide.

The stakes have never been higher. Right now in the U.S. there are almost 3 million students in special-education classes specifically because they can't read. Most of them are probably dyslexic. But there are other slow readers who are simply overlooked—ignored in crowded classrooms or dismissed as discipline problems. Unless corrective action is taken, their self-confidence often crumbles as they see other students progressing. Even worse, their peers may taunt or ostracize them—a situation that Sean Slattery's mother Judy remembers all too well. "Sean cried for four hours every day after kindergarten," she says. "He was so unhappy."

To be sure, researchers still don't understand everything there is to know about learning disabilities. Dyslexia, for one, may consist of several subtypes. "It would be very dangerous to assume that every child with reading problems is uniform and has the same kinds of breakdowns preventing him from learning to read," says Dr. Mel Levine, a pediatrician and author of several influential books about learning disabilities and dyslexia, including *A Mind at a Time*. But whatever the exact nature of the deficit, the search for answers begins with the written word.

When you think about it, that anyone can read at all is something of a miracle. Reading requires your brain to rejigger its visual and speech processors in such a way that artificial markings, such as the letters on a piece of paper, become linked to the sounds they represent. It's not enough simply to hear and understand different words. Your brain has to pull them apart into their constituent sounds, or phonemes. When you *see* the written word cat, your brain must *hear* the sounds /k/ ... /a/... /t/ and associate the result with an animal that purrs.

Unlike speech, which any developmentally intact child will eventually pick up by imitating others who speak, reading must be actively taught. That makes sense from an evolutionary point of view. Linguists believe that the spoken word is 50,000 to 100,000 years old. But the written word—and therefore the possibility of reading—has probably been around for no more than 5,000 years. "That's not long enough for our brains to evolve certain regions for just that purpose," says Guinevere Eden, a professor of pediatrics at Georgetown University in Washington, who also uses brain scans to study reading. "We're probably using a whole network of areas in the brain that were originally designed to do something slightly different." As Eden puts it, the brain is moonlighting—and some of the resulting glitches have yet to be ironed out.

To understand what sorts of glitches we're talking about, it helps to know a little about how the brain works. Researchers have long been aware that the two halves, or hemispheres, of the brain tend to specialize in different tasks. Although the division of labor is not absolute, the left side is particularly adept at processing language while the right is more attuned to analyzing spatial cues. The specialization doesn't stop there. Within each hemisphere, different regions of the brain break down various tasks even further. So reading a sonnet, catching a ball or recognizing a face requires the complex interaction of a number of different regions of the brain.

Most of what neuroscientists know about the brain has come from studying people who were undergoing brain surgery or had suffered brain damage. Clearly, this is not the most convenient way to learn about the brain, especially if you want to know more about what passes for normal. Even highly detailed pictures from the most advanced computer-enhanced X-ray imaging machines could reveal only the organ's basic anatomy, not how the various parts worked together. What researchers needed was a scanner that didn't subject patients to radiation and that showed which parts of the brain are most active in healthy subjects as they perform various intellectual tasks. What was needed was a breakthrough in technology.

That breakthrough came in the 1990s with the development of a technique called functional magnetic resonance imaging (fMRI). Basically, fMRI allows researchers to see which parts of the brain are getting the most blood—and hence are the most active—at any given point in time.

Neuroscientists have used fMRI to identify three areas of the left side of the brain that play key roles in reading. Scientifically, these are known as the left inferior frontal gyrus, the left parieto-temporal area and the left occipito-temporal area. But for our purposes, it's more helpful to think of them as the "phoneme producer," the "word analyzer" and the "automatic detector." We'll describe these regions in the order in which they are activated, but you'll get closer to the truth if you think of them as working simultaneously, like the sections of an orchestra playing a symphony.

Using fMRI, scientists have determined that beginning readers rely most heavily on the phoneme producer and the word analyzer. The first of these helps a person say things—silently or out loud—and does some analysis of the phonemes found in words. The second analyzes words more thoroughly, pulling them apart into their constituent syllables and phonemes and linking the letters to their sounds.

As readers become skilled, something interesting happens: the third section—the automatic detector—becomes more active. Its function is to build a permanent repertoire that enables readers to recognize familiar words on sight. As readers progress, the balance of the symphony shifts and the automatic detector begins to dominate. If all goes well, reading eventually becomes effortless.

In addition to the proper neurological wiring, reading requires good instruction. In a study published in the current issue of *Biological Psychiatry*, Shaywitz and colleagues identified a group of poor readers who were not classically dyslexic, as their phoneme producers, word analyzers and automatic detectors were all active. But the three regions were linked more strongly to the brain's memory processors than to its language centers, as if the children had spent more time memorizing words than understanding them.

The situation is different for children with dyslexia. Brain scans suggest that a glitch in their brain prevents them from easily gaining access to the word analyzer and the automatic detector. In the past year, several fMRI studies have shown that dyslexics tend to compensate for the problem by overactivating the phoneme producer.

Here at last is physical evidence that the central weakness in dyslexia is twofold. First, as many dyslexia experts have long suspected, there is an inherent difficulty in deriving sense from phonemes. Second, because recognizing words doesn't become automatic, reading is slow and labored. This second aspect, the lack of fluency, has for the most part not been widely appreciated outside the research community.

Imagine having to deal with each word you see as if you had never come across it before, and you will start to get the idea. That's exactly what Abbe Winn of Atlanta realized her daughter Kate, now 9, was doing in kindergarten. "I noticed that when her teacher sent home a list of spelling words, she had a real hard time," Abbe says. "We'd get to the word the and come back five minutes later, and she had no idea what it was."

So much for what dyslexia is. What many parents would like to know is what can be done about it. Fortunately, the human brain is particularly receptive to instruction. Otherwise practice would never make perfect. Different people respond to different approaches, depending on their personality and the nature of their disability. "The data we have don't show any one program that is head and shoulders above the rest," says Shaywitz. But the most successful programs emphasize the same core elements: practice manipulating phonemes, building vocabulary, increasing comprehension and improving the fluency of reading.

This kind of instruction leaves nothing to chance. "In most schools the emphasis is on children's learning to read sentences," says Gina Callaway, director of the Schenck School in Atlanta, which specializes in teaching dyslexic students using the Orton-Gillingham approach. "Here we have to teach them to recognize sounds, then syllables, then words and sentences. There's lots of practice and repetition." And a fair number of what the kids call tricks, or rules, for reading. (Among the most important and familiar: the magic *e* at the end of a word that makes a vowel say its name, as in *make* or *cute*.) A particularly good route to fluency is to practice reading aloud with a skilled reader who can gently correct mistakes. That way the brain builds up the right associations between words and sounds from the start.

Boys and girls are equally likely to suffer from dyslexia

There is no reason to assume that the public school system, despite its myriad problems, isn't up to the task. But it's a sad fact of life, particularly in larger or cash-starved institutions, that many kids fall through the cracks. A parent may have to keep up the pressure on the child's school district. Unfortunately, some have had to sue to get results. In extreme cases, parents can be reimbursed for private schooling, as two unanimous decisions by the Supreme Court, in 1985 and 1993, have made clear.

It helps to tap into a student's interests. For Monique Beltran, 13, of Los Angeles, the turning point came with the computer game Pokémon. "I had to read to get to more levels," she says matter-of-factly. The computer game also showed Monique the value of reading outside of schoolwork, and she is eagerly devouring the latest *Harry Potter* book.

As you might expect, early intervention gives the best results. Yet for decades most schools wouldn't consider special education for a child until he or she had fallen at least a year behind. That may be changing. In the U.S., Congress is considering legislation that would eliminate the need to show a discrepancy between a child's IQ and his or her achievements before receiving a diagnosis of dyslexia.

Ideally, all children should be screened in kindergarten—to minimize educational delay and preserve self-confidence. How do you know someone has dyslexia before he or she has learned to read? Certain behaviors—like trouble rhyming words—are good clues that something is amiss. Later you may notice that your child is memorizing books rather than reading them. A kindergarten teacher's observation that reading isn't clicking with your son or daughter should be a call to action.

If caught soon enough, can a child's dyslexia be reversed? The evidence looks promising. In her book, Shaywitz reports that brain scans of dyslexic kindergartners and first-graders who have benefited from a year's worth of targeted instruction start to resemble those of children who have never had any difficulty reading.

That doesn't mean older folks need despair. Shaywitz's brain scans of adult dyslexics suggest that they can compensate by tapping into the processing power on their brain's right side. Just don't expect what works for young children to work for adults. "If you're 18 and you're about to graduate and you don't have phonemic awareness, that may not be your top priority," says Chris Schnieders, director of teacher training at the Frostig Center in Pasadena, Calif. "It's a little bit late to start 'Buh is for baby' at that point."

Technology can play a supporting role. Some dyslexics supplement their reading with books on tape. (Indeed, in 1995, the Recording for the Blind organization changed its name to Recording for the Blind and Dyslexic in recognition of that fact.) Because their condition affects the ability to write as well as read, a growing number of dyslexics are turning to voice-recognition software for help in preparing term papers, memos and reports. A couple of small studies have shown that the software can also bolster the ability to read. "We found improvement in word recognition, in reading comprehension and spelling," says Marshall Raskind, director of research at the Frostig Center. He suspects that the ability to say, hear and see words almost simultaneously provides good training for the brain.

Up to 1 in 5 u.s. schoolchildren are living with dyslexia

There are, alas, no quick fixes. Dyslexic students often have to put many more hours into their course work than naturally skilled readers do. But the results are worth it. In the seventh grade, Sean Slattery was barely reading on a first-grade level.

Now, after four years at the Frostig Center, he has nearly caught up to where he should be. In May, on his third try, Slattery passed California's high school exit exam.

That's another thing about dyslexics: they learn to persevere. Now Slattery has his eye on a career as an underwater welder. "There's a lot of reading involved" between the course work and the instruction manuals, he says. "But I'm looking forward to it, actually." The written word is not going to hold him back anymore.

The Trouble with Boys

**They're kinetic, maddening and failing at school.
Now educators are trying new ways to help them succeed.**

PEG TYRE

Spend a few minutes on the phone with Danny Frankhuizen and you come away thinking, "What a *nice* boy." He's thoughtful, articulate, bright. He has a good relationship with his mom, goes to church every Sunday, loves the rock band Phish and spends hours each day practicing his guitar. But once he's inside his large public Salt Lake City high school, everything seems to go wrong. He's 16, but he can't stay organized. He finishes his homework and then can't find it in his backpack. He loses focus in class, and his teachers, with 40 kids to wrangle, aren't much help. "If I miss a concept, they tell me, 'Figure it out yourself'," says Danny. Last year Danny's grades dropped from B's to D's and F's. The sophomore, who once dreamed of Stanford, is pulling his grades up but worries that "I won't even get accepted at community college."

44%—The number of male undergraduates on college campuses; 30 years ago, the number was 58%.

His mother, Susie Malcom, a math teacher who is divorced, says it's been wrenching to watch Danny stumble. "I tell myself he's going to make something good out of himself," she says. "But it's hard to see doors close and opportunities fall away."

What's wrong with Danny? By almost every benchmark, boys across the nation and in every demographic group are falling behind. In elementary school, boys are two times more likely than girls to be diagnosed with learning disabilities and twice as likely to be placed in special-education classes. High-school boys are losing ground to girls on standardized writing tests. The number of boys who said they didn't like school rose 71 percent between 1980 and 2001, according to a University of Michigan study. Nowhere is the shift more evident than on college campuses. Thirty years ago men represented 58 percent of the undergraduate student body. Now they're a minority at 44 percent. This widening achievement gap, says Margaret Spellings, U.S. Secretary of Education, "has profound implications for the economy, society, families and democracy."

With millions of parents wringing their hands, educators are searching for new tools to help tackle the problem of boys.

Books including Michael Thompson's best seller "Raising Cain" (recently made into a PBS documentary) and Harvard psychologist William Pollack's definitive work "Real Boys" have become must-reads in the teachers' lounge. The Gurian Institute, founded in 1997 by family therapist Michael Gurian to help the people on the front lines help boys, has enrolled 15,000 teachers in its seminars. Even the Gates Foundation, which in the last five years has given away nearly a billion dollars to innovative high schools, is making boys a big priority. "Helping underperforming boys," says Jim Shelton, the foundation's education director, "has become part of our core mission."

The problem won't be solved overnight. In the last two decades, the education system has become obsessed with a quantifiable and narrowly defined kind of academic success, these experts say, and that myopic view is harming boys. Boys are biologically, developmentally and psychologically different from girls—and teachers need to learn how to bring out the best in every one. "Very well-meaning people," says Dr. Bruce Perry, a Houston neurologist who advocates for troubled kids, "have created a biologically disrespectful model of education."

Thirty years ago it was girls, not boys, who were lagging. The 1972 federal law Title IX forced schools to provide equal opportunities for girls in the classroom and on the playing field. Over the next two decades, billions of dollars were funneled into finding new ways to help girls achieve. In 1992, the American Association of University Women issued a report claiming that the work of Title IX was not done—girls still fell behind in math and science; by the mid-1990s, girls had reduced the gap in math and more girls than boys were taking high-school-level biology and chemistry.

'Often boys are treated like defective girls,' says Thompson.

Some scholars, notably Christina Hoff Sommers, a fellow at the American Enterprise Institute, charge that misguided feminism is what's been hurting boys. In the 1990s, she says, girls were making strong, steady progress toward parity in schools,

Elementary School

Boys start off with lower literacy skills than girls, and are less often encouraged to read, which only widens the gap.

■ Girls ages 3 to 5 are **5%** more likely than boys to be read to at home at least three times a week.

■ Girls are **10%** more likely than boys to recognize words by sight by the spring of first grade.

■ Boys ages 5 to 12 are **60%** more likely than girls to have repeated at least one grade.

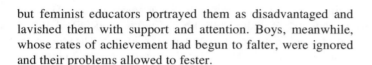

AVERAGE SCORES
FOURTH-GRADE STUDENTS

SOURCES: U.S. DEPARTMENT OF EDUCATION, CENTERS FOR DISEASE CONTROL

■ Girls' reading scores improve **6%** more than boys' between kindergarten and third grade.

■ First- to fifth-grade boys are **47%** more likely than girls to have disabilities such as emotional disturbances, learning problems or speech impediments.

■ Fourth-grade girls score **3%** higher on standardized reading tests than boys.

■ Fourth-grade girls score **12%** higher on writing tests than boys.

but feminist educators portrayed them as disadvantaged and lavished them with support and attention. Boys, meanwhile, whose rates of achievement had begun to falter, were ignored and their problems allowed to fester.

Standardized tests have become common for kids as young as 6.

Boys have always been boys, but the expectations for how they're supposed to act and learn in school have changed. In the last 10 years, thanks in part to activist parents concerned about their children's success, school performance has been measured in two simple ways: how many students are enrolled in accelerated courses and whether test scores stay high. Standardized assessments have become commonplace for kids as young as 6. Curricula have become more rigid. Instead of allowing teachers to instruct kids in the manner and pace that suit each class, some states now tell teachers what, when and how to teach. At the same time, student-teacher ratios have risen, physical education and sports programs have been cut and recess is a distant memory. These new pressures are undermining the strengths and underscoring the limitations of what psychologists call the "boy brain"—the kinetic, disorganized, maddening and sometimes brilliant behaviors that scientists now believe are not learned but hard-wired.

When Cris Messler of Mountainside, N.J., brought her 3-year-old son Sam to a pediatrician to get him checked for ADHD, she was acknowledging the desperation parents can feel. He's a high-energy kid, and Messler found herself hoping for a positive diagnosis. "If I could get a diagnosis from the doctor, I could get him on medicine," she says. The doctor said Sam is a normal boy. School has been tough, though. Sam's reading teacher said he was hopeless. His first-grade teacher complains he's antsy, and Sam, now 7, has been referring to himself as "stupid." Messler's glad her son doesn't need medication, but what, she wonders, can she do now to help her boy in school?

For many boys, the trouble starts as young as 5, when they bring to kindergarten a set of physical and mental abilities very different from girls'. As almost any parent knows, most 5-year-old girls are more fluent than boys and can sight-read more words. Boys tend to have better hand-eye coordination, but their fine motor skills are less developed, making it a struggle for some to control a pencil or a paintbrush. Boys are more impulsive than girls; even if they can sit still, many prefer not to—at least not for long.

Thirty years ago feminists argued that classic "boy" behaviors were a result of socialization, but these days scientists believe they are an expression of male brain chemistry. Sometime in the first trimester, a boy fetus begins producing male sex hormones that bathe his brain in testosterone for the rest of his gestation. "That exposure wires the male brain differently," says Arthur Arnold, professor of physiological science at UCLA. How? Scientists aren't exactly sure. New studies show that prenatal exposure to male sex hormones directly affects the way children play. Girls whose mothers have high levels of testosterone during pregnancy are more likely to prefer playing with trucks to playing with dolls. There are also clues that hormones influence the way we learn all through life. In a Dutch study published in 1994, doctors found that when males were given female hormones, their spatial skills dropped but their verbal skills improved.

In elementary-school classrooms—where teachers increasingly put an emphasis on language and a premium on sitting quietly and speaking in turn—the mismatch between boys and school can become painfully obvious. "Girl behavior becomes the gold standard," says "Raising Cain" coauthor Thompson. "Boys are treated like defective girls."

Two years ago Kelley King, principal of Douglass Elementary School in Boulder, Colo., looked at the gap between boys and girls and decided to take action. Boys were lagging 10 points behind girls in reading and 14 points in writing. Many more boys—than girls were being labeled as learning disabled, too. So King asked her teachers to buy copies of Gurian's book "The Minds of Boys," on boy-friendly classrooms, and in the fall of 2004 she launched a bold experiment. Whenever possi-

Middle School

Coming of age in a culture that discourages bookishness, boys are more likely to fall victim to drugs and violence.

- Eighth-grade girls score an average of **11 points** higher than eighth-grade boys on standardized reading tests.

- Eighth-grade girls score **21 points** higher than boys on standardized writing tests.

- Between 1993 and 2003, the number of ninth-grade

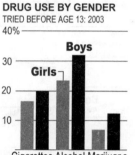

DRUG USE BY GENDER
TRIED BEFORE AGE 13: 2003

boys who skipped school at least once a month because they didn't feel safe increased **22%**.

- Boys between the ages of 5 and 14 are **200%** more likely to commit suicide than girls.

- Ninth-grade boys are **78%** more likely than girls to get injured in a fight at least once a year.

- Between the ages of 5 and 14, boys are **36%** more likely to die than their female counterparts.

ble, teachers replaced lecture time with fast-moving lessons that all kids could enjoy. Three weeks ago, instead of discussing the book "The View From Saturday," teacher Pam Unrau divided her third graders into small groups, and one student in each group pretended to be a character from the book. Classes are noisier, Unrau says, but the boys are closing the gap. Last spring, Douglass girls scored an average of 106 on state writing tests, while boys got a respectable 101.

Boys love video-games because when they lose, the defeat is private.

Primatologists have long observed that juvenile male chimps battle each other not just for food and females, but to establish and maintain their place in the hierarchy of the tribe. Primates face off against each other rather than appear weak. That same evolutionary imperative, psychologists say, can make it hard for boys to thrive in middle school—and difficult for boys who are failing to accept the help they need. The transition to middle school is rarely easy, but like the juvenile primates they are, middle-school boys will do almost anything to avoid admitting that they're overwhelmed. "Boys measure everything they do or say by a single yardstick: does this make me look weak?" says Thompson. "And if it does, he isn't going to do it." That's part of the reason that videogames have such a powerful hold on boys: the action is constant, they can calibrate just how hard the challenges will be and, when they lose, the defeat is private.

When Brian Johns hit seventh grade, he never admitted how vulnerable it made him feel. "I got behind and never caught up," says Brian, now 17 and a senior at Grand River Academy, an Ohio boarding school. When his parents tried to help, he rebuffed them. When his mother, Anita, tried to help him organize his assignment book, he grew evasive about when his homework was due. Anita didn't know where to turn. Brian's school had a program for gifted kids, and support for ones with special needs. But what, Anita asked his teachers, do they do about kids like her son who are in the middle and struggling? Those kids,

one of Brian's teachers told Anita, "are the ones who fall through the cracks."

It's easy for middle-school boys to feel outgunned. Girls reach sexual maturity two years ahead of boys, but other, less visible differences put boys at a disadvantage, too. The prefrontal cortex is a knobby region of the brain directly behind the forehead that scientists believe helps humans organize complex thoughts, control their impulses and understand the consequences of their own behavior. In the last five years, Dr. Jay Giedd, an expert in brain development at the National Institutes of Health, has used brain scans to show that in girls, it reaches its maximum thickness by the age of 11 and, for the next decade or more, continues to mature. In boys, this process is delayed by 18 months.

Middle-school boys may use their brains less efficiently than girls.

Middle-school boys may use their brains less efficiently, too. Using a type of MRI that traces activity in the brain, Deborah Yurgelun-Todd, director of the cognitive neuroimaging laboratory at McLean Hospital in Belmont, Mass., tested the activity patterns in the prefrontal cortex of children between the ages of 11 and 18. When shown pictures of fearful faces, adolescent girls registered activity on the right side of the prefrontal cortex, similar to an adult. Adolescent boys used both sides—a less mature pattern of brain activity. Teenage girls can process information faster, too. In a study about to be published in the journal Intelligence, researchers at Vanderbilt University administered timed tests—picking similar objects and matching groups of numbers—to 8,000 boys and girls between the ages of 5 and 18. In kindergarten, boys and girls processed information at about the same speeds. In early adolescence, girls finished faster and got more right. By 18, boys and girls were processing with the same speed and accuracy.

Scientists caution that brain research doesn't tell the whole story: temperament, family background and environment play

High School and Beyond

Many boys continue to fall behind girls in reading and writing proficiency, and fewer are going to college.

■ Boys are **33%** more likely than girls to drop out of high school.

■ Twelfth-grade girls score **16 points** higher than boys on standardized reading tests.

■ High-school boys are **30%** more likely to use cocaine than high-school girls.

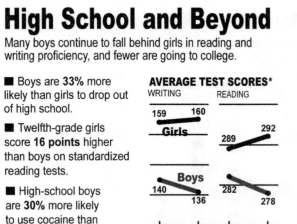

AVERAGE TEST SCORES*

WRITING   READING

159   160

Girls

289   292

Boys

140   136

282   278

1998   2002   1980   2004

*TWELFTH-GRADE SCORES

■ Twelfth-grade girls score **24 points** higher than boys on standardized writing tests.

■ High-school girls are **36%** more likely to take Advanced Placement or honors biology than high-school boys.

■ **22%** more high-school girls are planning to go to college than boys.

■ The percentage of male undergraduates dropped **24%** from 1970 to 2000.

big roles, too. Some boys are every bit as organized and assertive as the highest-achieving girls. All kids can be scarred by violence, alcohol or drugs in the family. But if your brain hasn't reached maturity yet, says Yurgelun-Todd, "it's not going to be able to do its job optimally."

Across the nation, educators are reviving an old idea: separate the girls from the boys—and at Roncalli Middle School, in Pueblo, Colo., administrators say, it's helping kids of both genders. This past fall, with the blessing of parents, school guidance counselor Mike Horton assigned a random group of 50 sixth graders to single-sex classes in core subjects. These days, when sixth-grade science teacher Pat Farrell assigns an earth-science lab on measuring crystals, the girls collect their materials—a Bunsen burner, a beaker of phenyl salicylate and a spoon. Then they read the directions and follow the sequence from beginning to end. The first things boys do is ask, "Can we eat this?" They're less organized, Farrell notes, but sometimes, "they're willing to go beyond what the lab asks them to do." With this in mind, he hands out written instructions to both classes but now goes over them step by step for the boys. Although it's too soon to declare victory, there are some positive signs: the shyest boys are participating more. This fall, the all-girl class did best in math, English and science, followed by the all-boy class and then coed classes.

One of the most reliable predictors of whether a boy will succeed or fail in high school rests on a single question: does he have a man in his life to look up to? Too often, the answer is no. High rates of divorce and single motherhood have created a generation of fatherless boys. In every kind of neighborhood, rich or poor, an increasing number of boys—now a startling 40 percent—are being raised without their biological dads.

Psychologists say that grandfathers and uncles can help, but emphasize that an adolescent boy without a father figure is like an explorer without a map. And that is especially true for poor boys and boys who are struggling in school. Older males, says Gurian, model self-restraint and solid work habits for younger ones. And whether they're breathing down their necks about grades or admonishing them to show up for school on time, "an older man reminds a boy in a million different ways that school is crucial to their mission in life."

A boy without a father figure is like an explorer without a map.

In the past, boys had many opportunities to learn from older men. They might have been paired with a tutor, apprenticed to a master or put to work in the family store. High schools offered boys a rich array of roles in which to exercise leadership skills—class officer, yearbook editor or a place on the debate team. These days, with the exception of sports, more girls than boys are involved in those activities.

In neighborhoods where fathers are most scarce, the high-school dropout rates are shocking: more than half of African-American boys who start high school don't finish. David Banks, principal of the Eagle Academy for Young Men, one of four all-boy public high schools in the New York City system, wants each of his 180 students not only to graduate from high school but to enroll in college. And he's leaving nothing to chance. Almost every Eagle Academy boy has a male mentor—a lawyer, a police officer or an entrepreneur from the school's South Bronx neighborhood. The impact of the mentoring program, says Banks, has been "beyond profound." Tenth grader Rafael Mendez is unequivocal: his mentor "is the best thing that ever happened to me." Before Rafael came to Eagle Academy, he dreamed about playing pro baseball, but his mentor, Bronx Assistant District Attorney Rafael Curbelo, has shown him another way to succeed: Mendez is thinking about attending college in order to study forensic science.

'An older man reminds a boy that school is crucial to life,' says Gurian.

Colleges would welcome more applications from young men like Rafael Mendez. At many state universities the gender balance is already tilting 60-40 toward women. Primary and secondary schools are going to have to make some major changes, says Ange Peterson, president-elect of the American Association of Collegiate Registrars and Admissions Officers, to restore the gender balance. "There's a whole group of men we're losing in education completely," says Peterson.

For Nikolas Arnold, 15, a sophomore at a public high school in Santa Monica, Calif., college is a distant dream. Nikolas is smart: he's got an encyclopedic knowledge of weaponry and war. When he was in first grade, his principal told his mother he was too immature and needed ADHD drugs. His mother balked. "Too immature?" says Diane Arnold, a widow. "He was six and a half!" He's always been an advanced reader, but his grades are erratic. Last semester, when his English teacher assigned two girls' favorites—"Memoirs of a Geisha" and "The Secret Life of Bees" Nikolas got a D. But lately, he has a math teacher he likes and is getting excited about numbers. He's reserved in class sometimes. But now that he's more engaged, his grades are improving slightly and his mother, who's pushing college, is hopeful he will begin to hit his stride. Girls get A's and B's on their report cards, she tells him, but that doesn't mean boys can't do it, too.

With Andrew Murr, Vanessa Juarez,
Anne Underwood, Karen Springen and Pat Wingert

Why We Need "The Year of Languages"

"2005: The Year of Languages" will focus on educating the U.S. public about the benefits of learning another language.

SANDY CUTSHALL

Q: What do you call a person who speaks three languages?
A: Trilingual.
Q: What do you call a person who speaks two languages?
A: Bilingual.
Q: What do you call a person who speaks one language?
A: An American.

The late Paul Simon, senator from Illinois and a champion of foreign language learning, once called the United States "linguistically malnourished" compared with other nations (Simon, 1980). People from different cultural and linguistic backgrounds have always come together to season the American melting pot, yet we have nevertheless held monolingualism in English as the gold standard of U.S. citizenship for immigrants, often at the expense of heritage languages.

Sadly, a chronic case of *xenoglossophobia*—the fear of foreign languages—has marked U.S. history. Only a few generations back, 22 states had restrictions prohibiting the teaching of foreign languages; it was not until 1923 that the U.S. Supreme Court overturned those laws. In 1954, only 14.2 percent of U.S. high school students were enrolled in foreign language classes; most public high schools (56 percent) offered no foreign language instruction at all (Clifford, 2004).

Studies have frequently reported on this area of national weakness. In 1979, the President's Commission on Foreign Language and International Studies noted that "Americans' incompetence in foreign languages is nothing short of scandalous, and it is becoming worse" (Clifford, 2004). Two decades later, a senior Department of Defense official said that the United States' greatest national challenge was its "general apathy toward learning foreign languages" (Clifford, 2004). In August 2001—one month before the September 11 terrorist attacks against the United States—the National Foreign Language Center at the University of Maryland noted that the country faced "a critical shortage of linguistically competent professionals across federal agencies and departments responsible for national security" (Simon, 2001).

This apathy plays out in the education landscape as well. Fewer than 1 in 10 students at U.S. colleges major in foreign languages, and most of those language majors choose French, German, Italian, or Spanish. Only 9 percent learn Arabic, Chinese, Japanese, Russian, or Indonesian—languages that are spoken by the majority of the planet's people (Strauss, 2002).

The current lack of accurate U.S. intelligence has heightened awareness of our lack of foreign language prowess. Many are hoping that the United States will finally change its priorities and find new and better ways to encourage and support language learning. Multilingualism carries many benefits. Individuals who speak, read, and understand more than one language can communicate with more people, read more literature, and benefit more fully from travel to other countries. Further, people who can communicate in at least two languages are a great asset to the communities in which they live and work. Jobs today are increasingly requiring workers who can interact with those who speak languages other than English and who can adapt to a wide range of cultural backgrounds. Every year, more than 200,000 Americans lose out on jobs because they do not know another language (Simon, 1980).

Allen Over Geld

So are we putting our money where our "tongues" are? Total federal funding for foreign language education was approximately $85 million for 2003, which represents less than one-sixth of 1 percent of the overall Department of Education budget. This means that for every $100 spent by the Department of Education in 2003, approximately $0.15 went to foreign language education (Keatley, 2004).

According to Thomas Keith Cothrun, president of the American Council on the Teaching of Foreign Languages (ACTFL), there is clearly a disconnect in the government: On one hand, the military and intelligence communities decry the lack of language experts; on the other hand, the Department of Education underemphasizes the importance of language learning. A recent study by the Council for Basic Education (CBE) indicates that the No Child Left Behind Act (NCLB) has forced a narrow focus on reading, math, and science at the expense of languages. Instruction time in foreign languages has decreased—particularly in schools serving minority populations—as a direct result of NCLB (CBE, 2004). The National Association of State Boards of Education (NASBE) also recently reported that both arts and foreign language education are increasingly at risk of being eliminated from the core curriculum (NASBE, 2003).

Non è Facile

Foreign language learning is not something that happens overnight; it takes a commitment of time and money. U.S. schools compound the problem by waiting too long to start foreign language instruction. According to ACTFL Professional Programs Director Elvira Swender, U.S. students often start learning foreign languages at puberty, "an age at which their brains are least receptive to language learning." Swender also notes the relative unimportance that schools assign to languages. "It doesn't occur to anyone that we should wait to teach students math," she points out, "so why do we wait with foreign languages?"

ACTFL recommends that elementary school language programs include classes three to five days a week for 30 to 40 minutes; middle schools should hold classes daily for 40 to 50 minutes. Few public schools do this even in Spanish and French, the most commonly taught languages (Strauss, 2002).

Further, some of the languages that are most crucial for Americans to learn are the most challenging for English speakers, thus requiring the greatest commitment of time and effort. Research estimates that it takes between 2,400 and 2,760 hours of instruction for someone with a superior aptitude for languages to attain the highest level of achievement in Arabic, for example (Strauss, 2002).

Quel est le Problème?

It's not that people in the United States don't want to learn languages; rather, they often believe that they are unable to do so or that they simply don't need to. As ACTFL Executive Director Bret Lovejoy points out,

> This perception that languages are too difficult to learn can often be traced to the fact that a person didn't start early enough, didn't have enough time devoted to the language, or had a difficult time in a language course in the past. (Personal communication, April 7, 2004)

People in the United States may travel hundreds of miles in their own nation and never hear a language other than English spoken, a decidedly different situation from that of European countries, whose citizens live in much more multilingual world. In addition, the widespread perception of English as the international language of business has contributed to a pervasive belief in the United States that everyone should learn English and that Americans simply don't need to learn another language. In fact, the international language of business is always the language of the client or customer. If businesses in the United States don't speak the language of their customers, those businesses end up at a competitive disadvantage.

Beginning language learning at an early age is crucial to increasing our language capabilities. A primary difference between the United States and nations that boast greater language strengths is the latter countries' emphasis on learning languages at younger ages. The Center for Applied Linguistics (CAL) is-

sued a report on approaches to language learning that compared the United States with 22 other nations. Seven countries—Australia, Austria, Germany, Italy, Luxembourg, Spain, and Thailand—had widespread or compulsory education in additional languages by age 8, and another eight—Canada, the Czech Republic, Denmark, Finland, Israel, Kazakhstan, Morocco, and the Netherlands—introduced a foreign language in the upper elementary grades. In many cases, a *second* foreign language was offered or required in the elementary grade.

In stark contrast, the majority of students in the United States do not start studying foreign language until age 14 (Pufahl, Rhodes, & Christian, 2000). Most foreign language study in the United States takes place in grades 9–12, during which time more than one-third (39 percent) of students study a foreign language. Only 6 percent of U.S. students study a foreign language in grades 1–6.

The shortage of language teachers in the United States is yet another challenge. Because early language learning has not been part of the traditional U.S. education model and most communities don't have access to foreign languages in elementary schools, there is a lack of well-trained language teachers at these levels.

People who can communicate in at least two languages are a great asset to the communities in which they live and work.

El Año de Lenguas

Language learning is a complex, long-term issue. In a culture unfortunately known for its short attention span, we need to do something dramatic to draw sustained attention to this issue.

Enter "2005: The Year of Languages," a national public awareness campaign that may be our best hope to put language learning in the spotlight and engage in a fruitful national conversation about the relationship between Americans and foreign language learning. Under the guidance and stewardship of ACTFL, 2005: The Year of Languages advances the concept that every person in the United States should develop proficiency in at least one language in addition to English. Each month of the yearlong endeavor will focus on a different area—such as language policy, higher education, language advocacy, heritage languages, and early language learning—with specific events reflecting the monthly focus.

For example, in February—the month that will tackle international engagement—a panel of Fulbright Exchange participants and representatives from other international programs will discuss the importance of study-abroad programs. There are currently more than 3,000 study-abroad programs for U.S. students to choose from. Although the number of U.S. students studying abroad for credit doubled in the past decade to more than 150,000 in the 2000-2001 school year, this number represents only 1 percent of college enrollments (Institute of International Education, 2003). Many students lack access to study-abroad programs through their institutions.

July's focus will be on languages and communities; during that month, the annual Folk Life Festival sponsored by the Smithsonian Institution will feature communities within and outside the United States and their respective languages and cultures. October will emphasize the benefits of early language learning: Activities cosponsored by the National Council of PTAs will provide parents with information on the benefits of learning languages at an early age and will feature K-12 programs that highlight language learning.

Language teachers in a school or district may choose to meet as a group to brainstorm ideas for promoting foreign language awareness, using the official Year of Languages Calendar of Events as a starting point. The calendar (available at **www.yearoflanguages.org**) may be used as a guide in planning local school events. ACTFL state and regional organizations have also coordinated plans for 2005: The Year of Languages and can serve as a local resource for schools to get involved with activities planned in their areas.

Alle Sind Optimistisch

There is great hope that the 2005: The Year of Languages campaign will not only draw U.S. attention to the important issue of foreign language learning but also inspire actions like those that resulted from a similar European effort in 2001, such as an ongoing annual National Language Day/Week, a national language agenda, and an official language policy.

With so much at stake—international relations, global competitiveness, support for internal diversity, and national security—it may well be time for everyone involved in education to think about what they can personally do to make this a successful Year of Languages.

References

Clifford, R. (2004, Jan. 16). Remarks at *National briefing on language and national security*, National Press Club, Washington, DC. Available: **www.ndu.edu/nsep/january16_briefing.htm**

Council for Basic Education. (2004). *Academic atrophy: The condition of the liberal arts in America's public schools*. Washington, DC: Author.

Institute of International Education. (2003). *Open doors 2003: Report on international educational exchange*. New York: Author.

Keatley, C. (2004, March). Who is paying the bills? The federal budget and foreign language education in U.S. schools and universities. *The Language Resource Newsletter*. Available: **www.nclrc.org/caidlr82.htm#no2**

National Association of State Boards of Education. (2003). *The complete curriculum: Ensuring a place for the arts and foreign languages in America's schools*. Alexandria, VA: Author.

Pufahl, I., Rhodes, N., & Christian, D. (2000, December). *Foreign language teaching: What the United States can learn from other countries*. Washington, DC: Center for Applied Linguistics. Available: **www.cal.org/resources/countries.html**

Simon, P. (1980). *The tongue-tied American: Confronting the foreign language crisis*. New York: Continuum.

Strauss, V. (2002, May 28). Mastering Arabic's nuances no easy mission. *The Washington Post,* p. A9.

Author's note: Thomas Keith Cothrun, Bret Lovejoy, Mary Louise Pratt, Nancy Rhodes, and Elvira Swender contributed to this article. For more information about 2005: The Year of Languages, visit **www.yearoflanguages.org** or contact the American Council on the Teaching of Foreign Languages (ACTFL) at 703-894-2900.

SANDY CUTSHALL is Managing Editor of *Foreign Language Annals*, the quarterly journal of the American Council on the Teaching of Foreign Languages, and a teacher of English as a second language to adults in Mountain View, California.

Failing Our Children

No Child Left Behind Undermines Quality and Equity in Education

LISA GUISBOND AND MONTY NEILL

The No Child Left Behind Act (NCLB), the title of the federal Elementary and Secondary Education Act, describes a worthy goal for our nation. Tragically the reality is that NCLB is aggravating, not solving, the problems that cause many children to be left behind. For the federal government to truly contribute to enhancing the quality of education for low-income and minority group students, NCLB must be overhauled.

FairTest, our nonprofit organization that strives to end misuses of standardized testing and promote fair evaluation of both teachers and students, has tracked the first two years of NCLB's implementation and identified fundamental errors in its conception, design, and execution. Rather than accept NCLB's dangerous prescriptions for public education, we propose a new approach to accountability as the basis for a comprehensive revamp of NCLB (Neill and Guisbond 2004).

Many false assumptions undergird NCLB. The most serious of the suppositions are the following:

1. *Boosting standardized test scores should be the primary goal of schools.* This assumption leads to one-size-fits-all teaching that focuses primarily on test preparation and undermines efforts to give all children a high-quality education. This exclusive focus on test scores ignores the widespread desire for schools that address a broad range of academic and social goals, as reported in public opinion polls. One recent public opinion survey found Americans believe the most important thing schools should do is prepare responsible citizens. The next most important role for public schools was to help students become economically self-sufficient (Rose and Gallup 2000). Another recent survey found that people's key concerns about schools were mostly social issues not addressed by standards, tests, or accountability (Goodwin 2003).

2. *Because poor teaching is the primary cause of unsatisfactory student performance, schools can best be improved by threats and sanctions.* Such threats encourage teachers to focus narrowly on boosting test scores. However, these punitive actions fail to address underlying problems such as family poverty and inadequate school funding, which are major reasons that many students start off behind and never catch up.

A new accountability system must start from accurate assumptions, including a richer vision of schooling that will lead away from NCLB's test-and-punish methodology. This new approach assumes that educators want to do their jobs but need assistance to do better. We believe that rather than threatening educators with sanctions based on test results, our more effective approach focuses on gathering multiple forms of evidence about many aspects of schooling and using them to support school improvements. Because schools need to build the capacity to ensure that all children receive a high-quality education, all levels of government, therefore, must fulfill their responsibilities to provide adequate and equitable resources. FairTest's proposal also gives parents and the community central roles in the accountability process rather than excluding them through incomprehensible statistical procedures and bureaucratically mandated reports currently required by NCLB.

Set Up to Fail

At NCLB's destructive core is a link between standardized testing and heavy sanctions through the rigid and unrealistic "adequate yearly progress" (AYP) formula. The problem is that NCLB's AYP provision is not grounded in any proven theory of school improvement. As Harvard Graduate School of Education Professor Richard Elmore explains: "The AYP requirement, a completely arbitrary mathematical function grounded in no defensible knowledge or theory of school improvement, could, and probably will, result in penalizing and closing schools that are actually experts in school improvement" (Elmore 2003, 6–10).

Moreover, many other expert analysts also have concluded that the AYP mechanism, the heart of the NCLB accountability provisions, guarantees failure for a substantial majority of the nation's schools. For example, the National Conference of State Legislatures estimated that, according to these standards, some 70 percent of schools nationwide will fail (Prah 2002). More recently, a study conducted for the Connecticut Education Association projected that more than nine out of ten Connecticut elementary and middle schools will fail to meet AYP targets within ten years (Moscovitch 2004).

The reason for the high failure rate is that the pace of progress envisioned in the law—that all students will reach the proficient level within fourteen years of its passage—is implausible. Part of the problem lies in the word "proficiency," which Education Secretary Rod Paige defines as solid, grade-level achievement. In fact, the term comes from the National Assessment of Educational Progress (NAEP), where it has been widely criticized for being an unrealistic and inaccurate standard, as well as a political construct engineered to depict a national academic crisis (Bracey 2003). Only about three in ten American students now score at the proficient level on NAEP reading and math tests (NCES 2004). Thus, within a little more than a decade, all students are expected to do as well as only a third now do—a goal far more stringent than simply "grade level."

Based on trends on NAEP tests over the past decade, prominent measurement expert Robert Linn calculated that it would take 166 years for all twelfth graders to attain proficiency, as defined by NCLB, in both reading and math (Linn 2003; Linn, Baker, and Herman 2002). In addition, due to requirements that all demographic groups make AYP, several studies have concluded that schools with more integrated student bodies are far more likely to fail than schools that lack diversity (Kane and Staiger 2002; Novak and Fuller 2003). Adding to the confusion, states' definitions of proficiency vary wildly, making it difficult to make meaningful state-to-state comparisons (Kingsbury et al. 2003).

The AYP provisions further reflect the flawed reasoning behind NCLB by assuming that schools already have adequate resources to get all students to a proficient level, if they would only use those resources better. The implication is that administrators and teachers are not working hard enough, not working well, or both. Thus, with willpower and effort, schools and districts can bootstrap their way to unprecedented results. This reasoning ignores real factors that impede improvements in teaching and learning, such as large class sizes, inadequate books, and outmoded technology, as well as nonschool factors like poverty and high student mobility.

The Limits of Test Scores

For NCLB proponents, the law's near-total reliance on test scores to determine the progress of students, teachers, and schools reflects a desire for objective assessments of educational outcomes. For example, President Bush has said, "Without yearly testing, we don't know who is falling behind and who needs help. Without yearly testing, too often we don't find failure until it is too late to fix" (Bush 2001). But standardized test scores offer nothing more than snapshots, often fuzzy ones, of student achievement at a single moment in time. When used to make important decisions about students and schools, they can be misleading and damaging. Moreover, good teachers already know which students are falling behind.

The national obsession with using standardized test scores to drive school improvement and reform is not new. Education researchers have examined this trend only to come up with results that cast serious doubts about the efficacy of test-based reform. Among the findings:

- Test scores do not necessarily indicate real progress when they rise or deterioration when they fall. Annual fluctuations should not be used to reward or sanction schools, teachers or school officials (Haney 2002).
- Many of the tests used to judge our students, teachers, and schools are norm-referenced, meaning they are specifically designed to ensure a certain proportion of "failures" (Haney 2002).
- Errors in question design, scoring and reporting have always been a part of standardized testing and are likely to increase substantially with the increase in testing mandated by NCLB (Rhoades and Madaus 2003).

NCLB's rigid AYP mechanism and the sanctions it triggers exacerbate standardized exams' weaknesses, such as their cultural biases, their failure to measure higher-order thinking, and the problem of measurement error. Exams with such narrow scopes and strong sanctions promote intensive teaching to the test, which undermines efforts to improve educational quality (von Zastrow 2004).

As one seventh-grade Kentucky student explained, "The test is taking away the real meaning of school. Instead of learning new things and getting tools for life, the mission of the schools is becoming to do well on the test" (Mathison 2003).

Even before NCLB became law, there was ample evidence that many of its assumptions and the model on which it was based had fundamental flaws:

- Little evidence supports the idea that the model of standards, testing, and rewards and punishments for achievement is the cure for public schooling's ailments. On the contrary, several studies show a decline in achievement in states with high-stakes testing programs relative to those with low-stakes testing (Stecher, Hamilton, and Gonzalez 2003; Amrein and Berliner 2002).
- Surveys of educators confirm that the model promotes teaching to the test and narrowed curricula, particularly in schools that serve low-income and minority students (Pedulla et al. 2003; Clarke et al. 2002).
- Independent analysts have found that tests often fail to measure the objectives deemed most important by educators who determine academic standards. Thus, students taught to such tests will not be exposed to high-quality curricula, and the public will not be informed about student achievement relative to those standards (Rothman et al. 2002).
- The instructional quality suffers under such a model because it is often assumed that all students who fail need the same type of remediation. On the contrary, researchers have found that students fail for a variety of reasons and need different instructional approaches to get on track (Riddle Buly and Valencia 2002; Moon, Callahan, and Tomlinson 2003; Hinde 2003; Mabry et al. 2003).
- Research refutes the assumption that low-achieving students are motivated to work harder and learn more in a

high-stakes context. On the contrary, low-achieving students are most likely to become discouraged and give up in that environment (Harlen and Deakin-Crick 2002; Ryan and La Guardia 1999).

- There is evidence of falling graduation rates in highstakes states, as well as evidence that schools retain additional students in hopes of reaping higher test scores in key grades. Decades of research support the contention that retained students are more likely to drop out of school (Haney 2003).

Within its more than one thousand pages, NCLB does include some potentially helpful provisions. However, the law's flaws overwhelm them and end up damaging educational quality and equity. For example:

- NCLB calls for multiple measures that assess higher-order thinking and are diagnostically useful. However, these provisions are neither enforced nor embedded in most state practices.
- The law mandates school (or district) improvement plans. In practical terms, however, improvement means boosting test scores. Disruptive sanctions based on unrealistic rates of AYP deny schools the opportunity to see if their own improvement efforts work.

Another potentially useful component of NCLB is the call for high-quality teachers for all students. Unfortunately, the law's requirements fall short of the attractive label: A teacher may be deemed "highly qualified" if she or he has a bachelor's degree and passes a paper-and-pencil standardized exam. This minimal definition can in no way ensure that all children have good teachers.

There is no persuasive evidence demonstrating a strong relationship between passing a standardized test and being competent in the classroom. A National Academy of Sciences report, *Testing teaching candidates: The role of licensure tests in improving teacher quality*, offers the most comprehensive study of this issue. It found that raising cut-off scores on the exams may reduce racial diversity in the teaching profession without improving quality (Mitchell et al. 2001). Furthermore, the study concludes that the tests cannot "predict who will become effective teachers" (FairTest 2001).

NCLB, however, allows groups such as the American Board for Certification of Teacher Excellence (ABCTE) to promote quick and inadequate fixes. For example, the group offers a standardized test as a solution to the serious problem low-income areas have attracting strong teachers to their schools (Jacobson 2004). ABCTE is a project of the conservative, pro-NCLB Education Leaders Council, cofounded by Department of Education Deputy Secretary Eugene Hickok. ABCTE has received roughly $40 million in federal support for this scheme, although two of the three members of the department's own review panel rejected it.

A strong definition of "highly qualified" ensures that teachers work successfully with a variety of students to attain a range of important outcomes, not just test scores. And although NCLB does contain some good ideas for improving the teach-

ing force, such as mentoring and ongoing professional development, they must be separated from the drive to narrow schooling to test preparation. These favorable elements easily could become key parts of a revamped accountability and school improvement system that would replace NCLB.

NCLB also harms rather than helps schools in need in other ways. Sanctions intended to force school improvement eventually divert funds away from efforts to help all children succeed toward helping a few parents obtain transfers and tutoring for their children. The law's ultimate sanctions—privatizing school management, firing staff, state takeovers, and similar measures—have no proven record of success.

As many educators have pointed out, the federal government has failed to adequately fund the law (National Conference of State Legislatures 2004). Just as schools are hit with the demands of the current law, most states' education budgets are shrinking. Worse, neither federal nor state governments address either the dearth of resources required to bring all children to educational proficiency or the deepening poverty that continues to hinder some children's learning.

A Movement for Authentic Accountability

These problems have catalyzed a growing movement seeking to overhaul NCLB. State officials, parents, teachers, and students are mobilizing against the law. Unfortunately, some efforts, such as proposals to modify the AYP formula or spend more money without changing the law, seek only to minimize the damage caused by NCLB and would further perpetuate educational inequality. Others address only peripheral issues rather than the law's faulty premises and assumptions.

Effective opposition to NCLB must embrace genuine accountability, stronger equity, and concrete steps toward school improvement. FairTest has been working with educators, civil rights organizations, parent groups, and researchers across the nation to devise new models of accountability. Based on a set of draft principles, core elements of a better accountability system include:

1. *Getting federal, state, and local governments to work together to provide a fair opportunity for all children to learn a rich curriculum.* Current governments have failed to meet this fundamental accountability requirement because they have not ensured adequate, equitable funding and have overemphasized test scores.
2. *Using multiple forms of evidence to assess student learning.* If we want to know how well students are doing, we need to look at a range of real student work. If we want students to learn more or better, we have to provide teachers and students with useful feedback based on high-quality classroom assessments that reflect the various ways children really learn.
3. *Focusing on helping teachers and schools ensure educational success for all students.* Reaching that goal requires schools to be safe, healthy, supportive, and challenging environments. This means providing schools

with data that can help improve academic and social aspects of education and making certain that the schools are equipped to use the data.

4. *Localizing the primary accountability mechanisms.* These mechanisms must involve educators, parents, students, and the local community. Open, participatory processes, including local school councils, annual reports, and meetings to review school progress, are necessary.

5. *Focusing the primary responsibility of state governments to provide tools and support for schools and teachers while maintaining equity and civil rights.* Intervention should take place only when localities have been given adequate resources and support but still fail to improve performance or when uncorrected civil rights violations occur.

In the short term, NCLB's rigid AYP provisions and draconian penalties should be amended. States should no longer have to annually test all students in grades 3–8 in reading and math, and the amount of required testing should be reduced. Additional measures of school performance and student learning should be included in progress evaluations. Congress also should appropriate the full amount authorized under NCLB.

FairTest's report. *Failing our children*, uses work in Nebraska and the Massachusetts Coalition for Authentic Reform in Education's community-based assessment systems as models in the construction of a different approach to accountability.

More fundamentally, policymakers must seriously consider both the damage that NCLB has wrought and the problem of inadequate educational funding around the nation. They should begin by listening to the voices of educators, parents, and community people asking for high-quality education, not test preparation, for children.

Stripped of its bureaucratic language, NCLB is a fundamentally punitive law that uses flawed standardized tests to label many schools as failures and then punishes them with harmful sanctions. NCLB must be transformed into a law that supports lasting educational improvement and makes good on the promise, in the words of the Children's Defense Fund, to "leave no child behind."

Note

FairTest's report on NCLB, *Failing our children: How "No Child Left Behind" undermines quality and equity in education and an accountability model that supports school improvement*, is available at **http:// www.fairtest.org/Failing_Our_Children_ Report.html.**

References

Amrein, A., and D. Berliner. 2002. An analysis of some unintended and negative consequences of high-stakes testing. Tempe, AZ: Education Policy Studies Laboratory, Arizona State Univ. **http:// www.asu.edu/educ/epsl/EPRU/documents/EPSL-0211-125-EPRU.pdf (accessed June 18, 2004).**

Bracey, G. 2003. NCLB—A plan for the destruction of public education: Just say no! *NoChildLeft.com* 1, no. 2 (February). **http://www.nochildleft.com/2003/feb03no.html** (accessed June 29, 2004).

Bush, G. W. 2001. Press conference with President Bush and Education Secretary Rod Paige to introduce the President's education program. **http://www.whitehouse.gov/news/releases/2001/01/20010123-2.html** (accessed June 18, 2004).

Clarke, M., A. Shore, K. Rhoades, L. Abrams, J. Miao, and J. Lie. 2002. *Perceived effects of state-mandated testing programs on teaching and learning: Findings from interviews with educators in low-, medium-, and high-stakes states.* Boston: National Board on Educational Testing and Public Policy, Boston College. **http://www.bc.edu/research/nbetpp** (accessed June 18, 2004).

Elmore, R. F. 2003. A plea for strong praise. *Education Leadership* 61 (3): 6–10.

FairTest. 2001. Reports blast teacher tests. *Examiner.* **http://www.fairtest.org/examarts/Winter%2000-01/Reports%20Blast%20Teacher%20Tests.html** (accessed April 29, 2004).

Goodwin, B. 2003. *Digging deeper: Where does the public stand on standards-based education?* Aurora, CO: Mid-continent Research for Education and Learning.

Haney, W. 2002. Lake Woebeguaranteed: Misuse of test scores in Massachusetts, Part I. *Education Policy Analysis Archive* 10 (24), **http://epaa.asu.edu/epaa/vl0n24/** (accessed June 14, 2004).

———. 2003. Attrition of students from New York schools. Invited testimony at public hearing, "Regents Learning Standards and High School Graduation Requirements," before the New York Senate Standing Committee on Education, New York. **http://www.timeoutfromtesting.org/testimonies/923_Testimony_Haney.pdf** (accessed June 16, 2004).

Harlen, W., and R. Deakin-Crick. 2002. A systematic review of the impact of summative assessment and tests on students' motivation for learning. Evidence for Policy and Practice Information and Coordinating Centre (EPPI-Centre), Univ. of London.

Hinde, E. R. 2003. The tyranny of the test. *Current Issues in Education* 6, no. 10 (May 27), **http://cie.asu.edu/volume6/number10/** (accessed June 16, 2004).

Jacobson, L. 2004. Education Dept. ignored reviewers in issuing grant for teachers' test. *Education Week* 23 (27): 10. **http://www.edweek.org/ew/ewstory.cfm?slug =27Amboard.h23&keywords=education %20leaders%20council** (accessed June 21, 2004).

Kane, T. J., and D. O. Staiger. 2002. Volatility in school test scores: Implications for test-based accountability systems. Brookings Papers on Education Policy. Washington, DC: Brookings Institution.

Kingsbury, G. G., A. Olson, J. Gronin, G. Hauser, and R. Houser. 2003. *The state of standards.* Portland, OR: Northwest Evaluation Association. **http://www.young-roehr.com/nwea/** (accessed June 14, 2004).

Linn, R. L. 2003. *Accountability: Responsibility and reasonable expectations.* Los Angeles: National Center for Research on Evaluation, Standards, and Student Testing, Univ. of California.

Linn, R. L., E. L. Baker, and J. L. Herman. 2002. Minimum group size for measuring adequate yearly progress. *The CRESST Line* 1 (Fall): 4–5. Los Angeles: National Center for Research on Evaluation, Standards, and Student Testing, Univ. of California. **http://www.cse.ucla.edu/products/newletters/CL2002fall.pdf.**

Mabry, L., J. Poole, L. Redmond, and A. Schultz. 2003. Local impact of state testing in Southwest Washington. *Education Policy Analysis Archives* 11, no. 21 (July 18), **http://epaa.asu.edu/epaa/v11n22** (accessed June 16, 2004).

Mathison, S. 2003. The accumulation of disadvantage: The role of educational testing in the school career of minority children. *Workplace* 5, no. 2, **http://www.louisville. edu/journal/ workplace/issue5p2/mathison. html** (accessed April 26, 2004).

Mitchell, K. J., D. Z. Robinson, B. S. Plake, and K. T. Knowles, eds. 2001. *Testing teacher candidates: The role of licensure tests in improving teacher quality.* Committee on Assessment and Teacher Quality, Board on Testing and Assessment, National Research Council. Washington, DC: National Academy Press.

Moon, T. R., C. M. Callahan, and C. A. Tomlinson. 2003. Effects of state testing programs on elementary schools with high concentrations of student poverty: Good news or bad news? *Current Issues in Education* 6, no. 8 (April 28), **http:// cie.asu.edu/volume6/number8/index.html** (accessed July 15, 2004).

Moscovitch, E. 2004. Projecting AYP in Connecticut Schools. Prepared for the Connecticut Education Association. Gloucester, MA: Cape Ann Economics.

National Center for Education Statistics. 2004. *The nation's report card.* Washington, DC: National Center for Education Statistics, Institute of Education Sciences, U.S. Department of Education. **http://nces.ed.gov/nationsreportcard/** (accessed June 14, 2004).

National Conference of State Legislatures. 2004. *Mandate Monitor* 1, no. 1 (March 31). **http://www.ncsl.org/programs/ press/2004/ pr040310.htm** (accessed June 18, 2004).

Neill, M., and Guisbond, L. 2004. *Failing our children: How "No Child Left Behind" undermines quality and equity in education and an accountability model that supports school improvement.* Cambridge, MA: FairTest. **http://www.fairtest.org/ Failing_Our_Children_Report.html** (accessed June 14, 2004).

Novak, J. R., and B. Fuller. 2003. Penalizing diverse schools? Similar test scores but different students bring federal sanctions. Policy Analysis for California Education (PACE), policy brief 03-4. **http://pace.berkeley.edu/pace_publications.html** (accessed June 18, 2004).

Pedulla, J., L. Abrams, G. Madaus, M. Russell, M. Ramos, and J. Miao. 2003. *Perceived effects of state-mandated testing programs on teaching and learning: Findings from a national survey of teachers.* Boston: National Board on Educational Testing and Public Policy, Boston College. **http://www.bc.edu/ research/nbetpp/reports.html** (accessed June 18, 2004).

Prah, P. M. 2002. New rules may guarantee "F's" for many schools. *Stateline.org*, December 9. **http://stateline.org/ stateline/ ?pa=story&sa=showStoryInfo &id=275753.**

Rhoades, K., and G. Madaus. 2003. Errors in standardized tests: A systemic problem. National Board on Educational Testing and Public Policy, Boston College. **http://www.bc.edu/nbetpp** (accessed June 14, 2004).

Riddle Buly, M., and S. W. Valencia. 2002. Below the bar: Profiles of students who fail state reading assessments. *Educational Evaluation and Policy Analysis* 24 (3): 219–39. **http:// depts.washington.edu/ctpmail/PDFs/Reading-MRBSV-04-2003.pdf** (accessed June 14, 2004).

Rose, L. C., and A. M. Gallup. 2000. The 32nd annual Phi Delta Kappan Gallup poll of the public's attitudes toward the public schools. *Phi Delta Kappan* 82 (1): 41–58.

Rothman, R., J. B. Slattery, J. L. Vranek, and L. B. Resnick. 2002. *Benchmarking and alignment of standards and testing.* Los Angeles: National Center for Research on Evaluation, Standards, and Student Testing. **http://www.cse.ucla.edu/CRESST/ Reports/TR566.pdf.**, Univ. of California.

Ryan, R. M., and J. G. La Guardia, 1999. Achievement motivation within a pressured society: Intrinsic and extrinsic motivations to learn and the politics of school reform. In *Advances in motivation and achievement,* ed. T. Urdan, 45–85. Greenwich, CT: JAI Press.

Stecher, B., L. Hamilton, and G. Gonzalez. 2003. *Working smarter to leave no child behind: Practical insights for school leaders.* Santa Monica, CA: RAND Corp.

von Zastrow, G. 2004. *Academic atrophy: The condition of the liberal arts in America's public schools.* Washington, DC: Council for Basic Education. **http://www.c-b-e.org/PDF/ cbe_principal_Report.pdf.**

LISA GUISBOND is a researcher and advocate for the National Center for Fair and Open Testing (FairTest), where **MONTY NEILL, EDD**, is the executive directo*r.*

From *The Clearing House,* Vol. 78, No. 1, September–October 2004, pp. 12-16. Reprinted by permission of the Helen Dwight Reid Educational Foundation. Published by Heldref Publications, 1319, Eighteenth St., NW, Washington, DC 20036-1802. Copyright © 2004. www.heldref.org

StrengthsQuest in Application: The Experience of Four Educators

The Power of Teaching Students Using Strengths

GLORIA HENDERSON

Like Chip Anderson, I was initially taught to use the deficit-remediation model with my students. Even in that negative context, though, and with no exposure at all to strengths-based education, I unconsciously based my early teaching on four of my five Clifton StrengthsFinder signature themes: *Significance* (I wanted to be recognized for having made a difference to each student); *Achiever* (I focused on individual students and tried to energize them to establish and reach their goals); *Restorative* (I was confident that I would create success in even those students who had lost all hope); and *Futuristic* (I developed a vision for my students with the identified deficits reduced or eliminated).

As I learned about strengths-based education after I entered Azusa Pacific University's doctoral program, I came to realize the importance of systematic research and the application of research results in developing the most effective instructors possible. I became determined to use my own strengths consciously and deliberately.

Consciously Applying Strengths to Decide on a Job

I knew I had found my calling when I saw a position posting for a late-term-replacement teacher of at-risk kids in a program structured as a school-within-a-school. The school offers more Advanced Placement, International Baccalaureate, and honors classes than regular classes. The students I would teach composed the "school within." They had covered only a minimal amount of content and had not met the state standards.

Being Restorative, I found it natural to identify and take a constructive approach to the students' deficits in skills and the lack of decorum in the classroom. I looked at each student as an individual to determine areas in which performance was satisfactory and those in which it needed improvement. Being Futuristic, I dreamed big for my new students, and being an Achiever, I developed a plan to make my vision a reality. I conducted research to find lessons, discipline plans, and other resources to assist my students. I also sought advice from other teachers, who brought different strengths to bear. Although I endured many tests from those students, I became a much more effective teacher by consciously using my strengths and encouraging them to use theirs.

Consciously Applying Strengths to Develop Teaching Style

I now teach a sophomore English class for at-risk students at the same school. As an Achiever I set high expectations because I know that if I lower the bar and set expectations that are too easy to reach, the students will meet the expectations yet still not pass the required high school exit exam.

Although I fully intend that every student will pass the exit exam (Significance), I employ a Restorative teaching style that seems to fit my students particularly well. I tease them, cajole them, encourage them, tell them they are better than they think they are, and express my concerns and my hopes for them. I do not focus my efforts on content, but they seem to have a huge impact on how well the students learn the content.

So far the fit between my strengths and my job seems to be working well for the students. I have overheard students telling their friends, "Our English class is fun," "We didn't learn how to do that last year," "Can I take this class next semester?" and "I got a B on a test!" And although it is expected that my at-risk students will not perform as well as the others in the school, they did perform as well, if not better, on recent vocabulary benchmark tests.

After I initiated a video-technology program for the school, my at risk students successfully took on the challenge of learning theory and abstract application with very limited experiential learning. Even though the equipment arrived late, the students completed a number of well done projects—remakes, public service announcements, school- and community-focused films, music videos, instructional videos, independent films, and trailers—in only a few short weeks.

For years my students have been told that they are not the best—or worse than that. Evidently, though, many students simply did not understand what was expected of them or lacked the incentive to perform. By consciously using my own strengths, I have been able to address such specific needs. In return I have found it gratifying to make a real, measurable difference. By consciously matching the challenges I undertake with my strengths, I have been able to enjoy greater initial success than I would have otherwise. I have come to believe that although most people already use their strengths intuitively, any teacher will foster greater student achievement and success by clearly identifying and consciously applying strengths.

GLORIA HENDERSON teaches English, video technology, and psychology at Diamond Bar High School in Diamond Bar, California.

From *Educational Horizons*, Vol. 83, Spring 2005, pp. 202-204. Copyright © 2005 by Gloria Henderson. Educational Horizons is the quarterly journal of Pi Lambda Theta Inc., International Honor Society and Professional Association in Education. Reprinted with permission of the author.

UNIT 4

Development During Childhood: Family and Culture

Unit Selections

Key Points to Consider

- Why do American parents find it so difficult to say "no" to their children?

- Which is worse, a parent who torments, a parent who hovers, an uninvolved parent, or are all behaving badly?

- Can bad behavior in children be blamed on bad parenting? Are good behaviors the result of good parenting? What roles do genetic factors play in behaviors?

- Should immigrant children, who have learned a little English, be used as translators for their immigrant parents, who have not yet learned the language? What are the results of using children as translators?

- Are American schools equal? If not, why not? What is the future for school desegregation?

Student Website

www.mhcls.com/online

Internet References

Further information regarding these websites may be found in this book's preface or online.

Childhood Injury Prevention Interventions
http://depts.washington.edu/hiprc/
Families and Work Institute
http://www.familiesandwork.org/index.html
Parentsplace.com: Single Parenting
http://www.parentsplace.com/

Most people accept the proposition that families and cultures have substantial effects on child outcomes. How? Are the anti-American, anti-Israeli terrorists in the Middle East socialized to hate? Alternatively, does something in their childhood environment "turn on" the hate genes that all humans possess? New interpretations of behavioral genetic research suggest that genetically predetermined child behaviors may be having substantial effects on how families parent, how children react, and how cultures evolve. Nature and nurture are very interactive. Is it possible that there is a genetic predisposition toward more war-like, aggressive, and violent behaviors in children? Do some child-rearing practices suppress this genetic trait? Do others aggravate it? The answers are not yet known.

If parents and societies have a significant impact on child outcomes, is there a set of cardinal family values? Does one culture have more correct answers than another culture? Some Middle Eastern spokesmen have called the Western culture corrupt and decadent. Laypersons often assume that children's behaviors and personalities have a direct correlation with the behaviors and personality of the person or persons who provided their socialization during infancy and childhood. Have Americans become paranoid about weapons of mass destruction and the extent of terrorist intentions? Do we try to justify our culture's flaws by claims that other cultures are worse? Do we teach our children this fear? Conversely, do other cultures try to hide their atrocities and war-mongering behaviors behind the screen that Americans are worse, or that they must be stopped first?

Are you a mirror image of the person or persons who raised you? How many of their beliefs, preferences, and virtuous behaviors do you reflect? Did you learn their hatreds and vices as well? Do you model your family, your peers, your culture, all of them, or none of them? If you have a sibling, are you alike because the same person or persons raised you? What accounts for all the differences between people with similar genes, similar parenting, and the same cultural background? These and similar questions are fodder for future research.

During childhood, a person's family values get compared to and tested against the values of schools, community, and culture. Peers, schoolmates, teachers, neighbors, extracurricular activity leaders, religious leaders, and even shopkeepers play increasingly important roles. Culture influences children through holidays, styles of dress, music, television, world events, movies, slang, games played, parents' jobs, transportation, exposure to sex, drugs, and violence, and many other variables. The ecological theorist Urie Bronfenbrenner called these cultural variables exosystem and macrosystem influences. The developing personality of a child has multiple interwoven influences: from genetic potentialities through family values and socialization practices to community and cultural pressures for behaviors.

The first article discusses "Raising Happy Achieving Children in the New Millennium," Alice Honig gives advice on how parents and teachers can build child self-esteem, how parents and teachers can cooperate in education, how to discipline positively, how to apply insights from the new brain research, and how parents can partner with professionals to increase children's happiness and achievement.

"The Power of No," discusses contemporary childrearing. The authors state that for many parents, the pendulum has swung too far in the permissive direction. They quote psychologists warning of the dangers of overindulgence and the inability to say "no."

The following article continues to look at contemporary parents, but in a different light. Nancy Gibbs discusses the arena of parent-school interactions. Teachers want parent involvement in education. However, they sometimes get more than they require. Parents may hover like helicopters and volunteer too much. Other parents may torment them with criticisms and accusations. Teachers and parents need mutually supportive, not adversarial, relationships.

The next article cautions that parents are not the only force shaping behavior in children. Many behaviors are inherent in human nature, predetermined by genetic factors. They are found in peoples of every culture, regardless of parenting practices. Parents are important. Good parenting is vital to a civilized society. Parents, however, should not be blamed or credited for every action taken by normally behaving members of the human race in their childhoods.

Unit 4, subsection B (Culture), begins with an exposition on miscommunication between recent American immigrants and the professionals who serve them. With our increasing population diversity, it is imperative that time and effort be spent to avoid life-threatening misunderstandings.

The last article in this subsection deals with the question of school desegregation in the United States. A Supreme Court decision ended segregated schools over 50 years ago. Other court decisions in the 1970s, 1980s, and 1990s weakened compliance with the 1954 *Brown v. Board of Education* ruling. Many inner-city schools are not only segregated, but also have fewer resources, more crowded conditions, and fewer teachers than schools in the affluent suburbs. Ellis Cose describes the historical changes in education since the *Brown* decision.

Raising Happy Achieving Children in the New Millennium*

ALICE STERLING HONIG
Syracuse University

Raising happy achieving children is a tall order. The recipe is complicated. The ingredients are awesomely many! Some of the ingredients involve educators and the training of high quality caregivers and teachers. Some of the recipe requirements involve political advocacy for the poor. Some ingredients are challenging—such as how to provide sexual information and information about unwanted pregnancies and AIDS and how to provide internship opportunities for practicing excellent caregiving within a high school model childcare—for teens who need clear and helpful knowledge and skills. These recipe requirements mean changes in offering school courses in junior high and senior high school. Required courses in positive communication techniques and required courses in family life education are as urgent as studying the invasions of Ghenghis Khan or the history of the Norman invasion in England and its effect on enriching the vocabulary of the English language.

Changes in the way education is offered for medical, nursing, and legal professionals to include more knowledge about children's interests and needs must also be part of the complex societal recipe to support children's flourishing. Thus, part of the recipe lies in enhancing the training of obstetricians and nurses caring for pregnant first time parents. Sensitivity training and knowledge, in dealing with birthing situations for single parents and high-risk teens, are important for professionals involved with childbirth. They will be more likely then to provide nurturance to promote early bonding with the newborn and to support breast feeding for those who may be physically able to nurse but have no clue as to how or why.

Another political ingredient in this recipe will mean much wider monetary support for home visitation personnel who work with at-risk pregnant women PRIOR to the birth of the baby. Honig and Morin's (2000) research has shown that IF high-risk teens who dropped out of an intensive home visitation program had about 7 home visits, then they still had much lower rates of confirmed neglect/abuse several years later. These rates were actually comparable to rates for high risk teen moms who stayed in program for 18 to 24 months regardless of whether program teens' entry was prebirth or postbirth.

High risk teens who started program after the birth of the baby and then dropped out had markedly higher confirmed abuse/neglect rates.

Loving, Knowledgeable, Skilled Caregivers: The Priceless Ingredient

The priceless ingredient in the recipe for a happy achieving child is a strong and loving family foundation and highly competent caregivers in group care. Parents are young children's most precious resource. No other caregiver and no material resources can take the place of parents who genuinely treasure their children and are deeply committed to nourish their children's growth and optimal development. The dream of every family is a child who is able to grow up independent yet lovingly related to family and achieving work success and satisfaction in life. We still cannot improve on this formula of the old master, Sigmund Freud!

After their needs for food and comforting, for protection from distress and from danger are taken care of, young children most need a special person whom they know in their deepest self is their loving protector, teacher, and friend. This fundamental security base, this unpaid worker who puts in countless overtime hours without pay and often without much recognition from society, is a PARENT. Thus, this presentation will focus particularly on positive parental ingredients for raising happy achieving children.

Many excellent enrichment programs such as Head Start, Even Start, HIPPY, and Parent Child Development Centers actively work to enlist parental help in young children's learning. Yet sometimes programs that attempt to work with low-income, low education parents, or very young parents or upper class dual career busy parents, report frustrations they were not prepared to cope with. Often the program staff goal is to assist new parents in positive ways to deepen the love relationship with a child, become primary educators of their preschoolers and to encourage parents to work actively in partnership with child care providers. Yet staff report low turnout for meetings, missed appointments for home visits, and lack of parent attunement to program messages.

> **...quality parenting is the secret indispensable ingredient to provide the inner core of self-love and self-esteem that sustains each growing child.**

What are the sources of difficulties? Part of the problem lies in the stressful lives of parents with limited time and often with aggravating lack of means of transportation to program sites. Some families may not have learned in their own families of origin the ability to empathize with child neediness. Struggling to cope with their own adult problems, some parents are not even aware of how important early consistent tender nurturing is in order to promote early child emotional attachment to parents. Chaos, drug abuse, spousal or partner abuse, depression and current lack of family supports account for some of the frustrations for families and for program staff. The deep reverberations of what Fraiberg (1980) calls "ghosts in the nursery"—angers, jealousies, resentments over being rejected or unloved or terrorized in own's own childhood—intrude in dangerous ways into the parent's current relationship with a young child. Some staff frustrations stem from lack of access to technical skills, such a specific therapeutic techniques, book reading techniques, anger management skills, etc. on the part of staff. Sometimes staff is strong on wishing to do good but not trained thoroughly enough in sensitivity to client needs nor community mores. This can lead, for example, to family outreach workers becoming discouraged with parents and gradually working more and more directly with the child even though the program goals were to empower parents to become their children's most special enrichment person.

Part of the problem also results when service providers lack materials for parents with low literacy skills or for immigrant parents from different culture groups. Programs need to be proactive and create lending libraries that contain both videos (on infant massage and well-baby care, for example) and materials written in easy to read words or in a family's native language. Many publications available for encouraging optimal parenting are geared toward families with more resources, higher literacy, and fewer stresses.

Family support and information programs for parents need to brainstorm creatively to find ways to engage parents with their children. For example, a home visiting program can provide a weekly xeroxed "How to play the game" sheet with suggestions for **varying** an interactive learning game if a child needs more help OR, if a child needs more challenge (Honig, 1982b). And of course, staff needs to affirm steadily for parents how priceless is their role in supporting their children's emotional and intellectual learning.

Parents and Teachers Build Child Self Esteem

A caring adult committed to children's secure well-being is a person every society should honor or cherish. There could not be enough "awards" or medals for such special persons! Responsive caregivers permit hope that the fabric of society will not be rent with violence, alienation, school dropouts, suicides, drug abuse, and other tragic attempts by youngsters attempting to deaden their personal pain or to carve out a feeling of power. Watch the new films about kids in high school, for example. So many "in" youngsters in school cliques behave in ruthlessly ridiculing ways. Girls who aren't considered "sexy" or "beautiful" are called unkind names and treated with contempt socially. Boys who are shy or intellectual are labelled "nerds". Teachers need specialized training in working on cutting out bullying in classrooms, corridors, rest rooms and playing fields! In Norway, thanks to the work of Olweus on the noxious effects of school bullying, teachers are trained to address this issue and are responsible for proactive handling of bullying. Teaching as a profession needs more respect from society, and more in-depth training on how to enhance emotional intelligence as well as intellectual intelligence and knowledge! Teaching staff in childcare has very high turnover each year. Many caregivers earning minimum wage also have minimum training. We need to enhance the respect for quality caregiving. We need to support campaigns for worth wages! An even more intriguing question is how to help parents to see how important a quality child care provider in each child's life—not as paid servant but as a concerned, talented, hardworking extra "parenting" person in that young child's life.

> **Children need parents who provide for them as the parents in the fairy tale of the Three Bears, where the porridge was not too hot and not too cold, but just right!**

Because of the hazards of changing providers and inconsistent care, we must still emphasize that quality parenting is the secret indispensable ingredient to provide the inner core of self-love and self-esteem that sustains each growing child. As Erik Erikson taught us long ago, this consistent core of cherishing permits that child in turn to grow up to care for others in ways that sustain family and community. As a young one is given unto, so does that little one grow up learning how to become a giver. Such caring gives inner courage to cope with problems so that the child can both lead a productive personal life as well as contribute to society (Honig, 1982a). Parents are the **mirror** wherein young children find their inner true selves reflected as either essentially lovable or sadly unworthy (Briggs, 1975).

In a women's dress store, a toddler wandered among the clothes. As she walked around, babbling "Da" and touching clothing, the mother called out over and over either "No! No! Don't touch!". Mostly she kept saying

"I don't want you. I don't want you!" The toddler looked bewildered and started to cry. "It must feel frustrating to be among all these clothes racks while the grown ups are busy shopping" I remarked sympathetically to the mother. "Yeah, I've been frustrated with her every minute since she's born!" replied the mother as she reluctantly picked up the tiny tot and continued down the store aisle.

Just giving birth to a child is not the same as parenting! Bettelheim (1987) and Winnicott (1987), wise psychiatrists, remind us, however, the young children do not need perfect parents to thrive. They will do very well with a "good enough parent". There is no "How-to" book that works for every child in every life situation.

Parents with profound good will for their children remember that cherishing does not mean smothering or intrusiveness.

A teen mother was waiting in the well-baby clinic for the pediatrician to see her child. The toddler, playing with a ring stack set (provided with other toys by a caring nursing staff in a play corner in the waiting room) put the rings on haphazardly. "That's not how you do it", the mom remarked with contempt. She snatched the ring stack from her child and put the rings on in graduated sizes. "There, that's the right way", she announced triumphantly as she handed back the toy to her child. The toddler took the ring stack, and turned it upside down as she let all the rings tumble in disarray to the floor. She gave her mother an angry look and walked silently away from her.

Insightful adults understand developmental stages. They understand that wanting a child to do well cannot be forced but must be supported. They let children have the leisure to try toys on their own. They don't constantly intrude with trying to force the child's attention. They LURE kids to new experiences. But they do not dominate the play situation. Rather they are responsive to children's cues, to children's curiosity, to children's explorations when the child seems calm and engrossed in play. If a toy seems too frustrating, they may move in quietly to provide a bit of unobtrusive support (such as steadying the elbow of a child trying to stack boxes), a quiet suggestion, a turning of a puzzle piece so that the child can better notice where it goes. TEMPO is an important skill in childrearing and in lovemaking! We need to talk more about tempo just as we need to address power issues more in society, with respect to marriages and childrearing as well as in business and politics!

Keeping the see-saw of daily life from bumping down too hard for some children is a major challenge!

Havighurst, a half-century ago, wrote about the developmental tasks of childhood. As a theorist he may be out of fashion nowadays. But he observed wisely that many adults need to become more aware emotionally that a young child first needs to be **allowed to be dependent** and kept safe in order to grow up brave enough to become **independent** and separate from the parents. Youth who feel they must belong to a gang, must cut classes and smoke and drink to be "cool" and grownup, who must act violent with a sex partner are NOT independent persons. They are acting out ancient wounds and scenarios. Their immature and scary actions show how much they lack skills for being independent, contributing helpful adults in society. As one adult remarked quietly to me about her teen years:

> I cut out emotionally. My parents were both quarreling a lot. They were so busy with their careers. They did not seem to have time really to talk with me or to see that their intellectual interest were not the same as my interests in music and sports. So I gave up caring about their world. I turned to peers and to drugs so my friends became my "family" support. It took me years to become my own person.

Parents and teachers together need to notice how special and *individual* each child is in a family. Children do not have the same temperament or wishes or abilities as a parent or as another youngster. A child who is very shy may be quite unlike a gregarious younger sibling. Children need parents who provide for them as the parents in the fairy tale of the Three Bears, where the porridge was not too hot and not too cold, but just right!

Too Much Enmeshment or Too Much Isolation Emotionally Withers The Souls of Young Children

What a strange job parenting is! We cherish and protect, worry over sniffles, blow noses, tie shoelaces, read stories, help with homework, patiently teach moral values and courtesies toward others (Lickona, 1983). Yet we do the job of parenting so that children can grow up to make their own choices and be able to live calmly and effectively on their own without parental help. If the job of parenting is done well, it is done so that parents work themselves OUT of a job!

Flexibility and Adaptability Help Caregivers and Parents Survive

Caregiving requirements change with children's ages and stages. Caregivers who are perceptive will note when to drop the baby talk that so delighted the 10-month-old and truly encouraged her to try words. Now they will use clearly pronounced adult words like "water" rather than "wa-wa" with their toddler whose vocabulary is growing by leaps and bounds. Adults will note that a toddler expresses fierce independence about what he wants, how much he wants and how he wants it right away. They cannot let that child run in the street or go out without clothes on a winter morning! But, they will also note that a No-saying defiant toddler who tries adult patience in the household still needs his thumb or pacifier and definitely needs the reassurance of his parent's lap when tired, crabby, or coming down with a cold. Parents who are perceptive will note that the five-year-old can feed and dress herself rather well now and can even be allowed to choose clothes to lay out the night before going to kindergarten.

The mystery of growth and development is not steady or predictable. Perceptive caregivers balance firmness with sensible tuning in to a child's stages and needs. They work hard to figure out where each child is at in each domain in his or her learning career. Some children love tinkering with tools and are good at helping Mom or granddad with a repair job. But they may have many frustrations with reading and math in school work. Ridicule and nagging only increase a child's smoldering resentment or stubborn refusal to cooperate at home or school. Finding a warm caring tutor and also exploring the community for an excellent vocational high school may open the path to real job satisfaction later in life for this youngster. Adults need to be good noticers and good balancers in order to promote each child's well being. Keeping the see-saw of daily life from bumping down too hard for some children is a major challenge!

Parents As Teachers: Teachers As Parent Supporters

Parents and caregivers must both be the emotional teachers of young children. They can teach empathy (sensitivity to feelings—of one's own and of other persons) and trustfulness; or they can teach mistrust and anger, insensitivity and uncaring.

> On the toddler playground, Donny pushed at another boy and snatched his shiny toy auto. Mama came over, kneeled down, held his hands and firmly reminded him of the social rules: "Donny, no pushing or hitting." The toddler nodded and added tearfully "And no biting and kicking!" Self-control is so hard to learn. But with the help of his mother's clear and patient teachings, Donny was learning.

Authoritative parents (as opposed to permissive parents or to authoritarian "Do as I say because I say so!" parents) bring up children who are easiest to live with at home and teachers report that they are a pleasure to have in the classroom (Baumrind, 1977). Such parents show genuine interest in their children. They provide firm clear rules and reasons for rules. And they need, of course, to be flexible about rules. A feverish school child may be excused from family chores. A child just starting a new daycare placement needs more lap time and more tolerance for his crankiness until he feels more secure in the new environment. A teenager who comes home with a really difficult and long set of homework problems feels grateful when a concerned parent offers to take on the teenager's chore of loading the dishwasher to free up some extra study time that evening. Teach generosity by being generous. Teach kindness by showing kindness.

Thus, every child needs caring adults who will promote emotional intelligence (Goleman, 1995). How to be assertive as differentiated from angry and hostile is a challenging emotional task. Children and parents need to focus on how to reframe daily hassles as opportunities to strengthen positive emotional skills, such as: giving a peer a chance to explain, being able to articulate well your point of view and trying to see another's point of view as well; searching for win-win reasonable solutions to social hassles; asking for help in ways that affirm the role of the helper, whether teacher or parents. Some folks believe that the job of teacher and the job of parent are totally different. Those of you who have cared for infants and toddlers know so well that diaper changing, holding a frightened tiny person, feeding, and soothing are intimate ministrations. The roles are indeed blurred when we care for the youngest little persons. Maybe a high school teacher can be sarcastic and put down a student in front of the class. Maybe that student will not feel resentment and anger. Maybe. Sometimes an adolescent with strong family supports achieves ego serenity and resilience and can handle such classroom stresses fairly well. The provider of care for your children is working with a small person whose ego is gradually building. Be sure that all the builders are cooperating, caring and knowledgeable or the structure being built will have troublesome flaws!

Learning Values

Parents are also on the frontiers of a child's learning values in the family. If parents deal their own problems by screaming and lashing out, or being sharply jeering and critical of weaknesses or mistakes made by a family member, then children will **model** their folks and learn those ways to cope with frustrations. If parents struggle to keep a family organized and functioning, then even though financial resources are limited, if they cherish children through hard times and good, their children will learn courage and caring (Honig, 1982a).

Children's empathy flows from experiencing their own parent's empathic response to their early fears and emotional upsets. Research by Yarrow and Zahn-Waxler reveals that during the first two years of life, the parent who shows empathy by soothing a child's hurt after a scare or a kneebruising fall, and who, in addition, clearly does not allow a child to hurt others as a way of solving social disagreements, will have a socially empathic child who is more likely to tune into and try to help other children who are hurt or scared (Pines, 1979).

If families provide models for punitive and vengeful actions, they need to realize that their children may gloat over the misfortune of others or else be indifferent to others' pain. Parents need to become aware of the emotional response that the old master, Sigmund Freud, called "Identification with the aggressor".

> In a rigidly organized household with innumerable rules posted on the refrigerator, the ten-year-old was being punished. She had tried to add her cuddly teddy bear, her comfort object for years, to her school backpack. The parents were angry. The toy animal could have been lost at school or taken by another child. They "punished" the child by having her sit for several hours at an empty dining room table without moving. The five-year-old in the family declared that her older sister "deserved" her punishment and announced that she "did not care" if her sister felt sad.

Parents Prime the Pump of Learning

How does a parent become the first, best teacher who ensures the child's early learning success? Varied are the programs that have been developed to teach parents how best to help their children learn. Some involve parents in groups together. Some programs invite parents as aides into classrooms. Some programs provide Home Visitation in order to promote parenting skills (see Honig, 1979 for an in-depth description of types of parent involvement programs).

Respect for the child is the foundation of good teaching. As parents notice early skills just emerging, they **scaffold, support, and lure** the child to a slightly more difficult accomplishment, to a slightly more subtle level of understanding, to a somewhat higher and more mature level of skill. I have called this technique "Dancing developmental ladders of learning" (Honig, 1982b). In each area of learning, the parent takes CUES from the child: Is the baby making new babbling sounds? Talk delightedly with a cooing baby. Express genuine interest in what baby seems to be trying to communicate. Turn-taking-talk primes language learning (Honig, 1985a). Does the baby smile when he sees animals? Snuggle together and point to pictures of animals during picture book story time with your little one and be sure to label objects baby points to.

Is your year-old child trying to feed herself? Provide Cheerios on the high chair tray to facilitate thumb and forefinger precise pincer prehension. Is your five-year old asking questions about where babies come from? Be an askable parent and provide simple, short calm explanations easy for that young child to understand (Gordon, 1983). Is your six-year-old determined to learn to ride a two-wheeler? Be sure that she is skillful with her tricycle; then advance to training wheels.

Facilitate learning by creating easy "steps" upward toward skill mastery. Figure out the **prerequisites** for success in any area of learning. If a parent provides more toeholds on the ladders of learning, children are more likely to succeed as they push upward in their growth toward achievements.

Preparations ahead of time boost the effectiveness of parent efforts to prime new learning, to scaffold opportunities for learning. Provide lots of discarded paper and crayons for children to draw. Keep assorted "beautiful junk" in a special place; empty egg cartons, pine cones collected on a walk, bubble paper from packaging, old greeting cards, and paper towel rolls plus some paste, blunt scissors, and Magic Markers are good ingredients for rainy day art activities.

Every parent needs a large repertoire of [discipline] techniques to use at different ages and stages of a child's growing up. Not all techniques work all the time with all youngsters!

Take children on small outdoor walks and to parks often. Give them opportunities to learn to swing, climb, balance, and coordinate their bodies with ease and grace. Also, teach them the names of weeds and flowers (dandelions and daisies are great!) growing by the roadside. Encourage children to notice and feel with their fingers the contrasting roughness and smoothness of the bark of different trees, such as a maple and a beech. Delight in the way clouds and sunshine light the land, the way cool air rustles and sways a flower stem, the way the earth smells fresh after a rain.

Express joy! Your own joy in the glories of the natural world sparks in your young child a deep pleasure, awareness, and appreciation for the world's beauty.

Creativity Turns Living Experiences into Learning Opportunities

Caregivers with limited financial resources need to scout their living space to use every opportunity to turn a household chore or routine into a learning experience. Store-bought toys may be too expensive; but adult creativity transforms every homey experience into a learning adventure (Honig, 1982b; Honig & Brophy, 1996). *Laundry time* can be used to teach colors, shapes, comparative sizes (of socks and of washcloths and towels), and the names for different materials and garments. Kids will love to feel important as they measure out laundry detergent up to the one-cup line and pour it into a wash tub or machine.

Cooking and baking times are a wonderful opportunity to increase hand dexterity skills in rolling, kneading, shaping, and measuring. And the tastes afterward are an extra reward for the helping youngster.

Grocery shopping is a superb perceptual and language learning experience for young children. Meat, dairy and fruit/vegetable departments give children opportunities to form conceptual categories. Why are peppers and celery and broccoli all in bins near one another? Where would hamburger be found? What items will need refrigeration? Which cartons or cans are heavier than others?

Encourage numerical estimations. As children grow and learn about numbers and letters, many take pride in being able to find a nutritious cereal box by the special letter on the box. They like to help stuff a plastic bag with string beans for supper. Many children by early school age can do estimates; they add up a dollar for this item (rounded off) and three dollars for that item, and so forth, and then come up with a fairly close estimate of how much the groceries will add up to. How proud your child feels. And how much practice in addition such estimates give her!

Teach children about money. People work to earn money. When money is in short supply, a child learns early that food and rent come first. Money, whether in pounds or dollars, for extras such as toys or snacks must be carefully budgeted.

Learning categories and learning gradations (such as little, big, bigger, biggest) are important cognitive tasks of the early years. The real world of shopping, cooking, clean-up times, and yard work provides rich opportunities for learning about number, shape, color, weight, bulk, categories of object, and other cognitive concepts. **Reframe** ordinary household experiences. Transform them into potential lesson times.

Positive Discipline Ideas: A Gift For Every Caregiver And Parent

All parents, not just parents with limited resources, need help in acquiring discipline techniques beyond the dreary "hit" and "scold" and "go to your room" many folks learned in their families of origin. Every parent needs a large repertoire of techniques to use at different ages and stages of a child's growing up. Not all techniques work all the time with all youngsters!

Most of the time, a young child is just acting like a child, not thinking in logical sequences, acting in-the-present time rather than planning ahead.

Parents who were raised by being belted or whipped in turn sometimes show powerful urges to use physical punishment. They hated the type of discipline they received but often believe it was justified. They need support to learn more appropriate child management skills. Sometimes young children's boisterous or overly intrusive games spark a feeling of rage in an adult. Grim and hostile parents are reflecting the anger they felt from adults far back in their own childhoods, when family members, furious with some of their behaviors, punished them harshly and branded them as "bad!"

Research has shown that **severe physical punishment (SPP)** was the major discipline method of parents whose youngsters ended up convicted of juvenile crimes. And, the worst crimes (as judged by independent professionals) were committed by the youths who had received the most SPP! (Welsh, 1976).

Let us cull from clinicians and researchers useful ideas about positive discipline that parents CAN use in order to raise responsible and cooperative children without instilling fear and deep anger against parental power (Briggs, 1975; Crary, 1990; Gordon, 1975; Honig, 1985b, 1996; Lickona, 1983). For example, the **redirection technique** helps a parent avoid willful battles with a toddler intent on messing up his big brother's model airplane. The parent invests a different, appropriate activity, such as wooden train tracks or a puzzle, or a jack-in-the-box, with interest so that the toddler turns toward the new and safer game.

Below are some further ideas to help adults re-think what discipline is about and how to use effective teaching techniques and avoid a punishment perspective.

Positive Attributions

Build up self esteem by generous use of **positive attributions** (Honig, 1996). Tell children what you admire about their behaviors and interactions.

Anger Management Techniques

Anger management techniques (such as counting to ten, or using words instead of fists) help children achieve self-control (Eastman & Rozen, 1984).

Teach Sharing

During a play group time, if two toddlers are struggling for a toy, supply an additional toy so each can play with a truck or have a supply of blocks. Talk about taking turns as a reasonable way to share a toy. Tell each child you will help with the taking turns by reminding each child in turn when the toy has been played with for an agreed upon number of minutes. Use a back rub and caress to soothe that child who has snatched a toy from another and as well the aggrieved child who is crying. Thus, you teach both the children that gentleness and kindness are necessary and important for each child.

Time Out as "Teach In"

Use time-out sparingly, and as a *"teach-in"* technique so that children can re-evaluate their inappropriate interactions and choose other ways to get their needs met (Honig, 1996).

Reframe a Problem in Terms of a Developmental Perspective

Adults can take a giant step toward devising new coping skills when they look at certain behaviors in terms of the stage a child is at or the curiosity a child has, or the need the child has to keep moving and exploring. Then certain behaviors, sometimes regarded as "bad" begin to seem just developmentally ordinary, such as a toddler's joy in jumping off a couch (find him someplace else that is appropriate and safe to jump off) or an infant's squeezing a banana through her fingers while watching in wonder.

How can a caregiver steer a child into more appropriate ways to experience vigorous body motions or to experience textures and squish clay?

Be Mindful of the Importance of Practising New Skills

Remember that children have to learn the initial steps for every new learning (and then practice that new skill). This helps an adult be tolerant even of toileting accidents or clumsy spills while a toddler pours juice. Perhaps a two-year-old cannot sit still but needs to run about a lot. He may not have the words for "poop" and "pee" yet. He may get intensely absorbed in his play and forget totally any signals coming from bladder or bowel. Punishing a two-year-old for a toileting accident when that particular child may not be ready to give up diapers for another year shows a lack of awareness of developmental norms for sphincter control. Toilet learning takes several years for some children to master. Male children have higher rates of enuresis. Little boys need particular understanding from parents who want compliance with their toilet training efforts (Honig, 1993).

Develop Realistic Expectations

More realistic expectations of young children's development supports a better understanding of how and when to discipline, and best of all, how to **prevent** discipline problems from arising. Expecting a newly cruising-about baby not to touch breakables or garbage in a bag left on a floor is more than the young one is capable of managing (Honig & Wittmer, 1990). Baby proofing a room full of interesting breakable art objects is a wise idea when curiosity is in full bloom. A toddler has little understanding of the difference between a shiny toy OK to play with and a shiny porcelain vase. Quite possibly, parental yelling if a toddler touches a treasured and fragile knick-knack on a coffee table will surely endow that particular item with increasing fascination and interest as a potential play toy.

Remind yourself that no baby, no school child, no parent, no spouse can ever be "perfect".

After hearing me at a morning public lecture talk about what children need from their folks, a beautiful young teen mom with a nine-month-old child came to me with tears in her eyes. "Dr. Honig, you seem to know so much about little children. Teach me how to make my baby perfect so I won't have to hit her so much?"

Avoid Hostile Blame

Another danger sign among adults is when they assume that a child is doing unwanted or disapproved actions "on purpose" to displease or act mean to the adult. Babies soak their diapers. Preschoolers love to get all muddy and splash in puddles. They do not "mean" to cause more laundry work for a parent. Beware the dangers of **Projecting Evil** (a Freudian defense mechanism) onto young children. Parental rage is too often fueled in abuse cases by the adult's feeling that a small child deliberately set out to "hurt" or "defy" the adult. If we expect that young children have the same thinking skills as adults we will be very mad at some of their actions and "blame" them—for being children! Most of the time, a young child is just acting like a child, not thinking in logical sequences, acting in-the-present time rather than planning ahead. This focused-on-own-needs small person is sometimes messy, sometimes in short supply of inner controls, sometimes needing to dawdle or say "No". A year-old baby cannot comply perfectly with "No-no". A young preschooler finds it very hard to sit still comfortably for hours without a toy or books or playmates in a dentist's waiting room or at a religious ceremony.

Professionals must help parents gain more **realistic expectations** and understandings of young children's growth needs. Projecting evil onto children is a danger that regrettably leads to violence and inappropriate punishments rather than behavior guidance to help a youngster gain more mature behaviors.

Importance Of The New Brain Research

Apply Insights From the New Brain Research Findings

New brain research reveals that toddlers by 24 months have twice as many brain synapses as adults. Somewhere during the early school years, and by 10 years of age, nature starts to prune away brain connections that have not been wired well by fre-

quent teaching and learning experiences. The motto for rich neural connections is "Use it or lose it!"

It is interesting that in England, compared with the United States, far fewer children are labelled "ADHD" (Attention Deficit and Hyperactivity Disorder) and British teachers are more likely to use behavior modification techniques rather than advocate the use of drugs.

Many families do not realize how early they CAN teach their little ones many kinds of lessons. By three weeks, if a baby has been talked to regularly, and a caregiver has waited with loving calmness for baby to respond with cooing throaty vowels, a baby can keep on cooing back in response to the caregivers' slow delighted talk with the baby held in "en face" position about one foot from the adult's face. The latest brain research reveals that **Parentese** (talk with babies using long drawn out vowels, short phrases, and a high pitched voice) is great for wiring in many rich neuron connections in the brain. This news means that to become good "teachers of the brain", caregivers need to have rich conversations with kids, read picture books frequently, sing songs, and offer their children experiences and adventures such as trips to the zoo, the public library, the supermarket, and local museums.

Figure Out Who Owns A Problem

Decide who owns a particular discipline problem. A teenager who dawdles in the mornings so long that she misses the school bus owns her problem. If a baby tears plant leaves from a favorite plant left on a low ledge, the parent owns the problem. If a parent expects a child with learning disabilities to do as well in school as an older brother who got high grades, the parent owns the problem. A parent's strong disapproval rather than support may contribute to possible school failure, and low child self esteem.

Some problems, of course, are owned by both parent and child. Have family meetings where each person can say what is bothering him about a rule, or an interaction, or a discipline in the family. When such meetings let each person have a say honestly about the week's positives and negatives, then such problems can be identified and hashed out with good will and a desire for reasonable compromise (Gordon, 1975).

Offer Choices

Toddlers who are contrary will often settle more easily into cooperation if offered a choice: "Do you want apple juice or orange juice? Do you want to sleep with your head at this end of the crib or the other end?" (when a tot has trouble setting into nap time). "You go choose two story books that you want me to read to you tonight". Offering choices often heads off a potential problem of crankiness or non-cooperation.

Think Through Household and Classroom Rules

How clear are your rules? Some children are scared that they will do something "wrong" inevitably because of the long lists of strict rules their folks insist on. Have few and clear house rules and be sure there are good reasons for the rules. Drinking milk is not a "must". A child can get calcium and Vitamin A from yellow cheese and from yoghurt. But not hurting a sibling IS a must in a family. *Make sure young children really understand your rules.* Ask a child who is not following a rule of the family to repeat to you what the household rule was. If the child is confused, he may not be aware of his "misbehavior."

Children have to learn about equity as well as fairness. Equity means taking into account special needs at special times for each person.

Adults get weary but need dogged persistence in explaining rules and the reasons for them over and over, especially for toddlers just learning to share, or children just learning how to balance homework responsibilities with their desire to rush out to play after school. "Don't need to wash my hands for supper 'cause they are clean" may mean that the preschooler needs to learn more about germs and the importance of keeping safe from sickness.

Do Not Ignore When Children Harm Others

Ignoring misbehavior only works for minor infractions. For example, if two children are verbally fussing or arguing, they may well be able to settle by themselves who gets to pull the wagon with blocks first. Aggression that is ignored will often escalate; it will not go away. If a child hits or kicks another, and the adult ignores this, the undesirable actions will not decrease but continue. Children then assume that the adult thinks hurting another child is allowed. Be firm about not allowing children to hurt others; but express that firmness without modeling physical hurt yourself. Talk so your child will listen; and be sure to listen so your child will open up to you (Faber & Mazlish, 1980).

Respect Each Child As A Person

Every person, big or little has a viewpoint and feelings of his or her own. A child is not personal property like furniture! Don't make comparisons between kids that make one child feel unloved, unpretty, or untalented compared with another. Screaming at or cursing a child, telling him he is rotten—these behaviors reflect parental anger and anguish, but in no way show that the adult remembers that this little child is a person and deserves to be treated with courtesy even when being disciplined.

Teach To Each Child's Temperament Style

Respect also means that the adult needs to tune into a child's personality style and cluster of temperature traits. Children differ in their threshold of tolerance for distress. They differ in whether they approach or avoid the NEW—whether babysitters or foods or an unknown visiting relative.

Children may be impulsive or quietly reflective. Some are very active, always on the go. Others are quieter. Perceptive parents do not lump all children together. They notice the small differences in mood, in shyness or worrying, in adaptability or rigidity among their children and they are generous in tailoring their demands for more mature behaviors to the temperaments and abilities of each UNIQUE child. It is interesting that in England, compared with the United States, far fewer children are labelled "ADHD" (Attention Deficit and Hyperactivity Disorder) and British teachers are more likely to use behavior modification techniques rather than advocate the use of drugs.

Is a child shy and slow to warm up to new events, people and experiences? Is a child triggery and intense in responding to frustrations? Is a child's mood mostly upbeat and does the child bounce back fairly quickly from upsets? *Tuning into temperament helps you head off potential tantrums* and gives you better clues to guide your child into more peaceable ways of interacting with others (Honig, 1997).

Break Up Tasks Into Manageable Parts

Nobody likes being dictated to. When we give a vague order such as "Go clean up your messy room" a child may have no clear idea how and where to begin. But he sure feels that he cannot succeed and he may grumble and show morose resentment of his folks. Suggest smaller parts of this big task so that the child realizes what has to be done specifically. If you break the task down into manageable bits (put clothes in the hamper; stack books on the shelves; put away toy trucks and cars into the toybox) then a child feels more hopeful about being able to carry out small portions of a task that seemed initially so huge and vague.

Find Out How A Child Reasons When He Or She Misbehaves

When children seem unreasonable in their requests, try to require reasons. Sometimes young children give amusing reasons, such as "I should get four cookies because I am four." "I should go first because I am bigger." As children grow, let them know that you expect them to **think** about their actions and to think through reasons for how they are choosing to act.

Children's acting out gives a strong message that they have "empty" insides and deep needs for adult acceptance and caring.

Adults have to help young children actively learn how to reason and to think causally and sequentially. By asking children for reasons without putting them down, we encourage them to think more clearly: "Can you think of a **different** idea to get Bobby to let you hold his pet puppy?" "Can you think why Grandpa asked you to hold his hand before crossing this wide avenue?" "Can I get dinner ready and read to you at the same time? I can find time to read to you **after** I have all the food cooking on the stove?" Children learn "polar opposites", such as "before" and "after" "same" and "different" more easily when they are actively utilized in real life discipline situations.

Offer Appropriate Incentives

If your school-age child wants you to take him to the park to play with some friends later in the day, think out loud together (Camp & Bash, 1985). He can finish his homework first and read his little brother a picture book story while you get dinner ready early so that you can then take the time off to go to the park with the children. "After you clean up your room we can play a game of checkers." "If you can take turns with Tanisha playing with the new dump truck or if you can figure out a way to play together, then you can have more play dates with her." This technique is sometimes called "*Grandma's Rule*". That is, a low preferred activity, such as cleaning up, is followed by a highly preferred activity, such as a privilege or a treat. This timing pattern is more likely to result in an increase in the low-preferred activity. Unfortunately, many parents switch the timing. "Honey, be sure to do your homework after you come back from playing soccer!" is far less likely to result in completed homework!

Teach Ideas of Fairness

Introduce the language of fairness into your talks with children in their play with peers or siblings: "Each child needs to get a turn. Every child in the game needs to play by the same rules. Games will end up in fighting and they will not be fun if children do not follow the rules." Still, fairness may not always work. If one child has disabilities or is ill, then that child may need special attention and care. Children have to learn about **equity as well as fairness. Equity means taking into account special needs at special times for each person.**

Fantasy and Truth are Fuzzy Ideas For Preschoolers

Children have such strong longings and they often believe sincerely and strongly in the reality of fantasy characters, such as Ninja Turtles or He-Man. They sometimes have trouble distinguishing reality from their own wishes. A six-year old reported enthusiastically that she was a terrific swimmer, when she could barely take a few strokes in the water. In Menotti's Christmas opera about the three Wise Men, "Amahl and the night visitors", the boy Amahl tells his mother excitedly that he has seen a star with a tail as long as the sky. Parents may need to ask their children: "Is that a true-true story or a true-false one?" Do not be quick to brand a child as a "liar" when she makes up a fanciful

tale or declares her imaginary playmate is sitting on the couch just where visiting Uncle Jim is about to seat himself. Remember how vivid children's imaginations are. Many young children are scared of "monsters" under the bed or in the closet. Many still blend fantasy and reality in ways adults find difficult to imagine!

Some make-believe tall tales of children represent deep longings. If your child pretends to others that she has a fabulously rich uncle who has promised her a pony, you may want to spend more real time doing loving activities together to help your youngster feel more at peace with the real world.

Be A Good Gatekeeper with TV

Be careful and judicious in the use of television. Some programs are prosocial. They give messages about how to handle impulsiveness or mean or mad feelings. Other television programs aimed at youngsters are incubators for teaching violent means of solving social problems. The cartoons are colorful. The animation is awesome. But the messages are pernicious. Sending kids to the television as a babysitter constantly is like using a narcotic to keep a child still. Enjoy activities, even peeling green peas or baking bread, or stripping the bed—together! Caring adults are good gatekeepers for choosing nourishing foods instead of junk food for children. Adults also need to be good gatekeepers for choosing programs that support self-reflectivity, positive solutions to social problems, and mistrust of easy or violent solutions. For example, in the United States there have recently been all too many violent solutions to ostracism and feelings of social rejection in schools with children shooting other children. Television programs with the Aardvark Arthur, the Teletubbies characters, Mr. Roger's Neighborhood neighbors, and the dragons in Dragon Tales all promote positive messages in solving social problems or personal issues. Be sure you are a good gatekeeper for television. Don't nag. Do arrange viewing situations, whether programs or videos or for positive learning.

Try To Figure Out What Is Worrying or Angering A Child

Anger, jealousy, resentment, and fear lead to acting out and misbehavior. Understanding your child's negative emotions may help you figure out how to approach and help your child.

Be careful about deciding what "causes" angry actions or misbehavior. Some families think a child should know right from wrong long before a child's thinking skills are well developed. Some children who were drug addicted in the womb show unmotivated and sudden aggressive actions, such as coming up behind an adult and biting the leg hard. Some children struggle with subtle thinking or perceptual deficits, a legacy from alcohol or drug addiction before they were born.

Blaming the Other Parent is Not a Useful Discipline Technique

Some folks blame the other parent. They say "The child gets his bad temper from his father. It's in his genes." Blaming the other parent for a child's troubling behaviors is guaranteed not to bring peace and good feelings in a family.

Use Victim-Centered Discipline Talk

Help children understand how others feel if they are attacked or hurt. Describe in vivid short sentences how a punch, a nasty word, a bite, a sneering remark hurts another's body and feelings. Galvanize your child to feel how it would be if the hurt had been done to him or her. Be firm in not accepting hurting as a means for your child to solve social conflicts. We do not shame children. They are not bad because they have a toileting accident sometimes or clumsily spill juice when they are toddlers. But if a child hurts another deliberately during the preschool years, we need to summon Eriksonian guilt. A child who understands how she would feel if someone hurt her or how he would feel if someone was mean to him is ready for you to lay your discipline talk on thick! Combine loving kindness with victim-centered discipline talk so that gradually the child comes to understand how kind ways help ease social difficulties far more than hurting ways. With your help, children learn inner self-control.

Use Empathic Listening

"Reflective Listening", sometimes called "Active listening" to the child's emotional message of aggravation, is a powerful tool that communicates an important message to your child: "My parent cares about me. My feelings are important to my folks. My parents want to help me figure out how to resolve my troubles rather than preaching at me or just getting angry." Simple "door-openers" help children open up and pour out their troubles. Try: "Looks like you had a rough day today, honey" (Gordon, 1975).

As you listen to a child's aggravations and woes with a peer or a parent or a teacher, try to reflect back to the child as best you can the genuine feelings you catch when he acts troubled or upset. Ridicule, put-downs, impatience—these are the swords that drive deep into children's hearts to make them feel that adults do not truly care about their feelings. Listen to your child's miseries. Listen and try to express your empathy with the child's upset feelings even when you do not agree with the scenario or think she or he is being childish.

Suppose Ricky is sad because his favorite friend now prefers a neighbor child as playmate and Ricky feels he has no one to play with. This problem seems as serious to a preschooler as adult problems seem to a parent. A teenage girl's worries about her weight or her popularity seem overblown to a parent, but desperately important to that girl. Don't suffer with her. Empathize and try to listen in a caring and supportive way.

Show Genuine Interest in Each Child

Be available and truly interested in talking with children in your care. Give them your full attention. Children hunger so deeply for personal attention. If adults are too involved in their own lives and needs, children express this emptiness in a variety of ways. They may turn away from parents and run with gangs of peers. They will sometimes steal coins out of parents' pockets. Sometimes they fight terribly with siblings or classmates. Children's acting out gives a strong message that they have "empty" insides and deep needs for adult acceptance and caring. Children have deep **emotional hunger for focused adult attention and emotional acceptance. Unconditional acceptance of each person heals the soul.** Can you think of a person in your own life who gave you that precious gift? Hopefully, a parent, a teacher, a spouse, a childcare provider, a religious leader in your faith community. And this gift makes a profound difference in healing past hurts.

Help Children Consider the Consequences of Their Actions

Many a youngster has never thought through exactly what will happen IF he hits Johnny or tears up his big brother's homework. It is really important for parents to probe and ask a lot: "What do think will happen next if you do that?" If Johnny fights with Billy over a toy, you may send Billy home and then Johnny will have nobody to play with the rest of the rainy weekend afternoon. Kids need encouragement to THINK, out loud, about what might happen IF they act in a certain way. When children are challenged to think of the consequences they often themselves decide that their action or idea is not helpful for themselves (Shure, 1994).

Challenge Children To Think Up Alternatives to Fighting

Help children get used to making a plan before a social problem arises. Encourage children to think up other ways of handling their social conflicts besides "not playing" with another child, or "hitting him". The more that teachers daily encouraged children to think up *alternative solutions* to their peer problems, the more likely they have been found to solve their social problems more appropriately after three months of such classroom work (Shure & Spivack, 1978).

Find Community Resources, Books, and Programs That Support Families

To cope with the complex stresses and forces in society today, families need a lot of skills, a lot of insights, a lot of supports. Job loss, divorce, a child born with disabilities, death and illness, all impact on the family. Teachers and social service personnel can reach out to offer supports and services to increase peaceable family functioning and enhance children's lives.

Encourage Excellence, Not Perfection

Expect children to try hard. They know they can never be perfect and may deliberately fail or act clumsy if they feel very anxious that adults expect perfection. Praise good trying. Appreciate hard work and good efforts even when a child's grades are not as high as you would wish or even when she is clumsy when she gets to bat in a ball game.

Find Each Child's Gifts: Play as a Wonderful Discovery Channel for Learning a Child's Skills!

Sometimes a parent wants a child to be a terrific ball player because that was the parent's secret desire as a child. Or parents are so anxious about a child doing well in science and math that they do not realize that this child is talented in art but not as gifted for science. Learn the gifts of each child. The child who draws and doodles a lot in class may not be showing disrespect to the teacher. He may be showing a budding gift for cartooning or drawing. Children whose parents ignore their gifts and push other agendas on them (such as getting into a prestigious college 12 years later!) may start to lie and even to cheat on tests in school.

Some children do need help to develop their learning skills. Perhaps a child's family has moved and changed classrooms often. That child may not be able to keep up with school work. Be aware of when a child needs tutoring in school. Other children have more stable schooling situations, but they may have dyslexia or difficulties with reading or math. For example, some school age children reverse letters. They have troubles with figure-ground relationships (of black print on a white page) and do not see words clearly against the background of the page. Other children have perceptual-motor difficulties that make using a pencil to write clearly a very arduous task. Search for professional help when you see a clear need.

But also learn to appreciate the gifts your children do have. Some young children carry a tune flawlessly (Honig, 1995). Some kids can run with fleet feet. Some can recognize the model of every car that passes on the road. Some kids can tell you the baseball batting statistics of every player on their favorite team. Some kids can soothe a playmate's upset by kind words. Be a not-so-secret admirer of your child and discover each gift with joy and gladness. If you watch your children at play with peers, you may catch their ingenuity at solving a social problem, such as trying to enter a peer group already playing house or pretending to be explorers on Mars.

Promote Children's Play

Provide rich play experiences by arranging for play dates and for quality preschool experiences. And then become a tuned-in NOTICER of the world of play. Read Vivien Paley's books, such as "The boy who would be a helicoptert" or "You can't say you can't play" to get more insights into the power of the world of play to socialize children just as the family is powerful in socializing children. Never permit bullying! Never permit catty clique behaviors. Talk about kindness with others and practice it yourself.

Don't Denigrate The Child's Other Parent

More and more marriages end in divorce, and second marriages tend to end even more frequently in divorce. In separations and divorce, parental bitterness and resentment belong to the adult, but so often heavy negative emotions spill over onto the children. Parental anger should not be sent as an arrow through the soul of a child where there has been a separation or divorce. Professionals need to help parents work through rage and grief so that these sorrowful poisons do not afflict children unduly. Already, young children in divorce often feel that it was their fault. Parents who feel betrayed or abandoned sometimes try to influence a child to turn against and hate the other parent. When possible, children need to feel that they are still loved by the other parent and they have total permission to love each parent. Enrolling children embroiled in divorce/custody issues in the "Banana Splits" programs social workers run in many schools is a good idea. Try to provide books and other materials to answer children's questions (Rofes, 1982). When mothers raise children alone, they may not realize that fathers are very precious to children (Biller & Meredith, 1975). Fathers are the preferred playmates of babies, and loss of affection from a divorced and absent father can cause long-lasting distress for children. Try to promote a climate of surety about each parent's caring for the children even when the parents cannot manage to live with each other.

Use Bibliotherapy

When children feel scared of the dark or worried about starting in a new school, stories have a wonderful power to heal. With stories, you find a way to reassure children so they feel more secure. Children identify with the loyal elephant in Dr. Seuss' "Horton hears a who". They do not always have to act out their resentments or disappointments. They can also identify with kind characters in stories.

In addition, children love mischievous characters, such as Pippo the monkey. They grin at the "Cat in the Hat". Everything gets fixed up just fine at the end of that Dr. Seuss story. Yet the Cat in the Hat surely acted naughty for a while!

Children sometimes misbehave when they want more attention. They act out with misbehavior in order to get attention, even when that attention is negative, such as yelling and spanking! A neighborhood library has good books about children's troubles. If you are going through a troubled time in your family, search for books such as "The boy who could make his mother stop yelling", for example.

Some children misbehave because they desperately want to feel powerful or exact revenge (for example, because they felt unwanted and unimportant when the new baby was born). Many problems hurt a child's soul, such as loss of a grandparent, or living with an alcoholic parent who humiliates the child so that he is afraid ever to invite a friend over to the home. Some children feel abandoned when a parent remarries and the stepparent obviously does not want the child around and never offers any affection to the child. The local library has many books you can read to help your child identify with a story child who has lived through such a problem and has managed to cope despite sorrow and worries.

Read stories that resonate for a child over and over. One youngster loved me to read daily for weeks Dr. Seuss' "The king's stilts". This is a story of a courageous little boy who digs up the king's buried stilts and returns them to the monarch (who loves to play on them at the end of a work day) and thus returns the king's joy and ability to govern well. That message, that a child could be scared of a mean and menacing adult (the king's prime minister in the story) and still finally become brave enough to do the right thing, seemed to resonate so deeply for this child. Another child, much younger, loved me to read "The enormous turnip" over and over. Somehow, naming all the family members as helpers in getting that huge turnip out of the ground was so satisfying. And he loved to point out that even Petya, the tiny beetle really helped too.

Toddlers love the Sam books too. Sam and Lisa quarrel over a toy car. Each one wants it. Each one smacks the other. Mama comes with another car so that each has a car to play with and they play together. These books resonate for toddlers who are learning, struggling, with the idea of sharing and taking turns. Choose your books to help children wrestle with such issues at every level. Choose books with cadences and poetry so that preschoolers can learn the refrains as in the book "Something from nothing". Preschoolers enthusiastically join in saying "Grandpa can fix it!". This is the positive refrain of the little boy Jacob every time his mama wants him to throw out something old and torn.

Create Your Own Stories to Reassure Worried Children

If a child has terrors or fears, for example, about starting kindergarten, make up stories about a little child (who very much resembles your child) who had a similar problem and how a healing, reassuring, good ending happened in that situation (Brett, 1986).

When parents are separating and getting a divorce, children often feel torn in pieces. They are afraid that something they did caused the breakup. They worry that if one parents has left, they may also be abandoned by the other parent. Make up stories that have endings clearly showing how each parent loves the child and showing the child where she will be living and how she will be kept safe and secure.

Help Siblings Get Along More Peacefully

Jealousy, the green-eyed monster, is often alive and well in families. Tattling and reporting important news are different. Make a distinction to your children between 1) tattling to hurt a sibling to get even or as one way to show jealousy, and 2) the importance of telling information to parents if there is a really important trouble where an adult **must** get involved. Praise each time that the siblings try to talk courteously and not trade sneering put downs. Talk with your children about the far future when they are all grown up and will have each other as the only close family persons. Share a good book about jealous siblings and how they dealt with the green eyed monster. Try to find time alone for meeting the special needs of each child. Take one grocery shopping while a friend or relative watches the other children. Bring one down to the laundry room to work together while the others are busy doing homework.

Use relaxation and vivid imagination techniques to help children relax, especially where there is sibling jealousy and too much rush and tension in the children's lives. Deep breathing exercises and conjuring peaceful scenes sometimes help bring down child tensions (Hendricks & Wills, 1975).

Assign Required and Admired Chores

Be sure that chores are not assigned just to get daily jobs done the parents don't want to do! Chores should depend on the age and ability of each child. Children should not feel that they are their parents' "slaves" but family helpers pitching in to make the household work easier. Give children a feeling that when they do their chores they are important, contributing members of the family so they feel proud to be useful and helpful. "I am a big helper. I clear the table after dinner. My papa needs me to hold the nails and hand him a nail as he repairs the ripped porch screens." Swan and Stavros' work among poor inner-city families showed that children with required chores, whose parents praised their participation and gave them genuine admiration and appreciation felt very secure in the bosom of the family and performed with high achievement in the kindergarten and first grade classroom. "Me a big helper" is a proud and splendid boast from an older toddler!

Be a Good Matchmaker

Make the tasks you expect from each child be ones that the child can do. Encourage efforts and support early attempts to master new tasks in accordance with each child's ability (Honig, 1982b).

In a research study in New Orleans, Swan and Stavros (1973) found that low-income parents who required helpfulness (not coerced, but required) had children who were successful as kindergarten learners and in their social relationships with peers. They noted that fathers were mostly present in these low-income families with self-motivated learners. Parents had neat clean living environments, read daily to their young children, ate meals and talked together at dinner time, and found their children genuinely interesting persons.

Express Personal Pleasure With Each Child

Tell a child that you love him, that you love her. Hug that child frequently. Caress a child with warm (rather than cold or disapproving) voice tones. Shine your eyes at a child so that the sunshine of your smile and the pleasure in your tone of voice warm the deepest corners of your child's self.

Talk About Peer Pressure With Children

Peer pressure is very powerful in coercing some youngsters to misbehave. Sometimes peer pressure to have special sneakers or clothes or possessions will lead to children's stealing another's prized clothing item to gain peer admiration. Peer pressure can lead a teenager to drink immoderately, try drugs, or engage in unsafe sex. Families must talk frankly about peer pressure and how their child feels about it. A youngster can accept and more likely live by family values and family circumstances. IF the child feels a strong sense of rootedness and reassurance within the family rather than from the peer group.

Avoid the Use of Shame

Shame is an acid that corrodes the soul. Shame is often twinned with rage that fuels serious misbehavior. Do not shame your children or they may well feel that they need to get revenge on you and on the world. Perhaps a child acts defiant just to show that you cannot really make him eat a food he detests, you cannot make him fall asleep at a too-early bedtime for him. To get even, he will lie awake angry for hours. Power and revenge games are dangerous. They destroy a child's feelings of security and trust in responsible adults.

Encourage Competence

Even very young children need to feel they "can do it"—put a peg into a pegboard, roll a ball, pick up a wiggly spaghetti strand to feed themselves, throw a used Kleenex in the wastebasket, or other simple skills. Let them try, even if they are not expert, to accomplish tasks they are capable of doing, such as putting on a coat, or setting a table or pouring out dog food into the bowl on the floor. Children who give up easily or feel that they can never do their homework, never learn to ride a bide, for example, are **discouraged** children. Try patiently to support their small accomplishments. Figure out ways to decrease their discouraged feelings.

> Felicia asked for a wastebasket right by the table where she struggled nightly with homework math problems. She did not want all the papers with wrong answers and scribbles to pile up in front of her, almost accusing her of being "stupid". But with the handy wastebasket nearby, she was willing to struggle anew with a fresh sheet to try her math homework.

Provide Positive Attributions

Give praise for **specific** actions. Cheerfully tossing off "You're terrific!" or "That's wonderful!" makes a child feel uncomfortable. She knows how much she still has to learn, and how many times she goofs up. Notice specific times when praise can really boost self-esteem and brighten a child's day. For example, an adult could say: "You are a really good friend to Robbie. Did you notice how happy he was when you shared your markers with him. You know how to make another child feel comfortable and welcome here!"

Work Alongside A Young Child

By expecting too much, too fast, we sometimes force children to act incompetent to get out from under the disapproval they feel will be inevitable if they aren't superior (Dinkmeyer & McKay, 1982). When a job seems overwhelming to a young child, make sure you work alongside. "Clean up your room" may send a child into a temper tantrum or into trying to avoid the job entirely. But if you tackle the task cheerfully **together**, the child will enjoy your company and feel pride as he works together with you. When you break a task into smaller manageable bits, you **scaffold** the task for a youngster: "Which do you want to pick up first—the toys on the floor that go into your toy box or the clothes that go into the wash hamper?"

Professionals As Partners With Parents

Professionals who work together with parents are not only teachers with a lot of information to share. They sometimes act as therapists. Sometimes they become caring friends of the family. Sometimes, as in Fraiberg's kitchen therapy model of home visitation, they become caring surrogate parents. They re-parent new parents whose ghosts of anguish and violence from the past are strongly impacting on the children in the present. Teachers especially need to "partner" with parents to form a strong team to support a child's early learning.

Sometimes, with very young mothers, professionals need to assist them in the process of **reflectivity**. The more that a new mother can reflect on her family of origin and how much during childhood she resented or was scared of harsh discipline, and decide that she does not want those feelings for her baby, the more affectionate and close will be her relationship with the new baby (Brophy & Honig, 1999).

In addition to support and knowledge, what other functions can personnel carry out to enhance positive family functioning?

Help Parents Find Ways To Give Themselves A Lift

Parents who feel happier with their own lives discipline more effectively and can share their happiness with children. Something as simple and inexpensive as a long bubble bath may relax an adult. Cleanup as a team after dinner with an adult partner helps any parent feel appreciated.

In a family with limited material resources, encourage parents to enlist imagination rather than material objects in order to bring special highlights into the family's day and into life. When rainy days in a row have resulted in short tempers, a family can plan to serve supper as a picnic on the living room floor. The children help make sandwiches. They spread the tuna salad and peanut butter on bread slices and wrap each sandwich. The family places all the picnic fixings in a basket and pretends they are walking to the picnic grounds—an old green sheet spread on the floor. Pretend games can break into the crankiness or hassles of daily living where severe financial constraints do not permit entertainments that "cost money".

Making collages out of bits of plastic egg cartons and other collected throw-aways can brighten an afternoon and provide art decorations to display on a refrigerator door so that children feel how proud you are of their talents.

Help Families to Network

Professionals need to introduce parents to others sometimes so they can form a support group when families feel isolated and alone. They could meet together at one another's home to talk about child issues with professional help or they can choose parenting materials to discuss. Help families feel comfortable in the world of the free public library or in a "Please Touch" museum. Introduce families to a drop-in store front center that welcomes families with respite child care, opportunities to swap children's used clothing and shopping coupons, as well as providing parenting classes and guitar lessons.

Find Respite Care For Overwhelmed Parents

Arrange for respite care when a parent is overwhelmed with caring for a disabled or emotionally disturbed child. Safe and secure respite care that a parent can count on and trust is one of the greatest gifts to give an exhausted parent. In a neighborhood, maybe parents can give each other coupons for helping out with childcare for each other. Such barter systems can provide needed respite without any money changing hands.

Assist Parents Trying to Join the Work Force

Help in finding job training and help in acquiring a high school diploma are other precious supports that families need as the bottom line in order to qualify for work positions to support their children. A resource room in a school or clinic can set out easy-to-read materials that focus on job training and on agencies that can help families in their search to become self sufficient.

Galvanize Specialist Help

When parents are behaving in seriously dysfunctional ways with children you need to act quickly and pinpoint the agencies and service to mobilize. Stresses can unnerve and make life difficult for parents. The five kinds of abuse that do occur in some families are: physical abuse, sexual abuse, physical neglect, emotional hostility, and emotional unavailability. Sometimes counseling and insight from child development experts and therapists can help. In urgent cases, when legal systems are threatening to remove a child from a home, then more strenuous professional help, such as Homebuilders provides (Kinney, Haapala & Booth, 1991), may be required. Homebuilders is an emergency service whereby a caseworker spends a great many hours for about six weeks in the home teaching the family members Gordon's (1975) Active Listening and I-statement techniques so that they can manage their severe difficulties and get along more positively. Specialists in anger management can be enlisted to "tame the dragon of anger" in children and parents (Eastman & Rozen, 1994).

Conclusions

Enhancing parent involvement and training a highly skilled child-care provider workforce must become priority goals for nations if we are to improve children's lives and learning careers. As we support parents, particularly parents whose lives include undue stress from limited resources and chaotic and inappropriate role models from the past, we will be ensuring a brighter future not only for the families and children served but for our entire society. And as we support teachers in schools and care providers in nurseries and preschools with money, prestige, training, and our deep appreciation, we will also be ensuring that our children grow up to be happy, responsible, achieving citizens.

References

Baumrind, D. (1977). Some thoughts about childrearing. In S. Cohen and T. Comiskey (Eds.), *Child development: Contemporary perspectives* (pp. 248–258). Itasca, IL: F. E. Peacock.

Bettelheim, B. (1987). *A good enough parent: A book on childrearing.* New York: Random House.

Biller, H. and Meredith, D. (1975). *Father power: The art of effective fathering and how it can bring joy and freedom to the whole family.* New York: McKay.

Brett, D. (1986). *Annie stories.* Australia: Penguin.

Briggs, D. C. (1975). *Your child's self esteem.* New York: Doubleday.

Brophy-Herb, H. E. and Honig, A. S. (1999). Reflectivity: Key ingredient in positive adolescent parenting. *The Journal of Primary Prevention,* **19** (3), 241–250.

Camp, B. N. and Bash, M. A. (1985). *Think aloud. Increasing social and cognitive skills—a problem solving program for children.* Champaign, IL: Research Press.

Crary, E. (1990). *Pick up your socks and other skills growing children need: A practical guide to raising responsible children.* Seattle, WA: Parenting Press.

Dinkmeyer, D. and McKay, G. D. (1982). *The parent's handbook: STEP. Systematic training for effective parenting.* Circle Pines, MN: American Guidance Service.

Eastman, M. and Rozen, S. C. (1994). *Taming the dragon in your child: Solutions for breaking the cycle of family anger.* New York: John Wiley.

Erikson, E. (1970). *Childhood and society.* New York: Norton.

Faber, A. and Mazlish, E. (1980). *How to talk so kids will listen and listen so kids will talk.* New York: Rawson Wade.

Fraiberg, S. (Ed.) (1980). *Clinical studies in infant mental health: The first year of life.* New York: Basic Books.

Goleman, D. (1995). *Emotional intelligence.* New York: Basic Books.

Gordon, S. (1983). *Parenting: A guide for young people.* New York: Oxford.

Gordon, T. (1975). *Parent effectiveness training.* New York:

Hart, B. and Risley, T. R. (1995). *Meaningful differences in the everyday experiences of young American children.* Baltimore, MD: Paul H. Brookes.

Henricks, G. and Wills, R. (1975). *The centering book: Awareness activities for children, parents, and teachers.* Engelwood Cliffs, NJ: Prentice Hall.

Honig, A. S. (1979). *Parent involvement in early childhood education.* Washington, DC.: National Association for the Education of Young Children.

Honig, A. S. (1982a). The gifts of families: Caring, courage, and competence. In N. Stinnett, J. Defrain, K. King, H. Hingren, G. Fowe, S. Van Zandt, and R. Williams (Eds.), *Family strengths 4: Positive support systems* (pp. 331–349). Lincoln, NE: University of Nebraska Press.

Honig, A. S. (1982b). *Playtime learning games for young children.* Syracuse, NY: Syracuse University Press.

Honig, A. S. (1985a). The art of talking to a baby. *Working Mother,* **8** (3), 72–78.

Honig, A. S. (1985b). Research in review; Compliance, control and discipline. *Young Children,* Part 1, **40** (2), 50–58; Part 2, **40** (3), 47–52.

Honig, A. S. (1993, Fall). Toilet learning. *Day Care and Early Education.*

Honig, A. S. (1995). Singing with infants and toddlers. *Young Children,* **50** (5), 72–78.

Honig, A. S. (1996). *Behavior guidance for infants and toddlers.* Little Rock, AR: Southern Early Childhood Association.

Honig, A. S. (1997). Infant temperament and personality: What do we need to know? *Montessori Life, 9* (3), 18–21.

Honig, A. S. and Brophy, H. E. (1996). *Talking with your baby: Family as the first school.* Syracuse, NY: Syracuse University Press.

Honig, A. S. and Morin, C. (2000). When should programs for teen parents and babies begin? *Journal of Primary Prevention, 21* (1).

Honig, A. S. and Wittmer, D. S. (1990). Infants, toddlers and socialization. In J. R. Lally (Ed.,), *A caregiver's guide to social emotional growth and socialization* (pp. 62–80). Sacramento, CA: California State Department of Education.

Kinney, J. Haapala, D. and Booth, C. (1991). *Keeping families together: The Homebuilders model.* Hawthorne, NY: Aldine De Gruyter.

Lickona, T. (1983). *Raising good children: From birth through the teenage years.* New York: Bantam Books.

Rofes, E. (Ed.) (1982). *The kids' book of divorce.* New York: Vintage.

Shure, M. B. (1994). *Raising a thinking child: Help your young child to resolve everyday conflicts and get along with others.* New York: Henry Holt.

Shure, M. and Spivack, G. (1978). *Problem-solving techniques in child-rearing.* San Francisco, CA: Jossey Bass.

Swan, R. W. and Stavros, H. (1973A). Child-rearing practices associated with the development of cognitive skills of children in a low socio-economic area. *Early Child Development and Care, 2,* 23–38.

Welsh, R. (1976). Violence, permissiveness and the overpunished child. *Journal of Pediatric Psychology, 1,* 68–71.

Winnicott, D. W. (1987). *Babies and their mothers.* Reading, MA: Addison-Wesley.

---

*Keynote address presented at the Child and Family Development Conference, Charlotte, North Carolina, March, 2000.

The Blank Slate

The long-accepted theory that parents can mold their children like clay has distorted choices faced by adults trying to balance their lives, multiplied the anguish of those whose children haven't turned out as hoped, and mangled the science of human behavior

STEVEN PINKER

If you read the pundits in newspapers and magazines, you may have come across some remarkable claims about the malleability of the human psyche. Here are a few from my collection of clippings:

- Little boys quarrel and fight because they are encouraged to do so.
- Children enjoy sweets because their parents use them as rewards for eating vegetables.
- Teenagers get the idea to compete in looks and fashion from spelling bees and academic prizes.
- Men think the goal of sex is an orgasm because of the way they were socialized.

If you find these assertions dubious, your skepticism is certainly justified. In all cultures, little boys quarrel and fight, children like sweets, teens compete for status, and men pursue orgasms, without the slightest need of encouragement or socialization. In each case, the writers made their preposterous claims without a shred of evidence—without even a nod to the possibility that they were saying something common sense might call into question.

Intellectual life today is beset with a great divide. On one side is a militant denial of human nature, a conviction that the mind of a child is a blank slate that is subsequently inscribed by parents and society. For much of the past century, psychology has tried to explain all thought, feeling, and behavior with a few simple mechanisms of learning by association. Social scientists have tried to explain all customs and social arrangements as a product of the surrounding culture. A long list of concepts that would seem natural to the human way of thinking—emotions, kinship, the sexes—are said to have been "invented" or "socially constructed."

At the same time, there is a growing realization that human nature won't go away. Anyone who has had more than one child, or been in a heterosexual relationship, or noticed that children learn language but house pets don't, has recognized that people are born with certain talents and temperaments. An acknowledgment that we humans are a species with a timeless and universal psychology pervades the writings of great political thinkers, and without it we cannot explain the recurring themes of literature, religion, and myth. Moreover, the modern sciences of mind, brain, genes, and evolution are showing that there is something to the commonsense idea of human nature. Although no scientist denies that learning and culture are crucial to every aspect of human life, these processes don't happen by magic. There must be complex innate mental faculties that enable human beings to create and learn culture.

Sometimes the contradictory attitudes toward human nature divide people into competing camps. The blank slate camp tends to have greater appeal among those in the social sciences and humanities than it does among biological scientists. And until recently, it was more popular on the political left than it was on the right.

But sometimes both attitudes coexist uneasily inside the mind of a single person. Many academics, for example, publicly deny the existence of intelligence. But privately, academics are *obsessed* with intelligence, discussing it endlessly in admissions, in hiring, and especially in their gossip about one another. And despite their protestations that it is a reactionary concept, they quickly invoke it to oppose executing a murderer with an IQ of 64 or to support laws requiring the removal of lead paint because it may lower a child's IQ by five points. Similarly, those who argue that gender differences are a reversible social construction do not treat them that way in their advice to their daughters, in their dealings with the opposite sex, or in their unguarded gossip, humor, and reflections on their lives.

No good can come from this hypocrisy. The dogma that human nature does not exist, in the face of growing evidence from science and common sense that it does, has led to contempt among many scholars in the humanities for the concepts of evidence and truth. Worse, the doctrine of the blank slate often distorts science itself by making an extreme position—that culture alone determines behavior—seem moderate, and by making the moderate position—that behavior comes from an interaction of biology and culture—seem extreme.

Although how parents treat their children can make a lot of difference in how happy they are, placing a stimulating mobile over a child's crib and playing Mozart CDs will not shape a child's intelligence.

For example, many policies on parenting come from research that finds a correlation between the behavior of parents and of their children. Loving parents have confident children, authoritative parents (neither too permissive nor too punitive) have well-behaved children, parents who talk to their children have children with better language skills, and so on. Thus everyone concludes that parents should be loving, authoritative, and talkative, and if children don't turn out well, it must be the parents' fault.

Those conclusions depend on the belief that children are blank slates. It ignores the fact that parents provide their children with genes, not just an environment. The correlations may be telling us only that the same genes that make adults loving, authoritative, and talkative make their children self-confident, well-behaved, and articulate. Until the studies are redone with adopted children (who get only their environment from their parents), the data are compatible with the possibility that genes make all the difference, that parenting makes all the difference, or anything in between. Yet the extreme position—that parents are everything—is the only one researchers entertain.

The denial of human nature has not just corrupted the world of intellectuals but has harmed ordinary people. The theory that parents can mold their children like clay has inflicted child-rearing regimes on parents that are unnatural and sometimes cruel. It has distorted the choices faced by mothers as they try to balance their lives, and it has multiplied the anguish of parents whose children haven't turned out as hoped. The belief that human tastes are reversible cultural preferences has led social planners to write off people's enjoyment of ornament, natural light, and human scale and forced millions of people to live in drab cement boxes. And the conviction that humanity could be reshaped by massive social engineering projects has led to some of the greatest atrocities in history.

The phrase "blank slate" is a loose translation of the medieval Latin term tabula rasa—scraped tablet. It is often attributed to the 17th-century English philosopher John Locke, who wrote that the mind is "white paper void of all characters." But it became the official doctrine among thinking people only in the first half of the 20th century, as part of a reaction to the widespread belief in the intellectual or moral inferiority of women, Jews, nonwhite races, and non-Western cultures.

Part of the reaction was a moral repulsion from discrimination, lynchings, forced sterilizations, segregation, and the Holocaust. And part of it came from empirical observations. Waves of immigrants from southern and eastern Europe filled the cities of America and climbed the social ladder. African Americans took advantage of "Negro colleges" and migrated northward, beginning the Harlem Renaissance. The graduates of women's colleges launched the first wave of feminism. To say that women and minority groups were inferior contradicted what people could see with their own eyes.

Academics were swept along by the changing attitudes, but they also helped direct the tide. The prevailing theories of mind were refashioned to make racism and sexism as untenable as possible. The blank slate became sacred scripture. According to the doctrine, any differences we see among races, ethnic groups, sexes, and individuals come not from differences in their innate constitution but from differences in their experiences. Change the experiences—by reforming parenting, education, the media, and social rewards—and you can change the person. Also, if there is no such thing as human nature, society will not be saddled with such nasty traits as aggression, selfishness, and prejudice. In a reformed environment, people can be prevented from learning these habits.

In psychology, behaviorists like John B. Watson and B. F. Skinner simply banned notions of talent and temperament, together with all the other contents of the mind, such as beliefs, desires, and feelings. This set the stage for Watson's famous boast: "Give me a dozen healthy infants, well-formed, and my own specified world to bring them up in, and I'll guarantee to take any one at random and train him to become any type of specialist I might select—doctor, lawyer, artist, merchant-chief, and yes, even beggar-man and thief, regardless of his talents, penchants, tendencies, abilities, vocations, and race of his ancestors."

Watson also wrote an influential child-rearing manual recommending that parents give their children minimum attention and love. If you comfort a crying baby, he wrote, you will reward the baby for crying and thereby increase the frequency of crying behavior.

In anthropology, Franz Boas wrote that differences among human races and ethnic groups come not from their physical constitution but from their *culture*. Though Boas himself did not claim that people were blank slates—he only argued that all ethnic groups are endowed with the same mental abilities—his students, who came to dominate American social science, went further. They insisted not just that *differences* among ethnic groups must be explained in terms of culture (which is reasonable), but that *every aspect* of human existence must be explained in terms of culture (which is not). "Heredity cannot be allowed to have acted any part in history," wrote Alfred Kroeber. "With the exception of the instinctoid reactions in infants to sudden withdrawals of support and to sudden loud noises, the human being is entirely instinctless," wrote Ashley Montagu.

In the second half of the 20th century, the ideals of the social scientists of the first half enjoyed a well-deserved victory. Eugenics, social Darwinism, overt expressions of racism and sexism, and official discrimination against women and minorities were on the wane, or had been eliminated, from the political and intellectual mainstream in Western democracies.

At the same time, the doctrine of the blank slate, which had been blurred with ideals of equality and progress, began to show cracks. As new disciplines such as cognitive science, neuroscience, evolutionary psychology, and behavioral genetics flourished, it became clearer that thinking is a biological process, that the brain is not exempt from the laws of evolution, that the sexes differ above the neck as well as below it, and that people are not psychological clones. Here are some examples of the discoveries.

Hundreds of traits, from romantic love to humorous insults, can be found in every society ever documented.

Natural selection tends to homogenize a species into a standard design by concentrating the effective genes and winnowing out the ineffective ones. This suggests that the human mind evolved with a universal complex design. Beginning in the 1950s, linguist Noam Chomsky of the Massachusetts Institute of Technology argued that a language should be analyzed not in terms of the list of sentences people utter but in terms of the mental computations that enable them to handle an unlimited number of new sentences in the language. These computations have been found to conform to a universal grammar. And if this universal grammar is embodied in the circuitry that guides babies when they listen to speech, it could explain how children learn language so easily.

Similarly, some anthropologists have returned to an ethnographic record that used to trumpet differences among cultures and have found an astonishingly detailed set of aptitudes and tastes that all cultures have in common. This shared way of thinking, feeling, and living makes all of humanity look like a single tribe, which the anthropologist Donald Brown of the University of California at Santa Barbara has called the universal people. Hundreds of traits, from romantic love to humorous insults, from poetry to food taboos, from exchange of goods to mourning the dead, can be found in every society ever documented.

One example of a stubborn universal is the tangle of emotions surrounding the act of love. In all societies, sex is at least somewhat "dirty." It is conducted in private, pondered obsessively, regulated by custom and taboo, the subject of gossip and teasing, and a trigger for jealous rage. Yet sex is the most concentrated source of physical pleasure granted by the nervous system. Why is it so fraught with conflict? For a brief period in the 1960s and 1970s, people dreamed of an erotopia in which men and women could engage in sex without hang-ups and inhibitions. "If you can't be with the one you love, love the one you're with," sang Stephen Stills. "If you love somebody, set them free," sang Sting.

But Sting also sang, "Every move you make, I'll be watching you." Even in a time when, seemingly, anything goes, most people do not partake in sex as casually as they partake in food or conversation. The reasons are as deep as anything in biology.

One of the hazards of sex is a baby, and a baby is not just any seven-pound object but, from an evolutionary point of view, our reason for being. Every time a woman has sex with a man, she is taking a chance at sentencing herself to years of motherhood, and she is forgoing the opportunity to use her finite reproductive output with some other man. The man, for his part, may be either implicitly committing his sweat and toil to the incipient child or deceiving his partner about such intentions.

On rational grounds, the volatility of sex is a puzzle, because in an era with reliable contraception, these archaic entanglements should have no claim on our feelings. We should be loving the one we're with, and sex should inspire no more gossip, music, fiction, raunchy humor, or strong emotions than eating or talking does. The fact that people are tormented by the Darwinian economics of babies they are no longer having is testimony to the long reach of human nature.

Although the minds of normal human beings work in pretty much the same way, they are not, of course, identical. Natural selection reduces genetic variability but never eliminates it. As a result, nearly every one of us is genetically unique. And these differences in genes make a difference in mind and behavior, at least quantitatively. The most dramatic demonstrations come from studies of the rare people who *are* genetically identical, identical twins.

Identical twins think and feel in such similar ways that they sometimes suspect they are linked by telepathy. They are similar in verbal and mathematical intelligence, in their degree of life satisfaction, and in personality traits such as introversion, agreeableness, neuroticism, conscientiousness, and openness to experience. They have similar attitudes toward controversial issues such as the death penalty, religion, and modern music. They resemble each other not just in paper-and-pencil tests but in consequential behavior such as gambling, divorcing, committing crimes, getting into accidents, and watching television. And they boast dozens of shared idiosyncrasies such as giggling incessantly, giving interminable answers to simple questions, dipping buttered toast in coffee, and, in the case of Abigail van Buren and the late Ann Landers, writing indistinguishable syndicated advice columns. The crags and valleys of their electroencephalograms (brain waves) are as alike as those of a single person recorded on two occasions, and the wrinkles of their brains and the distribution of gray matter across cortical areas are similar as well.

Identical twins (who share all their genes) are far more similar than fraternal twins (who share just half their genes). This is as true when the twins are separated at birth and raised apart as when they are raised in the same home by the same parents. Moreover, biological siblings, who also share half their genes, are far more similar than adoptive siblings, who share no more genes than strangers. Indeed, adoptive siblings are barely similar at all. These conclusions come from massive studies employing the best instruments known to psychology. Alternative explanations that try to push the effects of the genes to zero have by now been tested and rejected.

People sometimes fear that if the genes affect the mind at all they must determine it in every detail. That is wrong, for two reasons. The first is that most effects of genes are probabilistic. If one identical twin has a trait, there is often no more than an even chance that the other twin will have it, despite having a complete genome in common (and in the case of twins raised together, most of their environment in common as well).

The second reason is that the genes' effects can vary with the environment. Although Woody Allen's fame may depend on genes that enhance a sense of humor, he once pointed out that "we live in a society that puts a big value on jokes. If I had been an Apache Indian, those guys didn't need comedians, so I'd be out of work."

Studies of the brain also show that the mind is not a blank slate. The brain, of course, has a pervasive ability to change the strengths of its connections as the result of learning and experience—if it didn't, we would all be permanent amnesiacs. But that does not mean that the structure of the brain is mostly a product of experience. The study of the brains of twins has shown that much of the variation in the amount of gray matter in the prefrontal lobes is genetically caused. And these variations are not just random differences in anatomy like fingerprints; they correlate significantly with differences in intelligence.

People born with variations in the typical brain plan can vary in the way their minds work. A study of Einstein's brain showed that he had large, unusually shaped inferior parietal lobules, which participate in spatial reasoning and intuitions about numbers. Gay men are likely to have a relatively small nucleus in the anterior hypothalamus, a nucleus known to have a role in sex differences. Convicted murderers and other violent, antisocial people are likely to have a relatively small and inactive prefrontal cortex, the part of the brain that governs decision making and inhibits impulses. These gross features of the brain are almost certainly not sculpted by information coming in from the senses. That, in turn, implies that differences in intelligence, scientific genius, sexual orientation, and impulsive violence are not entirely learned.

The doctrine of the blank slate had been thought to undergird the ideals of equal rights and social improvement, so it is no surprise that the discoveries undermining it have often been met with fear and loathing. Scientists challenging the doctrine have been libeled, picketed, shouted down, and subjected to searing invective.

This is not the first time in history that people have tried to ground moral principles in dubious factual assumptions. People used to ground moral values in the doctrine that Earth lay at the center of the universe, and that God created mankind in his own image in a day. In both cases, informed people eventually reconciled their moral values with the facts, not just because they had to give a nod to reality, but also because the supposed connections between the facts and morals—such as the belief that the arrangement of rock and gas in space has something to do with right and wrong—were spurious to begin with.

We are now living, I think, through a similar transition. The blank slate has been widely embraced as a rationale for morality, but it is under assault from science. Yet just as the supposed foundations of morality shifted in the centuries following Galileo and Darwin, our own moral sensibilities will come to terms with the scientific findings, not just because facts are facts but because the moral credentials of the blank slate are just as spurious. Once you think through the issues, the two greatest fears of an innate human endowment can be defused.

One is the fear of inequality. Blank is blank, so if we are all blank slates, the reasoning goes, we must all be equal. But if the slate of a newborn is not blank, different babies could have different things inscribed on their slates. Individuals, sexes, classes, and races might differ innately in their talents and inclinations. The fear is that if people do turn out to be different, it would open the door to discrimination, oppression, or eugenics.

But none of this follows. For one thing, in many cases the empirical basis of the fear may be misplaced. A universal human nature does not imply that *differences* among groups are innate. Confucius could have been right when he wrote, "Men's natures are alike; it is their habits that carry them far apart."

Regardless of IQ or physical strength, all human beings can be assumed to have certain traits in common.

More important, the case against bigotry is not a factual claim that people are biologically indistinguishable. It is a moral stance that condemns judging an *individual* according to the average traits of certain *groups* to which the individual belongs. Enlightened societies strive to ignore race, sex, and ethnicity in hiring, admissions, and criminal justice because the alternative is morally repugnant. Discriminating against people on the basis of race, sex, or ethnicity would be unfair, penalizing them for traits over which they have no control. It would perpetuate the injustices of the past and could rend society into hostile factions. None of these reasons depends on whether groups of people are or are not genetically indistinguishable.

Far from being conducive to discrimination, a conception of human nature is the reason we oppose it. Regardless of IQ or physical strength or any other trait that might vary among people, all human beings can be assumed to have certain traits in common. No one likes being enslaved. No one likes being humiliated. No one likes being treated unfairly. The revulsion we feel toward discrimination and slavery comes from a conviction that however much people vary on some traits, they do not vary on these.

Parents often discover that their children are immune to their rewards, punishments, and nagging. Over the long run, a child's personality and intellect are largely determined by genes, peer groups, and chance.

A second fear of human nature comes from a reluctance to give up the age-old dream of the perfectibility of man. If we are forever saddled with fatal flaws and deadly sins, according to this fear, social reform would be a waste of time. Why try to make the world a better place if people are rotten to the core and will just foul it up no matter what you do?

But this, too, does not follow. If the mind is a complex system with many faculties, an antisocial desire is just one component among others. Some faculties may endow us with greed or lust or malice, but others may endow us with sympathy, foresight, self-respect, a desire for respect from others, and an ability to learn from experience and history. Social progress can come from pitting some of these faculties against others.

For example, suppose we are endowed with a conscience that treats certain other beings as targets of sympathy and inhibits us from harming or exploiting them. The philosopher Peter Singer of Princeton University has shown that moral improvement has proceeded for millennia because people have expanded the mental dotted line that embraces the entities considered worthy of sympathy. The circle has been poked outward from the family and village to the clan, the tribe, the nation, the race, and most recently to all of humanity. This sweeping change in sensibilities did not require a blank slate. It could have arisen from a moral gadget with a single knob or slider that adjusts the size of the circle embracing the entities whose interests we treat as comparable to our own.

Some people worry that these arguments are too fancy for the dangerous world we live in. Since data in the social sciences are never perfect, shouldn't we err on the side of caution and stick with the null hypothesis that people are blank slates? Some people think that even if we were certain that people differed genetically, or harbored ignoble tendencies, we might still want to promulgate the fiction that they didn't.

This argument is based on the fallacy that the blank slate has nothing but good moral implications and a theory that admits a human nature has nothing but bad ones. In fact, the dangers go both ways. Take the most horrifying example of all, the abuse of biology by the Nazis, with its pseudoscientific nonsense about superior and inferior races. Historians agree that bitter memories of the Holocaust were the main reason that human nature became taboo in intellectual life after the Second World War.

But historians have also documented that Nazism was not the only ideologically inspired holocaust of the 20th century.

Many atrocities were committed by Marxist regimes in the name of egalitarianism, targeting people whose success was taken as evidence of their avarice. The kulaks ("bourgeois peasants") were exterminated by Lenin and Stalin in the Soviet Union. Teachers, former landlords, and "rich peasants" were humiliated, tortured, and murdered during China's Cultural Revolution. City dwellers and literate professionals were worked to death or executed during the reign of the Khmer Rouge in Cambodia.

And here is a remarkable fact: Although both Nazi and Marxist ideologies led to industrial-scale killing, *their biological and psychological theories were opposites*. Marxists had no use for the concept of race, were averse to the notion of genetic inheritance, and were hostile to the very idea of a human nature rooted in biology. Marx did not explicitly embrace the blank slate, but he was adamant that human nature has no enduring properties: "All history is nothing but a continuous transformation of human nature," he wrote. Many of his followers did embrace it. "It is on a blank page that the most beautiful poems are written," said Mao. "Only the newborn baby is spotless," ran a Khmer Rouge slogan. This philosophy led to persecution of the successful and of those who produced more crops on their private family plots than on communal farms. And it made these regimes not just dictatorships but totalitarian dictatorships, which tried to control every aspect of life, from art and education to child rearing and sex. After all, if the mind is structureless at birth and shaped by its experience, a society that wants the right kind of minds must control the experience.

None of this is meant to impugn the blank slate as an evil doctrine, any more than a belief in human nature is an evil doctrine. Both are separated by many steps from the evil acts committed under their banners, and they must be evaluated on factual grounds. But the fact that tyranny and genocide can come from an anti-innatist belief system as readily as from an innatist one does upend the common misconception that biological approaches to behavior are uniquely sinister. And the reminder that human nature is the source of our interests and needs as well as our flaws encourages us to examine claims about the mind objectively, without putting a moral thumb on either side of the scale.

From the book *The Blank Slate* by Steven Pinker. Copyright © Steven Pinker, 2002. Printed by arrangement with Viking Penguin, a member of Penguin Putman Inc. Published in September 2002.

From *Discover* magazine, October 2002, pp. 34–40. © 2002 by Steven Pinker. Reprinted by permission of the author.

The Power of NO

It's an unanticipated legacy of the affluent '90s: parents who can't, or won't, set limits. Now a growing number of psychologists are warning of the dangers of overindulgence and teaching how—and where—to draw the line.

PEG TYRE, JULIE SCELFO AND BARBARA KANTROWITZ

Eloise Goldman struggled to hold the line. She knew it was ridiculous to spend $250 on a mini iPod for her 9-year-old son Ben. The price tag wasn't the biggest issue for Goldman, a publicist, and her fund-raiser husband, Jon. It was the idea of buying such an extravagant gadget for a kid who still hasn't mastered long division. If she gave in, how would Ben ever learn that you can't always get what you want? Goldman knew there was a good chance the iPod would soon be lost or abandoned, just like Ben's toy-of-choice from last year, a bright blue drum set that now sits forlornly in the basement of their suburban New York home. But Ben nagged and pestered and insisted that "everyone has one." Goldman began to weaken. Ben's a good kid, she reasoned; she wanted him to have what the other kids had. After doing a neighborhood-mom check and finding that Ben's peers were indeed wired for sound, Goldman caved—but not without one last attempt to salvage some lesson about limits. She offered her son a deal. We give you an iPod, you forfeit your birthday party. "Done," he said. Then, without missing a beat: "Now what about getting me my own Apple G4?"

It's an unexpected legacy of the affluent '90s: parents who can't say no. With school starting, the annual assault on the family budget to fill backpacks with all the cool stuff that "everyone" else has is just beginning. This generation of parents has always been driven to give their kids every advantage, from Mommy & Me swim classes all the way to that thick envelope from an elite college. But despite their good intentions, too many find themselves raising "wanting machines" who respond like Pavlovian dogs to the marketing behemoth that's aimed right at them. Even getting what they want doesn't satisfy some kids—they only want more. Now, a growing number of psychologists, educators and parents think it's time to stop the madness

---

CASE STUDY
Fairview H.S.,
BOULDER, COLO.

Even before they graduated from high school in May, these 18-year-olds drove cars that many adults can only dream of owning. Area parents, concerned that kids are getting too much too soon, created a support network to set standards. Now they're improving their parenting skills by learning new techniques for communicating with one another.

53% of kids say buying certain products makes them feel better about themselves

---

and start teaching kids about what's really important—values like hard work, delayed gratification, honesty and compassion. In a few communities, parents have begun to take action by banding together to enforce limits and rules so that no one has to feel guilty for denying her 6-year-old a $300 Nokia cell phone with all the latest bells and whistles. "It's almost like parents have lost their parenting skills," says Marsha Moritz, 54, who helped found the Parent Engagement Network, a support group in Boulder, Colo. "They want to be their kids' best friend and make sure they're having fun, but what the kids really need is for parents to be parents."

While it's certainly true that affluent parents can raise happy and well-adjusted children, the struggle to set limits has never been tougher. Saying no is harder when you can afford to say yes. But the stakes have also never been higher. Recent studies of adults who were overindulged as children paint a discouraging picture of their future. Kids who've

CASE STUDY
The Villaverdes,

CORAL GABLES, FLA.

After emigrating from Cuba as a child, Raul Villaverde, 43, now takes pride in providing for his family. "We try to give them everything they want," he says for Lauren 12, this includes a pink bedroom stocked with a TV, DVD player, laptop and several boom boxes. Chandler 14, also has his own TV and DVD player, as well as several Play Stations. In exchange, though, the kids are required to do chores. Grandma thinks they should do even more to help out at home. Says mom Toni: "They've got a good work ethic."

75% of parents say their kids do fewer chores than children did 10 or 15 years ago

been given too much too soon grow up to be adults who have difficulty coping with life's disappointments. They have a distorted sense of entitlement that gets in the way of success both in the workplace and in relationships. Psychologists say parents who overindulge their kids may actually be setting them up to be more vulnerable to future anxiety and depression. "The risk of overindulgence is self-centeredness and self-absorption, and that's a mental-health risk," says William Damon, director of the Stanford University Center on Adolescence. "You sit around feeling anxious all the time instead of figuring out what you can do to make a difference in the world."

Today's parents—who themselves were raised on Greatest Generation values of thrift and self-sacrifice—grew up in a culture where "no" was a household word. Goldman remembers that as a teenager, she had to beg for a phone in her room. In a world where families spend "quality time" at the mall instead of in the backyard, her request seems almost quaint. Today's kids want much more, partly because there's so much more to want. The oldest members of this Generation Excess were born in the late 1980s, just as PCs and videogames were making their assault on the family room. They think of MP3 players and flat-screen TVs as essential utilities and they've developed strategies to get them. One survey of grade-school children found that when they crave something new, most expect to ask nine times before their parents give in. By every measure, parents are shelling out record amounts. According to market researchers Packaged Facts, families with 3- to 12-year-olds spend $53.8 billion annually on entertainment, personal-care items and reading materials for their children. This is $17.6 billion more than parents spent in 1997. Teens are spending huge amounts of money themselves, some of it cadged from their families and the rest from after-school jobs. Last year 12- to 19-year-olds spent roughly

$175 billion, $53 billion more than in 1997, according to Teen Research Unlimited.

In the heat of this buying blitz, even parents who desperately need to say no find themselves reaching for their credit cards. Kechia Williams is a 32-year-old single mother of five who works as a custodian at Emory University in Atlanta. She rises at 4 a.m. to get to work at 6 in order to make $9 an hour. She has to work overtime to pay for basics like new school clothes and supplies. And yet, her children do demand and often get costly gifts. The oldest boys, Darryl, 15, and Kwentavius, 12, have a PlayStation 2 and several games that cost $60 apiece that they play on a big-screen TV. "They're always begging for brand names—FUBU, Polo, Tommy, Gucci, Nike—especially the ones the rappers are talking about," says Williams. "I constantly have to remind them my paycheck will go only so far," she says. "But that doesn't stop them from wanting it. The stuff is all over the TV, and the videos, then some of the other kids have it." Williams knows how they feel; she had very little growing up. "I can see it in their eyes sometimes, how bad they want something, and I want to get it for them."

Darryl and Kwentavius are responding to a tidal wave of marketing aimed at kids. According to the American Academy of Pediatrics, the average American child sees more than 40,000 commercials a year. That's in addition to fast-food outlets in schools, product placements in TV shows and movies, even corporate sponsorship of sports stadiums. "There's virtually no escape from it," says Susan Linn, a Harvard psychologist and the author of "Consuming Kids: The Hostile Takeover of Childhood." "The marketers call it 'cradle-to-grave brand loyalty.' They want to get kids from the moment they're born."

And this generation of parents is uniquely ill equipped to counter the relentless pressure. Baby boomers, raised in the contentious 1960s and '70s (the era of the "generation gap"), swore they would do things differently and have a much closer relationship with their own children. Many even wear the same Gap clothes as their kids and listen to the same music. "So whenever their children get angry at them, it makes this generation feel a lot guiltier than previous generations," says Laurence Steinberg, a psychologist at Temple University and the author of "The 10 Basic Principles of Good Parenting." Today's parents put in more hours on the job, too; at the end of a long workweek, it's tempting to buy peace with "yes," rather than mar precious family time with conflict. Anxiety about the future is a factor as well. How do well-intentioned parents say no to all the sports equipment and arts and language lessons they believe will help their kids thrive in an increasingly competitive world? But these parents are confusing permissiveness with love. Experts agree: too much love won't spoil a child, but too few limits will.

In their zeal to make their kids happy, parents fail to impart the very values they say they want to teach. Jenn Andrlick, a

CASE STUDY
The Bourgoignies,

Seeking a simpler life, Georges and Denise Bourgoignie sold their suburban home and moved to rural Florida. But for a time their teenage girls, Chelsea, 17 and Gaia, 15, opted to stay with Grandma in order to be closer to school, their friends and their favorite malls. The girls are wild for pricey handbags from Vuitton, Dior, Kate Spade and Gucci. But Mom worries that over-indulgence has made them careless. "They have a total disregard for the things because they don't have to work for it."

73% of parents say today's kids are too focused on buying and consuming things

23-year-old editorial assistant in New York, describes herself as a recovering "spoiled brat." As a child in Omaha, she says, she regularly manipulated her hardworking parents into fulfilling her every whim—special toys, dance lessons, fashionable clothes and a car. "I told them if they loved me, they'd get it for me," she recalls. Now, as a young adult perched precariously on the first rung of her career ladder, she's finding it impossible to live within her means and still relies on handouts from Mom and Dad. Once she was the envy of all her friends because "I always had more than anyone." But these days, she says, she envies her roommates who know how to stick to a budget. And her mother, Debbie Love, keeps asking herself if it might finally be time to "cut her off."

No one is suggesting Scrooge as a parental role model. What parents need to find, psychologists say, is a balance between the advantages of an affluent society and the critical life lessons that come from waiting, saving and working hard to achieve goals. That search for balance has to start early. Eve and Jay Gagné, both 30, were both brought up by single moms in New Hampshire, so they know what it's like to go without. Now that Eve, an at-home mother, and Jay, a computer executive, have income for luxuries that their parents didn't, they love to treat their daughter, Sydney, 3, to clothes and toys. But Eve says they're trying hard to be reasonable and not spend too much money on perfect party dresses. "She's going to get dirty," Eve says, "and she'll grow out of it and it ends up costing a fortune ... When it comes down to it, nobody really notices the outfit. They notice her behavior." Recently, the Gagnes let Sydney play with a giant stuffed rocking horse at a toy store. Sydney wanted to ride it home, but the Gagnes said no. They could easily afford it, Eve said, "but we didn't want to give in to every whim." Sydney had a meltdown and her parents held firm. "We would like to run the show," says Eve.

Psychologists like Temple University's Steinberg say that's exactly what they should be doing. "Children need limits on their behavior because they feel better and more secure when they live within a certain structure." Parents should not make the mistake of projecting their own needs or feelings on their children. "As adults, we don't like it when other people tell us what we can and can't do," he says. "To children, it doesn't feel that way." Children learn self-control by watching how other people behave, especially their parents.

Learning how to overcome challenges is essential to becoming a successful adult. Whether it's having to earn money to buy Stila cosmetics in this season's palette or adding more hours in the library to pull up a grade, kids need to have parents who are on the sideline cheering them on but not caving in. Raul and Toni Villaverde, who live in a suburb outside Miami, say they've tried to walk the line between giving their children what they want and providing them with a strong enough work ethic so that they will become self-reliant. With an older sister at Brown University, 10th grader Chandler Villaverde has set his sights on MIT. Toni has made it clear she expects him to keep his grades up. So far he's gotten mostly A's and B's. "I got one C one time," says Chandler. His mom's very palpable disappointment was enough to get him back on track: "I never got a C again." Toni sometimes gave Chandler a hand with school projects in middle school. Not anymore. "Most things I try to do on my own," he says. The Villaverdes also insist their kids do chores. Chandler takes care of the garbage and dishes, while his sister Lauren, 12, gets the mail, makes coffee and is learning to do the laundry.

Kids who get too much too soon often have trouble coping with the inevitable ups and downs of life

Families like the Villaverdes are in the minority. Few parents ask kids to do anything around the house because they think their kids are already overwhelmed by social and academic pressures; adding lawn mowing or laundry almost seems cruel. And who wants to nag a 12-year-old (for the fifth time) about taking out the garbage? "When parents have so little time with their kids," says Irene Goldenberg, a family therapist and professor emeritus at UCLA, "they don't want it to be filled with conflict." But kids who have no responsibilities never learn one of life's most basic lessons: that every individual can be of service to others and that life has meaning beyond one's own immediate happiness.

That means parents who want to teach values have to take a long, hard look at their own. "It's going to be a tough sell to your kids if you're not walking the walk," says Thomas Lickona, a development psychologist at the State University of New York at Cortland. "It starts with parents' leading a life that centers on higher values so you have credibility when you try to teach that standard."

Across the country, many parents and educators are reaching out for guidance on how to say no. The American Society of Professional Education, a continuing-education

17 Variations on a Theme

In theory, setting limits with your children should be easy. In practice, though, when they beg and whine, it can be very tough. Minnesota parenting expert Jean Illsley Clarke came up with this handy crib sheet. Read it aloud. Then repeat.

1. No.
2. No, for sure.
3. No, and that's final.
4. No! Do not ask me again.
5. I have thought about it and the answer is no.
6. We don't have money for that right now.
7. You already have enough of those.
8. I don't approve of it.
9. Nice try.
10. I already know you know how to nag.
11. Go find something else to do.
12. I'm starting to get really angry with you.
13. Your whining makes me think you already have too many toys.
14. I remember saying no.
15. Who is the grown-up here?
16. I'm not going to change my mind about this.
17. It's your money, but I'm in charge.

CASE STUDY
The Williamses,

ATLANTA, GA.

Despite the financial strain of raising five kids on a custodian's salary, mom Kechia struggles to get her brood the same toys as everyone else. High on the wish list? A Barbie Jeep, FUBU clothes, top-of-the line Nike sneakers and an electric scooter that retails for about $300. They're good kids who keep their grades up, she says. And while they understand that "sometimes Mama just can't afford it," they still want the stuff they see on TV.

30% of parents say that brand preference is of 'major importance' when buying for kids

sues so everyone sticks to the same rules, and to find other families who share their values: "Create your own village."

That's exactly what some parents in Boulder, Colo., are trying to do. The scenic college town on the border of the Rockies has long been home to progressive families who eschew cars in favor of bike rides to the local organic grocery. But over the past decade, an influx of wealthy families brought an infusion of SUVs and Starbucks. Boulder parents were alarmed by a rise in teenage alcohol and drug abuse. Christine Denning, a local psychotherapist who specializes in adolescent and parent issues, treated one 17-year-old patient who always insisted on getting her own way. "She felt everything would be fine if everybody moved out of the house and she could have it" all to herself, says Denning. "That's her fantasy."

Lamenting that their kids were out of control, a group of parents and educators last year formed the Parent Engagement Network, which now offers monthly workshops that cover such topics as parenting skills, morality and ethics for children, and understanding the impact of media on kids. The group also distributes a pamphlet (from Assets for Colorado Youth) listing ways parents can show they care without buying things: notice them, tell them how thoughtful a certain action is, acknowledge their insights in a conversation, show excitement in their discoveries, listen to their stories.

But change doesn't come easily. The senior parking lot at Boulder's Fairview High School remains overrun with luxury cars, and many members of the most recent graduating class spent their spring break in Puerto Vallarta. Parents still feel they have a lot to learn about how to work with their neighbors to enforce the same values. At one network meeting, a woman raised her hand and requested that the speakers role-play what she should say if she called another parent to check on her kids. "I thought it was a joke," says Fran Raudenbush, a school administrator and a founder of the group. "But it wasn't. Parents are starving for information."

Psychologists say even the simplest steps can yield tremendous benefits. When Mary Pipher's son, Zeke, now 34, was a

firm based in North Carolina, last year launched a seminar for mental-health professionals (which includes psychologists, social workers, family therapists and school counselors) to learn about dealing with overindulged children and their "enabling parents." Demand was so great that the $169 daylong seminar was repeated more than 350 times in the last year. "We've been to every state except Montana," says spokesman Conrad Stuntz. But not because parents there are any different. "We just couldn't work it into our schedule," he says. In one session, the seminar explains the "distorted thoughts" of overindulgent parents, including the self-imposed pressure they feel to constantly keep their kids happy. In another, attendees learn how to convert overindulgent parents into "mentoring" parents.

In Eden Prairie, Minn., a group of concerned mothers recently invited Jean Illsley Clarke—a parent educator and author of "How Much Is Enough?"—to come help them deal with what one said was "the problem we're having with our neighbors." They all complained that it was other parents who eroded their hard-fought efforts to set appropriate limits for their kids. Sitting in the meeting room of the Assembly of God Church, 20 moms expressed their genuine frustration. "How do we keep grandparents from buying and buying and buying?" "How many birthday gifts should my kid get?" "How many Game Boys are enough?" Clarke urged the mothers to band together. "Parents have trouble knowing what is enough," she told them. Even children can understand that treats are reserved for special occasions: "Thanksgiving is really great, but if we had it every week, wouldn't it be awful?" She encourages parents and grandparents to discuss these is-

teenager, he had nothing in common with his psychologist mother, author of "Reviving Ophelia." She is bookish, an introvert who likes to spend time in the garden. He was a jock and a partier who stayed out too late and bugged her constantly for more spending money. Finally, she instituted a free zone: once a week, the pair would go out to breakfast with no haranguing or begging for money. Sometimes, the two would have deep conversations and sometimes they would say barely anything at all. But it was a big relief, says Pipher. "Going shopping together is not much better quality time than no time at all. That free zone is what parents want." And it's what kids want, too—even if they won't admit it.

Parents Behaving Badly

Inside the new classroom power struggle: what teachers say about pushy moms and dads who drive them crazy

NANCY GIBBS

If you could walk past the teachers' lounge and listen in, what sorts of stories would you hear?

An Iowa high school counselor gets a call from a parent protesting the C her child received on an assignment. "The parent argued every point in the essay," recalls the counselor, who soon realized why the mother was so upset about the grade. "It became apparent that she'd written it."

A sixth-grade teacher in California tells a girl in her class that she needs to work on her reading at home, not just in school. "Her mom came in the next day," the teacher says, "and started yelling at me that I had emotionally upset her child."

A science teacher in Baltimore, Md., was offering lessons in anatomy when one of the boys in class declared, "There's one less rib in a man than in a woman." The teacher pulled out two skeletons—one male, the other female—and asked the student to count the ribs in each. "The next day," the teacher recalls, "the boy claimed he told his priest what happened and his priest said I was a heretic."

A teacher at a Tennessee elementary school slips on her kid gloves each morning as she contends with parents who insist, in writing, that their children are never to be reprimanded or even corrected. When she started teaching 31 years ago, she says, "I could make objective observations about my kids without parents getting offended. But now we handle parents a lot more delicately. We handle children a lot more delicately. They feel good about themselves for no reason. We've given them this cotton-candy sense of self with no basis in reality. We don't emphasize what's best for the greater good of society or even the classroom."

When our children are born, we study their every eyelash and marvel at the perfection of their toes, and in no time become experts in all that they do. But then the day comes when we are expected to hand them over to a stranger standing at the head of a room full of bright colors and small chairs. Well aware of the difference a great teacher can make—and the damage a bad teacher can do—parents turn over their kids and hope. Please handle with care. Please don't let my children get lost. They're breakable. And precious. Oh, but push them hard and don't let up, and make sure they get into Harvard.

But if parents are searching for the perfect teacher, teachers are looking for the ideal parent, a partner but not a pest, engaged but not obsessed, with a sense of perspective and patience. And somehow just at the moment when the experts all say the parent-teacher alliance is more important than ever, it is also becoming harder to manage. At a time when competition is rising and resources are strained, when battles over testing and accountability force schools to adjust their priorities, when cell phones and e-mail speed up the information flow and all kinds of private ghosts and public quarrels creep into the parent-teacher conference, it's harder for both sides to step back and breathe deeply and look at the goals they share.

> ## "The parent doesn't know what you're giving and accepts what the child says. Parents are trusting children before they trust us. They have lost faith in teachers."

Ask teachers about the best part of their job, and most will say how much they love working with kids. Ask them about the most demanding part, and they will say dealing with parents. In fact, a new study finds that of all the challenges they face, new teachers rank handling parents at the top. According to preliminary results from the MetLife Survey of the American Teacher, made available exclusively to TIME, parent management was a bigger struggle than finding enough funding or maintaining discipline or enduring the toils of testing. It's one reason, say the Consortium for Policy Research in Education and the Center for the Study of Teaching and Policy, that 40% to 50% of new teachers leave the profession within five years. Even master teachers who love their work, says Harvard education professor Sara Lawrence-Lightfoot, call this "the most treacherous part of their jobs."

"Everyone says the parent-teacher conference should be pleasant, civilized, a kind of dialogue where parents and teachers build alliances," Lawrence-Lightfoot observes. "But what most teachers feel, and certainly what all parents feel, is anxiety, panic and vulnerability." While teachers worry most about the parents they never see, the ones who show up faithfully pose a whole different set of challenges. Leaving aside the monster parents who seem to have been born to torment the teacher, even "good" parents can have bad days when their virtues exceed their boundaries: the eager parent who pushes too hard, the protective parent who defends the cheater, the homework helper who takes over, the tireless advocate who loses sight of the fact that there are other kids in the class too. "I could summarize in one sentence what teachers hate about parents," says the head of a private school. "We hate it when parents undermine the education and growth of their children. That's it, plain and simple." A taxonomy of parents behaving badly:

"You get so angry that you don't care what the school's perspective is. This is my child. And you did something that negatively impacted my child. I don't want to hear that you have 300 kids."

The Hovering Parent

It was a beautiful late morning last May when Richard Hawley, headmaster at University School in Cleveland, Ohio, saw the flock of mothers entering the building, eager and beaming. "I ask what brings them to our halls," he recalls. "They tell me that this is the last day the seniors will be eating lunch together at school and they have come to watch. To watch their boys eat lunch? I ask. Yes, they tell me emphatically. At that moment, a group of lounging seniors spot their mothers coming their way. One of them approaches his mother, his hands forming an approximation of a crucifix. 'No,' he says firmly to his mother. 'You can't do this. You've got to go home.' As his mother draws near, he hisses in embarrassment, 'Mother, you have no life!' His mother's smile broadens. 'You are my life, dear.'"

Parents are passionate, protective creatures when it comes to their children, as nature designed them to be. Teachers strive to be dispassionate, objective professionals, as their training requires them to be. Throw in all the suspicions born of class and race and personal experience, a culture that praises teachers freely but pays them poorly, a generation taught to question authority and a political climate that argues for holding schools ever more accountable for how kids perform, and it is a miracle that parents and teachers get along as well as they do. "There's more parent involvement that's good—and bad," notes Kirk Daddow, a 38-year veteran who teaches Advanced Placement history in Ames, Iowa. "The good kind is the 'Make yourself known to the teacher; ask what you could do.' The bad kind is the 'Wait until something happens, then complain about it and try to get a grade changed.'" Overall, he figures, "we're seeing more of the bad."

Long gone are the days when the school was a fortress, opened a couple of times a year for parents' night and gradua-

tion but generally off limits to parents unless their kids got into trouble. Now you can't walk into schools, public or private, without tripping over parents in the halls. They volunteer as library aides and reading coaches and Mentor Moms, supplement the physical-education offerings with yoga and kickboxing, sponsor faculty-appreciation lunches and fund-raising barbecues, supervise field trips and road games and father-daughter service projects. Even the heads of boarding schools report that some parents are moving to live closer to their child's school so that they can be on hand and go to all the games. As budgets shrink and educational demands grow, that extra army of helpers can be a godsend to strapped schools.

In a survey, 90% of new teachers agreed that involving parents in their children's education is a priority at their school, but only 25% described their experience working with parents as "very satisfying." When asked to choose the biggest challenge they face, 31% of them cited involving parents and communicating with them as their top choice. 73% of new teachers said too many parents treat schools and teachers as adversaries.

But parents, it turns out, have a learning curve of their own. Parents who are a welcome presence in elementary school as library helpers need to learn a different role for junior high and another for high school as their children's needs evolve. Teachers talk about "helicopter parents," who hover over the school at all times, waiting to drop in at the least sign of trouble. Given these unsettled times, if parents feel less in control of their own lives, they try to control what they can, which means everything from swooping down at the first bad grade to demanding a good 12 inches of squishy rubber under the jungle gym so that anyone who falls will bounce right back. "The parents are not the bad guys," says Nancy McGill, a teacher in Johnston, Iowa, who learned a lot about handling parents from being one herself. "They're mama grizzly bears. They're going to defend that cub no matter what, and they don't always think rationally. If I can remember that, it defuses the situation. It's not about me. It's not about attacking our system. It's about a parent trying to do the best for their child. That helps keep the personal junk out of the way. I don't get so emotional."

While it's in the nature of parents to want to smooth out the bumps in the road, it's in the nature of teachers to toss in a few more: sometimes kids have to fail in order to learn. As children get older, the parents may need to pull back. "I believe that the umbilical cord needs to be severed when children are at school," argues Eric Paul, a fourth- and fifth-grade teacher at Roosevelt Elementary School in Santa Monica, Calif. He goes to weekend ball games and piano recitals in an effort to bond with families but also tries to show parents that there is a line that shouldn't be crossed. "Kids need to operate on their own at school, advocate on their own and learn from each other. So in my class, parents' involvement is limited," he says.

High schools, meanwhile, find themselves fending off parents who expect instant responses to every e-mail; who request a change of teacher because of "poor chemistry" when the real issue is that the child is getting a poor grade; who seek out a doctor who will proclaim their child "exceptionally bright but with a learning difference" that requires extra time for testing; who insist that their child take five Advanced Placement classes, play three varsity sports, perform in the school orchestra and be in student government—and then complain that kids are stressed out because the school doesn't do enough to prevent scheduling conflicts. Teachers just shake their heads as they see parents so obsessed with getting their child into a good college that they don't ask whether it's the right one for the child's particular interests and needs.

> **"They'll misbehave in front of you. You see very little of that 'I don't want to get in trouble' attitude because they know Mom or Dad will come to their defense."**

And what if kids grow so accustomed to these interventions that they miss out on lessons in self-reliance? Mara Sapon-Shevin, an education professor at Syracuse University, has had college students tell her they were late for class because their mothers didn't call to wake them up that morning. She has had students call their parents from the classroom on a cell phone to complain about a low grade and then pass the phone over to her, in the middle of class, because the parent wanted to intervene. And she has had parents say they are paying a lot of money for their child's education and imply that anything but an A is an unacceptable return on their investment.

These parents are not serving their children well, Sapon-Shevin argues. "You want them to learn lessons that are powerful but benign. Your kid gets drunk, they throw up, feel like crap—that's a good lesson. They don't study for an exam, fail it and learn that next time they should study. Or not return the library book and have to pay the fine. But when you have a kid leave their bike out, it gets run over and rusty, and you say, 'O.K., honey, we'll buy you a new one,' they never learn to put their bike away."

The Aggressive Advocate

Marguerite Damata, a mother of two in Silver Spring, Md., wonders whether she is too involved in her 10-year-old son's school life. "Because he's not in the gifted and talented group, he's almost nowhere," she says. "If I stopped paying attention, where would he be?" Every week she spends two hours sitting in his math class, making sure she knows the assignments and the right vocabulary so that she can help him at home. And despite all she sees and all she does, she says, "I feel powerless there."

Parents understandably argue that there is a good reason to keep a close watch if their child is one of 500 kids in a grade level. Teachers freely admit it's impossible to create individual

teaching programs for 30 children in a class. "There aren't enough minutes in the day," says Tom Loveless, who taught in California for nine years and is now director of the Brown Center on Education Policy at the Brookings Institution. "You have to have kids tackling subject matter together as a group. That's a shoe that will pinch for someone." Since the passage of the No Child Left Behind Act, which requires schools to show progress in reading and math test scores in Grades 3 through 8 across all racial and demographic groups, parents are worried that teachers will naturally focus on getting as many students as possible over the base line and not have as much time to spur the strongest kids or save the weakest. Some educators argue that you can agree on the goals of accountability and achievement, but given the inequalities in the system, not all schools have the means to achieve them. "A really cynical person who didn't want to spend any more money on an educational system might get parents and teachers to blame each other and deflect attention away from other imperfect parts of the system," observes Jeannie Oakes, director of the Institute for Democracy, Education and Access at UCLA.

> **"With the oldest, I think I micromanaged things. I had to come to a point where I said, These are his projects. They're not my projects. I'm not helping him."**

Families feel they have to work the system. Attentive parents study the faculty like stock tables, looking for the best performer and then lobbying to get their kids into that teacher's class. "You have a lot of mothers who have been in the work force, supervising other people, who have a different sense of empowerment and professionalism about them," notes Amy Stuart Wells, professor of sociology and education at Columbia University's Teachers College. "When they drop out of the work force to raise their kids, they see being part of the school as part of their job." Monica Stutzman, a mother of two in Johnston, Iowa, believes her efforts helped ensure that her daughter wound up with the best teacher in each grade. "We know what's going on. We e-mail, volunteer on a weekly basis. I ask a lot of questions," she says. "I'm not there to push my children into things they're not ready for. The teachers are the experts. We've had such great experiences with the teacher because we create that experience, because we're involved. We don't just get something home and say, 'What's this?'"

> **"Most teachers will do what they need to, but there are teachers who are uncomfortable, who turn their backs or close their eyes or ears because they do not want what they perceive might be a confrontation."**

Parents seeking to stay on top of what's happening in class don't have to wait for the report card to arrive. "Now it's so easy for the parents through the Internet to get ahold of us, and they expect an immediate response," notes Michael Schaffer, a classroom veteran who teaches AP courses at Central Academy in Des Moines, Iowa. "This e-mail—'How's my kid doing?'— could fill my day. That's hyperbole. But it's a two-edged sword here, and unfortunately it's cutting to the other side, and parents are making demands on us that are unreasonable. Yeah, they're concerned about their kids. But I'm concerned about 150 kids. I don't have time during the day to let the parent know when the kid got the first B." As more districts make assignments and test scores available online, it may cut down on the "How's he doing" e-mails but increase the "Why did she get a B?" queries.

Beneath the ferocious jostling there is the brutal fact that outside of Lake Wobegon, not all children are above average. Teachers must choose their words carefully. They can't just say, "I'm sorry your child's not as smart as X," and no parent wants to hear that there are five other kids in the class who are a lot smarter than his or hers. Younger teachers especially can be overwhelmed by parents who announce on the first day of school that their child is going to be the smartest in the class and on the second day that he is already bored. Veteran teachers have learned to come back with data in hand to show parents who boast that their child scored in the 99th percentile on some aptitude test that 40 other students in the class did just as well.

It would be nice if parents and teachers could work together to improve the system for everyone, but human nature can get in the way. Both sides know that resources are limited, and all kinds of factors play into how they are allocated—including whose elbows are sharpest. Many schools, fearful of "bright flight," the mass departure of high-achieving kids, feel they have no choice but to appease the most outspoken parents. "I understand, having been a parent, the attitude that 'I don't have time to fix the whole system; I don't have time and energy to get rid of systemic injustice, racism, poverty and violence; I have to get what's right for my kid,'" says Syracuse's Sapon-Shevin. "But then the schools do educational triage. They basically attend to the most vocal, powerful people with more resources. They say, 'Don't get angry. We'll take care of this issue.' And they mean, 'We'll take care of it for your child. We'll get your kid out of the class with the bad teacher and leave the other kids in there.'"

At the deepest level, teachers fear that all this parental anxiety is not always aimed at the stuff that matters. Parents who instantly call about a grade or score seldom ask about what is being taught or how. When a teacher has spent the whole summer brightening and deepening the history curriculum for her ninth-graders, finding new ways to surprise and engage them, it is frustrating to encounter parents whose only focus is on test scores. "If these parents were pushing for richer, more meaningful instruction, you could almost forgive them their obnoxiousness and inattention to the interests of all the other children," says Alfie Kohn, a Boston-based education commentator and author of *Unconditional Parenting*. But "we have pushy parents pushing for the wrong thing." He argues that test scores often measure what matters least—and that even high test scores should invite parents to wonder what was cut from the curriculum to make room for more test prep.

"It's a challenge to be a good parent of a high school student. You want to help our kids without putting too much pressure on."

Kohn knows a college counselor hired by parents to help "package" their child, who had perfect board scores and a wonderful grade-point average. When it was time to work on the college essay, the counselor said, "Let's start with a book you read outside of school that really made a difference in your life." There was a moment of silence. Then the child responded, "Why would I read a book if I didn't have to?" If parents focus only on the transcript—drive out of children their natural curiosity, discourage their trying anything at which they might fail—their definition of success will get a failing grade from any teacher watching.

The Public Defenders

By the time children turn 18, they have spent only 13% of their waking lives in the classroom. Their habits of mind, motivation and muscles have much more to do with that other 87%. But try telling that to an Ivy-educated mom and dad whose kids aren't doing well. It can't be the genes, Mom and Dad conclude, so it must be the school. "It's the bright children who aren't motivated who are most frustrating for parents and teachers," says Nancy McGill, a past president of the Iowa Talented and Gifted Association. "Parents don't know how to fix the kid, to get the kid going. They want us to do it, and discover we can't either." Sometimes bright kids intentionally work just hard enough to get a B because they are trying to make a point about what should be demanded of them, observes Jennifer Loh, a math teacher at Ursuline Academy in Dallas. "It's their way of saying to Mom and Dad, 'I'm not perfect.'" Though the best teachers work hard to inspire even the most alienated kids, they can't carry the full burden of the parents' expectations. In his dreams, admits Daddow, the Iowa history teacher, what he would like to say is "Your son or daughter is very, very lazy." Instead, he shows the parents the student's work and says, "I'm not sure I'm getting Jim's best effort."

When a teacher asks parents to be partners, he or she doesn't necessarily mean Mom or Dad should be camping in the classroom. Research shows that though students benefit modestly from having parents involved at school, what happens at home matters much more. According to research based on the National Education Longitudinal Study, a sample of nearly 25,000 eighth-graders, among four main areas of parental involvement (home discussion, home supervision, school communication and school participation), home discussion was the most strongly related to academic achievement.

Any partnership requires that both sides do their part. Teachers say that here again, parents can have double standards: Push hard, but not too hard; maintain discipline, but don't punish my child. When teachers tell a parent that a child needs to be reprimanded at home, teachers say they often get the response, "I don't reprimand, and don't tell me how to raise my child."

Older teachers say they are seeing in children as young as 6 and 7 a level of disdain for adults that was once the reserve of adolescents. Some talk about the "dry-cleaner parents" who drop their rambunctious kids off in the morning and expect them to be returned at the end of the day all clean and proper and practically sealed in plastic.

At the most disturbing extreme are the parents who like to talk about values but routinely undermine them. "You get savvier children who know how to get out of things," says a second-grade teacher in Murfreesboro, Tenn. "Their parents actually teach them to lie to dodge their responsibilities." Didn't get your homework done? That's O.K. Mom will take the fall. Late for class? Blame it on Dad. Parents have sued schools that expelled kids for cheating, on the grounds that teachers had left the exams out on a desk and made them too easy to steal. "Cheating is rampant," says Steve Taylor, a history teacher at Beverly Hills High School in California. "If you're not cheating, then you're not trying. A C means you're a loser." Every principal can tell a story about some ambitious student, Ivy bound, who cheats on an exam. Teacher flunks her. Parents protest: She made a mistake, and you're going to ruin her life. Teachers try to explain that good kids can make bad decisions; the challenge is to make sure the kids learn from them. "I think some parents confuse advocating on behalf of their student with defending everything that the student does," says Scott Peoples, a history teacher at Skyview High School outside Denver.

> **"I called the parents on a discipline issue with their daughter. Her father called me a total jerk. Then he said, "Well, do you want to meet someplace and take care of this man to man?"**

Student-teacher disputes can quickly escalate into legal challenges or the threat of them. The fear of litigation that has given rise to the practice of defensive medicine prompts educators to practice defensive teaching. According to Forrest T. Jones Inc., a large insurer of teachers, the number of teachers buying liability insurance has jumped 25% in the past five years. "A lot of teachers are very fearful and don't want to deal with it," says Roxsana Jaber-Ansari, who teaches sixth grade at Hale Middle School in Woodland Hills, Calif. She has learned that everything must be documented. She does not dare accuse a student of cheating, for instance, without evidence, including eyewitness accounts or a paper trail. When a teacher meets with a student alone, the door always has to be open to avoid any suspicion of inappropriate behavior on the teacher's part. "If you become angry and let it get to you, you will quit your job," says Jaber-Ansari. "You will hate what you do and hate the kids."

Teacher's Pests

Some parents ask too much of the school or too little of their kids

Helicopter Parents

In order to grow, kids need room to fail; the always hovering parent gets in the way of self-reliance

Monster Parents

The lurking moms and dads always looking for reasons to disagree are a teacher's worst nightmare

Dry-cleaner Parents

They drop their rambunctious kids off and want them all cleaned up and proper by the end of the day

---

The Culture Warriors

Teachers in schools with economically and ethnically diverse populations face a different set of challenges in working with parents. In less affluent districts, many parents don't have computers at home, so schools go to some lengths to make contact easier. Even 20 minutes twice a year for a conference can be hard for families if parents are working long hours at multiple jobs or have to take three buses to get to the school. Some teachers visit a parent's workplace on a Saturday or help arrange language classes for parents to help with communication. Particularly since a great goal of education is to level the playing field, teachers are worried that the families that need the most support are least able to ask for it. "The standards about what makes a good parent are always changing," notes Annette Lareau, a professor of sociology at Temple University, who views all the demand for parent involvement as a relatively recent phenomenon. "And it's middle-class parents who keep pace."

Lareau also sees cultural barriers getting in the way of the strong parent-teacher alliance. When parents don't get involved at school, teachers may see it as a sign of indifference, of not valuing education—when it may signal the reverse. Some cultures believe strongly that school and home should be separate spheres; parents would no more interfere with the way a teacher teaches than with the way a surgeon operates. "Working-class and poor families don't have a college education," says Lareau. "They are looking up to teachers; they respect teachers as professionals. Middle-class parents are far less respectful. They're not a teacher, but they could have been a teacher, and often their profession has a higher status than teachers'. So they are much more likely to criticize teachers on professional grounds."

And while she views social class as a major factor in shaping the dynamic, Lareau finds that race continues to play a role. Middle-class black parents, especially those who attended segregated schools, often approach the teacher with caution. Roughly 90% of teachers are white and middle class, and, says

Lareau, many black parents are "worried that teachers will have lowered expectations of black children, that black boys will be punished more than white boys. Since teachers want parents to be positive and supportive, when African-American parents express concerns about racial insensitivity, it can create problems in their relationship."

Finally, as church-state arguments boil over and principals agonize over what kids can sing at the Winter Concert, teachers need to be eternally sensitive to religious issues as well. This is an arena where parents are often as concerned about content as grades, as in the debate over creationism vs. evolution vs. intelligent design, for instance. Teachers say they have to become legal scholars to protect themselves in a climate where students have "rights." Jaber-Ansari was challenged for hanging Bible quotes on her classroom walls. But she had studied her legal standing, and when she was confronted, "the principal supported me 100%," she says.

Perhaps the most complicated part of the conversation—beyond all the issues of race and class and culture, the growing pressures to succeed and arguments over how success should be defined—is the problem of memory. When they meet in that conference, parent and teacher bring their own school experiences with them—what went right and wrong, what they missed. They are determined for it to be different for the child they both care about. They go into that first-grade room and sit in the small chairs and can easily be small again themselves. It is so tempting to use the child's prospects to address their own regrets. So teachers learn to choose their words with care and hope that they can build a partnership with parents that works to everyone's advantage and comes at no one's expense. And parents over time may realize that when it comes to their children, they still have much to learn. "I think that we love our children so much that they make us a little loony at times," says Arch Montgomery, head of the Asheville School in North Carolina. He winces at parents who treat their child as a cocktail-party trophy or a vanity sticker for the window of their SUV, but he also understands their behavior. "I think most parents desperately want to do what is right for their kids. This does not bring out the better angels of our natures, but it is understandable, and it is forgivable."

—With reporting by Amanda Bower, New York, Melissa August, Washington, Anne Berryman, Athens, Cathy Booth Thomas, Dallas, Rita Healy, Denver, Elizabeth Kauffman, Nashville, Jeanne McDowell, Los Angeles and Betsy Rubiner, Des Moines

Where Personality Goes Awry

A multifaceted research approach is providing more clues to the origins of personality disorders.

CHARLOTTE HUFF

Over the years, few large-scale prospective studies have targeted the causes of personality disorders (PDs). But recently, a new body of research has begun to explore the potential influences of several factors, from genetics and parenting to peer influences, and even the randomness of life events.

Indeed, says Patricia Hoffman Judd, PhD, clinical professor of psychiatry at the University of California, San Diego, research into the origins of PDs is just beginning to take off. "I think for years people thought, 'It's just personality—you can't do anything about it,'" she explains. "There's also been moralism [that people with such disorders] are evil, that they are lazy," adds Judd, author of "A Developmental Model of Borderline Personality Disorder" (American Psychiatric Publishing, 2003).

But research is helping to turn such misconceptions around. Genetics researchers, for example, are closer to identifying some of the biological underpinnings that may influence PDs. Last year, for example, a team located—and described in *Molecular Psychiatry* (Vol, 8. No. 11)—a malfunctioning gene they believe may be a factor in obsessive-compulsive disorder. Other researchers are investigating genetic links to aggression, anxiety and fear—traits that could be influential in the later development of a personality disorder.

However, genetics don't work in a vacuum. Studies continue to indicate that abuse, even verbal abuse, can amplify the risk of developing a personality disorder.

For some disorders, such as antisocial PD, the evidence suggests that genetic factors play a significant role, while others, such as dependent personality disorder, appear to be more environmentally influenced, says longtime PD researcher Theodore Millon, PhD, DSc, editor of an ongoing book series, "Personality-guided Psychology" (APA).

But regardless of the specific disorder, researchers increasingly observe a back-and-forth interplay between genetic and environmental influences.

"We see a paradigm shift taking place in the field now toward a more interactionist perspective," says Jeffrey G. Johnson, PhD, associate professor of clinical psychology in Columbia University's psychiatry department. "I think the field is getting away from genetics versus environment—it's a major change."

The Genetic/Environmental Convergence

One of the largest efforts to look at PDs, the Collaborative Longitudinal Personality Disorders Study (CLPS), is attempting to gain insight into a cross-section of the disorders' characteristics, stability and progression. The multisite study, funded by the National Institute of Mental Health until 2005, has since 1996 enrolled 668 people with the diagnoses of avoidant, borderline, obsessive-compulsive or schizotypal personality disorders. A summary of the study's aims appeared in the *Journal of Personality Disorders* (Vol. 14. No. 4).

Although the study is not looking directly at causes, it's collecting historical information that may one day provide some insights, says Tracie Shea, PhD, associate professor in the department of psychiatry and human behavior at Brown Medical School and one of CLPS's principal investigators. "I like to think of it as generating hypotheses that can be tested," she says.

Shea co-authored a 2002 study in the *Journal of Nervous and Mental Disease* (Vol. 190, No. 8) that looked at CLPS data and found an association between the severity of specific PDs and the number and type of childhood traumas. In particular, people with borderline PDs reported particularly high rates of childhood sexual trauma—55 percent detailing physically forced, unwanted sexual contact. The researchers note, however, that the type of analysis couldn't determine if the personality adaptations occurred in response to the trauma or whether the individuals' underlying character pathology predisposed them.

Among those exploring the genetic and environmental influences linking normal and abnormal personality is Robert Krueger, PhD, associate professor of psychology at the University of Minnesota. In 2002, Krueger co-authored a study in the *Journal of Personality* (Vol. 70, No. 5) that looked at the personality traits of 128 twin pairs who had been raised apart. The study found that the identical twins were more similar in personality traits than the fraternal twins.

Thus, although both genetics and environment contributed to the association between normal and abnormal personality, genetics appeared to play the greater role overall, Krueger says. "The predominant reason normal and abnormal personality are linked to each other is because they are linked to the same underlying genetic mechanisms," he explains.

With borderline PD, for example, ongoing research indicates that there may be a genetic base for the problems with impulsivity and aggression, says the University of California's Judd. But environmental influences are significant and can extend deep into childhood, even infancy, Judd adds.

"There is a pretty high prevalence of maltreatment by caregivers across all personality disorders," she notes. "One of the key problems appears to be neglect. Probably more of an emotional neglect—more of a lack of attention to a child's emotional needs."

Judd points to several studies by Johnson, including one published in 1999 in the *Archives of General Psychiatry* (Vol. 56, No. 7) that followed 639 New York state families and their children for nearly two decades. Children with documented instances of childhood abuse or neglect were more than four times as likely to develop a PD in early adulthood, according to the research.

Another study, led by Johnson and published in 2001 in *Comprehensive Psychiatry* (Vol. 42, No. 1), came to a similar conclusion when examining maternal verbal abuse in the same New York group of families, involving this time 793 mothers and their children. The prospective study asked mothers a variety of questions, including whether they had screamed at their children in the previous month and whether they had told their child they didn't love them or would send them away. Offspring who experienced verbal abuse in childhood—compared with those who didn't—were more than three times as likely to be diagnosed as adults with borderline, narcissistic, obsessive-compulsive and paranoid PDs.

Shea cautions, though, that at this point research into childhood neglect and abuse, albeit intriguing, has largely been suggestive because prospective studies remain limited.

"It's likely that these childhood abuse factors do play an important role," he explains. "It's hard to say what and how big that role is, more specifically."

The Parent-Blame Problem

The role of abuse is particularly controversial among family members of people with a borderline disorder, who say they are being unfairly blamed—similar to what happened in the early days of schizophrenia research. Emphasizing maltreatment and abuse is misleading and has a devastating effect on families, says Valerie Porr, president of a New York-based nonprofit group, Treatment and Research Advancements National Association for Personality Disorder (**www.tara4bpd.org/tara.html**).

Porr doesn't deny that parental behavior can play a role in borderline PD. "But it's not like it's the evil mother beating her children," she says. Rather, she explains, the child's "behavior is so off the wall [that] the family's responses are off the wall."

Porr, who has a family member with borderline personality disorder, points to emerging research, including that of Harvard University-based psychologist Jerome Kagan, PhD, identifying the high sensitivity to outside stimuli of some children as significant. Family members of people with borderline PD report unusual responses even in the first months of life, Porr says, noting that, "They say, 'The light bothers them. They are sensitive to noise. Texture bothers them.'"

But Kagan, in a 2002 *Dialogues in Clinical Neuroscience* article (Vol. 4, No. 3), says that the role of high reactivity in infancy is far from clear-cut. It's true, he says, that highly reactive infants are more likely to develop shy, timid or anxious personalities. Still, there are puzzling questions, including the significant gap between the percentage of children—20 percent—who are highly reactive infants and the prevalence—less than 10 percent—of those who develop social phobias.

"This fact suggests that many high reactives find an adaptive niche in their society that allows them to titer unpredictable social encounters," Kagan writes.

In the end, says Johnson, the goal of research into environmental influences is not to blame, but to help parents. "We must understand what parenting behaviors are associated with greater risk to the child," he says. "When we identify those parenting behaviors, we can use them to design intervention."

The Role of Peers

Psychologists' findings also suggest that caregivers, teachers and even peers may play a role in PDs—both in positive as well as negative ways. Even a single strong positive relationship—say a close bond with a grandmother—can offset negative influences in a dysfunctional household.

"The child with a predisposition toward developing a personality disorder doesn't need the perfect teacher or the perfect friends to not develop the disorder," says Judith Beck, PhD, director of the Beck Institute for Cognitive Therapy and Research in suburban Philadelphia. "If the child is in an extreme environment, such as abuse or neglect, that may make the difference in terms of developing a personality disorder."

And life events can help tip the balance, Beck says. For example, a child with obsessive-compulsive tendencies who has alcoholic parents may assume the responsibility of caring for his younger siblings—a move that may amplify his propensities until he meets the diagnosis of a disorder. "It's the fit between your environment and your personality," Beck explains.

Over time, researchers will continue probing that fit and will likely identify more than a few causes even for a single personality disorder, says Millon, dean of the Florida-based

Institute for Advanced Studies in Personology and Psychopathology. Narrowing down potential causes will help psychologists more quickly isolate what might be influencing a particular patient, he says.

Millon explains: "Once you identify the one cause that seems most probable and most significant, then you can design your therapy in order to unlearn what seemed most problematic for that individual."

CHARLOTTE HUFF is a freelance writer in Fort Worth, Texas.

When Cultures Clash

ANNE UNDERWOOD AND JERRY ADLER

Urdu, Mandarin, Haitian Creole... By the thousands each week, they pass through the doors of Elmhurst Hospital in Queens, the borough of New York City that contains Kennedy airport and is home to perhaps a greater diversity of foreign-born immigrants than any comparable community in the nation or the world.

Spanish, Korean, Albanian...

A broken bone is the same in any language, but not so diabetes or hypertension—abstractions for which many people do not have words. The very concept of organic illness varies from culture to culture. If you were brought up to believe that your symptoms arise from sorcery or from something you did in a previous life, you might not grasp the necessity for a course of chemotherapy whose most immediate and obvious effect will be to make you feel a hundred times worse. And if well-educated Americans sometimes find it hard to keep track of the complicated regimen of medications for, say, heart failure and diabetes together, it surely is no easier for a Pashto speaker relying on her grandson to explain how to measure her blood sugar. There are barriers to communication even among people who speak the same language, like a white AIDS specialist and the African-American patient who knows that the only people he sees dying of the disease are black.

A growing medical challenge: doctors and patients often can't communicate.

The languages were different—Polish, Yiddish or Italian—but even a century ago, poor immigrant patients and upper-middle-class physicians faced each other suspiciously across a vast cultural gap. But probably never in our history has this country had to absorb so many newcomers from such a diversity of cultures, and medicine, which touches so intimately on their lives, has never been more specialized and technological. "Hmong [a Laotian ethnic group with a pastoral culture] will smile and nod when they're with the doctor, but they have no intention of taking the pills," says Sa Vang, a fourth-year medical student at the University of California, Davis, whose parents came to the United States in 1979. "My grandmother would only take her blood-pressure medication when she had a headache." Vang has seen this happen many times in her community: patients who take their pills in response to a specific symptom, which may or may not be related to the condition the drugs are supposed to treat. The patient doesn't want to offend the doctor, so he says he's been taking his medicine; the condition hasn't improved, so the doctor increases the dosage, to the point where the patient starts to experience unwanted side effects. The result: "Patients think the doctors don't know what they're doing."

The best-documented case of such misunderstandings involved Lia Lee, the daughter of a Hmong family in Merced County, Calif., in the late 1980s. When she was 3 months old, she fainted on hearing the sound of a door slamming. Doctors assumed the seizures she suffered after that were from epilepsy, but her parents provided their own diagnosis, the temporary disappearance of her soul out of her body, a condition whose name translates as "the spirit catches you and you fall down" (which was the title of an excellent book by Anne Fadiman on Lia's case). Whether modern medicine could have controlled her epilepsy is unknown; what Fadiman found was that her highly competent and dedicated doctors prescribed more than a dozen different drugs in various dosages and combinations that changed 23 times in four years. Her well-meaning parents, illiterate even in Hmong, followed the doctors' orders only sporadically, but sent away to Thailand for sacred amulets, and changed Lia's name to fool the evil spirits—a plan that failed, according to her mother, because the doctors insisted on calling her Lia. Four years after her first symptoms, she suffered a massive seizure that left her in a persistent vegetative state, where she remains today. She is 22.

Few other groups have as great a cultural distance to traverse as the Hmong, but even native-born Americans may suffer from poor communication with their doctors. Minorities often carry a burden of suspicion with them into the examination room, as shown in a RAND Corp. study this year; 53 percent of African-Americans surveyed agreed that there is a drug to cure AIDS, but poor people aren't being told about it, and nearly one in six believed that AIDS was created by government scientists to control the black population. Lead researcher Laura Bogart noted that men who held those beliefs were significantly less likely to use condoms.

Minorities carry a burden of suspicion into the examination room.

"When I was in medical school, there was lots of talk about [racial] disparities in health care, but it focused on access," says Dr. Maren Grainger-Monsen, director of the Bioethics in Film Program at Stanford. "Then we learned that minorities with equal insurance and access still had drastically worse outcomes in cardiac surgery and lung cancer." Grainger-Monsen believes the "shocking" disparity can be attributed, in large part, to cultural differences and failures of communication, which afflict minorities. Her new film, "Hold Your Breath," recounts the case of Mohammad Kochi, an Afghan immigrant who was treated in California for stomach cancer. After his surgery, doctors recommended chemotherapy, but Kochi refused to undergo an unpleasant treatment that might not work. His real objection emerged much later: his doctor had prescribed a continuous intravenous infusion of chemotherapy, which would have minimized the side effects. But Kochi was a devout Muslim who prayed five times a day and could not let foreign fluids enter his body after he had cleansed himself for prayer—a prohibition that he believed extended to an IV drip. He never knew there were other ways to receive chemotherapy—and by the time this got straightened out, it was too late to help.

A trained medical interpreter might have gotten to the root of Kochi's problem sooner, but he had relied on one of his daughters, who had her own ideas about which information her father should receive. When his doctor told him that he still had cancer after the surgery, she refused to translate that information, fearing it would upset him. Dr. Joseph Betancourt, director of multicultural education at Massachusetts General Hospital, recalls how as a 7-year-old he was asked to serve as the intermediary between a doctor and his Spanish-speaking grandmother from Puerto Rico. Simple ignorance of medical terms was compounded by embarrassment; his grandmother was suffering from uterine cancer. "We still see kids acting as the cultural brokers for their families," says Betancourt, "but it's no way to run a hospital."

The medical profession has its own traditions, of course, and humility did not always rank high among them. But physicians increasingly realize that, simple human dignity aside, respecting patients' cultural beliefs can avoid tragedies like Lia Lee's. Fadiman's book on the case is now assigned in many medical schools; at Yale, incoming students discuss it on the very first day of class. And more than 100 medical programs use the saga of Kochi to help teach "cultural competence." As Sa Vang shows by her own example, many of the problems will lessen as immigrants assimilate. It would be unthinkable for her to do as her parents did, when they sacrificed goats and chickens to cure her grandmother. She knows that disease is not caused by evil spirits snatching the soul out of the body. Her husband doesn't really believe that either, but neither does he let their two young sons attend funerals, where the evil spirits are especially active. And Sa Vang, the medical student, doesn't object.

Brown v. Board

A Dream Deferred

Fifty years ago, a landmark ruling seemed to break Jim Crow's back and usher in an era of hope for integrated education. But the reality has fallen short of the promise. The fight for decent schooling for black kids goes on.

ELLIS COSE

Sometimes history serves as a magnifying mirror—making momentous what actually was not. But *Brown v. Board of Education of Topeka, Kansas,* is the real thing: a Supreme Court decision that fundamentally and forever changed America. It jump-started the modern civil-rights movement and excised a cancer eating a hole in the heart of the Constitution.

So why is the celebration of its 50th anniversary so bittersweet? Why, as we raise our glasses, are there tears in our eyes? The answer is simple: *Brown,* for all its glory, is something of a bust.

Clearly *Brown* altered forever the political and social landscape of an insufficiently conscience-stricken nation. "*Brown* led to the sit-ins, the freedom marches... the Civil Rights Act of 1964... If you look at *Brown* as... the icebreaker that broke up... that frozen sea, then you will see it was an unequivocal success," declared Jack Greenberg, former head of the NAACP Legal Defense & Educational Fund Inc. and one of the lawyers who litigated *Brown*. Still, measured purely by its effects on the poor schoolchildren of color at its center, *Brown* is a disappointment—in many respects a failure. So this commemoration is muted by the realization that *Brown* was not nearly enough.

While most white and Hispanic Americans (59 percent for each group) think their community schools are doing a good or excellent job, only 45 percent of blacks feel that way, according to an exclusive NEWSWEEK Poll. That is up considerably from the 31 percent who thought their schools were performing well in 1998, but it means a lot of people are still unhappy with the deck of skills being dealt to black kids.

Only 38 percent of blacks think those schools have the resources necessary to provide a quality education, according to the poll. And African-Americans are not alone in feeling that funding should increase. A majority of the members of all ethnic groups support the notion that schools attended by impoverished minority children ought to have equivalent resources to those attended by affluent whites. Indeed, most Americans go even further. They say schools should be funded at "whatever level it takes to raise minority-student achievement to an acceptable national standard." Sixty-one percent of whites, 81 percent of Hispanics and a whopping 93 percent of blacks agree with that statement—which is to say they agree with the proposition of funding schools at a level never seriously countenanced by the political establishment: a total transformation of public education in the United States.

Increasingly, black and Latino kids are likely to find themselves in classrooms with few, if any, nonminority faces. The shift is due in part to Supreme Court decisions that undermined *Brown*.

Most white and Hispanic Americans (59% for each group) think their local schools do a good or excellent job. Only 45% of blacks feel that way.

So now, 50 years after the court case that changed America, another battle is upon us—and only at this moment becoming clear. It began at the intersection of conflicting good intentions, where the demands of politicians and policymakers for high educational standards collided with the demands of educators and children's advocates for resources. Throw in a host of initiatives spawned, at least in part, by frustration at low student achievement—vouchers, charter schools, privatization, curbs on social promotion, high-stakes testing (all issues now swirling around the presidential campaign)—and you have the making of an educational upheaval that may rival *Brown* in its ramifications. It may in some ways be the second phase of *Brown*: a continuation by other means of the battle for access to a decent education by those whom fortune left behind.

On May 17, 1954, the day the walls of segregation fell, the Supreme Court actually handed down two decisions, involving five separate cases—in South Carolina, Virginia, Delaware, Kansas and Washington, D.C.—all of which came collectively to be known as *Brown*. Instead of abolishing segregation straightaway, the justices sought advice on how—and when—desegregation was to come about. So *Brown* spawned what came to be known as *Brown* II—a decision in May 1955 that provided neither a timetable nor a plan. Instead it ordered the South to proceed with "all deliberate speed," which the South took as an invitation to stall. But something more was wrong.

The decision rested on an assumption that simply wasn't true: that once formal, state-mandated segregation ended, "equal educational opportunities" would be the result. A half century later, school segregation is far from dead and the goal of educational equality is as elusive as ever. Since the early 1990s, despite the continued growth of integration in other sectors of society, black and Latino children are increasingly likely to find themselves in classes with few, if any, non-minority faces.

The shift is due, at least in part, to Supreme Court decisions that essentially undermined *Brown*. In 1974 the court ruled that schools in white suburbs were not obliged to admit black kids from the inner city. And in 1992 the court decided that local school boards, even if not in full compliance with desegregation orders, should be released from court supervision as quickly as possible. "Racial balance is not to be achieved for its own sake," proclaimed the court.

For most black parents, of course, *Brown* was never about integration "for its own sake"—though blacks strongly support integration. Instead, it was about recognition of the fact that unless their children went to school with the children of the whites who controlled the purse strings, their children were likely to be shortchanged.

Most blacks are no longer convinced their kids necessarily do better in integrated settings. Some 57 percent of black parents say the schools' racial mixture makes no difference, significantly more than the 41 percent who said that in 1988. But they also know resource allocation is not colorblind. Hence, 59 percent of blacks, 52 percent of Hispanics and 49 percent of whites agree that it will be impossible to provide equal educational opportunities for all "as long as children of different races in this country basically go to different schools."

Today, by virtually any measure of academic achievement, blacks, Puerto Ricans and Mexican-Americans are, on average, far behind their white and Asian-American peers. A range of factors, from bad prenatal care to intellectually destructive neighborhood or home environments, have been implicated to explain the disparity. Certainly one reason for the difference is that blacks (and Puerto Ricans and Mexican-Americans) do not, for the most part, go to the same schools, or even the same types of schools, as do the majority of non-Hispanic whites. They are more likely to go to schools such as those found in parts of rural South Carolina—schools that, were it not for the American flags proudly flying over the roofs, might have been plucked out of some impoverished country that sees education as a luxury it can barely afford.

Take a tour of Jasper County and you will find a middle school with a drainpipe in the corridor, which occasionally spills sewage into the hallway. You'll find labs where the equipment doesn't work, so children have to simulate, rather than perform, experiments. In nearby Clarendon County resources are also lacking. Were Thurgood Marshall to find himself in Clarendon County today, "he would think [*Brown*] had been reversed," state Sen. John Marshall told a visitor. So Clarendon County is again in court, refighting the battle for access to a decent education that Clarendon's children, and all the children of *Brown*, presumably won a long time ago.

In 1951, kids walked out to protest school conditions in Farmville, Va. Despite Brown, relief did not come. The schools were shuttered for five years. Today the dream of integration is thriving there.

The saga of Clarendon County began in 1947 with a simple request for a bus. The county's white schoolchildren already had 30 schoolbuses at their disposal. Though black children outnumbered whites by a margin of nearly three to one, they had not a single bus. So a local pastor, J. A. DeLaine, went on a crusade. His request for transportation led angry whites to burn down his church and his home, to shoot at him and to literally run him out of town under cover of night. It also spawned a lawsuit known as *Briggs v. Elliot*, which challenged the doctrine of "separate but equal" and was later bundled into *Brown*.

Instead of integrating its school systems, as *Brown* had decreed, South Carolina maneuvered to keep segregation alive. It structured school districts in such a way that blacks were largely lumped together, and having clustered them together, the state "systematically neglected to adequately fund those districts," says Steve Morrison, a partner in the law firm that is currently suing the state for additional resources for Clarendon and more than 30 other counties.

Blacks (83%) and Hispanics (91%) are more likely than whites (73%) to feel it's important to use standardized tests to raise academic standards

It is a sign of how much, in some respects, attitudes have changed that the state's largest law firm—Nelson Mullins Riley & Scarborough—is on the side of the plaintiffs. During a conversation in the offices of the law firm that bears his name, Richard Riley, former governor of South Carolina and former U.S. secretary of Education, remarked, "If *Brown* had been 100 percent successful, we wouldn't have this situation." In opening arguments Carl Epps, another Nelson Mullins attorney, compared the suit to Brown itself, calling it the kind of case that comes along only "every generation or two."

Certainly, when aggregated with a multitude of similar cases, the Clarendon case—known as *Abbeville County School District, et al. v. The State of South Carolina, et al.*—represents a major shift in tactics among those fighting for the educational rights of poor people. Once upon a time the emphasis was on "equity": on trying to ensure that the most economically deprived students were provided with resources equal to those lavished on the children of the rich. Now the cases are about whether states are providing sufficient resources to poor schools to allow the students who attend them to effectively compete in society. They are called "adequacy" cases, and they aspire to force states to produce graduates capable of functioning competently as citizens and as educated human beings.

The shift in strategy stems, in part, from the Supreme Court's making equity cases more difficult to win but leaving the door open to adequacy claims. In a seminal moment for this new movement, the Kentucky Supreme Court decided in 1989 that students in Kentucky had a right to a much better education than they were receiving. In response, the legislature totally overhauled the state's educational system.

Elsewhere, legislative reforms—so far—have been less dramatic as politicians have fought efforts to mandate spending increases. But in several states, including New York, judges are looking on adequacy suits with favor. Indeed, last week a group of high-profile businessmen called on New York politicians to heed the call for more and smarter education funding. The notion that schools ought to invest more in those whose need is greatest goes against American tradition, but it seems an idea whose time is coming. Conversely, the notion that integration ought to be an explicit goal driving policy seems to be an idea whose time (at least among most whites) has passed. While close to two thirds of blacks and

Hispanics feel that "more should be done" to integrate schools, only one third of whites agree. And only 18 percent of whites think whites receive a better education if they are in a racially mixed environment.

This is not to say that the push for integration has been a total failure. Indeed, in Farmville, Va., a small town little more than an hour's drive southwest of Richmond, the state capital, the dream of school integration is thriving. In the early 1950s, black high-school students in Farmville were relegated to a tiny structure. Students who could not be accommodated in the main building were relegated to flimsy shacks covered with tar paper, each heated with a single wood-burning stove. As former student leader John Stokes recalls, "The buildings were so bad that the people sitting near the windows or the door had to wear an overcoat, and the person sitting near the stove burned up." In 1951 the students walked out and took their complaints to the NAACP. That led to a case called *Davis v. County School Board of Prince Edward County,* which was eventually made part of *Brown.*

After the Supreme Court declared the era of separate but equal over, Virginia's legislature prohibited expenditure of funds on integrated schools. And when delay was no longer an option, Prince Edward County closed its public schools altogether. From the fall of 1959 through much of 1964 the schools were shuttered. Those whites whose parents had a little money could go to Prince Edward Academy, the newly established "private" school. But most blacks, who were barred from the (state subsidized) segregation academies, saw their educational hopes wither.

On May 25, 1964, the Supreme Court finally brought Prince Edward County's resistance to an end. "The time for mere 'deliberate speed' has run out," wrote Justice Hugo Black. But it was only this year that the Virginia State Legislature (prodded by Viola Baskerville, a black delegate, and Ken Woodley, editor of The Farmville Herald) passed a bill to provide some belated scholarship assistance to those who had missed school so long ago.

For Farmville's current generation of high-school students, integration has become a way of life. The racial composition (60 percent black, 39 percent white, in a high school of nearly 3,000) is a source of delight: "I talk about being proud that we are diverse," says school superintendent Margaret Blackmon. And nearly three fourths of those who graduate from Prince Edward County High go to college.

One reason Prince Edward County was able to integrate successfully no doubt has to do with size. Once desegregation was forced on it, tiny Farmville didn't really have the option of carving out separate black and white districts. And once the region's racial madness ended and the segregation academy fell on hard times, the public school seemed a less objectionable alternative. There was, in other words, no real room for whites to flee and, as time wore on, increasingly less reason to do so. In much of the rest of America, there are plenty of places to run. Nonetheless, to visit a place like Farmville, with full knowledge of its wretched history, is to experience a certain wistfulness—to wonder about what might have been.

66% of blacks and 67% of Hispanics favor vouchers, as do 54% of whites. But they're unlikely to get vouchers to send kids to any school they want

If integration is not the answer (at least not now), what is? If the heat generated around the issue is any indication, there are two popular answers: testing and choice, considered either separately or in combination.

In one state after another, politicians have seized on tests as the solution. Without question, testing is popular with the public. And though it may come as a surprise to some, testing is particularly popular with the black and Latino public. Blacks (83 percent) and Hispanics (91 percent) are much more likely than whites (73 percent) to believe that it is important or very important to use "standardized tests to raise academic standards and student achievement." Some 74 percent of blacks and 64 percent of Hispanics think "most" or "some" minority students would show academic improvement if required to pass standardized tests before being promoted from one grade to another.

My guess is that the numbers measure support more for the idea of testing than for the reality of what testing has become. The idea—that ability can be recognized and developed, that deficiencies can be diagnosed and remedied—is impossible to argue with. It is far from clear at this juncture that that is what is happening.

When it comes to children of color, we ask the wrong question. We ask, 'Why are you such a problem?' when we should ask, 'What have we not given you that we routinely give to upper-middle-class white kids?'

In a report assessing the first-year results of the No Child Left Behind Act in 11 urban districts, researchers from the Civil Rights Project at Harvard concluded: "In each of the districts we studied, fewer than 16% of eligible students requested and received supplemental educational services. In most of these districts it was less than 5% of the eligible students, and in some it was less than 1%."

The use of choice as a tool of educational reform has also been controversial, particularly when it comes to the issue of vouchers. On one side are those who claim that poor kids in ghettos and barrios have the right (and ought to receive public money) to leave crummy schools and seek a quality education

elsewhere. On the other side are those who say that vouchers will not appreciably increase the options of children attending wretched schools but will instead deprive public schools of resources they can ill afford to lose.

In the last several years, voucher programs have sprouted in a number of states. Florida's program—actually three different programs—is the most ambitious. In December 2003 an audit of those programs by the state's chief financial officer led to several probes for criminal irregularities. In a blistering editorial in February, The Palm Beach Post, which had written several critical investigative pieces on the programs, concluded that "as the state is running it, the entire voucher program is a fraud." Even the Florida Catholic Conference, a presumptive beneficiary of the programs, appealed for reforms. At the very least the conference wanted schools to be accredited, to have some kind of track record and to give standardized tests so parents would know how the schools were performing relative to others.

Certainly there is evidence that voucher programs can help some students. And most people view vouchers in a positive light. Some 66 percent of blacks and 67 percent of Hispanics favor vouchers, as do 54 percent of whites. But most people understand quite clearly that in the real world they are not likely to get a voucher that will allow them to send a child to any school of their dreams. So it is not inconsistent that a majority of Americans favor increasing funding for public education over providing parents with vouchers. Nor it is surprising that blacks, even more than whites, strongly support funding for public schools.

The voucher debate is bound to rage for years to come. With the backing of the Bush administration, Washington, D.C., is launching an ambitious new voucher experiment. Indeed, George W. Bush is running for re-election as the education president, as the leader who championed No Child Left Behind and who is making schools accountable with testing regimes and more demanding curricula. Not to be outdone, John Kerry has come up with his own education proposals, which include programs to keep young people, particularly people of color, in school and more funding for NCLB and special education.

The national dialogue on education that is emerging from the rhetoric of warring politicians—and from all these suits, all this testing and all these experiments with choice—must ultimately get beyond what happens in the school to what is happening in the larger society, and in the larger environment in which children exist.

In too many ways, when it comes to children of color, we continue to ask the wrong questions. We poke and probe and test those kids as we wrinkle our brows and ask, with requisite concern, "Why are you such a problem? What special programs do you need?" when we should be asking, "What have we not given to you that we routinely give to upper-middle-class white kids? What do they have that you don't?"

The answer is simple. They have a society that grants them the presumption of competence and the expectation of success; they have an environment that nurtures aspiration, peers who provide support and guardians who provide direction. If we are serious about realizing the promise of *Brown*, about decently educating those who begin with the least, we will have to ponder deeply how to deliver those things where they are desperately needed.

In the end, it may be that the true and lasting legacy of *Brown* has little to do with desegregation as such. It may instead be that *Brown* put us on a path that will, ideally, let us see children of color—and therefore our entire country—in a wholly new and beautiful light.

UNIT 5

Development During Adolescence and Young Adulthood

Unit Selections

Key Points to Consider

- What brain changes occur during adolescence? How do these changes affect behavior?

- What parental behaviors help ensure a peaceful adolescence?

- Should incarcerated adolescents continue their education in jail? What would a jail-school teach?

- Why are college students so stressed out? What can be done to reduce campus pressures?

- How do spiritual values impact on the American psyche?

- Can brain power be boosted with drugs? If so, should it be?

- Who are the "twixters?" Why do they find it so difficult to grow up?

Student Website

www.mhcls.com/online

Internet References

Further information regarding these websites may be found in this book's preface or online.

ADOL: Adolescent Directory On-Line
http://education.indiana.edu/cas/adol/adol.html

Adolescence: Change and Continuity
http://inside.bard.edu/academic/specialproj/darling/adolesce.htm

AMA—Adolescent Health On-Line
http://www.ama-assn.org/ama/pub/category/1947.html

American Academy of Child and Adolescent Psychiatry
http://www.aacap.org/

The term "adolescence" was coined in 1904 by G. Stanley Hall, one of the world's first psychologists. He saw adolescence as a discrete stage of life bridging the gap between sexual maturity (puberty) and socioemotional and cognitive maturity. He believed it to be characterized by "storm and stress." At the beginning of the twentieth century, it was typical for young men to begin working in middle childhood (there were no child labor laws), and for young women to become wives and mothers as soon as they were fertile and/or spoken for. At the turn of the twenty-first century, the beginning of adolescence is marked by the desire to be independent of parental control. The end of adolescence, which once coincided with the age of legal maturity (usually 16 or 18, depending on local laws), has now been extended upward. Although legal maturity is now 18 (voting, enlisting in the armed services, owning property, marrying without permission), the social norm is to consider persons in their late teens as adolescents, not adults. The years between 18 and 21 are often problematic for youth tethered between adult and not-adult status. They can be married, with children, living in homes of their own, running their own businesses, yet not be able to drive their cars in certain places or at certain times. They can go to college and participate in social activities, but they cannot legally drink. Often the twenty-first birthday is viewed as a rite of passage into adulthood in the United States because it signals the legal right to buy and drink alcoholic beverages. "Maturity" is usually reserved for those who have achieved full economic as well as socioemotional independence as adults.

Erik Erikson, the personality theorist, marked the passage from adolescence to young adulthood by a change in the nuclear conflicts of two life stages: identity versus role confusion and intimacy versus isolation. Adolescents struggle to answer the question, "Who am I?" Young adults struggle to find a place within the existing social order where they can feel intimacy rather than isolation. In the 1960s, Erikson wrote that females resolve both their conflicts of identity and intimacy by living vicariously through their husbands, an unacceptable idea to many females today.

As adolescence has been extended, so too has young adulthood. One hundred years ago, life expectancy did not extend too far beyond menopause for women and retirement for men. Young adulthood began when adolescents finished puberty. Parents of teenagers were middle-aged, between 35 and 55. Later marriages and delayed childbearing have redefined the line between young adulthood and middle age. Many people today consider themselves young adults well into their 40s.

Jean Piaget, the cognitive theorist, marked the end of the development of mental processes with the end of adolescence. Once full physical maturity, including brain maturity, was achieved, one reached the acme of his or her abilities to assimilate, accommodate, organize, and adapt to sensations, perceptions, associations, and discriminations. Piaget did not feel cognitive processing of information ceased with adulthood. He believed, however, that cognitive judgments would not reach a stage higher than the abstract, hypothetical, logical reasoning of formal operations. Today many cognitive theorists believe postformal operations are possible. The dialectics and the relativistic processes described in this book's preface are descriptive of some ideas about post-formal thinking.

The first article in this section addresses the Piagetian belief that brain maturity coincides with physical maturity. In "What Makes Teens Tick," Claudia Wallis presents new evidence, from sophisticated functional magnetic resonance imaging (fMRI) of the brain, that the brain may not reach final maturation until age 25. This opens the possibility of post-formal thinking.

The second article, "A Peaceful Adolescence," addresses the G. Stanley Hall belief that adolescence was a stage of life marked by "storm and stress." While some teenagers do have conflicts with their parents, new research documents that many teenagers have peaceful passages through adolescence. The authors of this article, Barbara Kantrowitz and Karen Springen, report on what adults do to nurture successful teen years.

The third selection, "Jail Time Is Learning Time," describes efforts to help jailed youth acquire GED instruction and earn high school equivalency diplomas. The program described also teaches anger management and vocational/job skills. Many adolescents are incarcerated in the United States every year. They should not be forgotten.

The last selection in the adolescence portion of this unit addresses some of the pressures and stressors that are weighing down our college students. Jane Brody, in "Hello to College Joys: Keep Stress Off Campus," gives an antithetical description of what happens to young people attending institutions of higher learning. Campus counseling centers are reporting an alarming increase in the numbers of students with serious psychological problems. She presents some fresh approaches to alleviating emotional distress. These include self-help practices and low cost mental health services.

The first article in the young adulthood portion of this unit, "How Spirit Blooms," describes the mid-20s faith journey of a woman raised in the Roman Catholic religion. It gives factual information about many contemporary spiritual belief systems, without being preachy. Readers will be stimulated to discuss many of Suzanne Clores' travel discoveries.

The second article of this section reviews some of the ways in which neuroscientific discoveries may boost our brain power in the years to come. "The Battle for Your Brain" discusses the pros and cons of doing so. Bioethicists weigh in with their opinions about changing the human brain in order to improve mood, memory, intelligence, and perhaps more.

This unit ends with Lev Grossman's introduction to a group he calls "The Twixters." They are young adults who find it difficult to settle down. In "Grow Up? Not So Fast," he asks the question, "Could growing up be harder than it used to be?" Twixters move around, experiment with jobs, spend more money than they earn, and consider their friends their new families. What roadmap can they follow to maturity?

What Makes Teens Tick

A flood of hormones, sure. But also a host of structural changes in the brain. Can those explain the behaviors that make adolescence so exciting—and so exasperating?

CLAUDIA WALLIS

Five young men in sneakers and jeans troop into a waiting room at the National Institutes of Health Clinical Center in Bethesda, Md., and drape themselves all over the chairs in classic collapsed-teenager mode, trailing backpacks, a CD player and a laptop loaded with computer games. It's midafternoon, and they are, of course, tired, but even so their presence adds a jangly, hormonal buzz to the bland, institutional setting. Fair-haired twins Corey and Skyler Mann, 16, and their burlier big brothers Anthony and Brandon, 18, who are also twins, plus eldest brother Christopher, 22, are here to have their heads examined. Literally. The five brothers from Orem, Utah, are the latest recruits to a giant study that's been going on in this building since 1991. Its goal: to determine how the brain develops from childhood into adolescence and on into early adulthood.

It is the project of Dr. Jay Giedd (pronounced Geed), chief of brain imaging in the child psychiatry branch at the National Institute of Mental Health. Giedd, 43, has devoted the past 13 years to peering inside the heads of 1,800 kids and teenagers using high-powered magnetic resonance imaging (MRI). For each volunteer, he creates a unique photo album, taking MRI snapshots every two years and building a record as the brain morphs and grows. Giedd started out investigating the developmental origins of attention-deficit/hyperactivity disorder (ADHD) and autism ("I was going alphabetically," he jokes) but soon discovered that so little was known about how the brain is supposed to develop that it was impossible to figure out where things might be going wrong. In a way, the vast project that has become his life's work is nothing more than an attempt to establish a gigantic control group. "It turned out that normal brains were so interesting in themselves," he marvels. "And the adolescent studies have been the most surprising of all."

Before the imaging studies by Giedd and his collaborators at UCLA, Harvard, the Montreal Neurological Institute and a dozen other institutions, most scientists believed the brain was largely a finished product by the time a child reached the age of 12. Not only is it full-grown in size, Giedd explains, but "in a lot of psychological literature, traced back to [Swiss psychologist] Jean Piaget, the highest rung in the ladder of cognitive development was about age 12—formal operations." In the past, children entered initiation rites and started learning trades at about the onset of puberty. Some theorists concluded from this that the idea of adolescence was an artificial construct, a phenomenon invented in the post–Industrial Revolution years. Giedd's scanning studies proved what every parent of a teenager knows: not only is the brain of the adolescent far from mature, but both gray and white matter undergo extensive structural changes well past puberty. "When we started," says Giedd, "we thought we'd follow kids until about 18 or 20. If we had to pick a number now, we'd probably go to age 25."

Now that MRI studies have cracked open a window on the developing brain, researchers are looking at how the newly detected physiological changes might account for the adolescent behaviors so familiar to parents: emotional outbursts, reckless risk taking and rule breaking, and the impassioned pursuit of sex, drugs and rock 'n' roll. Some experts believe the structural changes seen at adolescence may explain the timing of such major mental illnesses as schizophrenia and bipolar disorder. These diseases typically begin in adolescence and contribute to the high rate of teen suicide. Increasingly, the wild conduct once blamed on "raging hormones" is being seen as the by-product of two factors: a surfeit of hormones, yes, but also a paucity of the cognitive controls needed for mature behavior.

In recent years, Giedd has shifted his focus to twins, which is why the Manns are such exciting recruits. Although most brain development seems to follow a set plan, with changes following cues that are preprogrammed into genes, other, subtler changes in gray matter reflect experience and environment. By following twins, who start out with identical—or, in fraternal twins, similar—programming but then diverge as life takes them on different paths, he hopes to tease apart the influences of nature and nurture. Ultimately, he hopes to find, for instance, that Anthony Mann's plan to become a pilot and Brandon's to study law will lead to brain differences that are detectable on future MRIs. The brain, more than any other organ, is where experience becomes flesh.

Throughout the afternoon, the Mann brothers take turns completing tests of intelligence and cognitive function. Between sessions they occasionally needle one another in the waiting room. "If the other person is in a bad mood, you've got to provoke it," Anthony asserts slyly. Their mother Nancy Mann, a sunny paragon of patience who has three daughters in addition to the five boys, smiles and rolls her eyes.

Shortly before 5 p.m., the Manns head downstairs to the imaging floor to meet the magnet. Giedd, a trim, energetic man with a reddish beard, twinkly blue eyes and an impish sense of humor, greets Anthony and tells him what to expect. He asks Anthony to remove his watch, his necklace and a high school ring, labeled KEEPER. Does Anthony have any metal in his body? Any piercings? Not this clean-cut, soccer-playing Mormon. Giedd tapes a vitamin E capsule onto Anthony's left cheek and one in each ear. He explains that the oil-filled capsules are opaque to the scanner and will define a plane on the images, as well as help researchers tell left from right. The scanning will take about 15 minutes, during which Anthony must lie completely still. Dressed in a red sweat shirt, jeans and white K-Swiss sneakers, he stretches out on the examining table and slides his head into the machine's giant magnetic ring.

MRI, Giedd points out, "made studying healthy kids possible" because there's no radiation involved. (Before MRI, brain development was studied mostly by using cadavers.) Each of the Mann boys will be scanned three times. The first scan is a quick survey that lasts one minute. The second lasts two minutes and looks for any damage or abnormality. The third is 10 minutes long and taken at maximum resolution. It's the money shot. Giedd watches as Anthony's brain appears in cross section on a computer screen. The machine scans 124 slices, each as thin as a dime. It will take 20 hours of computer time to process the images, but the analysis is done by humans, says Giedd. "The human brain is still the best at pattern recognition," he marvels.

Some people get nervous as the MRI machine clangs noisily. Claustrophobes panic. Anthony, lying still in the soul of the machine, simply falls asleep.

Construction Ahead

One reason scientists have been surprised by the ferment in the teenage brain is that the brain grows very little over the course of childhood. By the time a child is 6, it is 90% to 95% of its adult size. As a matter of fact, we are born equipped with most of the neurons our brain will ever have—and that's fewer than we have in utero. Humans achieve their maximum brain-cell density between the third and sixth month of gestation—the culmination of an explosive period of prenatal neural growth. During the final months before birth, our brains undergo a dramatic pruning in which unnecessary brain cells are eliminated. Many neuroscientists now believe that autism is the result of insufficient or abnormal prenatal pruning.

What Giedd's long-term studies have documented is that there is a second wave of proliferation and pruning that occurs later in childhood and that the final, critical part of this second wave, affecting some of our highest mental functions, occurs in the late teens. Unlike the prenatal changes, this neural waxing and waning alters not the number of nerve cells but the number of connections, or synapses, between them. When a child is between the ages of 6 and 12, the neurons grow bushier, each making dozens of connections to other neurons and creating new pathways for nerve signals. The thickening of all this gray matter—the neurons and their branchlike dendrites—peaks when girls are about 11 and boys 12 1/2, at which point a serious round of pruning is under way. Gray matter is thinned out at a rate of about 0.7% a year, tapering off in the early 20s. At the same time, the brain's white matter thickens. The white matter is composed of fatty myelin sheaths that encase axons and, like insulation on a wire, make nerve-signal transmissions faster and more efficient. With each passing year (maybe even up to age 40) myelin sheaths thicken, much like tree rings. During adolescence, says Giedd, summing up the process, "you get fewer but faster connections in the brain." The brain becomes a more efficient machine, but there is a trade-off: it is probably losing some of its raw potential for learning and its ability to recover from trauma.

Most scientists believe that the pruning is guided both by genetics and by a use-it-or-lose-it principle. Nobel prizewinning neuroscientist Gerald Edelman has described that process as "neural Darwinism"—survival of the fittest (or most used) synapses. How you spend your time may be critical. Research shows, for instance, that practicing piano quickly thickens neurons in the brain regions that control the fingers. Studies of London cab drivers, who must memorize all the city's streets, show that they have an unusually large hippocampus, a structure involved in memory. Giedd's research suggests that the cerebellum, an area that coordinates both physical and mental activities, is particularly responsive to experience, but he warns that it's too soon to know just what drives the buildup and pruning phases. He's hoping his studies of twins will help answer such questions: "We're looking at what they eat, how they spend their time—is it video games or sports? Now the fun begins," he says.

No matter how a particular brain turns out, its development proceeds in stages, generally from back to front. Some of the brain regions that reach maturity earliest—through proliferation and pruning—are those in the back of the brain that mediate direct contact with the environment by controlling such sensory functions as vision, hearing, touch and spatial processing. Next are areas that coordinate those functions: the part of the brain that helps you know where the light switch is in your bathroom even if you can't see it in the middle of the night. The very last part of the brain to be pruned and shaped to its adult dimensions is the prefrontal cortex, home of the so-called executive functions—planning, setting priorities, organizing thoughts, suppressing impulses, weighing the consequences of one's actions. In other words, the final part of the brain to grow up is the part capable of deciding, I'll finish my homework and take out the garbage, and then I'll IM my friends about seeing a movie.

"Scientists and the general public had attributed the bad decisions teens make to hormonal changes," says Elizabeth Sowell, a UCLA neuroscientist who has done seminal MRI work on the developing brain. "But once we started mapping where and when the brain changes were happening, we could say, Aha, the part of the brain that makes teenagers more responsible is not finished maturing yet."

Raging Hormones

Hormones, however, remain an important part of the teen-brain story. Right about the time the brain switches from proliferating to pruning, the body comes under the hormonal assault of puberty. (Research suggests that the two events are not closely linked because brain development proceeds on schedule even when a child experiences early or late puberty.) For years, psychologists attributed the intense, combustible emotions and unpredictable behavior of teens to this biochemical onslaught. And new research adds fresh support. At puberty, the ovaries and testes begin to pour estrogen and testosterone into the bloodstream, spurring the development of the reproductive system, causing hair to sprout in the armpits and groin, wreaking havoc with the skin, and shaping the body to its adult contours. At the same time, testosterone-like hormones released by the adrenal glands, located near the kidneys, begin to circulate. Recent discoveries show that these adrenal sex hormones are extremely active in the brain, attaching to receptors everywhere and exerting a direct influence on serotonin and other neurochemicals that regulate mood and excitability.

The sex hormones are especially active in the brain's emotional center—the limbic system. This creates a "tinderbox of emotions," says Dr. Ronald Dahl, a psychiatrist at the University of Pittsburgh. Not only do feelings reach a flash point more easily, but adolescents tend to seek out situations where they can allow their emotions and passions to run wild. "Adolescents are actively looking for experiences to create intense feelings," says Dahl. "It's a very important hint that there is some particular hormone-brain relationship contributing to the appetite for thrills, strong sensations and excitement." This thrill seeking may have evolved to promote exploration, an eagerness to leave the nest and seek one's own path and partner. But in a world where fast cars, illicit drugs, gangs and dangerous liaisons beckon, it also puts the teenager at risk.

That is especially so because the brain regions that put the brakes on risky, impulsive behavior are still under construction. "The parts of the brain responsible for things like sensation seeking are getting turned on in big ways around the time of puberty," says Temple University psychologist Laurence Steinberg. "But the parts for exercising judgment are still maturing throughout the course of adolescence. So you've got this time gap between when things impel kids toward taking risks early in adolescence, and when things that allow people to think before they act come online. It's like turning on the engine of a car without a skilled driver at the wheel."

Dumb Decisions

Increasingly, psychologists like Steinberg are trying to connect the familiar patterns of adolescents' wacky behavior to the new findings about their evolving brain structure. It's not always easy to do. "In all likelihood, the behavior is changing because

the brain is changing," he says. "But that is still a bit of a leap." A critical tool in making that leap is functional magnetic resonance imaging (fMRI). While ordinary MRI reveals brain structure, fMRI actually shows brain activity while subjects are doing assigned tasks.

At McLean Hospital in Belmont, Mass., Harvard neuropsychologist Deborah Yurgelun-Todd did an elegant series of FMRI experiments in which both kids and adults were asked to identity the emotions displayed in photographs of faces. "In doing these tasks," she says, "kids and young adolescents rely heavily on the amygdala, a structure in the temporal lobes associated with emotional and gut reactions. Adults rely less on the amygdala and more on the frontal lobe, a region associated with planning and judgment." While adults make few errors in assessing the photos, kids under 14 tend to make mistakes. In particular, they identify fearful expressions as angry, confused or sad. By following the same kids year after year, Yurgelun-Todd has been able to watch their brain-activity pattern—and their judgment—mature. Fledgling physiology, she believes, may explain why adolescents so frequently misread emotional signals, seeing anger and hostility where none exists. Teenage ranting ("That teacher hates me!") can be better understood in this light.

At Temple University, Steinberg has been studying another kind of judgment: risk assessment. In an experiment using a driving-simulation game, he studies teens and adults as they decide whether to run a yellow light. Both sets of subjects, he found, make safe choices when playing alone. But in group play, teenagers start to take more risks in the presence of their friends, while those over age 20 don't show much change in their behavior. "With this manipulation," says Steinberg, "we've shown that age differences in decision making and judgment may appear under conditions that are emotionally arousing or have high social impact." Most teen crimes, he says, are committed by kids in packs.

Other researchers are exploring how the adolescent propensity for uninhibited risk taking propels teens to experiment with drugs and alcohol. Traditionally, psychologists have attributed this experimentation to peer pressure, teenagers' attraction to novelty and their roaring interest in loosening sexual inhibitions. But researchers have raised the possibility that rapid changes in dopamine-rich areas of the brain may be an additional factor in making teens vulnerable to the stimulating and addictive effects of drugs and alcohol. Dopamine, the brain chemical involved in motivation and in reinforcing behavior, is particularly abundant and active in the teen years.

Why is it so hard to get a teenager off the couch and working on that all important college essay? You might blame it on their immature nucleus accumbens, a region in the frontal cortex that directs motivation to seek rewards. James Bjork at the National Institute on Alcohol Abuse and Alcoholism has been using fMRI to study motivation in a challenging gambling game. He found that teenagers have less activity in this region than adults do. "If adolescents have a motivational deficit, it may mean that they are prone to engaging in behaviors that have either a really high excitement factor or a really low effort factor, or a combination of both." Sound familiar? Bjork believes his work may hold valuable lessons for parents and society. "When presenting suggestions, anything parents can do to emphasize more immediate payoffs will be more effective," he says. To persuade a teen to quit drinking, for example, he suggests stressing something immediate and tangible—the danger of getting kicked off the football team, say—rather than a future on skid row.

Persuading a teenager to go to bed and get up on a reasonable schedule is another matter entirely. This kind of decision making has less to do with the frontal lobe than with the pineal gland at the base of the brain. As nighttime approaches and daylight recedes, the pineal gland produces melatonin, a chemical that signals the body to begin shutting down for sleep. Studies by Mary Carskadon at Brown University have shown that it takes longer for melatonin levels to rise in teenagers than in younger kids or in adults, regardless of exposure to light or stimulating activities. "The brain's program for starting nighttime is later," she explains.

Pruning Problems

The new discoveries about teenage brain development have prompted all sorts of questions and theories about the timing of childhood mental illness and cognitive disorders. Some scientists now believe that ADHD and Tourette's syndrome, which typically appear by the time a child reaches age 7, may be related to the brain proliferation period. Though both disorders have genetic roots, the rapid growth of brain tissue in early childhood, especially in regions rich in dopamine, "may set the stage for the increase in motor activities and tics," says Dr. Martin Teicher, director of developmental biopsychiatry research at McLean Hospital. "When it starts to prune in adolescence, you often see symptoms recede."

Schizophrenia, on the other hand, makes its appearance at about the time the prefrontal cortex is getting pruned. "Many people have speculated that schizophrenia may be due to an abnormality in the pruning process," says Teicher. "Another hypothesis is that schizophrenia has a much earlier, prenatal origin, but as the brain prunes, it gets unmasked." MRI studies have shown that while the average teenager loses about 15% of his cortical gray matter, those who develop schizophrenia lose as much as 25%.

What's a Parent to Do?

Brain scientists tend to be reluctant to make the leap from the laboratory to real-life, hard-core teenagers. Some feel a little burned by the way earlier neurological discoveries resulted in Baby Einstein tapes and other marketing schemes that misapplied their science. It is clear, however, that there are implications in the new research for parents, educators and lawmakers.

In light of what has been learned, it seems almost arbitrary that our society has decided that a young American is ready to drive a car at 16, to vote and serve in the Army at 18 and to drink alcohol at 21. Giedd says the best estimate for when the brain is truly mature is 25, the age at which you can rent a car. "Avis must have some pretty sophisticated neuroscientists," he jokes. Now that we have scientific evidence that the adolescent brain is not quite up to scratch, some legal scholars and child advocates argue that minors should never be tried as adults and should be spared the death penalty. Last year, in an official statement that summarized current research on the adolescent brain, the American Bar Association urged all state legislatures to ban the death penalty for juveniles. "For social and biological reasons," it read, "teens have increased difficulty making mature decisions and understanding the consequences of their actions."

Most parents, of course, know this instinctively. Still, it's useful to learn that teenage behavior is not just a matter of willful pigheadedness or determination to drive you crazy—though these, too, can be factors. "There's a debate over how much conscious control kids have," says Giedd, who has four "teenagers in training" of his own. "You can tell them to shape up or ship out, but making mistakes is part of how the brain optimally grows." It might be more useful to help them make up for what their brain still lacks by providing structure, organizing their time, guiding them through tough decisions (even when they resist) and applying those time-tested parental virtues: patience and love.

A Peaceful Adolescence

**The teen years don't have to be a time of family storm and stress.
Most kids do just fine and now psychologists are finding out why that is.**

BARBARA KANTROWITZ AND KAREN SPRINGEN

At 17, Amanda Hund is a straight-A student who loves competing in horse shows. The high school junior from Willmar, Minn., belongs to her school's band, orchestra and choir. She regularly volunteers through her church and recently spent a week working in an orphanage in Jamaica. Usually, however, she's closer to home, where her family eats dinner together every night. She also has a weekly breakfast date with her father, a doctor, at a local coffee shop. Amanda credits her parents for her relatively easy ride through adolescence. "My parents didn't sweat the small stuff," she says. "They were always very open. You could ask any question."

Is the Hund family for real? Didn't they get the memo that says teens and their parents are supposed to be at odds until ... well, until forever? Actually, they're very much for real, and according to scientists who study the transition to adulthood, they represent the average family's experience more accurately than all those scary TV movies about out-of-control teens. "Research shows that most young people go through adolescence having good relationships with their parents, adopting attitudes and values consistent with their parents' and end up getting out of the adolescent period and becoming good citizens," says Richard Lerner, Bergstrom chair of applied developmental science at Tufts University. This shouldn't be news—but it is, largely because of widespread misunderstanding of what happens during the teen years. It's a time of transition, just like the first year of parenthood or menopause. And although there are dramatic hormonal and physical changes during this period, catastrophe is certainly not preordained. A lot depends on youngsters' innate natures combined with the emotional and social support they get from the adults around them. In other words, parents do matter.

The roots of misconceptions about teenagers go back to the way psychologists framed the field of adolescent development a century ago. They were primarily looking for explanations of why things went wrong. Before long, the idea that this phase was a period of storm and stress made its way into the popular consciousness. But in the last 15 years, developmental scientists have begun to re-examine these assumptions. Instead of focusing on kids who battle their way through the teen years, they're studying the dynamics of success.

At the head of the pack are Lerner and his colleagues, who are in the midst of a major project that many other researchers are following closely. It's a six-year longitudinal study of exactly what it takes to turn out OK and what adults can do to nurture those behaviors. "Parents and sometimes kids themselves often talk about positive development as the absence of bad," says Lerner. "What we're trying to do is present a different vision and a different vocabulary for young people and parents."

The first conclusions from the 4-H Study of Positive Youth Development, published in the February issue of The Journal of Early Adolescence, show that there are quantifiable personality traits possessed by all adolescents who manage to get to adulthood without major problems. Psychologists have labeled these traits "the 5 Cs": competence, confidence, connection, character and caring. These characteristics theoretically lead to a sixth C, contribution (similar to civic engagement). The nomenclature grows out of observations in recent years by a number of clinicians, Lerner says, but his study is the first time researchers have measured how these characteristics influence successful growth.

The 5 Cs are interconnected, not isolated traits, Lerner says. For example, competence refers not just to academic ability but also to social and vocational skills. Confidence includes self-esteem as well as the belief that you can make a difference in the world. The value of the study, Lerner says, is that when it is completed next year, researchers will have a way to quantify these characteristics and eventually determine what specific social and educational programs foster them.

During these years, parents should stay involved as they help kids move on.

In the meantime, parents can learn a lot from this rethinking of the teen years. Don't automatically assume that your kids become alien beings when they leave middle school. They still care what their parents think and they still need love and guidance—although in a different form. Temple University psychology professor Laurence Steinberg, author of "The Ten Basic Principles of Good Parenting," compares raising kids to building a boat that you eventually launch. Parents have to build a strong underpinning so their kids are equipped to face whatever's ahead. In the teen years, that means staying involved as you slowly let go. "One of the things that's natural in adolescence is that kids are going to pull away from their parents as they become increasingly interested in peers," says Steinberg. "It's important for parents to hang in there, for them not to pull back in response to that."

Communication is critical. "Stay in touch with your kids and make sure they feel valued and appreciated," advises Suniya Luthar, professor of clinical and developmental psychology at Columbia University. Even if they roll their eyes when you try to hug them, they still need direct displays of affection, she says. They also need help figuring out goals and limits. Parents should monitor their kids' activities and get to know their friends. Luthar says parents should still be disciplinarians and set standards such as curfews. Then teens need to know that infractions will be met with consistent consequences.

Adolescents are often critical of their parents but they're also watching them closely for clues on how to function in the outside world. Daniel Perkins, associate professor of family and youth resiliency at Penn State, says he and his wife take their twins to the local Ronald McDonald House and serve dinner to say thank you for time the family spent there when the children had health problems after birth. "What we've done already is set up the notion that we were blessed and need to give back, even if it's in a small way." That kind of example sets a standard youngsters remember, even if it seems like they're not paying attention.

Parents should provide opportunities for kids to explore the world and even find a calling. Teens who have a passion for something are more likely to thrive. "They have a sense of purpose beyond day-to-day teenage life," says David Marcus, author of "What It Takes to Pull Me Through." Often, he says, kids who were enthusiastic about something in middle school lose enthusiasm in high school because the competition gets tougher and they're not as confident. Parents need to step in and help young people find other outlets. The best way to do that is to regularly spend uninterrupted time with teens (no cell phones). Kids also need to feel connected to other adults they trust and to their communities. Teens who get into trouble are "drifting," he says. "They don't have a web of people watching out for them."

Teens should build support webs of friends and adults.

At some point during these years, teen-agers should also be learning to build their own support networks—a skill that will be even more important when they're on their own. Connie Flanagan, a professor of youth civic development at Penn State, examines how kids look out for one another. "What we're interested in is how they help one another avoid harm," she says. In one of her focus groups, some teenage girls mentioned that they decided none would drink from an open can at a party because they wouldn't know for sure what they were drinking. "Even though you are experimenting, you're essentially doing it in a way that you protect one another," Flanagan says. Kids who don't make those kinds of connections are more likely to get in trouble because there's no one their own age or older to stop them from going too far. Like any other stage of life, adolescence can be tough. But teens and families can get through it—as long as they stick together.

With JULIE SCELFO

Jail Time Is Learning Time

Signe Nelson and Lynn Olcott

There is excitement in the large, well-lit classroom. Student work, including history posters and artwork, adorn the walls. A polite shuffling of feet can be heard, as names are called and certificates presented. It is the graduation ceremony at the Onondaga County Justice Center in Syracuse, N.Y. The ceremony is held several times a year, recognizing inmates in the Incarcerated Education Program who have passed the GED exam or completed a 108-hour vocational program. The courses in the Incarcerated Education Program are geared to prepare inmates to transition successfully to several different settings.

The Incarcerated Education Program is a joint effort by the Syracuse City School District and the Onondaga County Sheriff's Office, and is housed inside the nine-story Onondaga County Justice Center in downtown Syracuse. The Justice Center is a 250,000 square-foot maximum-security, nonsentenced facility, completed and opened in 1995. The facility was built to contain 616 beds, but currently houses 745 inmates. Between 13,000 and 14,000 inmates passed through booking during 2004. About 2,500 of them were minors.

The Justice Center

The Justice Center is a state-of-the-art facility, designed for and operating on the direct supervision model. Direct supervision is a method of inmate management developed by the federal government in 1974 for presentenced inmates in the Federal Bureau of Prisons. There are about 140 such facilities operating throughout the United States and a few hundred currently under construction. Direct supervision places a single deputy directly in a "housing pod" with between 32 and 64 inmates. Maximum pod capacity in the Onondaga County Justice Center is 56 inmates. Inmates are given either relative freedom of movement within the pod or confined to their cells based on their behavior.

The program has been providing courses and classes at the Justice Center for 10 years, but this partnership between the school district and the sheriff's office began almost 30 years ago with the provision of GED instruction. The Incarcerated Education Program was originally conceived to ensure education for inmates who are minors. The program has grown tremendously and now has more than 20 offerings in academic, vocational and life management areas.

The Syracuse City School District professional staff includes six full-time and 18 part-time teachers and staff members. The program is unique in that there are three Onondaga County Sheriff's sergeants who hold New York State Adult Education certification and who teach classes in the vocational component. An average of 250 inmates, or about one-third of the Justice Center's incarcerated population, are enrolled in day and/or evening classes. There are about 250 hours of class time in the facility per week.

Varied Educational and Training Opportunities

As in the public education sector, vocational programs have evolved with the times. The Basic Office Skills class now offers two sections, and includes computer repair and office production skills. A course in building maintenance can be complemented by a course in pre-application to pre-apprenticeship plumbing, or in painting and surface preparation, a class that includes furniture refinishing. A baking class and nail technology have been added in the past few years. All vocational courses, before implementation, are approved by the New York State Education Department and are designed to be consistent with New York State Department of Labor employment projections for Onondaga County. No vocational programming is implemented without first identifying whether the occupation is an area of growth in the community.

Additionally, a broadly inclusive advisory board, made up of community representatives who are stakeholders in the local economy and in the quality of life in the Syracuse metropolitan area has been established. The Incarcerated Education Advisory Board meets approximately three times a year to discuss the perceived needs of the community and to address strategies for transitioning students into employment. Ongoing topics of study are issues surrounding employment, continuing education and housing.

Incarcerated Education Program planners are very aware that job skills are ineffective without proper work attitudes. Job Readiness Training addresses work ethic, proper work behavior, communication and critical behavior skills. Vocational classes are voluntary for the nonsentenced population. However, because of their popularity, a waiting list is maintained for several courses. Among these popular courses are Basic Office Skills and Small Engine Repair. An additional section of Small Engine Repair has been added for female inmates in the class to ensure gender equity in this training opportunity.

New York State law requires that incarcerated minors continue their education while incarcerated. The Incarcerated Education Program enrolls inmates, ages 16 to 21, in Adult Basic Education/GED classes and addresses students with special needs. Other adult inmates attend on a voluntary basis. Inmates are given an initial placement test to determine math and reading skill levels. Because inmates work at a wide range of ability levels, instruction is individualized and materials are geared to independent work. English as a second Language and English Literacy/Civics are complementary offerings for inmates who are in need of assistance in English language proficiency and knowledge of American culture and history.

The GED exam is given at the Justice Center every 60 days or more often as needed. In the past three years, 225 students have taken the exam. Passing rates fluctuate between 63 percent and 72 percent. The average passing rate for correctional institutions in New York is about 51 percent. The state average passing rate for the general public in community-based courses is fairly stable at 50 percent.[1]

Of course, not everyone will take the GED. Student turnover is high, as inmates are released, bailed out, sent to treatment centers, or sentenced to county, state and federal correctional facilities. Judy Fiorini is a GED teacher who has been with the program for more than 10 years. "Many go back out into our community. We try to teach them something useful for their lives," Fiorini explains.

Transition services form an integral part of the program. The focus is on minors, but help is available for everyone. Two full-time staff members assist people upon release, with such important tasks as acquiring a driver's license, seeking housing, reenrolling in high school or preparing for job interviews. A very important part of transition services is helping people acquire birth certificates, social security cards and other documents crucial for identification.

Tackling Cognitive Issues

Corrections professionals and educators are aware that it is not enough to improve the skill base of an inmate. There must be cognitive changes as well. The justice center is not a treatment facility, but it has been evolving into a therapeutic community. As the Incarcerated Education Program has grown, there has been the flexibility to add several important courses dealing with life issues, attitude and decision-making. According to data provided by the justice center, about 80 percent of inmates have substance abuse-related issues at the time of their arrest. To support desired cognitive changes, the justice center began establishing "clean and sober" pods in 2002. Currently, there are several clean and sober pods, including pods for adult men, women and youths. There are waiting lists for placement in the clean and sober pods.

The Incarcerated Education Program has been offering anger management groups for several years. Anger management helps group members deal with compulsive behavior and focus on long-term goals. Other life management offerings include family education, action for personal choice and a course called

Parent and Child Together. Most courses of study are developed inhouse by experienced professional faculty. Additionally, the program established gender-specific courses, Men's Issues and Women's Issues, to help inmates become more directly aware of their own responsibilities, separate from the role of a partner or significant other in their lives. The Men's Issues class is led by certified professionals and focuses on actions and their consequences. As in most jails, male inmates significantly outnumber female inmates. Courses and groups continue to be added, though it is sometimes difficult to find space for the abundance of activity in the program.

The program is financially supported, using state and federal funds, via nine carefully coordinated grants. Also significant for the success of the program has been ongoing encouragement and technical assistance from the New York State Education Department, the New York State Association of Incarcerated Education Programs and support from the New York State Sheriffs' Association.[2]

The Incarcerated Education Program continues to encounter challenges. It takes energy and dedication to keep the varied curricula substantial and cohesive, despite high student turnover and complex student needs. With a large civilian staff, the program requires close coordination between security and civilian concerns to help civilian staff work most effectively within the safety and security priorities of the facility. Biweekly meetings facilitate ongoing communication.

Making the Most of Time

Every available square inch of classroom space is in constant use. Classes have exceeded available space and some classes meet in core areas of the justice center as well. Several classes are held in the residence pods, where heavy, white tables are pulled together and portable white-boards are erected to create nomadic classrooms. Overall, the program is succeeding in several ways. Incarcerated minors are directly and meaningfully involved in high school equivalency classes, and inmates older than 21 receive academic and vocational services on a voluntary basis. All inmates are offered the opportunity for life-skills classes and for transitional services upon release. Time served at the Onondaga County Justice Center can also be time used for valuable academic, vocational and life management achievements.

Endnotes

1. New York State Department of Education maintains statistics for educational activities at correctional facilities in New York state. Patricia Mooney directs the GED Program for the state through the GED Testing Office in the State Department of Education. Greg Bayduss is the State Department of Education coordinator in charge of Incarcerated Education Programs throughout New York state.
2. State Professional Organizations: The New York State Association of Incarcerated Education Programs Inc. is a professional organization for teachers, administrators and security personnel

(www.nysaiep.org). Its mission is to promote excellence in incarcerated education programs in the state, support research in this field and advocate for incarcerated education initiatives through collaboration with other professional organizations. The authors must mention the valuable assistance of the New York State Sheriffs' Association, supporting each county sheriff, as the chief law enforcement officer in his or her county (www.nyssheriffs.org). The association provides valuable information and technical assistance to county sheriffs to help implement programs in their jails.

SIGNE NELSON is the coordinator of the Incarcerated Education Program, and **LYNN OLCOTT** is a teacher at Auburn Correctional Facility in New York, formerly with the Incarcerated Education Program. The program could not have attained its present strength without the vision and support of law enforcement officials Sheriff Kevin Walsh, Chief Anthony Callisto, and Syracuse City School District administrator Al Wolf. Special thanks to Capt. John Woloszyn, commander of Support Services; Sgt. Joseph Powlina, administrative compliance supervisor; and Deputy Joseph Caruso, photographer. Their assistance in the production of this article was crucial and much appreciated.

Hello to College Joys: Keep Stress Off Campus

JANE E. BRODY

Adults are often quick to tell college students: "Enjoy yourselves. This is the best time of your lives." But for an increasing number of students, the college experience is marred by chronic anxiety, stress and distress.

College counselors report a sharp increase in the need and demand for mental health services, and that can sometimes result in long waiting lists, making the troubled students' problems even worse.

In recent years more than 80 percent of campuses have noted significant increases in serious psychological problems, including severe stress, depression, anxiety and panic attacks, according to an annual survey of counseling centers by Dr. Robert P. Gallagher of the University of Pittsburgh.

Causes of Stress Abound

Some of this emotional distress can be attributed to financial worries in these economically uncertain times. Looking at the dismal employment situation, many students with college loans fret about how they will be able to repay them.

Furthermore, family support systems are not what they used to be for students whose parents are separated, divorced or remarried. Even within colleges, there may now be less support from peers, with the increase in nontraditional students who live on their own off campus rather than in dormitories.

But also, a host of new drugs have enabled more students with mental illnesses to attend college.

These challenges can land on top of traditional causes of student distress like broken romantic relationships, bad grades, insufficient sleep, difficulty making friends, failing to join fraternities or sororities, homesickness or simply feeling overwhelmed by the amount of work that has to be done.

The burden is especially heavy for student athletes who constantly have to juggle the demands of schoolwork and teamwork and for students who have to work to help pay for their schooling.

It does not take much to send a vulnerable 18-year-old into an emotional descent. I recall feeling as if I were in an academic sinkhole and close to suffering an emotional meltdown at the start of my sophomore year.

Although I had good grades in hard courses as a freshman biochemistry major, I began to doubt my interest in the field and questioned whether I had even chosen the right college. I became anxious, depressed and paranoid, thinking that no one liked me and that everyone was speaking ill of me.

But before I abandoned my major and college, I consulted a psychologist at the campus health center, who helped to turn my academic goals and my outlook on college life in a more positive direction.

After tests and talk revealed no underlying mental illness, the therapist suggested that I find an activity that I might enjoy and that would help me feel more a part of college life. So I joined my college's monthly magazine, began writing and editing science-related articles and eventually realized that my passion lay in writing about science rather than doing it. The rest is history.

Strategies Gone Awry

Far too many students turn to tobacco and alcohol to assuage their emotional crises and, in the process, make them worse. Recent studies have shown, for example, that smoking cigarettes causes rather than alleviates stress.

The stress that smokers typically experience when not smoking is induced by nicotine withdrawal, prompting them to believe that they cannot cope with life without cigarettes. But if they had not become hooked on nicotine to begin with or if they broke their addictions by quitting cigarettes (and nicotine replacements), most would eliminate the need to smoke to relieve stress.

Smoking by college students soared in the 1990's, and by 1999 one-third of students were reportedly current smokers, many of them having started after entering college. But more and more colleges are making it very hard to be a smoker on campus. Many forbid smoking in all campus buildings. Some campuses have become entirely smoke free and instead offer smoking-cessation programs for students and faculty members.

Drinking alcohol—especially binge drinking—has long been a troublesome college pastime, even when most students are younger than the legal drinking age. Many students drink alcohol simply to be part of the crowd. Others drink to help them relax and forget their problems.

But what most students—in fact, most people—do not realize is that alcohol is a depressant that only temporarily masks ill feelings but in the end makes matters worse. And binge drinking is plain dangerous. A few students each year die directly from alcohol intoxication. Many more die indirectly by doing something stupid while drunk.

Meanwhile, some colleges are working hard to help students resist the temptation to drink and are providing alternative activities to those where alcohol is most likely to flow. Rather than being stigmatized for refusing alcohol, students who participate in such activities are increasingly seen as campus leaders.

Another all-too-common but ill-conceived mechanism for coping can lead to an eating disorder. The problem may start with stress-induced compulsive eating, leading to weight gain or a fear of it. Desperate attempts to control unwanted pounds may lead to risky diets or even bulimia, the binge-and-purge syndrome that is said to afflict up to 15 percent of young women on some campuses.

Fresh Approaches

Young people with emotional problems often think that they are the only ones so afflicted and that no one understands them. But few if any such problems are unique, and talking about them to a good listener, professional or otherwise, can often make matters seem less serious and more manageable.

It can also lead to creative solutions for even seemingly impossible problems.

A student overwhelmed by a difficult course load may find that dropping an especially troublesome course and taking it or an alternative in summer school or the next semester is far more workable.

Those plagued with monetary worries can consult financial aid offices and explore options like scholarships, part-time or summer jobs or government loans that do not have to be paid back until after graduation.

Instead of using food, drugs, alcohol or tobacco in a counter-productive attempt to relieve stress, students might consider any of a number of wholesome relaxation techniques including meditation, yoga and physical exercise.

Sometimes a short walk or bike ride can help gain a healthier perspective and renewed vigor for dealing with challenging tasks. No matter how busy a student is academically, everyone needs a break and some fun from time to time to restore emotional reserves.

Finally, when emotional distress seems beyond self-help solutions, troubled students should not hesitate to seek professional counseling on campus or off.

Often the campus medical clinic can provide free or low-cost mental health services.

Using such help no longer provokes a stigma. Rather, it is a smart move that can be lifesaving. Plus, you never know where it might lead. It led me, for example, to a very rewarding career.

How Spirit Blooms

Most people long for spirituality, but what path do you take, and what are its milestones? A writer who tried everything from Buddhism to voodoo describes the four steps to finding a spiritual connection.

SUZANNE CLORES

Occasionally, a strange feeling comes over you. You hear a call from inside your heart. A faint, faraway sound you can barely hear amid the office phones, the people who need you, the list of plans for the week, the month, the rest of your life. But when you breathe deeply, the sound is louder and you relax. Finally, one afternoon during your commute home, you hear yourself. You say you need to nurture your soul. But now that you have voiced this need, how do you respond?

I reluctantly began a spiritual search when I was 25. I hated my job—my entire direction—and entered an early midlife panic. Many told me it was just "the age," but I knew it was more. These were the symptoms: A dull sense of separation from my own heart. An uncertainty about what I loved. A feeling that even my family didn't really know me. Doubt that a career path was the only thing worth striving for. Everyone feels that way, said the people I knew. But I felt excluded, apart, even more than usual. I wished I could join the party everyone seemed to be having and wondered how I had become an outsider.

The fact that a recent Gallup poll found that some 84 percent of Americans long for spirituality suggests that many people feel like I did—dissatisfied.

But it's not so easy to suddenly have a relationship with God. There is cynicism, past experiences with organized religion, and the general unhipness of being "religious." There is also our very stressful culture. When the body is confronted by stress, as mine was, it enters a state of fight or flight that drains oxygen from the higher functions of the mind. This makes it difficult to sit still, let alone consider your concerns with God. At the time of my spiritual crisis I was often so stressed about my love life and urban living that spirituality for me was in the same category as TV—something that ate your time and turned your brain to mush. Of course now—like everyone with a meditation or yoga practice—I know better. God is accessible by getting quiet and turning inside. But hindsight is 20/20. And it doesn't account for the pain and suffering that is crucial to acknowledge when stepping onto the spiritual path.

Wicca

Roots: Derived from pre-Christian Celtic religion.
Philosophy/practice: Although many call themselves witches, Wiccans do not practice the evil spells or acts of sorcery commonly associated with the word. They believe in a ubiquitous force, which they refer to as the All or the One, and are guided by the cycles of nature, symbols, and deities of ancient Celtic society.
Modern take: Wicca has grown in popularity since its revival in the United Kingdom in the 1940s. It remains an earth-based religion, with an emphasis on preserving nature and working with natural forces to create harmony and healing.

Yet in the last several years numerous medical studies have linked the benefits of a spiritual practice to improved mental health, particularly coping with depression, anxiety, and long-term illness. Fifty-eight percent of female trauma survivors found that a relationship with God gave them strength to create positive relationships with others. But it takes time, trust, and self-inquiry to have a real spiritual practice. You have to want it. You have to make it happen, and often that means finding support in a strange new world all by yourself.

My trepidation, it turns out, is common. Studies have shown people in physical or psychological crisis often feel left out of their religious or spiritual traditions, even when faith is a priority in their lives. Why is it so hard to believe we belong? Plenty of scientific studies prove that spirituality is inherently part of us. Books like *The God Gene* by Dean Hamer and *The "God" Part of the Brain* by Matthew Alper propose that, like other cognitive functions, our spiritual instincts, cognitions, sensations, and behaviors are generated from a particular cluster of neurons in the brain. We are wired to believe in something larger. (See "Rate Your Spirituality" on page 110.) Then why do we have so many lapses in faith? Because in the face of extreme distress, we are also wired to forget.

While I could not walk the path of St. Catherine of Siena or St. Francis of Assisi and shun material items, social life, and other worldly things holy people relinquish, I still craved spiritual depth. Six years later, I am finally onto something. It took a three-year search before I finally found yoga, another year before I felt comfortable with meditation, and another two years before landing in a real community. In that time my whole life changed. I moved from New York City to Tucson, Arizona, traded the city for the desert, and became part of a yoga-based spiritual practice called Yoga Oasis, a group of Anusara yogis and meditators who create what senior yoga teacher John Friend calls a "kula," or community of the heart. We devote several hours a week to practicing at the yoga center, creating a safe environment where spiritual exploration is welcome. Finally, I know contentment is possible.

But there was a long time of discontent. And guilt about the discontent. (Why can't I just be happy like other people? Why can't I just be a good Catholic or a resigned atheist?) I doggedly moved from tradition to tradition. Each time I met with joy and astonishment and chaos. My life filled with elation. Then my life fell apart. It sounds dramatic, but I can tell you this: With effort and vigilance, you are safe on the spiritual path though it may mean that your life changes entirely.

From my journey I've distilled four steps. Along with the quiz on page 110, they may help your spirituality blossom.

1. Imagine What You Want

What do I want? It seems like an obvious question. But for a long time, I didn't know what I wanted. It is natural—and easier—to continue feeling dissatisfied with situations before actually articulating to yourself "I want something more." Like everyone, I needed the security of faith, a promise of survival. Think of spring flowers that wait to bloom until the summer sun is warm enough. Or underpaid employees who wait until they have another job before leaving the one they have. Spiritual seekers are similar. We seek not just the right spiritual perspective but a safe environment in which to explore it.

The overwhelming but wonderful news is that help is available. The quest for calm has made it into our consumer culture, for better or worse. I soon found many organizations, groups, chat sites, books, magazines, and products available to a practitioner of anything. I know what you're thinking; it sounds like a trend seeker on a shopping spree. But not all investments in mala beads and yoga mats lead to materialism. As seekers we use these tools to respond to that inner voice, that inner calling. Once responding to that voice, you will soon meet others doing the same.

I found others at classes offered by spiritual spas and resorts like Omega, Esalen, and Kripalu. On the cliffs of Big Sur, Esalen had been exploring America's consciousness movement since the 1960s. Omega had intoxicating-looking psychospiritual programs for the New York intellectual, and Kripalu welcomed all seekers with restorative weekends in the bosom of the Berkshires in Massachusetts. Eventually I attended all of these centers and learned various teachings that helped create more peace in my life. But at the beginning of my search, even these resorts were too organized—I wanted raw experience.

I went to the right place. Something about the secrecy and female-centrism of paganism (specifically Wicca), called to me. I stepped into this rich, earth-based religion and found tools for acquiring security: The four elements—water, earth, air, and fire—were frequently invoked in bonfire chants and used in ceremonies to unify all life. How did I stave off my Catholic guilt while on a Wicca retreat? Don't laugh, but on some level I believed chanting around a fire at midnight and Drawing Down the Moon (when the Goddess is invoked in the priestess) was similar to drinking the wine and taking Communion. On a bus ride back to Manhattan from an outdoor pagan festival, I marveled at the idea that through nature, I was connected to the divine.

I arrived back in the concrete jungle knowing what I wanted: security; community; philosophical consistency; but not dogma; a connection with the divine that felt rooted and physical, not magical. I also knew that I didn't need ceremonies in the woods to find those things. In quiet moments I consulted with my level of self-connection: Do I feel secure now? When do I feel secure? How can I cultivate more security? I didn't know it at the time, but creating those quiet moments was the first step to creating a space for spiritual experience to exist.

Yoga

Roots: India, 4th century B.C.
Philosophy/practice: Yoga, which in Sanskrit means "union," is a practice of unifying with the divine Self, that exists beyond the ego, or small self. Yogis maintain that through physical, psychological, and spiritual practice, we can transcend the small, ego-driven chatter of our minds and enter into a higher consciousness.
Modern take: The physical aspect of yoga has attained an unparalleled following in the United States. A meditative, relaxing practice that also strengthens and tones the body, it appeals to people looking to stretch their spiritual frontiers—and their legs.

Sufism

Roots: First brought to America by Hazrat Inayat Khan in 1910
Philosophy/practice: Sufism is best known as the mystical movement within the Islamic religion, emphasizing personal union with the divine. Ritual song and dance also play a role in Sufi tradition.
Modern take: *Adab*, a long-standing Sufi tradition that is still practiced, is defined as a "profound courtesy of heart that arises from the deep relationship with the Divine and expresses itself in refined behavior of all kinds with other beings." Today a small yet devoted group of about 500 to 600 Americans are actively associated with Sufi spiritual practice.

2. Walk Around the Temple

Once I began my search, I kept my interests under wraps at first. I said nothing to my family. Not because they were Catholic, and not because they worried about me, but because my trust was brittle. I needed support, not reactions like, "What the heck are you doing?" or "That sounds weird; what's wrong with you?" If you ask around generally, most people claim openness to religious and spiritual freedom. Still, ours is a culture where most people consider non-Christian religion to be outside of the norm.

My whole life I had tried to understand how to be a good Catholic. I was exhausted and badly needed a fresh take on spirituality. Any outside doubts would have fanned the flames of my own doubts. And since doubt and cynicism were default attitudes among my peers, I felt it best to keep quiet.

But that may have been a mistake. It wasn't until my cousin Mary confided to me that she had been part of a Sufi community for 25 years—a secret she had held from the family for just as long—that I could see it was really possible to change my life. My cousin Mary remembers the loneliness in the first few years of her search. "When I first started looking for spiritual solace, I went to churches, synagogues, even Quaker meetings, and found nice people, but not what I was looking for. Eventually I found a spiritual teacher who called that part of the investigative process 'walking around the temple.' It was the time of seeking before I was ready to go inside."

People in crisis often feel left out of their religious or spiritual traditions, even when faith is a priority in their lives.

Carefully, I began talking to people. I mentioned to a friend's mother that I sought a kind of personal spirituality, and she gladly loaned me her dusty Kabbalah books. My Aunt Maureen invited me to a psychic fair featuring Sylvia Browne and John Edward. (She was hoping my grandfather would play one of his

---

Shamanism

Roots: Origins date back more than 30,000 years
Philosophy/practice: Based on the belief that medicine men (shamans) in ancient hunter-gatherer societies possessed special healing powers that allowed them to act as mediums between the earth and spirit worlds. With these gifts, they were capable of everything from curing diseases to reviving weak crops.
Modern take: Modern-day medicine people continue to cultivate this subtle relationship. They are mostly found in Native American communities and come to their vocation in various ways. Some receive a calling in a dream state, others embark upon a "vision quest," and others apprentice with a skilled shaman.

---

famous practical jokes from the beyond. He didn't.) I didn't know whether or how these spiritual events would fulfill my yearning, but I accepted everything people gave me. I regarded them as gifts, tokens from worlds that promised me something fantastic. But what?

It helps to see all spiritual offerings as gifts, even if not exactly fashioned for you. Also, try giving a little yourself. If you know people who are interested in making the world a safer, more sensitive place, talk with them. Sharing spiritual interests with open minds and hearts gives permission to others to do the same. My yoga community grows because people share their experiences. We commemorate every life event—a war, a marriage, a birth, a death, a holy day—with a special yoga or meditation practice. Plus, there is a danger to keeping it all inside. If you don't share your needs, desires, or experiences with anyone, there is a chance the stress and alienation will cause psychic and bodily harm.

3. Conquer the Fear

So many of us spend time walking around the temple that it almost becomes a spiritual path in and of itself. Though my cousin Mary is now a devoted student of Indian teacher Meher Baba, she maintains that spiritual searching was an important part of finding her true teacher. I took her advice and for many months—years, actually—slowly confronted my spiritual longings. I didn't know what I wanted. So I tried this and that. With as much of my heart as I could, I took shamanic journeys. I attended pagan ceremonies. I sought out voodoo rituals. And while most of the time I had powerful spiritual experiences, there was a major problem: I was scared.

All heroic myths, fairy tales, and spiritual heroes encounter what is called "the dark night of the soul." It is a time when seekers are deeply frightened, lonely, and uncertain about going forward. Yet they are aware that they cannot turn back. Sometimes, I found, it lasts longer than a night. Even after I attended deeply meaningful ceremonies and found a yoga teacher I liked, I kept asking myself, Is this really necessary? Is it sacrilegious? Will I be punished somehow for leaving my old religion and trying to find something as abstract as spirituality? Despite my frustration at not having answers, asking questions was one of the most productive and helpful steps I could take to relieve myself of fear. Asking honest questions leads to hearing honest answers, and honest answers led me to the truth that I needed to surrender to the paths that felt right.

One man I met on the spiritual path encountered his darkest night after he had already been studying with a teacher. It came right after his teacher asked that he make a greater commitment. "I tried everything to bring about a transformation in myself," the man told me. "All of the deep experiences I'd had, all of my understanding of dharma, even my will and perseverance had nothing to do with the kind of radical transformation that lay ahead. I began to experience intense confusion and fear, which grew into even more intense paranoia. I didn't know what to trust."

It took a year for this pilgrim to realize the transformation he needed to make, but he eventually did as a result of staying with it. "Transformation," he told me, "is a process of active surren-

Buddhism

Roots: India, 525 B.C., where Prince Siddhartha received enlightenment under the bodhi tree at the river Neranjara. Thereafter he was known as the Buddha, or Awakened One.

Philosophy/practice: Buddhist religion is based on the theory that life is a continual cycle of birth, death, and rebirth, and that we live in constant suffering. Meditation, persistent self-inquiry, and observance of moral precepts are the way to liberation and freedom from suffering.

Modern take: Buddhism thrives today as the fourth largest religion in the world. Buddhists practicing in the West are drawn to varying sects, including Theravada, Tibetan, Mahayana, and Zen.

der. You cannot will your own transformation at the soul level; you can only allow transformation to be enacted by forces greater than yourself."

4. Cross to Safety

There is no guarantee that stepping more deeply onto a spiritual path will solve all your problems. Rather, it demands more empathy and honesty from yourself than a lot of other relationships demand.

Voodoo

Roots: The exact origins of voodoo are unknown, but it's generally believed to have begun in the West African nation of Benin during the slave trade. It's also practiced in Haiti, South America, and New Orleans.

Philosophy/practice: Voodoo practitioners believe in one god, but call upon spirits, the Loa, to heal the sick, help the needy and provide practical solutions to life's problems.

Modern take: Voodoo is a guiding force in communities where it's practiced, and voodoo priests are prominent, respected figures who perform many sacred functions.

I found this can be more complex than comfortable. About two years into my exploration of various spiritual paths, my life had changed dramatically: I had left my long-term relationship, moved in with others on a spiritual path, changed my line of work to do freelance projects with various people. Very little in my life was stable. And yet the space gave my passion room to burn. I felt clear. My resolve was strong that I had made the right choices and let my spiritual vision guide me.

And then everything started collapsing. The couple I lived with were ending their marriage. The people I worked with were terminating our agreement prematurely. I was losing my home and job, and I was angry. What had I done wrong?

I phoned a shamanic practitioner I trusted. After consulting with her own spirit guides, she gave me news I had difficulty swallowing. She said, "The structures you have created for yourself are dissolving of your own doing. You must manifest a new structure for yourself."

I had expected her to say, "You are doing everything right, none of this is your fault. The universe will save you," I answered, with an edge to my voice, "How do I manifest a new life?"

She said seriously; "Get really clear in your mind. Meditate, chant, do whatever you have to do to clear the anxiety. Then dream what you want and need. Write it down very clearly and keep it somewhere."

"Dream?" I asked.

"Yes."

"And write it on a piece of paper?" I asked.

"Yes," she said.

I hung up, annoyed. This advice did not sound concrete. I was losing my home, and she wanted me to dream. But I had spent a year cultivating spiritual awareness and trust. So I sat down and did it. I dreamed a house in a different city than where I lived, with work and people whom I had never met. And within three months I had moved out of town unexpectedly, found the house, community, and work situation I had written on the page, almost exactly.

The spiritual path is not linear. This makes it hard to clear a weekend in October for a "spiritually deep" day. Like love, spiritual life does not work like that. And yet every moment provides an opportunity to begin. Perhaps on the radio, or on the news, a report mentions the word "spirituality," and your heart softens. Or perhaps when you hear somewhere that, post 9/11, attendance at spiritual retreats has increased, and that lay members of churches, synagogues, and mosques have begun to organize nationally, you somehow feel included. You know you are part of this group, these new pilgrims—maybe even the old ones—but how do you respond?

The truth is, to think about it is to begin. You have taken a crucial step. And you are not alone. I can tell you, the most important thing to remember is that you are not alone.

The Battle for Your Brain

Science is developing ways to boost intelligence, expand memory, and more. But will you be allowed to change your own mind?

RONALD BAILEY

"We're on the verge of profound changes in our ability to manipulate the brain," says Paul Root Wolpe, a bioethicist at the University of Pennsylvania. He isn't kidding. The dawning age of neuroscience promises not just new treatments for Alzheimer's and other brain diseases but enhancements to improve memory, boost intellectual acumen, and fine-tune our emotional responses. "The next two decades will be the golden age of neuroscience," declares Jonathan Moreno, a bioethicist at the University of Virginia. "We're on the threshold of the kind of rapid growth of information in neuroscience that was true of genetics 15 years ago."

One man's golden age is another man's dystopia. One of the more vociferous critics of such research is Francis Fukuyama, who warns in his book *Our Posthuman Future* that "we are already in the midst of this revolution" and *"we should use the power of the state to regulate it"* (emphasis his). In May a cover story in the usually pro-technology *Economist* worried that "neuroscientists may soon be able to screen people's brains to assess their mental health, to distribute that information, possibly accidentally, to employers or insurers, and to 'fix' faulty personality traits with drugs or implants on demand."

There are good reasons to consider the ethics of tinkering directly with the organ from which all ethical reflection arises. Most of those reasons boil down to the need to respect the rights of the people who would use the new technologies. Some of the field's moral issues are common to all biomedical research: how to design clinical trials ethically, how to ensure subjects' privacy, and so on. Others are peculiar to neurology. It's not clear, for example, whether people suffering from neurodegenerative disease can give informed consent to be experimented on.

Last May the Dana Foundation sponsored an entire conference at Stanford on "neuroethics." Conferees deliberated over issues like the moral questions raised by new brain scanning techniques, which some believe will lead to the creation of truly effective lie detectors. Participants noted that scanners might also be able to pinpoint brain abnormalities in those accused of breaking the law, thus changing our perceptions of guilt and innocence. Most nightmarishly, some worried that governments could one day use brain implants to monitor and perhaps even control citizens' behavior.

But most of the debate over neuroethics has not centered around patients' or citizens' autonomy, perhaps because so many of the field's critics themselves hope to restrict that autonomy in various ways. The issue that most vexes *them* is the possibility that neuroscience might enhance previously "normal" human brains.

The tidiest summation of their complaint comes from the conservative columnist William Satire. "Just as we have antidepressants today to elevate mood," he wrote after the Dana conference, "tomorrow we can expect a kind of Botox for the brain to smooth out wrinkled temperaments, to turn shy people into extroverts, or to bestow a sense of humor on a born grouch. But what price will human nature pay for these nonhuman artifices?"

Truly effective neuropharmaceuticals that improve moods and sharpen mental focus are already widely available and taken by millions. While there is some controversy about the effectiveness of Prozac, Paxil, and Zoloft, nearly 30 million Americans have taken them, with mostly positive results. In his famous 1993 book *Listening to Prozac*, the psychiatrist Peter Kramer describes patients taking the drug as feeling "better than well." One Prozac user, called Tess, told him that when she isn't taking the medication, "I am not myself."

One Pill Makes You Smarter...

That's exactly what worries Fukuyama, who thinks Prozac looks a lot like *Brave New World*'s soma. The pharmaceutical industry, he declares, is producing drugs that "provide self-esteem in the bottle by elevating serotonin in the brain." If you need a drug to be your "self," these critics ask, do you really have a self at all?

Another popular neuropharmaceutical is Ritalin, a drug widely prescribed to remedy attention deficit hyperactivity disorder (ADHD), which is characterized by agitated behavior and an inability to focus on tasks. Around 1.5 million schoolchildren take Ritalin, which recent research suggests boosts the activity of the neurotransmitter dopamine in the brain. Like all psychoactive drugs, it is not without controversy. Perennial psychiatric critic Peter Breggin argues that millions of children are being "drugged into more compliant or submissive state[s]" to satisfy the needs of harried parents and school officials. For Fukuyama, Ritalin is prescribed to control rambunctious children because "parents and teachers...do not want to spend the time and energy necessary to discipline, divert, entertain, or train difficult children the old-fashioned way."

Unlike the more radical Breggin, Fukuyama acknowledges that drugs such as Prozac and Ritalin have helped millions when other treatments have failed. Still, he worries about their larger social consequences. "There is a disconcerting symmetry between Prozac and Ritalin," he writes. "The former is prescribed heavily for depressed women lacking in self-esteem; it gives them more the alpha-male feeling that comes with high serotonin levels. Ritalin, on the other hand, is prescribed largely for young boys who do not want to sit still in class because nature never designed them to behave that way. Together, the two sexes are gently nudged toward that androgynous median personality, self-satisfied and socially compliant, that is the current politically correct outcome in American society."

What really worries critics is that Prozac and Ritalin may be the pharmacological equivalent of bearskins and stone axes compared to the new drugs that are coming.

Although there are legitimate questions here, they're related not to the chemicals themselves but to who makes the decision to use them. Even if Prozac and Ritalin can help millions of people, that doesn't mean schools should be able to force them on any student who is unruly or bored. But by the same token, even if you accept the most radical critique of the drug—that ADHD is not a real disorder to begin with—that doesn't mean Americans who exhibit the symptoms that add up to an ADHD diagnosis should not be allowed to alter their mental state chemically, if that's an outcome they want and a path to it they're willing to take.

Consider Nick Megibow, a senior majoring in philosophy at Gettysburg College. "Ritalin made my life a lot better, he reports. "Before I started taking Ritalin as a high school freshman, I was doing really badly in my classes. I had really bad grades, Cs and Ds mostly. By sophomore year, I started taking Ritalin, and it really worked amazingly. My grades improved dramatically to mostly As and Bs. It allows me to focus and get things done rather than take three times the amount of time that it should take to finish something." If people like Megibow don't share Fukuyama's concerns about the wider social consequences of their medication, it's because they're more interested, quite reasonably, in feeling better and living a successful life.

What really worries critics like Satire and Fukuyama is that Prozac and Ritalin may be the neuropharmacological equivalent of bearskins and stone axes compared to the new drugs that are coming. Probably the most critical mental function to be en-

hanced is memory. And this, it turns out, is where the most promising work is being done. At Princeton, biologist Joe Tsien's laboratory famously created smart mice by genetically modifying them to produce more NMDA brain receptors, which are critical for the formation and maintenance of memories. Tsien's mice were much faster learners than their unmodified counterparts. "By enhancing learning, that is, memory acquisition, animals seem to be able to solve problems faster," notes Tsien. He believes his work has identified an important target that will lead other researchers to develop drugs that enhance memory.

A number of companies are already hard at work developing memory drugs. Cortex Pharmaceuticals has developed a class of compounds called AMPA receptor modulators, which enhance the glutamate-based transmission between brain cells. Preliminary results indicate that the compounds do enhance memory and cognition in human beings. Memory Pharmaceuticals, co-founded by Nobel laureate Eric Kandel, is developing a calcium channel receptor modulator that increases the sensitivity of neurons and allows them to transmit information more speedily and a nicotine receptor modulator that plays a role in synaptic plasticity. Both modulators apparently improve memory. Another company, Targacept, is working on the nicotinic receptors as well.

All these companies hope to cure the memory deficits that some 30 million baby boomers will suffer as they age. If these compounds can fix deficient memories, it is likely that they can enhance normal memories as well. Tsien points out that a century ago the encroaching senility of Alzheimer's disease might have been considered part of the "normal" progression of aging. "So it depends on how you define normal," he says. "Today we know that most people have less good memories after age 40 and I don't believe that's a normal process."

Eight Objections

And so we face the prospect of pills to improve our mood, our memory, our intelligence, and perhaps more. Why would anyone object to that?

Eight objections to such enhancements recur in neuroethicists' arguments. None of them is really convincing.

- *Neurological enhancements permanently change the brain.* Erik Parens of the Hastings Center, a bioethics think tank, argues that it's better to enhance a child's performance by changing his environment than by changing his brain—that it's better to, say, reduce his class size than to give him Ritalin. But this is a false dichotomy. Reducing class size is aimed at changing the child's biology too, albeit indirectly. Activities like teaching are supposed to induce biological changes in a child's brain, through a process called *learning*.

Fukuyama falls into this same error when he suggests that even if there is some biological basis for their condition, people with ADHD "clearly...can do things that would affect their final degree of attentiveness or hyperactivity. Training, character, determination, and environment more generally would all play important roles." So can Ritalin, and much more expeditiously, too. "What is the difference between Ritalin and the Kaplan SAT review?" asks the Dartmouth neuroscientist Michael Gazzaniga. "It's six of one and a half dozen of the other. If both can boost SAT scores by, say, 120 points, I think it's immaterial which way it's done."

- *Neurological enhancements are anti-egalitarian.* A perennial objection to new medical technologies is the one Patens calls "unfairness in the distribution of resources." In other words, the rich and their children will get access to brain enhancements first, and will thus acquire more competitive advantages over the poor.

This objection rests on the same false dichotomy as the first. As the University of Virginia's Moreno puts it, "We don't stop people from giving their kids tennis lessons," If anything, the new enhancements might *increase* social equality. Moreno notes that neuropharmaceuticals are likely to be more equitably distributed than genetic enhancements, because "after all, a pill is easier to deliver than DNA."

- *Neurological enhancements are self-defeating.* Not content to argue that the distribution of brain enhancements won't be egalitarian enough, some critics turn around and argue that it will be too egalitarian. Parens has summarized this objection succinctly: "If everyone achieved the same relative advantage with a given enhancement, then ultimately no one's position would change; the 'enhancement' would have failed if its purpose was to increase competitive advantage."

This is a flagrant example of the zero-sum approach that afflicts so much bioethical thought. Let's assume, for the sake of argument, that everyone in society will take a beneficial brain-enhancing drug. Their relative positions may not change, but the overall productivity and wealth of society would increase considerably, making everyone better off. Surely that is a social good.

- *Neurological enhancements are difficult to refuse.* Why exactly would everyone in the country take the same drug? Because, the argument goes, competitive pressures in our go-go society will be so strong that a person will be forced to take a memory-enhancing drug just to keep up with everyone else. Even if the law protects freedom of choice, social pressures will draw us in.

For one thing, this misunderstands the nature of the technology. It's not simply a matter of popping a pill and suddenly zooming ahead. "I know a lot of smart people who don't amount to a row of beans," says Gazzaniga. "They're just happy underachieving, living life below their potential. So a pill that pumps up your intellectual processing power won't necessarily give you the drive and ambition to use it."

Beyond that, it's not as though we don't all face competitive pressures anyway—to get into and graduate from good universities, to constantly upgrade skills, to buy better computers and more productive software, whatever. Some people choose to enhance themselves by getting a Ph.D. in English; others are happy to stop their formal education after high school. It's not clear why a pill should be more irresistible than higher education, or why one should raise special ethical concerns while the other does not.

- *Neurological enhancements undermine good character.* For some critics, the comparison to higher education suggests a different problem. We should strive for what we get, they suggest; taking a pill to enhance cognitive functioning is just too easy. As Fukuyama puts it: "The normal, and morally acceptable, way of overcoming low self-esteem was to struggle with oneself and with others, to work hard, to endure painful sacrifices, and finally to rise and be seen as having done so."

"By denying access to brain-enhancing drugs, people like Fukuyama are advocating an exaggerated stoicism," counters Moreno. "I don't see the benefit or advantage of that kind of tough love." Especially since there will still be many different ways to achieve things and many difficult challenges in life. Brain-enhancing drugs might ease some of our labors, but as Moreno notes, "there are still lots of hills to climb, and they are pretty steep." Cars, computers, and washing machines have tremendously enhanced our ability to deal with formerly formidable tasks. That doesn't mean life's struggles have disappeared—just that we can now tackle the next ones.

- *Neurological enhancements undermine personal responsibility.* Carol Freedman, a philosopher at Williams College, argues that what is at stake "is a conception of ourselves as responsible agents, not machines." Fukuyama extends the point, claiming that "ordinary people" are eager to "medicalize as much of their behavior as possible and thereby reduce their responsibility for their own actions." As an example, he suggests that people who claim to suffer from ADHD "want to absolve themselves of personal responsibility."

But we are not debating people who might use an ADHD diagnosis as an excuse to behave irresponsibly. We are speaking of people who use Ritalin to change their behavior. Wouldn't it be more irresponsible of them to not take corrective action?

- *Neurological enhancements enforce dubious norms.* There are those who assert that corrective action might be irresponsible after all, depending on just what it is that you're trying to correct. People might take neuropharmaceuticals, some warn, to conform to a harmful social conception of normality. Many bioethicists—Georgetown University's Margaret Little, for example—argue that we can already see this process in action among women who resort to expensive and painful cosmetic surgery to conform to a social ideal of feminine beauty. Never mind for the moment that beauty norms for both men and women have never been so diverse. Providing and choosing to avail oneself of that surgery makes one complicit in norms that are morally wrong, the critics argue. After all, people should be judged not by their physical appearances but by the content of their characters.

That may be so, but why should someone suffer from society's slights if she can overcome them with a nip here and a tuck there? The norms may indeed be suspect, but the suffering is experienced by real people whose lives are consequently diminished. Little acknowledges this point, but argues that those who benefit from using a technology to conform have a moral obligation to fight against the suspect norm. Does this mean people should be given access to technologies they regard as beneficial only if they agree to sign on to a bioethical fatwa?

Of course, we should admire people who challenge norms they disagree with and live as they wish, but why should others be denied relief just because some bioethical commissars decree that society's misdirected values must change? Change may come, but real people should not be sacrificed to some restrictive bioethical utopia in the meantime. Similarly, we should no doubt value depressed people or people with bad memories just as highly as we do happy geniuses, but until that glad day comes people should be allowed to take advantage of technologies that improve their lives in the society in which they actually live.

Furthermore, it's far from clear that everyone will use these enhancements in the same ways. There are people who alter their bodies via cosmetic surgery to bring them closer to the norm, and there are people who alter their bodies via piercings and tattoos to make them more individually expressive. It doesn't take much imagination to think of unusual or unexpected ways that Americans might use mind-enhancing technologies. Indeed, the war on drugs is being waged, in part, against a small but significant minority of people who prefer to alter their consciousness in socially disapproved ways.

- *Neurological enhancements make us inauthentic.* Parents and others worry that the users of brain-altering chemicals are less authentically themselves when they're on the drug. Some of them would reply that the exact opposite is the case. In *Listening to Prozac*, Kramer chronicles some dramatic transformations in the personalities and attitudes of his patients once they're on the drug. The aforementioned Tess tells him it was "as if I had been in a drugged state all those years and now I'm clearheaded."

Cars, computers, and washing machines have tremendously enhanced our ability to deal with formerly formidable tasks. That doesn't mean life's struggles have disappeared—just that we can now tackle the next ones.

Again, the question takes a different shape when one considers the false dichotomy between biological and "nonbiological" enhancements. Consider a person who undergoes a religious conversion and emerges from the experience with a more upbeat and attractive personality. Is he no longer his "real" self? Must every religious convert be deprogrammed?

Even if there were such a thing as a "real" personality, why should you stick with it if you don't like it? If you're socially withdrawn and a pill can give you a more vivacious and outgoing manner, why not go with it? After all, you're choosing to take responsibility for being the "new" person the drug helps you to be.

Authenticity and Responsibility

"Is it a drug-induced personality or has the drug cleared away barriers to the real personality?" asks the University of Pennsylvania's Wolpe. Surely the person who is choosing to use the drug is in a better position to answer that question than some bioethical busybody.

This argument over authenticity lies at the heart of the neuroethicists' objections. If there is a single line that divides the supporters of neurological freedom from those who would restrict the new treatments, it is the debate over whether a natural state of human being exists and, if so, how appropriate it is to modify it. Wolpe makes the point that in one sense cognitive enhancement resembles its opposite, Alzheimer's disease. A person with Alzheimer's loses her personality. Similarly, an enhanced individual's personality may become unrecognizable to those who knew her before.

Not that this is unusual. Many people experience a version of this process when they go away from their homes to college or the military. They return as changed people with new capacities, likes, dislikes, and social styles, and they often find that their families and friends no longer relate to them in the old ways. Their brains have been changed by those experiences, and they are not the same people they were before they went away. Change makes most people uncomfortable, probably never more so than when it happens to a loved one. Much of the neuro-Luddites' case rests on a belief in an unvarying, static personality, something that simply doesn't exist.

It isn't just personality that changes over time. Consciousness itself is far less static than we've previously assumed, a fact that raises contentious questions of free will and determinism. Neuroscientists are finding more and more of the underlying automatic processes operating in the brain, allowing us to take a sometimes disturbing look under our own hoods. "We're finding out that by the time we're conscious of doing something, the brain's already done it," explains Gazzaniga. Consciousness, rather than being the director of our activities, seems instead to be a way for the brain to explain to itself why it did something.

Haunting the whole debate over neuroscientific research and neuroenhancements is the fear that neuroscience will undercut notions of responsibility and free will. Very preliminary research has suggested that many violent criminals do have altered brains. At the Stanford conference, *Science* editor Donald Kennedy suggested that once we know more about brains, our legal system will have to make adjustments in how we punish those who break the law. A murderer or rapist might one day plead innocence on the grounds that "my amygdala made me do it." There is precedent for this: The legal system already mitigates criminal punishment when an offender can convince a jury he's so mentally ill that he cannot distinguish right from wrong.

> **Like any technology, neurological enhancements can be abused. But critics have not made a strong case for why individuals should not be allowed to take advantage of breakthroughs.**

Of course, there are other ways such discoveries might pan out in the legal system, with results less damaging to social order but still troubling for notions of personal autonomy. One possibility is that an offender's punishment might be reduced if he agrees to take a pill that corrects the brain defect he blames for his crime. We already hold people responsible when their drug use causes harm to others—most notably, with laws against drunk driving. Perhaps in the future we will hold people responsible if they fail to take drugs that would help prevent them from behaving in harmful ways. After all, which is more damaging to personal autonomy, a life confined to a jail cell or roaming free while taking a medication?

The philosopher Patricia Churchland examines these conundrums in her forthcoming book, *Brainwise: Studies in Neurophilosophy*. "Much of human social life depends on the expectation that agents have control over their actions and are responsible for their choices," she writes. "In daily life it is commonly assumed that it is sensible to punish and reward behavior so long as the person was in control and chose knowingly and intentionally." And that's the way it should remain, even as we learn more about how our brains work and how they sometimes break down.

Churchland points out that neuroscientific research by scientists like the University of Iowa's Antonio Damasio strongly shows that emotions are an essential component of viable practical reasoning about what a person should do. In other words, neuroscience is bolstering philosopher David Hume's insight that "reason is and ought only to be the slave of the passions." Patients whose affects are depressed or lacking due to brain injury are incapable of judging or evaluating between courses of action. Emotion is what prompts and guides our choices.

Churchland further argues that moral agents come to be morally and practically wise not through pure cognition but by developing moral beliefs and habits through life experiences. Our moral reflexes are honed through watching and hearing about which actions are rewarded and which are punished; we learn to be moral the same way we learn language. Consequently, Churchland concludes "the default presumption that agents are responsible for their actions is empirically necessary to an agent's learning, both emotionally and cognitively, how to evaluate the consequences of certain events and the price of taking risks."

It's always risky to try to derive an "ought" from an "is," but neuroscience seems to be implying that liberty—i.e., letting people make choices and then suffer or enjoy the consequences—is essential for inculcating virtue and maintaining social cooperation. Far from undermining personal responsibility, neuroscience may end up strengthening it.

For Neurological Liberty

Fukuyama wants to "draw red lines" to distinguish between therapy and enhancement, "directing research toward the former while putting restrictions on the latter." He adds that "the original purpose of medicine is, after all, to heal the sick, not turn healthy people into gods" He imagines a federal agency that would oversee neurological research, prohibiting anything that aims at enhancing our capacities beyond some notion of the human norm.

"For us to flourish as human beings, we have to live according to our nature, satisfying the deepest longings that we as natural beings have," Fukuyama told the Christian review *Books & Culture* last summer. "For example, our nature gives us tremendous cognitive capabilities, capability for reason, capability to learn, to teach ourselves things, to change our opinions, and so forth. What follows from that? A way of life that permits such growth is better than a life in which this capacity is shriveled and stunted in various ways." This is absolutely correct. The trouble is that Fukuyama has a shriveled, stunted vision of human nature, leading him and others to stand athwart neuroscientific advances that will make it possible for more people to take fuller advantage of their reasoning and learning capabilities.

Like any technology, neurological enhancements can be abused, especially if they're doled out—or imposed—by an unchecked authority. But Fukuyama and other critics have not made a strong case for why *individuals*, in consultation with their doctors, should not be allowed to take advantage of new neuroscientific breakthroughs to enhance the functioning of their brains. And it is those individuals that the critics will have to convince if they seriously expect to restrict this research.

It's difficult to believe that they'll manage that. In the 1960s many states outlawed the birth control pill, on the grounds that it would be too disruptive to society. Yet Americans, eager to take control of their reproductive lives, managed to roll back those laws, and no one believes that the pill could be re-outlawed today.

Moreno thinks the same will be true of the neurological advances to come. "My hunch," he says, "is that in the United States, medications that enhance our performance are not going to be prohibited." When you consider the sometimes despairing tone that Fukuyama and others like him adopt, it's hard not to conclude that on that much, at least, they agree.

RONALD BAILEY is *Reason's* science correspondent and the editor of Global Warming and Other Eco-Myths: How the Environmental Movement Uses False Science to Scare Us to Death (Prima Publishing).

Grow Up? Not So Fast

Meet the twixters. They're not kids anymore, but they're not adults either. Why a new breed of young people won't—or can't?—settle down

Lev Grossman

Michele, Ellen, Nathan, Corinne, Marcus and Jennie are friends. All of them live in Chicago. They go out three nights a week, sometimes more. Each of them has had several jobs since college; Ellen is on her 17th, counting internships, since 1996. They don't own homes. They change apartments frequently. None of them are married, none have children. All of them are from 24 to 28 years old.

Thirty years ago, people like Michele, Ellen, Nathan, Corinne, Marcus and Jennie didn't exist, statistically speaking. Back then, the median age for an American woman to get married was 21. She had her first child at 22. Now it all takes longer. It's 25 for the wedding and 25 for baby. It appears to take young people longer to graduate from college, settle into careers and buy their first homes. What are they waiting for? Who are these permanent adolescents, these twentysomething Peter Pans? And why can't they grow up?

Everybody knows a few of them—full-grown men and women who still live with their parents, who dress and talk and party as they did in their teens, hopping from job to job and date to date, having fun but seemingly going nowhere. Ten years ago, we might have called them Generation X, or slackers, but those labels don't quite fit anymore. This isn't just a trend, a temporary fad or a generational hiccup. This is a much larger phenomenon, of a different kind and a different order.

Social scientists are starting to realize that a permanent shift has taken place in the way we live our lives. In the past, people moved from childhood to adolescence and from adolescence to adulthood, but today there is a new, intermediate phase along the way. The years from 18 until 25 and even beyond have become a distinct and separate life stage, a strange, transitional never-never land between adolescence and adulthood in which people stall for a few extra years, putting off the iron cage of adult responsibility that constantly threatens to crash down on them. They're betwixt and between. You could call them twixters.

Where did the twixters come from? And what's taking them so long to get where they're going? Some of the sociologists, psychologists and demographers who study this new life stage see it as a good thing. The twixters aren't lazy, the argument goes, they're reaping the fruit of decades of American affluence and social liberation. This new period is a chance for young people to savor the pleasures of irresponsibility, search their souls and choose their life paths. But more historically and economically minded scholars see it differently. They are worried that twixters aren't growing up because they can't. Those researchers fear that whatever cultural machinery used to turn kids into grownups has broken down, that society no longer provides young people with the moral backbone and the financial wherewithal to take their rightful places in the adult world. Could growing up be harder than it used to be?

The sociologists, psychologists, economists and others who study this age group have many names for this new phase of life—"youthhood," "adultescence"—and they call people in their 20s "kidults" and "boomerang kids," none of which have quite stuck. Terri Apter, a psychologist at the University of Cambridge in England and the author of *The Myth of Maturity*, calls them "thresholders."

Apter became interested in the phenomenon in 1994, when she noticed her students struggling and flailing more than usual after college. Parents were baffled when their expensively educated, otherwise well-adjusted 23-year-old children wound up sobbing in their old bedrooms, paralyzed by indecision. "Legally, they're adults, but they're on the threshold, the doorway to adulthood, and they're not going through it," Apter says. The percentage of 26-year-olds living with their parents has nearly doubled since 1970, from 11% to 20%, according to Bob Schoeni, a professor of economics and public policy at the University of Michigan.

Jeffrey Arnett, a developmental psychologist at the University of Maryland, favors "emerging adulthood" to describe this new demographic group, and the term is the title of his new book on the subject. His theme is that the twixters are misunderstood. It's too easy to write them off as overgrown children, he argues. Rather, he suggests, they're doing important work to get themselves ready for adulthood. "This is the one time of their lives when they're not responsible for anyone else or to anyone else," Arnett says. "So they have this wonderful freedom to really focus on their own lives and work on becoming the kind of person they want to be." In his view, what looks like incessant, hedonistic play is the twixters' way of trying on jobs and partners and personalities and making sure that when they do settle down, they do it the right way, *their* way. It's not that they don't take adulthood seriously; they take it so seriously, they're spending years carefully choosing the right path into it.

But is that all there is to it? Take a giant step backward, look at the history and the context that led up to the rise of the twixters, and you start to wonder, Is it that they don't want to grow up, or is it that the rest of society won't let them?

School Daze

Matt Swann is 27. He took 6½ years to graduate from the University of Georgia. When he finally finished, he had a brand-spanking-new degree in cognitive science, which he describes as a wide-ranging interdisciplinary field that covers cognition, problem solving, artificial intelligence, linguistics, psychology, philosophy and anthropology. All of which is pretty cool, but its value in today's job market is not clear. "Before the '90s maybe, it seemed like a smart guy could do a lot of things," Swann says. "Kids used to go to college to get educated. That's what I did, which I think now was a bit naive. Being smart after college doesn't really mean anything. 'Oh, good, you're smart. Unfortunately your productivity's s___, so we're going to have to fire you.'"

College is the institution most of us entrust to watch over the transition to adulthood, but somewhere along the line that transition has slowed to a crawl. In a TIME poll of people ages 18 to 29, only 32% of those who attended college left school by age 21. In fact, the average college student takes five years to finish. The era of the four-year college degree is all but over.

Swann graduated in 2002 as a newly minted cognitive scientist, but the job he finally got a few months later was as a waiter in Atlanta. He waited tables for the next year and a half. It proved to be a blessing in disguise. Swann says he learned more real-world skills working in restaurants than he ever did in school. "It taught me how to deal with people. What you learn as a waiter is how to treat people fairly, especially when they're in a bad situation." That's especially valuable in his current job as an insurance-claims examiner.

There are several lessons about twixters to be learned from Swann's tale. One is that most colleges are seriously out of step with the real world in getting students ready to become workers in the postcollege world. Vocational schools like DeVry and Strayer, which focus on teaching practical skills, are seeing a mini-boom. Their enrollment grew 48% from 1996 to 2000. More traditional schools are scrambling to give their courses a practical spin. In the fall, Hendrix College in Conway, Ark., will introduce a program called the Odyssey project, which the school says will encourage students to "think outside the book" in areas like "professional and leadership development" and "service to the world." Dozens of other schools have set up similar initiatives.

As colleges struggle to get their students ready for real-world jobs, they are charging more for what they deliver. The resulting debt is a major factor in keeping twixters from moving on and growing up. Thirty years ago, most financial aid came in the form of grants, but now the emphasis is on lending, not on giving. Recent college graduates owe 85% more in student loans than their counterparts of a decade ago, according to the Center for Economic and Policy Research. In TIME's poll, 66% of those surveyed owed more than $10,000 when they graduated, and 5% owed more than $100,000. (And this says nothing about the credit-card companies that bombard freshmen with offers for cards that students then cheerfully abuse. Demos, a public-policy group, says credit-card debt for Americans 18 to 24 more than doubled from 1992 to 2001.) The longer it takes to pay off those loans, the longer it takes twixters to achieve the financial independence that's crucial to attaining an adult identity, not to mention the means to get out of their parents' house.

Meanwhile, those expensive, time-sucking college diplomas have become worth less than ever. So many more people go to college now—a 53% increase since 1970—that the value of a degree on the job market has been diluted. The advantage in wages for college-degree holders hasn't risen significantly since the late 1990s, according to the Bureau of Labor Statistics. To compensate, a lot of twixters go back to school for graduate and professional degrees. Swann, for example, is planning to head back to business school to better his chances in the insurance game. But piling on extra degrees costs precious time and money and pushes adulthood even further into the future.

Work in Progress

Kate Galantha, 29, spent seven years working her way through college, transferring three times. After she finally graduated from Columbia College in Chicago (major: undeclared) in 2001, she moved to Portland, Ore., and went to work as a nanny and as an assistant to a wedding photographer. A year later she jumped back to Chicago, where she got a job in a flower shop. It was a full-time position with real benefits, but she soon burned out and headed for the territories, a.k.a. Madison, Wis. "I was really busy but not accomplishing anything," she says. "I didn't want to stay just for a job."

She had no job offers in Madison, and the only person she knew there was her older sister, but she had nothing tying her to Chicago (her boyfriend had moved to Europe) and she needed a change. The risk paid off. She got a position as an assistant at a photo studio, and she loves it. "I decided it was more important to figure out what to do and to be in a new environment," Galantha says. "It's exciting, and I'm in a place where I can accomplish everything. But starting over is the worst."

Galantha's frenetic hopping from school to school, job to job and city to city may look like aimless wandering. (She has moved six times since 1999. Her father calls her and her sister gypsies.) But *Emerging Adulthood*'s Arnett—and Galantha—see it differently. To them, the period from 18 to 25 is a kind of sandbox, a chance to build castles and knock them down, experiment with different careers, knowing that none of it really counts. After all, this is a world of overwhelming choice: there are 40 kinds of coffee beans at Whole Foods Market, 205 channels on DirecTV, 15 million personal ads on Match.com and 800,000 jobs on Monster.com. Can you blame Galantha for wanting to try them all? She doesn't want to play just the hand she has been dealt. She wants to look through the whole deck. "My problem is I'm really overstimulated by everything," Galantha says. "I feel there's too much information out there at all times. There are too many doors, too many people, too much competition."

"I do not want to be a parent. I mean, hell, why would I?"
—Matt Swann

Twixters expect to jump laterally from job to job and place to place until they find what they're looking for. The stable, quasi-parental bond between employer and employee is a thing of the past, and neither feels much obligation to make the relationship permanent. "They're well aware of the fact that they will not work for the same company for the rest of their life," says Bill Frey, a demographer with the Brookings Institution, a think tank based in Washington. "They don't think long-term about health care or Social Security. They're concerned about their careers and immediate gratification."

Twixters expect a lot more from a job than a paycheck. Maybe it's a reaction to the greed-is-good 1980s or to the whatever-is-whatever apathy of the early 1990s. More likely, it's the way they were raised, by parents who came of age in the 1960s as the first generation determined to follow its bliss, who want their children to change the world the way they did. Maybe it has to do with advances in medicine. Twixters can reasonably expect to live into their 80s and beyond, so their working lives will be extended accordingly and when they choose a career, they know they'll be there for a while. But whatever the cause, twixters are looking for a sense of purpose and importance in their work, something that will add meaning to their lives, and many don't want to rest until they find it. "They're not just looking for a job," Arnett says. "They want something that's more like a calling, that's going to be an expression of their identity." Hedonistic nomads, the twixters may seem, but there's a serious core of idealism in them.

Still, self-actualization is a luxury not everybody can afford, and looking at middle- and upper-class twixters gives only part of the picture. Twixters change jobs often, but they don't all do it for the same reasons, and one twixter's playful experimentation is another's desperate hustling. James Côté is a sociologist at the University of Western Ontario and the author of several books about twixters, including *Generation on Hold* and *Arrested Adulthood*. He believes that the economic bedrock that used to support adolescents on their journey into adulthood has shifted alarmingly. "What we're looking at really began with the collapse of the youth labor market, dating back to the late '70s and early '80s, which made it more difficult for people to get a foothold in terms of financial independence," Côté says. "You need a college degree now just to be where blue- collar people the same age were 20 or 30 years ago, and if you don't have it, then you're way behind." In other words, it's not that twixters don't want to become adults. They just can't afford to.

One way society defines an adult is as a person who is financially independent, with a family and a home. But families and homes cost money, and people in their late teens and early 20s don't make as much as they used to. The current crop of twixters grew up in the 1990s, when the dotcom boom made Internet millions seem just a business proposal away, but in reality they're worse off than the generation that preceded them. Annual earnings among men 25 to 34 with full-time jobs dropped 17% from 1971 to 2002, according to the National Center for Education Statistics. Timothy Smeeding, a professor of economics at Syracuse University, found that only half of Americans in their mid-20s earn enough to support a family, and in TIME's poll only half of those ages 18 to 29 consider themselves financially independent. Michigan's Schoeni says Americans ages 25 and 26 get an average of $2,323 a year in financial support from their parents.

INSIDE THE WORLD OF THE TWIXTERS

BECOMING AN ADULT

The markers of adulthood haven't changed for people ages 18 to 29 ...

What makes you an adult?

Having first child	**22%**
Moving out of parents' home	**22%**
Getting a good job with benefits	**19%**
Getting married	**14%**
Finishing school	**10%**

... yet over a third of twixters don't consider themselves grown up ...

... and they cite a variety of reasons for their delayed entry into adulthood

How would you describe yourself?

An adult	**61%**
Entering adulthood	**29%**
Not there yet	**10%**

What is the main reason that you do not consider yourself an adult?

Just enjoying life the way it is	**35%**
Not financially independent yet	**33%**
Not out of school	**13%**

GETTING AN EDUCATION

College is traditionally the institution that serves as a transition to adulthood, but students are taking longer to leave ...

23% say they were 24 or older when they finished

... and when they do get out of college, many find themselves in debt ...

29%	say paying for their education is a major financial concern
52%	say they owed money when they finished school
66%	owe over $10,000
23%	owe over $30,000
5%	owe over $100,000

EARNING MONEY

Even though 43% worry about paying bills, they're big spenders ...

Percentage who say they spend more than most people do on:

Eating out	**32%**
Clothes	**26%**
Going to/renting movies	**17%**
Computers and software	**12%**

... but they don't consider money alone the key to job satisfaction

Which of these do you consider essential for your job?

Job security	**71%**
Health benefits	**62%**
Interesting work	**60%**
Good salary	**56%**

LIVING IN THE REAL WORLD

Despite the money they have spent on their education, they're not ready for careers

19%	say school didn't prepare them to be successful in their work life
36%	say they're just getting started on finding the job or career they want

They move around a lot ...

25%	have had three addresses in the past five years
22%	have had four or more addresses in the past five years

... and they seek a safe haven with family

70%	report spending time with their family in the previous week
48%	communicate with their parents every day by phone or e-mail
39%	say their parents have a great deal of influence over their lives
26%	say their parents were too protective of them when they were growing up

The transition to adulthood gets tougher the lower you go on the economic and educational ladder. Sheldon Danziger, a public-policy professor at the University of Michigan, found that for male workers ages 25 to 29 with only a high school diploma, the average wage declined 11% from 1975 to 2002. "When I graduated from high school, my classmates who didn't want to go to college could go to the Goodyear plant and buy a house and support a wife and family," says Steve Hamilton of Cornell University's Youth and Work Program. "That doesn't happen anymore." Instead, high school grads are more likely to end up in retail jobs with low pay and minimal benefits, if any. From this end of the social pyramid, Arnett's vision of emerging adulthood as a playground of self-discovery seems a little rosy. The rules have changed, and not in the twixters' favor.

Weddings Can Wait

With everything else that's going on—careers to be found, debts to be paid, bars to be hopped—love is somewhat secondary in the lives of the twixters. But that doesn't mean they're cynical about it. *Au contraire:* among our friends from Chicago—Michele, Ellen, Nathan, Corinne, Marcus and Jennie—all six say they are not ready for marriage yet but do want it someday, preferably with kids. Naturally, all that is comfortably situated in the eternally receding future. Thirty is no longer the looming deadline it once was. In fact, five of the Chicago six see marriage as a decidedly post-30 milestone.

> **"I have a lot of debt from school that is hard to pay off. My jobs just don't pay well."**
> —Shaniqwa Jarvis

"It's a long way down the road," says Marcus Jones, 28, a comedian who works at Banana Republic by day. "I'm too self-involved. I don't want to bring that into a relationship now." He expects to get married in his mid- to late 30s. "My wife is currently a sophomore in high school," he jokes.

"I want to get married but not soon," says Jennie Jiang, 26, a sixth-grade teacher. "I'm enjoying myself. There's a lot I want to do by myself still."

"I have my career, and I'm too young," says Michele Steele, 26, a TV producer. "It's commitment and sacrifice, and I think it's a hindrance. Lo and behold, people have come to the conclusion that it's not much fun to get married and have kids right out of college."

That attitude is new, but it didn't come out of nowhere. Certainly, the spectacle of the previous generation's mass divorces has something to do with the healthy skepticism shown by the twixters. They will spend a few years looking before they leap, thank you very much. "I fantasize more about sharing a place with someone than about my wed-

ding day," says Galantha, whose parents split when she was 18. "I haven't seen a lot of good marriages."

But if twixters are getting married later, they are missing out on some of the social-support networks that come with having families of their own. To make up for it, they have a special gift for friendship, documented in books like Sasha Cagen's *Quirkyalone* and Ethan Watters' *Urban Tribes*, which asks the not entirely rhetorical question Are friends the new family? They throw cocktail parties and dinner parties. They hold poker nights. They form book groups. They stay in touch constantly and in real time, through social-networking technologeist like cell phones, instant messaging, text messaging and online communities like Friendster. They're also close to their parents. TIME's poll showed that almost half of Americans ages 18 to 29 talk to their parents every day.

Marrying late also means that twixters tend to have more sexual partners than previous generations. The situation is analogous to their promiscuous job-hopping behavior—like Goldilocks, they want to find the one that's just right—but it can give them a cynical, promiscuous vibe too. Arnett is worried that if anything, twixters are too romantic. In their universe, romance is totally detached from pragmatic concerns and societal pressures, so when twixters finally do marry, they're going to do it for Love with a capital *L* and no other reason. "Everybody wants to find their soul mate now," Arnett says, "whereas I think, for my parents' generation—I'm 47—they looked at it much more practically. I think a lot of people are going to end up being disappointed with the person that's snoring next to them by the time they've been married for a few years and they realize it doesn't work that way."

Twixter Culture

When it comes to social change, pop culture is the most sensitive of seismometers, and it was faster to pick up on the twixters than the cloistered social scientists. Look at the Broadway musical *Avenue Q*, in which puppets dramatize the vagaries of life after graduation. ("I wish I could go back to college," a character sings. "Life was so simple back then.") Look at that little TV show called *Friends*, about six people who put off marriage well into their 30s. Even twice-married Britney Spears fits the profile. For a succinct, albeit cheesy summation of the twixter predicament, you couldn't do much better than her 2001 hit *I'm Not a Girl, Not Yet a Woman*.

The producing duo Edward Zwick and Marshall Herskovitz, who created the legendarily zeitgeisty TV series *thirtysomething* and *My So-Called Life*, now have a pilot with ABC called *1/4life*, about a houseful of people in their mid-20s who can't seem to settle down. "When you talk about this period of transition being extended, it's not what people intended to do," Herskovitz says, "but it's a result of the world not being particularly welcoming when they come into it. Lots of people have a difficult time dealing with it, and they try to stay kids as long as they can because they don't know how to make sense of all this. We're interested in this process of finding courage and one's self."

As for movies, a lot of twixters cite *Garden State* as one that really nails their predicament. "I feel like my generation is waiting longer and longer to get married," says Zach Braff, 29, who wrote, directed and starred in the film about a twentysomething actor who comes home for the first time in nine years. "In the past, people got married and got a job and had kids, but now there's a new 10 years that people are using to try and find out what kind of life they want to lead. For a lot of people, the weight of all the possibility is overwhelming."

Pop culture may reflect the changes in our lives, but it also plays its part in shaping them. Marketers have picked up on the fact that twixters on their personal voyages of discovery tend to buy lots of stuff along the way. "They are the optimum market to be going after for consumer electronics, Game Boys, flat-screen TVs, iPods, couture fashion, exotic vacations and so forth," says David Morrison, president of Twentysomething Inc., a marketing consultancy based in Philadelphia. "Most of their needs are taken care of by Mom and Dad, so their income is largely discretionary. [Many twentysomethings] are living at home, but if you look, you'll see flat-screen TVs in their bedrooms and brand-new cars in the driveway." Some twixters may want to grow up, but corporations and advertisers have a real stake in keeping them in a tractable, exploitable, pre-adult state—living at home, spending their money on toys.

Living with Peter Pan

Maybe the twixters are in denial about growing up, but the rest of society is equally in denial about the twixters. Nobody wants to admit they're here to stay, but that's where all the evidence points. Tom Smith, director of the General Social Survey, a large sociological data-gathering project run by the National Opinion Research Center, found that most people believe that the transition to adulthood should be completed by the age of 26, on average, and he thinks that number is only going up. "In another 10 or 20 years, we're not going to be talking about this as a delay. We're going to be talking about this as a normal trajectory," Smith says. "And we're going to think about those people getting married at 18 and forming families at 19 or 20 as an odd historical pattern."

There may even be a biological basis to all this. The human brain continues to grow and change into the early 20s, according to Abigail Baird, who runs the Laboratory for Adolescent Studies at Dartmouth. "We as a society deem an individual at the age of 18 ready for adult responsibility," Baird points out. "Yet recent evidence suggests that our neuropsychological development is many years from being complete. There's no reason to think 18 is a magic number." How can the twixters be expected to settle down when their gray matter hasn't?

> ## "I just don't understand what the definition of 'grownup' is."
> —Kate Galantha

A new life stage is a major change, and the rest of society will have to change to make room for it. One response to this very new phenomenon is extremely old-fashioned: medieval-style apprenticeship programs that give high school graduates a cheaper and more practical alternative to college. In 1996 Jack Smith, then CEO of General Motors, started Automotive Youth Educational Systems (AYES), a program that puts high school kids in shops alongside seasoned car mechanics. More than 7,800 students have tried it, and 98% of them have ended up working at the business where they apprenticed. "I knew this was my best way to get into a dealership," says Chris Rolando, 20, an AYES graduate who works at one in Detroit. "My friends are still at pizza-place jobs and have no idea what to do for a living. I just bought my own house and have a career."

But success stories like Rolando's are rare. Child welfare, the juvenile-justice system, special-education and support programs for young mothers usually cut off at age 18, and most kids in foster care get kicked out at 18 with virtually no safety net. "Age limits are like the time limits for welfare recipients," says Frank Furstenberg, a sociologist who heads a research consortium called the MacArthur Network on Transitions to Adulthood. "They're pushing people off the rolls, but they're not necessarily able to transition into supportive services or connections to other systems." And programs for the poor aren't the only ones that need to grow up with the times. Only 54% of respondents in the TIME poll were insured through their employers. That's a reality that affects all levels of society, and policymakers need to strengthen that safety net.

Most of the problems that twixters face are hard to see, and that makes it harder to help them. Twixters may look as if they have been overindulged, but they could use some judicious support. Apter's research at Cambridge suggests that the more parents sympathize with their twixter children, the more parents take time to discuss their twixters' life goals, the more aid and shelter they offer them, the easier the transition becomes. "Young people know that their material life will not be better than their parents'," Apter says. "They don't expect a safer life than their parents had. They don't expect more secure employment or finances. They have to put in a lot of work just to remain O.K." Tough love may look like the answer, but it's not what twixters need.

The real heavy lifting may ultimately have to happen on the level of the culture itself. There was a time when people looked forward to taking on the mantle of adulthood. That time is past. Now our culture trains young people to fear it. "I don't ever want a lawn," says Swann. "I don't ever want to drive two hours to get to work. I do not want to be a parent. I mean, hell, why would I? There's so much fun to be had while you're young." He does have a point. Twixters have all the privileges of grownups now but only some of the responsibilities. From the point of view of the twixters, upstairs in their childhood bedrooms, snuggled up under their Star Wars comforters, it can look all downhill.

If twixters are ever going to grow up, they need the means to do it—and they will have to want to. There are joys and satisfactions that come with assuming adult responsibility, though you won't see them on *The Real World*. To go to the movies or turn on the TV is to see a world where life ends at 30; these

days, every movie is *Logan's Run*. There are few road maps in the popular culture—and to most twixters, this is the only culture—to get twixters where they need to go. If those who are 30 and older want the rest of the world to grow up, they'll have to show the twixters that it's worth their while. "I went to a Poster Children concert, and there were 40-year-olds still rocking," says Jennie Jiang. "It gave me hope."

—**With reporting by Nadia Mustafa and Deirdre van Dyk/ New York, Kristin Kloberdanz/ Chicago and Marc Schultz/ Atlanta**

UNIT 6

Development During Middle and Late Adulthood

Unit Selections

Key Points to Consider

- Does laughter serve biological functions? If so, what are the uses of laughter that are regulated by our primitive instincts?

- What are the three deadly threats alcohol abuse poses?

- How has AIDS changed America, and the world, in the last 25 years?

- Are the middle adulthood years the best years of one's life? What new research suggests that this is true?

- Aging is inevitable. Should we fight off its signs and symptoms, or accept them gracefully?

- What plans for retirement will protect retirees, even if the economy turns bad?

- Why do some people live over 100 years in good health? What are their secrets?

- People with Alzheimer's disease have lost many of their memories. Can new therapies help them re-discover some of their past knowledge?

- What are the ethics of terminal care? Who should prepare advance care directives? When?

Student Website

www.mhcls.com/online

Internet References

Further information regarding these websites may be found in this book's preface or online.

Alzheimer's Disease Research Center
http://alzheimer.wustl.edu/adrc2//
Lifestyle Factors Affecting Late Adulthood
http://www.school-for-champions.com/health/lifestyle_elderly.htm
National Aging Information Center (NAIC)
http://www.aoa.dhhs.gov/naic/

Joseph Campbell, a twentieth-century sage, said that the privilege of a lifetime is being who you are. This ego confidence often arrives during middle and late adulthood, even as physical confidence declines. There is a gradual slowing of the rate of mitosis of cells of all the organ systems with age. This gradual slowing of mitosis translates into a slowed rate of repair of cells of all organs. By the 40s, signs of aging can be seen in skin, skeleton, vision, hearing, smell, taste, balance, coordination, heart, blood vessels, lungs, liver, kidneys, digestive tract, immune response, endocrine functioning, and ability to reproduce. To some extent, moderate use of any body part (as opposed to disuse or misuse) helps it retain its strength, stamina, and repairability. However, by middle and late adulthood persons become increasingly aware of the aging effects of their organ systems on their total physical fitness. A loss of height occurs as spinal disks and connective tissues diminish and settle. Demineralization, especially loss of calcium, causes weakening of bones. Muscles atrophy, and the slowing of cardiovascular and respiratory responses creates a loss of stamina for exercise. All of this may seem cruel, but it occurs very gradually and need not adversely affect a person's enjoyment of life.

Healthful aging, at least in part, seems to be genetically preprogrammed. The females of many species, including humans, outlive the males. The sex hormones of females may protect them from some early aging effects. Males, in particular, experience earlier declines in their cardiovascular system. Diet and exercise can ward off many of the deleterious effects of aging. A reduction in saturated fat (low density lipid) intake coupled with regular aerobic exercise contributes to less bone demineralization, less plaque in the arteries, stronger muscles (including heart and lung muscles), and a general increase in stamina and vitality. An adequate intake of complex carbohydrates, fibrous foods, fresh fruits, fresh vegetables, unsaturated fats (high density lipids), and water also enhances good health.

Cognitive abilities do not appreciably decline with age in healthy adults. Research suggests that the speed with which the brain carries out problems involving abstract (fluid) reasoning may slow but not cease. Complex problems may simply require more time to solve with age. On the other hand, research suggests that the memory banks of older people may have more crystallized (accumulated and stored) knowledge and more insight. Creativity also frequently spurts after age 50. One's ken (range of knowledge) and practical skills (common sense) grow with age and experience. Older human beings also become expert at the cognitive tasks they frequently do. Many cultures celebrate these abilities as the "wisdom of age."

The first article about middle adulthood speaks to the urge to laugh. New brain research reported in "Emotions and the Brain: Laughter" suggests that laughing is a form of instinctive social bonding. We do not make a conscious decision to laugh. We are often unaware that we are laughing. And laughter is contagious. It makes us healthier by enhancing our immune responsivity and reducing our stress hormones. The "wisdom of age" may allow us to be more frivolous and to take more pleasure in happy friendships within our families and communities. Children laugh freely. Somehow many adults learn to suppress laughter and to be more serious. Perhaps some wisdom and maturity is evidenced by not trying to suppress this important biological response.

The second article about middle adulthood speaks to "Alcohol's Deadly Triple Threat." Karen Springen and Barbara Kantrowitz discuss gender differences in alcohol abuse. Men drink openly and seek help if they become addicted. Women more often hide their drinking. They risk their children's health, as well as their own, with their alcohol abuse.

"How AIDS Changed America" reviews 25 years since AIDS appeared in the United States. It has killed more people than every war from WWII through Iraq. It has forced people to discuss safe sex, gay sex, rape, and promiscuity in new ways. It is a major reason for the contemporary debate on gay marriage. AIDS spawned new blood tests and new retroviral drug cocktails. It has not been cured. It affects females and heterosexuals and has changed the face of our world.

The last middle adulthood selection, "The Myth of the Midlife Crisis," dismisses midlife as the beginning of a downward that which suggests increased creativity, a new sense of self, deeper knowledge, and better judgment in the second half of life. It makes one anticipate aging with hope and joy.

Erik Erikson suggested that the most important psychological conflict of late adulthood is achieving a sense of ego integrity. This is fostered by self-respect, self-esteem, love of others, and a sense that one's life has order and meaning. The articles in the subsection on late adulthood reflect Erikson's concern with experiencing ego integrity rather than despair.

In the first article on late adulthood, "Aging Naturally," Dr. Andrew Weil summarizes some of the main points from his book, *Healthy Aging*. Dr. Weil is an advocate of accepting aging, not fighting it. He suggests ways to maximize health and happiness and ways to minimize disease and distress with the passing of years.

The second late adulthood article, "When Your Paycheck Stops," discusses the necessity of careful preretirement planning. The 21st century poses new risks for investments and insurance. Jane Bryant Quinn offers advice on how to develop a plan to assure that retirement savings will be sufficient for one's needs.

In "Secrets of the Centenarians," Maya Pines portrays the lives of several people who are over age 100 but who appear to be in their 70s or early 80s. Researchers have identified genetic markers on the fourth pair of chromosomes that may contribute to longevity and good health. It may be possible in the future to manipulate the single-nucleotide polymorphisms (SNPs) to allow everyone to live as long as the centenarians being studied.

The fourth late adulthood selection, "Lost & Found," deals with people with Alzheimer's disease. The author, Barbara Basler, describes new therapeutic methods devised by Cameron Camp, the head of the Myers Research Institute in Ohio. Dr. Camp's methods, deemed valid and reliable by researchers, help draw patients out of their confusion and recapture some of their basic skills and knowledge.

The last article describes end-of-life care. The author, Helen Sorenson, discusses the conflicting opinions that create turmoil for patients, family, friends, and health care professionals when death is imminent. "Navigating Practical Dilemmas in Terminal Care" gives useful information on how to reduce such conflicts. Family conferences should occur well ahead of the end of life to discuss the terms of advance care directives. Asking questions and communicating openly can prevent misunderstandings.

Emotions and the Brain: Laughter

If evolution comes down to survival of the fittest, then why do we joke around so much? New brain research suggests that the urge to laugh is the lubricant that makes humans higher social beings

STEVEN JOHNSON

Robert Provine wants me to see his tickle Me Elmo doll. Wants me to hold it, as a matter of fact. It's not an unusual request for Provine. A professor of psychology and neuroscience at the University of Maryland, he has been engaged for a decade in a wide-ranging intellectual pursuit that has taken him from the panting play of young chimpanzees to the history of American sitcoms—all in search of a scientific understanding of that most unscientific of human customs: laughter.

The Elmo doll happens to incorporate two of his primary obsessions: tickling and contagious laughter. "You ever fiddled with one of these?" Provine says, as he pulls the doll out of a small canvas tote bag. He holds it up, and after a second or two, the doll begins to shriek with laughter. There's something undeniably comic in the scene: a burly, bearded man in his mid-fifties cradling a red Muppet. Provine hands Elmo to me to demonstrate the doll's vibration effect. "It brings up two interesting things," he explains, as I hold Elmo in my arms. "You have a best-selling toy that's a glorified laugh box. And when it shakes, you're getting feedback as if you're tickling."

Provine's relationship to laughter reminds me of the dramatic technique that Bertolt Brecht called the distanciation effect. Radical theater, in Brecht's vision, was supposed to distance us from our too-familiar social structures, make us see those structures with fresh eyes. In his study of laughter, Provine has been up to something comparably enlightening, helping us to recognize the strangeness of one of our most familiar emotional states. Think about that Tickle Me Elmo doll: We take it for granted that tickling causes laughter and that one person's laughter will easily "infect" other people within earshot. Even a child knows these things. (Tickling and contagious laughter are two of the distinguishing characteristics of childhood.) But when you think about them from a distance, they are strange conventions. We can understand readily enough why natural selection would have implanted the fight-or-flight response in us or endowed us with sex drives. But the tendency to laugh when others laugh in our presence or to laugh when someone strokes our belly with a feather—what's the evolutionary

advantage of that? And yet a quick glance at the Nielsen ratings or the personal ads will tell you that laughter is one of the most satisfying and sought-after states available to us.

Funnily enough, the closer Provine got to understanding why we laugh, the farther he got from humor. To appreciate the roots of laughter, you have to stop thinking about jokes.

There is a long, semi-illustrious history of scholarly investigation into the nature of humor, from Freud's *Jokes and Their Relation to the Unconscious,* which may well be the least funny book about humor ever written, to a British research group that announced last year that they had determined the World's Funniest Joke. Despite the fact that the researchers said they had sampled a massive international audience in making this discovery, the winning joke revolved around New Jersey residents:

A couple of New Jersey hunters are out in the woods when one of them falls to the ground. He doesn't seem to be breathing; his eyes are rolled back in his head. The other guy whips out his cell phone and calls the emergency services. He gasps to the operator: "My friend is dead! What can I do?"

The operator says: "Take it easy. I can help. First, let's make sure he's dead." There is silence, then a shot is heard. The guy's voice comes back on the line. He says, "OK, now what?"

This joke illustrates that most assessments of humor's underlying structure gravitate to the notion of controlled incongruity: You're expecting x, and you get y. For the joke to work, it has to be readable on both levels. In the hunting joke there are two plausible ways to interpret the 911 operator's instructions—either the hunter checks his friend's pulse or he shoots him. The context sets you up to expect that he'll check his friend's pulse, so the—admittedly dark—humor arrives when he takes the more unlikely path. That incongruity has limits, of course: If the hunter chooses to do something utterly nonsensical—untie his shoelaces or climb a tree—the joke wouldn't be funny.

A number of studies in recent years have looked at brain activity while subjects were chuckling over a good joke—an at-

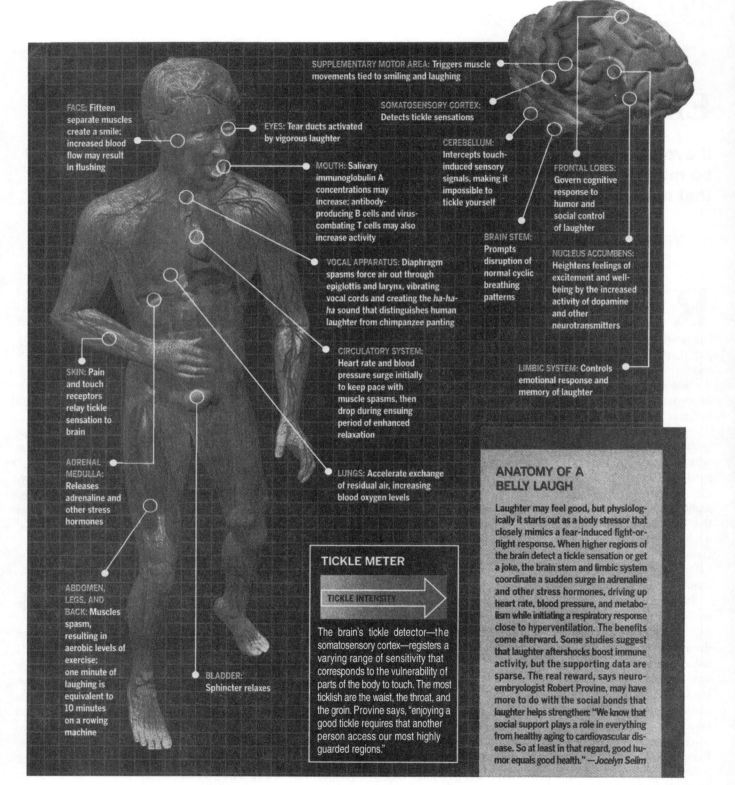

SUPPLEMENTARY MOTOR AREA: Triggers muscle movements tied to smiling and laughing

SOMATOSENSORY CORTEX: Detects tickle sensations

CEREBELLUM: Intercepts touch-induced sensory signals, making it impossible to tickle yourself

FRONTAL LOBES: Govern cognitive response to humor and social control of laughter

BRAIN STEM: Prompts disruption of normal cyclic breathing patterns

NUCLEUS ACCUMBENS: Heightens feelings of excitement and well-being by the increased activity of dopamine and other neurotransmitters

LIMBIC SYSTEM: Controls emotional response and memory of laughter

FACE: Fifteen separate muscles create a smile; increased blood flow may result in flushing

EYES: Tear ducts activated by vigorous laughter

MOUTH: Salivary immunoglobulin A concentrations may increase; antibody-producing B cells and virus-combating T cells may also increase activity

VOCAL APPARATUS: Diaphragm spasms force air out through epiglottis and larynx, vibrating vocal cords and creating the ha-ha-ha sound that distinguishes human laughter from chimpanzee panting

CIRCULATORY SYSTEM: Heart rate and blood pressure surge initially to keep pace with muscle spasms, then drop during ensuing period of enhanced relaxation

SKIN: Pain and touch receptors relay tickle sensation to brain

ADRENAL MEDULLA: Releases adrenaline and other stress hormones

LUNGS: Accelerate exchange of residual air, increasing blood oxygen levels

ABDOMEN, LEGS, AND BACK: Muscles spasm, resulting in aerobic levels of exercise; one minute of laughing is equivalent to 10 minutes on a rowing machine

BLADDER: Sphincter relaxes

TICKLE METER

TICKLE INTENSITY

The brain's tickle detector—the somatosensory cortex—registers a varying range of sensitivity that corresponds to the vulnerability of parts of the body to touch. The most ticklish are the waist, the throat, and the groin. Provine says, "enjoying a good tickle requires that another person access our most highly guarded regions."

ANATOMY OF A BELLY LAUGH

Laughter may feel good, but physiologically it starts out as a body stressor that closely mimics a fear-induced fight-or-flight response. When higher regions of the brain detect a tickle sensation or get a joke, the brain stem and limbic system coordinate a sudden surge in adrenaline and other stress hormones, driving up heart rate, blood pressure, and metabolism while initiating a respiratory response close to hyperventilation. The benefits come afterward. Some studies suggest that laughter aftershocks boost immune activity, but the supporting data are sparse. The real reward, says neuro-embryologist Robert Provine, may have more to do with the social bonds that laughter helps strengthen: "We know that social support plays a role in everything from healthy aging to cardiovascular disease. So at least in that regard, good humor equals good health." —Jocelyn Selim

Graphics by Don Foley

tempt to locate a neurological funny bone. There is evidence that the frontal lobes are implicated in "getting" the joke while the brain regions associated with motor control execute the physical response of laughter. One 1999 study analyzed patients with damage to the right frontal lobes, an integrative region of the brain where emotional, logical, and perceptual data converge. The brain-damaged patients had far more difficulty than control subjects in choosing the proper punch line to a series of jokes, usually opting for absurdist, slapstick-style endings rather than traditional ones. Humor can often come in coarse, lowest-common-denominator packages, but actually getting the joke draws upon our higher brain functions.

When Provine set out to study laughter, he imagined that he would approach the problem along the lines of these humor studies: Investigating laughter meant having people listen to jokes and other witticisms and watching what happened. He began by simply observing casual conversations, counting the number of times that people laughed while listening to someone speaking. But very quickly he realized that there was a fundamental flaw in his assumptions about how laughter worked. "I started recording all these conversations," Provine says, "and the numbers I was getting—I didn't believe them when I saw them. The speakers were laughing more than the listeners. Every time that would happen, I would think, 'OK, I have to go back and start over again because that can't be right.'"

Speakers, it turned out, were 46 percent more likely to laugh than listeners—and what they were laughing at, more often than not, wasn't remotely funny. Provine and his team of undergrad students recorded the ostensible "punch lines" that triggered laughter in ordinary conversation. They found that only around 15 percent of the sentences that triggered laughter were traditionally humorous. In his book, *Laughter: A Scientific Investigation,* Provine lists some of the laugh-producing quotes:

I'll see you guys later./Put those cigarettes away./I hope we all do well./It was nice meeting you too./We can handle this./I see your point./I should do that, but I'm too lazy./I try to lead a normal life./I think I'm done./I told you so!

The few studies of laughter to date had assumed that laughing and humor were inextricably linked, but Provine's early research suggested that the connection was only an occasional one. "There's a dark side to laughter that we are too quick to overlook," he says. "The kids at Columbine were laughing as they walked through the school shooting their peers."

As his research progressed, Provine began to suspect that laughter was in fact about something else—not humor or gags or incongruity but our social interactions. He found support for this assumption in a study that had already been conducted, analyzing people's laughing patterns in social and solitary contexts. "You're 30 times more likely to laugh when you're with other people than you are when you're alone—if you don't count simulated social environments like laugh tracks on television," Provine says. "In fact, when you're alone, you're more likely to talk out loud to yourself than you are to laugh out loud. Much more." Think how rarely you'll laugh out loud at a funny passage in a book but how quick you'll be to make a friendly laugh when greeting an old acquaintance. Laughing is not an instinctive physical response to humor, the way a flinch responds to pain or a shiver to cold. It's a form of instinctive social bonding that humor is crafted to exploit.

Provine's lab at the baltimore county campus of the University of Maryland looks like the back room at a stereo repair store—long tables cluttered with old equipment,

tubes and wires everywhere. The walls are decorated with brightly colored pictures of tangled neurons, most of which were painted by Provine. (Add some Day-Glo typography and they might pass for signs promoting a Dead show at the Fillmore.) Provine's old mentor, the neuroembryologist Viktor Hamburger, glowers down from a picture hung above a battered Silicon Graphics workstation. His expression suggests a sense of concerned bafflement: "I trained you as a scientist, and here you are playing with dolls!"

The more technical parts of Provine's work—exploring the neuromuscular control of laughter and its relationship to the human and chimp respiratory systems—draw on his training at Washington University in St. Louis under Hamburger and Nobel laureate Rita Levi-Montalcini. But the most immediate way to grasp his insights into the evolution of laughter is to watch video footage of his informal fieldwork, which consists of Provine and a cameraman prowling Baltimore's inner harbor, asking people to laugh for the camera. The overall effect is like a color story for the local news, but as Provine and I watch the tapes together in his lab, I find myself looking at the laughters with fresh eyes. Again and again, a pattern repeats on the screen. Provine asks someone to laugh, and they demur, look puzzled for a second, and say something like, "I can't just laugh." Then they turn to their friends or family, and the laughter rolls out of them as though it were as natural as breathing. The pattern stays the same even as the subjects change: a group of high school students on a field trip, a married couple, a pair of college freshmen.

At one point Provine—dressed in a plaid shirt and khakis, looking something like the comedian Robert Klein—stops two waste-disposal workers driving a golf cart loaded up with trash bags. When they fail to guffaw on cue, Provine asks them why they can't muster one up. "Because you're not funny," one of them says. They turn to each other and share a hearty laugh.

"See, you two just made each other laugh," Provine says.

"Yeah, well, we're coworkers," one of them replies.

The insistent focus on laughter patterns has a strange effect on me as Provine runs through the footage. By the time we get to the cluster of high school kids, I've stopped hearing their spoken words at all, just the rhythmic peals of laughter breaking out every 10 seconds or so. Sonically, the laughter dominates the speech; you can barely hear the dialogue underneath the hysterics. If you were an alien encountering humans for the first time, you'd have to assume that the laughing served as the primary communication method, with the spoken words interspersed as afterthoughts. After one particularly loud outbreak, Provine turns to me and says, "Now, do you think they're all individually making a conscious decision to laugh?" He shakes his head dismissively. "Of course not. In fact, we're often not aware that we're even laughing in the first place. We've vastly overrated our conscious control of laughter."

The limits of our voluntary control of laughter are most clearly exposed in studies of stroke victims who suffer from a disturbing condition known as central facial paralysis, which prevents them from voluntarily moving either the left side or the right side of their faces, depending on the location of the neurological damage. When these individuals are asked to smile or laugh on command, they produce lopsided grins: One side of the mouth curls up, the other remains frozen. But when they're told a joke or they're tickled, traditional smiles and laughs animate their entire faces. There is evidence that the physical mechanism of laughter itself is generated in the brain stem, the most ancient region of the nervous system, which is also responsible for fundamental functions like breathing. Sufferers of amyotrophic lateral sclerosis—Lou Gehrig's disease—which targets the brain stem, often experience spontaneous bursts of uncontrollable laughter, without feeling mirth. (They often undergo a comparable experience with crying as well.) Sometimes called the reptilian brain because its basic structure dates back to our reptile ancestors, the brain stem is largely devoted to our most primal instincts, far removed from our complex, higher-brain skills in understanding humor. And yet somehow, in this primitive region of the brain, we find the urge to laugh.

We're accustomed to thinking of common-but-unconscious instincts as being essential adaptations, like the startle reflex or the suckling of newborns. Why would we have an unconscious propensity for something as frivolous as laughter? As I watch them on the screen, Provine's teenagers remind me of an old Carl Sagan riff, which begins with his describing "a species of primate" that likes to gather in packs of 50 or 60 individuals, cram together in a darkened cave, and hyperventilate in unison, to the point of almost passing out. The behavior is described in such a way as to make it sound exotic and somewhat foolish, like salmon swimming furiously upstream to their deaths or butterflies traveling thousands of miles to rendezvous once a year. The joke, of course, is that the primate is *Homo sapiens,* and the group hyperventilation is our fondness for laughing together at comedy clubs or theaters, or with the virtual crowds of television laugh tracks.

I'm thinking about the Sagan quote when another burst of laughter arrives through the TV speakers, and without realizing what I'm doing, I find myself laughing along with the kids on the screen, I can't help it—their laughter is contagious.

We may be the only species on the planet that laughs together in such large groups, but we are not alone in our appetite for laughter. Not surprisingly, our near relatives, the chimpanzees, are also avid laughers, although differences in their vocal apparatus cause the laugher to sound somewhat more like panting. "The chimpanzee's laughter is rapid and breathy, whereas ours is punctuated with glottal stops," says legendary chimp researcher Roger Fouts. "Also, the chimpanzee laughter occurs on the inhale and exhale, while ours is primarily done on our exhales. But other than these small differences, chimpanzee laughter seems to me to be just like ours in most respects."

Chimps don't do stand-up routines, of course, but they do share a laugh-related obsession with humans, one that Provine believes is central to the roots of laughter itself: Chimps love tickling. Back in his lab, Provine shows me video footage of a pair of young chimps named Josh and Lizzie playing with a human caretaker. It's a full-on ticklefest, with the chimps panting

away hysterically when their bellies are scratched. "That's chimpanzee laughter you're hearing," Provine says. It's close enough to human laughter that I find myself chuckling along.

Parents will testify that ticklefests are often the first elaborate play routine they engage in with their children and one of the most reliable laugh inducers. According to Fouts, who helped teach sign language to Washoe, perhaps the world's most famous chimpanzee, the practice is just as common, and perhaps more long lived, among the chimps. "Tickling… seems to be very important to chimpanzees because it continues throughout their lives," he says. "Even Washoe at the age of 37 still enjoys tickling and being tickled by her adult family members." Among young chimpanzees that have been taught sign language, tickling is a frequent topic of conversation.

Like laughter, tickling is almost by definition a social activity. Like the incongruity theory of humor, tickling relies on a certain element of surprise, which is why it's impossible to tickle yourself. Predictable touch doesn't elicit the laughter and squirming of tickling—it's unpredictable touch that does the trick. A number of tickle-related studies have convincingly shown that tickling exploits the sensorimotor system's awareness of the difference between self and other: If the system orders your hand to move toward your belly, it doesn't register surprise when the nerve endings on your belly report being stroked. But if the touch is being generated by another sensorimotor system, the belly stroking will come as a surprise. The pleasant laughter of tickle is the way the brain responds to that touch. In both human and chimpanzee societies, that touch usually first appears in parent-child interactions and has an essential role in creating those initial bonds. "The reason [tickling and laughter] are so important," Roger Fouts says, "is because they play a role in maintaining the affinitive bonds of friendship within the family and community."

A few years ago, Jared Diamond wrote a short book with the provocative title *Why Is Sex Fun?* These recent studies suggest an evolutionary answer to the question of why tickling is fun: It encourages us to play well with others. Young children are so receptive to the rough-and-tumble play of tickle that even pretend tickling will often send them into peals of laughter. (Fouts reports that the threat of tickle has a similar effect on his chimps.) In his book, Provine suggests that "feigned tickle" can be thought of as the Original Joke, the first deliberate behavior designed to exploit the tickling-laughter circuit. Our comedy clubs and our sitcoms are culturally enhanced versions of those original playful childhood exchanges. Along with the suckling and smiling instincts, the laughter of tickle evolved as a way of cementing the bond between parents and children, laying the foundation for a behavior that then carried over into the social lives of adults. While we once laughed at the surprise touch of a parent or sibling, we now laugh at the surprise twist of a punch line.

Bowling Green State University professor Jaak Panksepp suggests that there is a dedicated "play" circuitry in the brain, equivalent to the more extensively studied fear and love circuits. Panksepp has studied the role of rough-and-tumble play in cementing social connections between juvenile rats. The play instinct is not easily suppressed. Rats that have been denied the opportunity to engage in this kind of play—which has a distinct choreography, as well as a chirping vocalization that may be the rat equivalent of laughter—will nonetheless immediately engage in play behavior given the chance. Panksepp compares it to a bird's instinct for flying. "Probably the most powerful positive emotion of all—once your tummy is full and you don't have bodily needs—is vigorous social engagement among the young," Panksepp says. "The largest amount of human laughter seems to occur in the midst of early childhood—rough-and-tumble play, chasing, all the stuff they love."

Playing is what young mammals do, and in humans and chimpanzees, laughter is the way the brain expresses the pleasure of that play. "Since laughter seems to be ritualized panting, basically what you do in laughing is replicate the sound of rough-and-tumble play," Provine says. "And you know, that's where I think it came from. Tickle is an important part of our primate heritage. Touching and being touched is an important part of what it means to be a mammal."

There is much that we don't know yet about the neurological underpinnings of laughter. We do not yet know precisely why laughing feels so good; one recent study detected evidence that stimulating the nucleus accumbens, one of the brain's pleasure centers, triggered laughter. Panksepp has performed studies that indicate opiate antagonists significantly reduce the urge to play in rats, which implies that the brain's endorphin system may be involved in the pleasure of laughter. Some anecdotal and clinical evidence suggest that laughing makes you healthier by suppressing stress hormones and elevating immune system antibodies. If you think of laughter as a form of behavior that is basically synonymous with the detection of humor, the laughing-makes-you-healthier premise seems bizarre. Why would natural selection make our immune system respond to jokes? Provine's approach helps solve the mystery. Our bodies aren't responding to wisecracks and punch lines; they're responding to social connection.

In this respect, laughter reminds us that our emotional lives are as much outward bound as they are inner directed. We tend to think of emotions as private affairs, feelings that wash over our subjective worlds. But emotions are also social acts, laughter perhaps most of all. It's no accident that we have so many delicately choreographed gestures and facial expressions—many of which appear to be innate to our species—to convey our emotions. Our emotional systems are designed to share our feelings and not just represent them internally—an insight that Darwin first grasped more than a century ago in his book *The Expression of the Emotions in Man and Animals.* "The movements of expression in the face and body, whatever their origin may have been, are in themselves of much importance for our welfare. They serve as the first means of communication between mother and infant; she smiles approval, and thus encourages her child on the right path.... The free expression by outward signs of an emotion intensifies it."

And even if we don't yet understand the neurological basis of the pleasure that laughing brings us, it makes sense that we should seek out the connectedness of infectious laughter. We are social animals, after all. And if that laughter often involves some pretty childish behavior, so be it. "I mean, this is why we're not like lizards," Provine says, holding the Tickle Me Elmo doll on his lap. "Lizards don't play, and they're not social the way we are. When you start to see play, you're starting to see mammals. So when we get together and have a good time and laugh, we're going back to our roots. It's ironic in a way: Some of the things that give us the most pleasure in life are really the most ancient."

Alcohol's Deadly Triple Threat

Women get addicted faster, seek help less often and are more likely to die from the bottle

KAREN SPRINGEN AND BARBARA KANTROWITZ

P at Staples's childhood gave birth to the demons that nearly killed her. Her father was a volatile alcoholic. "I was physically, verbally and emotionally abused," she says. "Nose broken, head into the walls." In kindergarten she started dreaming about running away; she finally escaped in 1959, at the age of 20, when she married young to get out of the alcoholic house. But she couldn't flee her past. Over the years she gradually became an addict herself first with pills and then with alcohol. Still, her life seemed good on the surface. The marriage endured, defying the odds, and she and her husband had two healthy daughters. "Our house was on the home tour," she says. "Our kids were perfect."

The reality was far more bleak. She felt constantly under stress, anxious and terrified. "I was taking pills and drinking to keep it up," she says. Her husband started marking the bottles in the bar area, but she would just add water so he couldn't tell how much she had drunk. He checked the trash, too, and when she could no longer hide the empty bottles under newspapers, she started stashing them on the hill behind their house. Finally, one day in 1985, Staples went into the kitchen to get more ice for her vodka and saw her younger daughter, Tracy, then a high-school senior, making soup. The sweet smile on Tracy's face triggered something in Staples. "I looked at her, and I walked over, and I put my arms around her, and I said, 'Tracy, I need help'." Tracy replied, "I'm so proud of you." A few weeks later, when Staples entered the Betty Ford Center in Rancho Mirage, Calif., she was hemorrhaging rectally. "The alcohol had stripped the veins in my stomach," says Staples, now 64. "I would be dead today if I hadn't gotten sober."

Staples's grim assessment echoes new research about the devastating effects of alcohol on women. "Women get addicted faster with less alcohol, and then suffer the consequences more profoundly than men do," says Susan Foster, director of policy research and analysis at the National Center on Addiction and Substance Abuse at Columbia University. A single drink for a woman has the impact of two drinks for a man. One reason: women's bodies contain proportionately less water than men's, and a given amount of alcohol produces a higher concentration in the bloodstream. For women, anything more than one drink a day (five ounces of wine or a 12-ounce bottle of beer) is consid-

ered risky. The limit for men is two. Women who start drinking young and become heavy drinkers as they get older are more vulnerable to a range of major health problems, from infertility to osteoporosis to cancer. At the same level of consumption, controlling for body size, women seem more likely than men to develop alcohol-related liver disease.

But new evidence about the dangers of alcohol hasn't stopped women from drinking. Researchers say that about 60 percent of American women consume alcohol on a regular basis and about 5 percent average two or more drinks a day. Many female alcoholics keep their drinking secret for years. "Our culture is still more critical of women who are intoxicated than of men who are intoxicated," says psychologist Nancy Waite-O'Brien of the Betty Ford Center. Women who drink heavily are denigrated as sluts, while a man may be praised for his hollow leg. That bias means many women drink in secret and don't seek help until major health problems make denial impossible.

Most experts say the best way to spare women from alcoholism is to get them when they're young. People who drink before they're 15 are four times as likely to be alcohol-dependent or have alcohol problems when they're adults. Drinking can also damage the still-developing teenage brain, according to the American Medical Association. Unfortunately, that message isn't getting out. Even though drinking under the age of 21 is illegal in all 50 states, 41 percent of ninth graders reported drinking in the past month, according to National Institutes of Health literature. Other studies have shown that more teen girls are getting drunk, and they're trying to keep up with the boys, drink for drink. "It puts them at risk of sexual assault, of physical violence," says Foster.

Many teen girls see drinking as cool, a way to be social. Elizabeth Anderson, now 26, started drinking with her friends when she was a 15-year-old high-school student in suburban Boulder, Colo. A year later she had her first blackout. Still, she did well in school, graduating in the top 10 percent of her class. She continued drinking at the University of Colorado, where she graduated with degrees in French and advertising. At 22 she crashed her car after drinking. At 23 she got a DUI. She doesn't remember much of the next year—there were more blackouts, and eventually she was fired. At 24 she was deep in debt and finally

174

called her father for help. He got her into rehab, and she says she's been sober ever since. She avoids drinking parties and begs off when friends go to bars. Instead, she cherishes the friends she has made through a 12-step program—people who can understand what she's been through. "More than anything, what keeps me sober is looking at my life today," she says.

As women get older, their drinking threatens their children's health as well. During pregnancy especially, doctors say, women should abstain completely. "We haven't established that there's any safe level of drinking during pregnancy or lactation," says Foster. Fetal alcohol syndrome is the leading preventable cause of mental retardation in the United States. And it's not the only risk children face when pregnant women drink. Fetal alcohol spectrum disorders, which affect as many as 40,000 infants a year, can include a range of physical, mental, behavioral and learning problems.

Some studies indicate that women in unhappy or stressful relationships are the most likely to turn to alcohol for comfort. Women who have never been married or who are divorced are more likely to drink heavily than married women. And women who were sexually abused as children are more than three times as likely to suffer from alcohol problems, according to Sharon Wilsnack of the University of North Dakota School of Medicine and Health Sciences, who has conducted a 20-year study of women and alcohol. Depression is a common trigger for drinking in women. What women should watch for, doctors say, is a pattern of using alcohol to be less stressed or angry. "Alcohol is pretty good in the early stages at dealing with bad feelings," says Wilsnack. But ultimately drinking becomes as big a problem as depression and can even exacerbate negative feelings.

Wilsnack and her colleagues found that women are less likely to drink as they age—which is a good thing, because older women who drink heavily are at much higher risk for diseases of aging. Heavy alcohol use irreversibly weakens bones, and while there's some evidence that one drink a day may decrease the risk of heart disease, there's also research suggesting that the same amount of alcohol can increase the risk of breast cancer. A woman with a family history of heart disease but no family history of alcoholism or breast cancer could have a drink a day, but a woman with a family history of those diseases might want to abstain.

If you drink at all, drink sensibly—aim for no more than one drink a day. Don't drink alone. And don't drink to medicate your moods. If you think you have a problem, seek help. "It's not a moral issue," says Staples. "It's a disease. It needs to be treated by professionals who understand the disease. If a person wants it, there is help and there is hope." That's a message you can't get in a bottle.

How AIDS Changed America

The plague years: It brought out the worst in us at first, but ultimately it brought out the best, and transformed the nation. The story of a disease that left an indelible mark on our history, our culture and our souls.

DAVID JEFFERSON

Jeanne White-Ginder sits at home, assembling a scrapbook about her son, Ryan. She pastes in newspaper stories about his fight to return to the Indiana middle school that barred him in 1985 for having AIDS. She sorts through photos of Ryan with Elton John, Greg Louganis and others who championed his cause. She organizes mementos from his PBS special, "I Have AIDS: A Teenager's Story." "I just got done with his funeral. Eight pages. That was very hard," says White-Ginder, who buried her 18-year-old son in 1991, seven years after he was diagnosed with the disease, which he contracted through a blood product used to treat hemophiliacs. The scrapbook, along with Ryan's bedroom, the way his mother left it when he died, will be part of an exhibit at the Children's Museum of Indianapolis on three children who changed history: Anne Frank. Ruby Bridges. And Ryan White. "He put a face to the epidemic, so people could care about people with AIDS," his mother says.

At a time when the mere threat of avian flu or SARS can set off a coast-to-coast panic—and prompt the federal government to draw up contingency plans and stockpile medicines—it's hard to imagine that the national response to the emergence of AIDS ranged from indifference to hostility. But that's exactly what happened when gay men in 1981 began dying of a strange array of opportunistic infections. President Ronald Reagan didn't discuss AIDS in a public forum until a press conference four years into the epidemic, by which time more than 12,000 Americans had already died. (He didn't publicly utter the term "AIDS" until 1987.) People with the disease were routinely evicted from their homes, fired from jobs and denied health insurance. Gays were demonized by the extreme right wing: Reagan adviser Pat Buchanan editorialized in 1983, "The poor homosexuals—they have declared war against nature, and now nature is exacting an awful retribution." In much of the rest of the culture, AIDS was simply treated as the punch line to a tasteless joke: "I just heard the Statue of Liberty has AIDS," Bob Hope quipped during the rededication ceremony of the statue in 1986. "Nobody knows if she got it from the mouth of the Hudson or the Staten Island Fairy." Across the river in Manhattan, a generation of young adults was attending more funerals than weddings.

In 1995, Americans regarded HIV/AIDS as the nation's most urgent health problem. Today, only 17% rank it as the top concern.

All poll results are from the Kaiser family foundation's 2006 "Survey of Americans on HIV/AIDS," conducted among 2,517 Americans nationwide.

As AIDS made its death march across the nation, killing more Americans than every conflict from World War II through Iraq, it left an indelible mark on our history and culture. It changed so many things in so many ways, from how the media portray homosexuality to how cancer patients deal with their disease. At the same time, AIDS itself changed, from a disease that killed gay men and drug addicts to a global scourge that has decimated the African continent, cut a large swath through black America and infected almost as many women as men worldwide. The death toll to date: 25 million and counting. Through the crucible of AIDS, America was forced to face its fears and prejudices—fears that denied Ryan White a seat in school for a year and a half, prejudices that had customers boycotting restaurants with gay chefs. "At first, a ton of people said that whoever gets AIDS deserves to have AIDS, deserves to literally suffer all the physical pain that the virus carries with it," says Tom Hanks, who won an Oscar for playing a gay lawyer dying of the disease in 1993's "Philadelphia." "But that didn't hold." Watching a generation of gay men wither and die, the nation came to acknowledge the humanity of a community it had mostly ignored and reviled. "AIDS was the great unifier," says Craig Thompson, executive director of AIDS Project Los Angeles and HIV-positive for 25 years.

Without AIDS, and the activism and consciousness-raising that accompanied it, would gay marriage even be up for debate today? Would we be welcoming "Will & Grace" into our living rooms or weeping over "Brokeback Mountain"? Without red ribbons, first worn in 1991 to promote AIDS awareness, would we be donning rubber yellow bracelets to show our support for cancer research? And without the experience of battling AIDS, would scientists have the strategies and technologies to develop the antiviral drugs we'll need to battle microbial killers yet to emerge?

AIDS, of course, did happen. "Don't you dare tell me there's any good news in this," says Larry Kramer, who has been raging against the disease—and those who let it spread unchecked—since it was first identified in 1981. "We should be having a national day of mourning!" True. But as we try to comprehend the carnage, it's impossible not to acknowledge the displays of strength, compassion and, yes, love, that were a direct result of all that pain and loss. Without AIDS, we wouldn't have the degree of patient activism we see today among people with breast cancer, lymphoma, ALS and other life-threatening diseases. It was Kramer, after all, who organized 10,000 frustrated AIDS patients into ACT UP, a street army chanting "Silence equals death" that marched on the White House and shut down Wall Street, demanding more government funding for research and quicker access to drugs that might save lives. "The only thing that makes people fight is fear. That's what we discovered about AIDS activism," Kramer says.

Fear can mobilize, but it can also paralyze—which is what AIDS did when it first appeared. And no one—not the government, not the media, not the gay community itself—reacted fast enough to head off disaster. In the fiscally and socially conservative climate of Reagan's America, politicians were loath to fund research into a new pathogen that was killing mostly gay men and intravenous drug users. "In the first years of AIDS, I imagine we felt like the folks on the rooftops during Katrina, waiting for help," says Dr. Michael Gottlieb, the Los Angeles immunologist credited as the first doctor to recognize the looming epidemic. When epidemiologist Donald Francis of the federal Centers for Disease Control in Atlanta tried to get $30 million in funding for an AIDS-prevention campaign, "it went up to Washington and they said f--- off," says Francis, who quit the CDC soon after, defeated.

"Gay Cancer," as it was referred to at the time, wasn't a story the press wanted to cover—especially since it required a discussion of gay sex. While the media had a field day with Legionnaire's disease, toxic shock syndrome and the Tylenol scare, few outlets paid much attention to the new syndrome, even after scores of people had died. The New York Times ran fewer than a dozen stories about the new killer in 1981 and 1982, almost all of them buried inside the paper. (NEWSWEEK, for that matter, didn't run its first cover story on what "may be the public-health threat of the century" until April 1983.) The Wall Street Journal first reported on the disease only after it had spread to heterosexuals: NEW, OFTEN-FATAL ILLNESS IN HOMOSEXUALS TURNS UP IN WOMEN, HETEROSEXUAL MALES, read the February 1982 headline. Even the gay press missed the story at first: afraid of alarming the community and inflaming antigay forces, editors at the New York Native slapped the headline DISEASE RUMORS LARGELY UNFOUNDED

atop the very first press report about the syndrome, which ran May 18, 1981. There were a few notable exceptions, particularly the work of the late Randy Shilts, an openly gay journalist who convinced his editors at the San Francisco Chronicle to let him cover AIDS as a full-time beat: that reporting led to the landmark 1987 book "And the Band Played On," a detailed account of how the nation's failure to take AIDS seriously allowed the disease to spread exponentially in the early '80s.

Many gay men were slow to recognize the time bomb in their midst, even as people around them were being hospitalized with strange, purplish skin cancers and life-threatening pneumonia. Kramer and his friends tried to raise money for research during the 1981 Labor Day weekend in The Pines, a popular gay vacation spot on New York's Fire Island. "When we opened the collection boxes, we could not believe how truly awful the results were," says Kramer. The total? $769.55. "People thought we were a bunch of creeps with our GIVE TO GAY CANCER signs, raining on the parade of Pines' holiday festivities." The denial in some corners of the gay community would continue for years. Many were reluctant to give up the sexual liberation they believed they'd earned: as late as 1984, the community was bitterly debating whether to close San Francisco's gay bathhouses, where men were having unprotected sex with any number of partners in a single night.

With death a constant companion, the gay community sobered up from the party that was the '70s and rose to meet the unprecedented challenge of AIDS. There was no other choice, really: they had been abandoned by the nation, left to fend for themselves. "It's important to remember that there was a time when people did not want to use the same bathroom as a person with AIDS, when cabdrivers didn't want to pick up patients who had the disease, when hospitals put signs on patients' doors that said WARNING. DO NOT ENTER," recalls Marjorie Hill, executive director of Gay Men's Health Crisis in New York. Organizations like GMHC sprang up around the country to provide HIV patients with everything from medical care to counseling to food and housing. "Out of whole cloth, and without experience, we built a healthcare system that was affordable, effective and humane," says Darrel Cummings, chief of staff of the Los Angeles Gay & Lesbian Center. "I can't believe our community did what it did while so many people were dying." Patients took a hands-on approach to managing their disease, learning the intricacies of T-cell counts and grilling their doctors about treatment options. And they shared what they learned with one another. "There's something that a person with a disease can only get from another person with that disease. It's support and information and inspiration," says Sean Strub, who founded the magazine Poz for HIV-positive readers.

It took a movie star to get the rest of the nation's attention. In the summer of 1985, the world learned that Rock Hudson—the romantic leading man who'd been a symbol of American virility—was not only gay, but had full-blown AIDS. "It was a bombshell event," says Gottlieb, who remembers standing on the helipad at UCLA Medical Center, waiting for his celebrity patient to arrive, as news helicopters circled overhead. "For many Americans, it was their first awareness at all of AIDS. This prominent man had been diagnosed, and the image of him looking as sick as he did really stuck." Six years later, basketball legend Magic Johnson announced he was HIV-positive, and the shock waves were even bigger. A straight, healthy-looking superstar athlete had contracted the "gay" disease. "It can happen to anybody, even me, Magic Johnson," the 32-year-old announced to a stunned nation, as he urged Americans to practice safe sex.

Given the tremendous stigma, most well-known public figures with AIDS tried to keep their condition a secret. Actor Brad Davis, the star of "Midnight Express," kept his diagnosis hidden for six years, until he died in 1991. "He assumed, and I think rightly so, that he wouldn't be able to find work," says his widow, Susan Bluestein, a Hollywood casting director. After Davis died, rumors flew that he must have been secretly gay. "That part of the gossip mill was the most hurtful to me and my daughter," says Bluestein, who acknowledges in her book "After Midnight" that her husband was a drug addict and unfaithful—but not gay.

With the disease afflicting so many of their own, celebrities were quick to lend support and raise money. Elizabeth Taylor was among the first, taking her friend Rock Hudson's hand in public, before the TV cameras and the world, to dispel the notion that AIDS was something you could catch through casual contact. Her gesture seems quaint today, but in 1985—when the tabloids were awash with speculation that Hudson could have infected actress Linda Evans by simply kissing her during a love scene in "Dynasty"—Taylor's gesture was revolutionary. She became the celebrity face of the American Foundation for AIDS Research. "I've lost so many friends," Taylor says. "I have so many friends who are HIV-positive and you just wonder how long it's going to be. And it breaks your heart."

Behind the scenes, Hollywood wasn't nearly as progressive as it likes to appear. John Erman recalls the uphill battle getting the 1985 AIDS drama, "An Early Frost," on TV. "The meetings we had with NBC's Standards and Practices [the network's censors] were absolutely medieval," says Erman. One of the censors' demands: that the boyfriend of the main character be portrayed as "a bad guy" for infecting him: "They did not want to show a positive gay relationship," Erman recalls. Ultimately, with the support of the late NBC Entertainment president Brandon Tartikoff, Erman got to make the picture he wanted—though major advertisers refused to buy commercial time during the broadcast. Within a decade, AIDS had changed the face of television. In 1991, "thirtysomething" featured a gay character who'd contracted the disease. And in 1994, on MTV's "The Real World," 23-year-old Pedro Zamora, who died later that same year, taught a generation of young people what it meant to be HIV-positive.

If TV was slow to deal with AIDS, cinema was downright glacial. "Longtime Companion," the first feature film about the disease, didn't make it to the screen until 1990, nine years into the epidemic. "There was a lot of talk before the movie came out about how this was going to hurt my career, the same way there was talk about Heath Ledger in 'Brokeback Mountain'," says Bruce Davison, who received an Oscar nomination for his role. As for "Philadelphia," Hanks is the first to admit " it was late to the game."

Broadway was the major exception when it came to taking on AIDS as subject matter—in part because so many early casualties came from the world of theater. "I remember in 1982 sitting in a restaurant with seven friends of mine. All were gay men either working or looking to work in the theater, and we were talking about AIDS," recalls Tom Viola, executive director of Broadway Cares/Equity Fights AIDS. "Of those eight guys, four are dead, and two, including myself, are HIV-positive." By the time Tony Kushner's Pulitzer Prize-winning "Angels in America" made its Broadway debut in 1993, some 60 plays about the disease had opened in New York. Producer Jeffrey Seller remembers how he was told he "could never do a show on Broadway that's about, quote unquote, AIDS, homosexuality and drug addiction." He's talking about "Rent," which a decade later still draws capacity crowds.

The world of "Rent" is something of an artifact now. Just before it hit Broadway in 1996, scientists introduced the antiretroviral drug cocktails that have gone on to extend the lives of millions of patients with HIV. Since then, the urgency that once surrounded the AIDS fight in the United States has ebbed, as HIV has come to be seen as a chronic, rather than fatal, condition. But the drugs aren't a panacea—despite the fact that many people too young to remember the funerals of the '80s think the new medications have made it safe to be unsafe. "Everywhere I go, I'm meeting young people who've just found out they've been infected, many with drug-resistant strains of the virus," says Cleve Jones, who two decades ago decided to start stitching a quilt to honor a friend who had died of AIDS. That quilt grew to become an iconic patchwork of more than 40,000 panels, each one the size of a grave, handmade by loved ones to honor their dead. Ever-expanding, it was displayed several times in Washington, transforming the National Mall into what Jones had always intended: a colorful cemetery that would force the country to acknowledge the toll of AIDS. "If I'd have known 20 years ago that in 2006 I'd be watching a whole new generation facing this tragedy, I don't think I would have had the strength to continue," says Jones, whose own HIV infection has grown resistant to treatment.

Inner strength is what has allowed people living with HIV to persevere. "They think I'm gonna die. You know what, they better not hold their breath," Ryan White once told his mother. Though given six months to live when he was diagnosed with HIV, Ryan lived five and a half years, long enough to prod a nation into joining the fight against AIDS. When he died in 1990 at the age of 18, Congress named a new comprehensive AIDS funding act after him. But the real tribute to Ryan has been the ongoing efforts of his mother. "I think the hostility around the epidemic is still there. And because of religious and moral issues, it's been really hard to educate people about this disease and be explicit," says White-Ginder, who continues to give speeches about watching her son live and die of AIDS. "We should not still be facing this disease." Sadly, we are.

The Myth of the Midlife Crisis

It's time we stopped dismissing middle age as the beginning of the end. Research suggests that at 40, the brain's best years are still ahead.

GENE COHEN, M.D., PH.D.

I was taken by surprise several years ago when my colleagues started to worry that I was going through some sort of midlife crisis. I was in my late 40s, and after two decades as a gerontologist I was pursuing a new passion: designing games for older adults. My first game, a joint effort with artist Gretchen Raber, was a finalist in an internationally juried show on games as works of art. Though I still had a day job directing George Washington University's Center on Aging, Health & Humanities, I was now working hard on a second game.

"Are you turning right on us?" one friend, a neuroscientist, kidded me. He wasn't talking about politics. He was asking whether I'd scrapped the logical, analytical tendencies of the brain's left hemisphere to embrace the more creative, less disciplined tendencies of the right brain. But I wasn't scrapping anything. As a researcher, I had spent years documenting the psychological benefits of intergenerational play. Now I was using both sides of my brain to create new opportunities for myself. Instead of just measuring and studying the benefits of mental stimulation, I was finding creative ways to put my findings to work. What my friends perceived as a crisis was, in truth, the start of a thrilling new phase of my life.

The mature mind gets better at reconciling thoughts and feelings.

In thinking about this experience, I realized that our view of human development in the second half of life was badly outmoded. We tend to think of aging in purely negative terms, and even experts often define "successful" aging as the effective management of decay and decline. Rubbish. No one can deny that aging brings challenges and losses. But recent discoveries in neuroscience show that the aging brain is more flexible and adaptable than we previously thought. Studies suggest that the brain's left and right hemispheres become better integrated during middle age, making way for greater creativity. Age also seems to dampen some negative emotions. And a great deal of scientific work has confirmed the "use it or lose it" adage,

showing that the aging brain grows stronger from use and challenge. In short, midlife is a time of new possibility. Growing old can be filled with positive experiences. The challenge is to recognize our potential—and nurture it.

Until recently, scientists paid little attention to psychological development in the second half of life, and those who did pay attention often drew the wrong conclusions. "About the age of 50," Sigmund Freud wrote in 1907, "the elasticity of the mental processes on which treatment depends is, as a rule, lacking. Old people are no longer educable." Freud—who wrote those words at 51 and produced some of his best work after 65—wasn't the only pioneer to misconstrue the aging process. Jean Piaget, the great developmental psychologist, assumed that cognitive development stopped during young adulthood, with the acquisition of abstract thought. Even Erik Erikson, who delineated eight stages of psychosocial development, devoted only two pages of his classic work "Identity and the Life Cycle" to later life.

My own work picks up where these past giants left off. Through studies involving more than 3,000 older adults, I have identified four distinct developmental phases that unfold in overlapping 20-year periods beginning in a person's early 40s: a midlife re-evaluation (typically encountered between 40 and 65) during which we set new goals and priorities; a liberation phase (55 to 75) that involves shedding past inhibitions to express ourselves more freely; a summing-up phase (65 to 85) when we begin to review our lives and concentrate on giving back, and an encore phase (75 and beyond) that involves finding affirmation and fellowship in the face of adversity and loss. I refer to "phases" instead of "stages" because people vary widely during later life. We don't all march through these phases in lock step, but I've seen thousands of older adults pass through them—each person driven by a unique set of inner drives and ideals.

What sparks this series of changes? Why, after finding our places in the world, do so many of us spend our 40s and 50s re-evaluating our lives? The impulse stems partly from a growing awareness of our own mortality. As decades vanish behind us, and we realize how relatively few we have left, we gain new perspective on who we are and what we really care about. This awakening isn't always easy—it often reveals conflicts between the lives we've built and the ones we want to pursue—but only 10 percent of the people I've studied describe the midlife transition as a crisis. Far more say they're filled with a new sense of quest and personal discovery. "I'm looking forward to pursuing the career I always wanted," one 49-year-old woman told me. "I'm tired of just working on other people's visions, rather than my own, even if I have to start on a smaller scale."

While changing our perspective, age also remodels our brains, leaving us better equipped to fulfill our own dreams. The most important difference between older brains and younger brains is also the easiest to overlook: older brains have learned more than young ones. Throughout life, our brains encode thoughts and memories by forming new connections among neurons. The neurons themselves may lose some processing speed with age, but they become ever more richly intertwined. Magnified tremendously, the brain of a mentally active 50-year-old looks like a dense forest of interlocking branches, and this density reflects both deeper knowledge and better judgment. That's why age is such an advantage in fields like editing, law, medicine, coaching and management. There is no substitute for acquired learning.

Knowledge and wisdom aren't the only fruits of age. New research suggests that as our brains become more densely wired, they also become less rigidly bifurcated. As I mentioned earlier, our brains actually consist of two separate structures—a right brain and a left brain—linked by a row of fibers called the corpus callosum. In most people, the left hemisphere specializes in speech, language and logical reasoning, while the right hemisphere handles more intuitive tasks, such as face recognition and the reading of emotional cues. But as scientists have recently discovered through studies with PET scans and magnetic resonance imaging, this pattern changes as we age. Unlike young adults, who handle most tasks on one side of the brain or the other, older ones tend to use both hemispheres. Duke University neuroscientist Robert Cabeza has dubbed this phenomenon Hemispheric Asymmetry Reduction in Older Adults—HAROLD for short—and his research suggests it is no accident.

In a 2002 study, Cabeza assigned a set of memory tasks to three groups of people: one composed of young adults, one of low-performing older adults and one of high-performing older adults. Like the young people, the low-performing elders drew mainly on one side of the prefrontal cortex to perform the assigned tasks. It was the high-scoring elders who used both hemispheres. No one knows exactly what this all means, but the finding suggests that healthy brains compensate for the depredations of age by expanding their neural networks across the bilateral divide. My own work suggests that, besides keeping us sharp, this neural integration makes it easier to reconcile our thoughts with our feelings. When you hear someone saying, "My head tells me to do this, but my heart says do that," the person is more likely a 20-year-old than a 50-year-old. One of my patients, a 51-year-old man, remembers how he agonized over

decisions during his 20s, searching in vain for the most logical choice. As he moved through his 40s and into his 50s, he found himself trusting his gut. "My decisions are more subjective," he said during one session, "but I'm more comfortable with many of the choices that follow."

As our aging brains grow wiser and more flexible, they also tend toward greater equanimity. Our emotions are all rooted in a set of neural structures known collectively as the limbic system. Some of our strongest negative emotions originate in the amygdalae, a pair of almond-shaped limbic structures that sit near the center of the brain, screening sensory data for signs of trouble. At the first hint of a threat, the amygdalae fire off impulses that can change our behavior before our conscious, thinking brains have a chance to weigh in. That's why our hearts pound when strangers approach us on dark sidewalks—and why we often overreact to slights and annoyances. But the amygdalae seem to mellow with age. In brain-imaging studies, older adults show less evidence of fear, anger and hatred than young adults. Psychological studies confirm that impression, showing that older adults are less impulsive and less likely to dwell on their negative feelings.

An editor I know at a New York publishing company provides a case in point. He was in his 60s, and contemplating retirement, when he realized that he had finally matured into his job. Despite a sharp intellect and a passion for excellence, this man had spent much of his career alienating people with brusque, critical comments and a lack of sensitivity. Now, he told me over lunch, he was finally beginning to master interpersonal communication. As his emotional development caught up to his intellectual development, he morphed from a brilliant but brittle loner into a mentor and a mediator of conflicts. "I feel like a changed man," he said with a bemused smile. His best work was still ahead of him.

Clearly, the aging brain is more resilient, adaptable and capable than we thought. But that doesn't mean we can sit back and expect good things to happen. Research has identified several types of activity that can, if practiced regularly, help boost the power, clarity and subtlety of the aging brain.

Exercise physically. Numerous studies have linked physical exercise to increased brainpower. This is particularly true when the exercise is aerobic—meaning continuous, rhythmic exercise that uses large muscle groups. The positive effects may stem from increased blood flow to the brain, the production of endorphins, better filtration of waste products from the brain and increased brain-oxygen levels.

Exercise mentally. The brain is like a muscle. Use it and it grows stronger. Let it idle and it will grow flabby. So choose something appealing and challenging—and don't be surprised if, once you start, you want to do more. One of the programs I co-chair, the Creativity Discovery Corps, strives to identify unrecognized, talented older adults in the community. A 93-year-old woman we recently interviewed advised us that she might find scheduling the next interview difficult because she was very busy applying for a Ph.D. program.

Pick challenging leisure activities. Getting a graduate degree isn't the only way to keep your brain fit. An important 2003 study identified five leisure activities that were associated with a lower risk of dementia and cognitive decline. In order of impact (from highest to lowest), the winners were dancing, playing board games, playing musical instruments, doing crossword puzzles and reading. Risk reduction was related to the frequency of participation. For example, older persons who did crossword puzzles four days a week had a risk of dementia 47 percent lower than subjects who did puzzles only once a week.

Achieve mastery. Research on aging has uncovered a key variable in mental health called "sense of control." From middle age onward, people who enjoy a sense of control and mastery stay healthier than those who don't. The possibilities for mastery are unlimited, ranging from playing a musical instrument to learning a new language to taking up painting or embroidery. Besides improving your outlook, the sense of accomplishment may also strengthen the immune system.

Establish strong social networks. Countless studies have linked active social engagement to better mental and physical health and lower death rates. People who maintain social relationships during the second half of life enjoy significantly lower blood pressure, which in turn reduces the risk of stroke and its resulting brain damage. Social relationships also reduce stress and its corrosive effects, including anxiety and depression.

The brain is like the foundation of a building—it provides the physical substrate of our minds, our personalities and our sense of self. As we've seen, our brain hardware is capable of adapting, growing and becoming more complex and integrated with age. As our brains mature and evolve, so do our knowledge, our emotions and our expressive abilities. In turn, what we do with those abilities affects the brain itself, forging the new connections and constellations needed for further psychological growth. This realization should embolden anyone entering the later phases of life. If we can move beyond our stubborn myths about the aging brain, great things are possible. Successful aging is not about managing decline. It's about harnessing the enormous potential that each of us has for growth, love and happiness.

GENE COHEN is founding director of the Center on Aging, Health & Humanities at George Washington University Medical Center. This article is adapted from "The Mature Mind: The Positive Power of the Aging Brain," published this month by Basic Books, a member of the Perseus Book Group.

As seen in *Newsweek,* January 16, 2006, pp. 82, 84-86. Adapted from THE MATURE MIND: THE POSITIVE POWER OF THE AGING BRAIN (Basic Books, 2006). Copyright © 2006 by Gene Cohen. All rights reserved. Reprinted by permission of Basic Books, a member of Perseus Book Group, LLC.

Aging Naturally

In an exclusive TIME book excerpt, Dr. Andrew Weil shares his secrets for maximizing health and happiness—no matter how old you are

DR. ANDREW WEIL

I recently turned 60. To help celebrate the occasion, friends organized a surprise party. After the festivities, there came a time to reflect, and I came to an uncomfortable conclusion: I am closer to that period in life when my energy and powers will diminish and I will lose my independence. At age 60, the organs of the body gradually begin to fail and the first hints of age-related disease begin to appear.

I hardly notice my aging on a day-to-day basis. When I look in the mirror each morning, my face and white beard seem the same as the day before. But in photographs from the 1970s, my beard is completely black. On closer inspection, I notice other changes in my body: more aches and pains, less resilience, less vigor. And my memory may not be quite what it used to be. At the same time, despite the evidence, some part of me feels unchanged. In fact, I feel the same as when I was 6.

Some years ago I went to my 25th high school reunion. I had not seen most of my classmates since our graduation in 1959. A few were just as I remembered them, hardly changed at all. Others looked so aged that I could barely find points of coincidence with the pictures of them I had in my head. Why the difference? Why are some individuals so outwardly altered by time and others not? Or, in other words, why is there often a discrepancy between chronological age and biological age?

I believe the answer has to do with complex interactions of genetics and environment. I also believe, on the basis of evidence I have reviewed, we actually have control over some of those factors.

I do not subscribe to the view that aging suddenly overtakes us at some point in life, whether at 60 or some other milestone. I meet researchers, physicians and others who believe that we are born, grow rapidly to maturity, and then coast along on a more or less comfortable plateau until we begin to decline. They call the period of decline *senescence* and consider it distinct and apart from what came before.

I find it more useful to think of aging as a continuous and necessary process of change that begins at conception. Wherever you are on the continuum, it is important to learn how to live in appropriate ways in order to maximize health and happiness. That should be an essential goal for all of us. What is appropriate when you are in your 20s is likely not going to be appropriate in your 50s.

We can mask the outward signs of the process or try to keep up old routines in spite of it, but we cannot change the fact that we are all moving toward physical change. The best we can do—and it is a lot—is to accept the inevitability of aging and try to adapt to it, to be in the best health we can at any age. To my mind the denial of aging and the attempt to fight it are counterproductive, a failure to understand and accept an important aspect of our existence. Such attitudes are major obstacles to aging gracefully.

Which brings me to the subject of antiaging medicine.

The Antiaging Business

Antiaging medicine is nothing new. What is remarkable, though, is its growth into an organized field, with journals, annual meetings and a concerted attempt by leaders to have it recognized as a legitimate specialty of orthodox medicine.

There are at present no effective antiaging medicines. Yet the field keeps expanding. Currently, popular practices include live-cell therapy (injecting the fetal cells of animals into human beings), caloric restriction (drastically limiting the number of calories a body takes in) and hormone therapy (to restore hormones to levels found in younger people).

Here is the crux of the difference between practitioners of antiaging medicine and more conventional colleagues: the former are using methods and making claims that the latter consider unsupported by scientific evidence. Most of those methods may be relatively harmless except to the bank accounts of clients; others may not.

Furthermore, I am dismayed by the emphasis on appearance in antiaging medicine. This is apparent not just in the use of senior bodybuilders as models of healthy aging but in the prominent inclusion of cosmetic surgery in the American Academy of Anti-Aging Medicine's conferences and publications. To my mind, all this represents attempts to deny or mask the outward signs of aging. It is nonacceptance of aging—one of the great obstacles to doing it gracefully.

If you are tempted by the promises of antiaging medicine, I would advise you to use it selectively. Always assess the potential for harm of any intervention. Then try to evaluate the evidence for any claimed benefits. Weigh potential benefits against possible risks, including exorbitant costs. Get second opinions from doctors who are not part of the antiaging enterprise. If you do decide to follow a special treatment regimen, set a time limit for judging whether it does you any good—say, three to six months. Then determine if it was worth the cost.

Before I leave this subject, I want to warn you that the promises you will hear from antiaging practitioners are going to become more extravagant in the coming years. A number of hardcore molecular biologists claim to have identified genetic mechanisms that control the aging process as well as ways of manipulating them. These researchers believe that the biological clock *can* be stopped or turned back, and as antiaging doctors learn about this work, they will use it to their advantage.

My bottom line for now is that these theoretical breakthroughs serve only as distractions from what's important—namely, learning to accept the inevitability of aging, understanding its challenges and promises, and knowing how to keep minds and bodies as healthy as possible while moving through life's successive stages.

To age gracefully means to let nature take its course while doing everything in our power to delay the onset of age-related disease. Or, in other words, to live as long and as well as possible, then have a rapid decline at the end of life.

In the following pages, I will share some of my recommendations for what you can do to experience healthy aging. They are not intended to help you grow younger, to extend life beyond its reasonable limits or to make it easier for you to deny the fact of aging. The goal is to adapt to the changes that time brings and to arrive at old age with minimal deficits and discomforts—in technical terms, to compress morbidity. I hope that you will discover and enjoy the benefits that aging can bring: wisdom, depth of character, the smoothing out of what is rough and harsh, the evaporation of what is inconsequential and the concentration of true worth.

An Ounce of Prevention

Taking care of the body means different things at different stages in life. For example, accidents are major causes of death and disability in people in their teens and 20s, often the result of thoughtless or reckless behavior, such as riding motorcycles without helmets, diving headfirst into murky bodies of water and using drugs and alcohol unwisely.

Habits acquired in those years—notably addiction to tobacco—can markedly increase the risk of chronic disease in later life. Men in their 30s and 40s often injure themselves by engaging in contact sports or exercising improperly, while men in their 50s and 60s are often too sedentary. One of the secrets of healthy aging is knowing how to evaluate the riskiness of your behavior. Another is being willing to let go of behaviors more suited to younger bodies.

Obviously you will not have a chance to experience healthy aging if you succumb to one of the common diseases that strike

people in midlife, such as a heart attack or a tobacco-related cancer. To avoid these, you must be aware of your personal health risks, as suggested by your medical history, your family history and your medical examinations. You also need to know how to take advantage of modern preventive medicine—for example, how to make the best use of diagnostic screening tests that are now available (and to avoid tests that are not accurate or sensitive enough to justify their use).

There is much you can do to prevent illness, including having a complete physical exam and regular checkups. But there are two specific points of preventive health care that I feel need emphasis:

Don't smoke. Tobacco addiction is the single greatest cause of preventable illness. Exposure to tobacco smoke not only increases the odds of developing many kinds of cancer but also raises the risks of cardiovascular and respiratory diseases. Inhalation of vaporized nicotine is as addictive as the smoking of crack cocaine or crystal methamphetamine. Almost all cases of tobacco addiction begin in the teenage years or earlier; therefore, I address this message to young readers. Do not experiment with smoking: the chance of becoming addicted is too great, and this is one of the hardest of all addictions to break.

Watch your weight. Morbid obesity, sometimes defined as being more than 100 lbs. above your "normal" weight, is incompatible with healthy aging because it increases the risk of a number of age-related diseases, including cardiovascular disease, Type 2 diabetes and osteoarthritis. Ordinary obesity—weighing at least 20% more than you should—correlates with milder forms of these diseases as well as with increased incidence of postmenopausal breast cancer and cancer of the uterus, colon, kidney and esophagus. But what is normal, and how much should you weigh?

It is quite possible that our criteria for obesity and our thinking about its medical implications have been warped by fashion. We all know morbid obesity when we see it; clearly, it interferes with activities of daily living and makes people unhappy and unhealthy. But being too lean may also compromise health and successful aging. I believe that those who are somewhat overweight but fit in middle age may enjoy a healthier and longer old age than those who are lean and not fit.

Diet

It should be obvious by now that diets don't work, except in the short term. By definition, diets are regimens that eventually end, and when people go off them the weight that was lost is almost always regained. I am going to urge you to follow a diet that I believe can increase the probability of healthy aging, but I hesitate even to call it a diet. It is absolutely not intended as a weight-loss program, nor is it an eating plan to stay on for a limited period of time. Rather, it is the nutritional component of a healthy lifestyle. I like to call it the Anti-Inflammatory Diet.

The word inflammation suggests "fire within," a graphic if inaccurate image. Normal inflammation is the healing system's response to localized injury and attack. It is confined to that location, serves a purpose and ends when the problem is resolved.

Abnormal inflammation extends beyond its appointed limits in space and time; it does not end when the problem is resolved. The inflammatory process unleashes some of the immune system's most sophisticated weaponry, including enzymes that can rupture cell walls and digest vital components of cells and tissues. When inflammation targets normal tissues, when it just won't quit, it is abnormal and promotes disease rather than healing. Abnormal inflammation has been linked to a wide range of diseases, including cancer, coronary heart disease and the autoimmune diseases—Type 1 diabetes, multiple sclerosis, rheumatic fever, rheumatoid arthritis and systemic lupus.

I believe without question that diet influences inflammation. The food choices we make can determine whether we are in a proinflammatory state or in an antiinflammatory one. The antiinflammatory diet on these pages (see box) offers specific recommendations for foods to include and foods to avoid.

Supplements

Whether or not to use dietary supplements is a contentious issue today.

Here are the facts as I see them. I have always maintained that supplemental nutrients are not substitutes for the whole foods that contain them. Taking supplements does not excuse you from eating a healthy diet. This is particularly true for the micronutrients. I take a good daily multivitamin-multimineral supplement, one that I formulated myself, as insurance against gaps in my diet—for example, to cover those days when I am on the road and simply can't get the fruits and vegetables I'd like. The more regularly we supply our bodies with antioxidants and phytonutrients, the better our health. Most of us simply can't do that with food, hence the need for supplements.

Apart from providing insurance against gaps in the diet, supplements can provide optimum dosages of natural therapeutic agents that may help prevent and treat age-related diseases. Consider vitamin E. Oil-rich seeds and nuts are the main food source of it. Many studies suggest that doses in the range of 200 IUs to 400 IUs of alpha-tocopherol (or, better, 80 mg to 160 mg of the whole complex, including tocotrienols) offer the best antioxidant protection against common age-related diseases. Nuts are good for you, but you would have to eat far too many to get that amount of vitamin E.

I should say too that I have always favored increased regulation of the dietary-supplement industry, which has proved incapable of policing itself. I would like to see the U.S. Food and Drug Administration create a new Division of Natural Therapeutic Agents to regulate herbs, vitamins, minerals and other products—not with the intent of thwarting consumer access to them but rather of ensuring that products on the market are safe, contain what they claim to contain, and do what they claim to do.

Exercise

It is probably possible to lead an inactive life and still experience healthy aging, but it isn't likely. Almost all the healthy seniors I know were physically active throughout life, and many of them still are. They walk, dance, play golf, swim, lift weights, do yoga and Tai Chi.

Of course, it is possible to get too much physical activity, not just because overactivity raises the possibility of damaging joints, muscles and bones, but also because of the possible adverse effects on body composition, the nervous system and reproductive and immune function. Knees are especially vulnerable, and surgical methods for repairing them are less than ideal. Repeated concussive injuries, as in football and soccer, may be associated with cognitive impairment in later life. That said, far more people in our culture err on the side of getting too little physical activity than too much.

Walking, if you do it vigorously enough, is the overall best exercise for regular aerobic activity. It requires no equipment, everyone knows how to do it and it carries the lowest risk of injury. The human body is designed to walk. You can walk in parks or shopping malls or in your neighborhood. To get maximum benefit from walking, aim for 45 minutes a day, an average of five days a week.

Strength training is another important component of physical activity. Its purpose is to build and maintain bone and muscle mass, both of which diminish with age. In general, you will want to do strength training two or three days a week, allowing recovery days between sessions. You should be able to develop a routine, whether with machines, free weights or tubing, that you can complete in half an hour.

Finally, flexibility and balance training are increasingly important as the body ages. Aches and pains are high on the list of complaints in old age. Many of them are avoidable, the result of chronic muscle tension and stiffness of joints; simple flexibility training can prevent these by toning muscles and keeping joints lubricated. Some of this you do whenever you stretch. If you watch dogs and cats, you'll get an idea of how natural it is. The general principle is simple: whenever the body has been in one position for a while, it is good to briefly stretch it in an opposite position.

The best-known formal system of stretching is yoga, now immensely popular in the West. Many different styles of yoga exist, some very vigorous and demanding, some quite gentle. I couldn't be more pleased to see yoga becoming so mainstream in our part of the world; I think it will increase the numbers of healthier and happier people here. But I do not recommend the strenuous forms for everyone. Older people will do best with gentle forms of hatha yoga.

Rest and Sleep

In addition to adequate and proper physical activity, the human body needs adequate and proper rest and sleep. Most children and young adults have no problem getting them. Older people often do.

The few memories I can retrieve of nursery school and kindergarten are of afternoon naps after milk (which I didn't like) and cookies (which I did), curled up on a blanket on the floor of a classroom, often in a patch of sunlight coming through a window. It was so easy then to nap and wake up refreshed. I've had to relearn that process in my 60s—without the cookies.

One change I notice is that I get sleepy earlier than I used to, sometimes by 8:30 or 9 if I am having a quiet evening at home. I don't want to go to bed that early, because if I do, I'll get too much sleep or wake up when it's still dark. Sleep experts call this "advancement of the sleep phase" and note that it is a common experience of older people.

So, here is my advice about rest and sleep for healthy aging:

Rest is important. Make time for daily periods when you can be passive, without stimulation, doing nothing.

Naps are good. Try to get into the habit of napping: 10 minutes to 20 minutes in the afternoon, preferably lying down in a darkened room.

To minimize early waking, try to postpone the evening meal until after dusk and schedule some kind of stimulating activity in the early evening.

If your mind is too active when you get into bed, you will not be able to fall asleep, no matter how tired you are. It is good to know one or more relaxation techniques that can help you disengage from thoughts. More on those later.

Touch and Sex

Touch is a basic requirement for optimum health: touch-deprived babies, both animal and human, do not develop normally. This need does not diminish with age, but older people often have fewer opportunities to give and receive health-promoting physical contact. I urge you as strongly as possible to find ways to touch and be touched as you move through life. One way, a perfectly good one, is to treat yourself to massage on a regular basis.

Lack of sex is not so easily remedied if one lives alone or with a partner who is no longer interested in or physically able to engage in it. Clearly, many older people have active sex lives and get pleasure from it as much as or more than ever.

The point is that sexuality changes as you grow older. If you agree that acceptance of aging is the goal, then you must work out your peace with changes in your sexual life. Here are some strategies that I recommend:

If you are older and living with a partner, try to express your needs, especially if they have changed. See if you can find areas of common ground where you can exchange some form of nurturing touch.

Self-stimulation is always an option. I consider it a healthy practice throughout life.

Everyone is different. Pay attention to how your interests and appetites change. Try to adapt to the changes. And keep in mind that for some people diminished interest in sex can be a liberating and welcome change.

Stress

Life is stressful and always has been. Eliminating stress entirely is not an option. If there are discrete sources of stress in your life—a relationship, a job, a health problem—you can and should take action to try to mitigate them. But my experience is that we all are subject to a kind of conservation law of stress. If stress recedes in one area, it seems to increase in another. Get your finances in order, and your relationship sours. Get your relationship together, and the kids cause you grief.

Whatever objective stress you have to deal with, you can learn to activate the so-called relaxation response, a shift within the autonomic nervous system from sympathetic dominance (the fight-or-flight response) to parasympathetic dominance (the heart rate slows, blood pressure falls and metabolism and immunity are optimal). You can evoke the relaxation response in many ways: by working on your breathing, practicing yoga, taking biofeedback training, floating in water or stroking a cat or dog that you love.

I have long promoted the benefits of working with the breath as the simplest, most efficient way of taking advantage of the mind-body connection to affect both physical and mental health. Here's a simple relaxing breath technique you can try at home:

1. Place the tip of your tongue against the ridge behind and above your front teeth, and keep it there throughout the exercise.
2. Exhale completely through your mouth, making a whoosh sound.
3. Inhale deeply and quietly through the nose to a count of four (with your mouth closed).
4. Hold for a count of seven.
5. Exhale audibly through your mouth to a count of eight.
6. Repeat steps 3, 4 and 5 for a total of four breaths.

Practice the exercise at least twice a day and whenever you feel stressed, anxious or off center. After a month, if you are comfortable with it, increase to eight breaths each time.

The obvious advantages of this kind of practice are that it requires no equipment, is free and can be done anywhere. It is the most cost- and time-efficient relaxation method I have discovered, and I teach it to all my patients and to all health professionals I train.

Thoughts, Emotions and Attitudes

Your thoughts, emotions and attitudes are key determinants of how you age. The most common forms of emotional imbalance—depression and anxiety—are so prevalent that they can properly be called epidemic. They affect people of all ages, including a large percentage of the elderly. Doctors manage them with antidepressants and antianxiety agents—the key word here being "manage." These drugs suppress depression and anxiety; they do not cure them or get to their roots.

Conventional psychotherapy can make people aware of the thought patterns that give rise to emotional problems, but it rarely helps people change them. Changing habits of thought requires conscious effort and practice and often outside help. The best sources of help I have found are innovative forms of psychotherapy and Buddhist psychology.

Dr. Andrew Weil's Wellness Diet

OVERVIEW: Aim for variety, and include as much fresh food as possible in your diet. Minimize your consumption of processed and fast food. Eat an abundance of fruits and vegetables, and try to include carbohydrates, fat and protein in every meal. Most adults need to consume between 2,000 and 3,000 calories a day. Women and smaller, less active people require fewer calories; men and larger, more active people need more calories. The distribution of calories you take in should be: 40% to 50% from carbohydrates, 30% from fat and 20% to 30% from protein.

Carbohydrates

- On a 2,000-calorie-a-day diet, adult women should eat about 160 g to 200 g of carbohydrates daily. (Most of this should be in the form of less refined, less processed foods.)
- Adult men should eat about 240 g to 300 g of carbohydrates a day.
- **REDUCE** your consumption of foods made with wheat flour and sugar, especially bread and most packaged snack foods.
- Eat more whole grains (not whole-wheat-flour products), beans, winter squashes and sweet potatoes.
- Cook pasta al dente and eat it in moderation.
- **AVOID** products made with high-fructose corn syrup.

Fat

- On a 2,000-calorie-a-day diet, 600 calories can come from fat—that is, about 67 g. This should be in a ratio of 1:2:1 of saturated to monounsaturated to polyunsaturated fat.
- **REDUCE** your intake of saturated fat by eating less butter, cream, cheese and other full-fat dairy products, unskinned chicken, fatty meats and products made with coconut and palm-kernel oils.
- Use extra-virgin olive oil as a main cooking oil. If you want a neutral-tasting oil, use expeller-pressed organic canola oil. High-oleic versions of sunflower and safflower oil are also acceptable.
- **AVOID** regular safflower and sunflower oils, corn oil, cottonseed oil and mixed vegetable oils.
- **STRICTLY AVOID** margarine, vegetable shortening and all products listing them as ingredients. Strictly avoid all products made with partially hydrogenated oils of any kind.
- Include in your diet avocados and nuts, especially walnuts, cashews and almonds and nut butters made from them.
- For omega-3 fatty acids, eat salmon (preferably wild—fresh or frozen—or canned sockeye), sardines, herring, black cod (sablefish, butterfish), omega-3 fortified eggs, hempseeds, flaxseeds and walnuts; or take a fish-oil supplement .

Protein

- On a 2,000-calorie-a-day diet, your daily intake of protein should be between 80 g and 120 g. Eat less protein if you have liver or kidney problems, allergies or autoimmune disease.
- **DECREASE** your consumption of animal protein except for fish and reduced-fat dairy products.
- Eat more vegetable protein, especially from beans in general and soybeans in particular.

Fiber

- Try to eat 40 g of fiber a day. You can achieve this by increasing your consumption of fruit, vegetables (especially beans) and whole grains.
- Ready-made cereals can be good fiber sources, but read labels to make sure they give you at least 4 g and preferably 5 g of bran per 1-oz. serving.

Phytonutrients

- To get maximum natural protection against age-related diseases, eat a variety of fruits, vegetables and mushrooms.
- Choose fruits and vegetables from all parts of the color spectrum, especially berries, tomatoes, orange and yellow fruits, and dark leafy greens.
- Choose organic produce whenever possible. Learn which conventionally grown crops are most likely to carry pesticide residues, and avoid them.
- Eat cruciferous (cabbage-family) vegetables regularly.
- Include soy foods in your diet.
- Drink tea instead of coffee, especially good-quality white, green or oolong tea.
- If you drink alcohol, use red wine preferentially.
- Enjoy plain dark chocolate (with a minimum cocoa content of 70%) in moderation.

Vitamins and Minerals

- The best way to obtain all your daily vitamins, minerals and micronutrients is by eating a diet high in fresh foods, with an abundance of fruits and vegetables.
- In addition, supplement your diet with this antioxidant cocktail:
- Vitamin C, 200 mg a day; vitamin E, 400 IUs of natural mixed tocopherols (d-alpha-tocopherol with other tocopherols or, better, a minimum of 80 mg of natural mixed tocopherols and tocotrienols).
- Selenium, 200 mcg of an organic (yeast-bound) form.
- Mixed carotenoids, 10,000 IUs to 15,000 IUs daily.
- In addition, take a daily multivitamin-multimineral supplement that provides at least 400 mcg of folic acid and at least 1,000 IUs of vitamin D. It should contain no iron and no preformed vitamin A (retinol).
- Take supplemental calcium, preferably as calcium citrate. Women need 1,200 mg to 1,500 mg a day, depending on their dietary intake of this mineral; men should get no more than 1,200 mg of calcium a day from all sources.

Other Dietary Supplements

- If you are not eating oily fish at least twice a week, take supplemental fish oil, 1 g to 2 g a day. Look for molecularly distilled products certified to be free of heavy metals and other contaminants.
- Talk to your doctor about going on low-dose aspirin therapy, 1 or 2 baby aspirins (81 mg or 162 mg) a day.
- If you are not regularly eating ginger and turmeric, consider taking them in supplemental form.
- Add coenzyme Q-10 to your daily regimen: 60 mg to 100 mg in a soft-gel form taken with your largest meal.
- If you are prone to metabolic syndrome, take alpha-lipoic acid, 100 mg to 400 mg a day.

Water

- Try to take 6 to 8 glasses of pure water or drinks that are mostly water (tea, very diluted fruit juice, sparkling water with lemon) every day.
- Use bottled water or get a home water purifier if your tap water tastes of chlorine or other contaminants.
- For more information, see **healthyaging.com**

The best we can do—and it is a lot—is to accept the inevitability of aging and try to adapt to it, to be in the best health we can at any age.

Cognitive behavioral therapy, or CBT, has become popular only in recent years. It traces its remote origins in part to the teachings of a Greek philosopher, Epictetus, a former slave who developed a science of happiness. Perhaps the best-known expression of Epictetus' philosophy is the Serenity Prayer, attributed to the Protestant theologian Reinhold Niebuhr and adopted by Alcoholics Anonymous: "God, grant me the Serenity to accept the things I cannot change, Courage to change the things I can, and Wisdom to know the difference."

Five hundred years ago, the Buddha taught his followers that unhappiness derives from the incessant habits of judging every experience as pleasant, unpleasant or neutral and of trying to hold on to the pleasant ones while shunning the unpleasant.

In the 1970s, a "cognitive revolution" in psychotherapy incorporated these ideas into modern psychology and inspired the development of practical methods of implementing them. The result is that technologies now exist to help people change their patterns of thought and the emotions and behavior that derive from them. (By "technologies," I mean therapeutic strategies like CBT, not the use of devices.) Moreover, these new forms of psychotherapy are effective—as effective as the latest psychiatric drugs in many studies—and they work quickly, not requiring the commitments of time and money that older forms of talk therapy do.

Spirit

One of the tenets of the integrative medicine that I practice is that health and illness involve more than the physical body. Good medicine must address the whole person: body, mind and spirit. My aim is to call attention to our unchanging essence—the part of us that remains the same no matter how much our appearance changes.

I consider it important for both doctors and patients to know how to assess spiritual health. Today there is a minor trend in medical education to offer some instruction in this area. More often than not, however, it is offered as an elective, and often it is linked to teaching about death and dying. At its best, it makes medical students aware of this other dimension of human life and gives them tools to help patients know their strengths and weaknesses, whether or not they have life-threatening illnesses.

One way to promote spiritual well-being is through the writing of an ethical will. An ordinary will or last testament mainly concerns the disposition of your material possessions at death. An ethical will has to do with nonmaterial gifts: the values and life lessons that you wish to leave to others.

In many cultures, elders, sages and saints have saved some of their pithiest teachings for students and disciples gathered at their deathbeds. Hindu saints, Zen masters and Jewish rabbis have been particularly good at this sort of thing; many of their final words have been written down for posterity. Jewish ethical wills almost 1,000 years old are preserved, and the practice of writing them appears to go back at least 1,000 years before that.

I can think of no better way to close this article than to recommend that you undertake the composition of an ethical will. No matter how old you are, it will make you take stock of your life experience and distill from it the values and wisdom you have gained. You can then put the document aside, read it over as the years pass and revise it from time to time as you see fit. It can be a wonderful gift to leave to your family at the end of your life, but I think its primary importance is what it can give you in the midst of life.

Aging brings rewards as well as challenges. And to age gracefully requires that we stop denying the fact of aging and learn and practice what we have to do to keep our bodies and minds in good working order through all phases of life. The first step toward aging gracefully is to look at the process squarely and honestly and understand it for what it is. My hope is that I have helped you to do just that.

DR. WEIL is clinical professor of medicine at the University of Arizona, where he founded and directs the program in integrative medicine, a healing-oriented form of medicine that draws on both conventional and alternative therapies. For more information, visit **integrativemedicine.arizona.edu**

As seen in *Time* Magazine, October 17, 2005, pp. 61-66, 69-70. Adapted from HEALTHY AGING, 2005, Knopf/Random House. Copyright © 2005 by Andrew Weil. Reprinted by permission of Alfred A. Knopf, a division of Random House, Inc.

Article 40

When Your Paycheck Stops

Ready to retire? Better make sure you can afford it. Here's how to make the most of what you've stashed in your piggy bank.

JANE BRYANT QUINN

One day, you'll look at your money and say, "That's all there is." No paycheck, no raises—only the income you generate from the work and savings you achieved in the past. Oof. What now? That's a scary question for boomers hitting the milestones of 60 and 55. For years, you've focused on earning, spending and (more recently) saving for the future. Now the future is heaving into view. You will retire—in fact, some of your friends are free already. Many went cheerfully; others were pushed. Some intend to work until 80, maybe including you. But you've entered the years when plans can go awry. Ready or not, everyone has to figure out how to make his or her savings last until 95. Wow.

There's no way of nailing the future down. But good preretirement planning can hold your anxiety down. Here's a start:

Figure Out What You Can Spend

Early retirement may turn into a pipe dream, once you calculate how much income you'll need for the rest of your life. "Some folks are realistic about their spending," says planner Lauren Klein of Newport Beach, Calif., but others—especially younger, executive-level retirees, have a harder time. "They want to front-load their retirement and spend early," she says. "For them, loss of status is a greater fear than outliving their money." (As if there's status in going broke.)

Smart preretirement planning begins with a budget—one that takes a first pass at separating future wants from needs. Will you still keep two cars? Should you drop your life insurance? Can you get out of debt before your paycheck stops? Living is cheaper without work expenses. On the other hand, medical costs will rise. Planner Susan Elser of Indianapolis tells her clients to figure on spending $3,000 a year, per person, for insurance premiums, deductibles, co-pays and drugs, when they go on Medicare.

36—Percentage of seniors who say they'll leave their home to heirs
Financial Freedom Senior Funding Corporation

On the income side, you'll be getting Social Security (watch the mail; three months before every birthday, the government sends you a notice, showing the current size of the benefit you can expect). Companies are shrinking their private pension plans, but full benefits are being paid in the public sector.

If you plan to draw an income from savings invested in stocks and bonds, the prudent annual limit is lower than you think. Planners advise that you spend no more than 4 percent of the total in the year you retire. On a $150,000 nest egg, that's just $6,000. In each subsequent year, increase your withdrawal by no more than the inflation rate. If you start with a 5 percent draw, you risk running out of money.

This comes as a shock to preretirees who'd planned to tap their savings for more. But that's what planning is all about. If you can't get by on the wise 4 percent withdrawal rate, you should have a serious talk with yourself and your spouse about your priorities, trade-offs and aspirations, says Paul Winter of Five Seasons Financial Planning in Holladay, Utah. Are you willing to work longer, slash expenses, work part time or move to a cheaper part of the country? The sooner you decide, the better your chance of right-sizing your retirement.

For Alice Sidwell, 64, early retirement didn't seem to be realistic. She worked for United Airlines as a flight attendant, but despite years of saving, her pension and 401(k) would not have been enough. "I could have lived," she says, "but couldn't have made extra purchases."

68—Percentage of retirees who take Social Security early
U.S. Social Security Administration

An inheritance saved her. In 1999 she sat down with planner Mark Brown, of Brown & Tedstrom in Denver, who looked at her spending and assets and told her that she could afford to retire. He also reorganized her money. Previously, it was run by a stockbroker who constantly bought and sold stocks (including risky penny stocks). Brown switched her investments into a diversified mix of stock and bond mutual funds. Her withdrawal rate is just 3 percent, so she's living well below her means.

Redo Your Investment Plan

When you're getting close to retirement, reconsider your investments. Bury any impulse to try to pick winning stocks—most of us aren't any good at it. Switch to mutual funds instead. (OK, keep a "mad money" fund—but if you lose it, take that as a sign.)

If you've piled up company stock in your 401(k), divest it now—not only the stock you bought yourself, but anything you received as a company match. Diversify into mutual funds no matter how good you think your company is.

Selling her company stock was one of the choices that helped Maria Bellon, 59, retire. A career BellSouth employee, she signed up 30 years ago to invest her 401(k) in stock and never looked back. She had a great run—but by 2000, BellSouth made up more than 80 percent of her retirement fund. Her planner, Mario Yngerto of Genesis Wealth Management in Plano, Texas, encouraged her to diversify. She scooted at $40 a share—not long before the stock bubble burst and the price plunged to less than $20. Bellon says she felt disloyal when she moved the money out, but is relieved she did. At retirement, she rolled her 401(k) and most of her lump-sum pension into an IRA invested in index mutual funds, which Yngerto tends.

When investing retirement assets, planners almost unanimously endorse what's called a total-return approach. That means taking all your financial assets—your 401(k) plus any taxable savings—and spreading them over a well-diversified group of mutual funds. The usual building blocks include large and small U.S. stocks, international and emerging-market stocks, and a mix of short- and long-term bonds. You calculate the safe 4 percent withdrawal rate and spend that much (or less) from your account each year. You're not specifically investing for income. You're investing for gain and taking the cash you need from the total pot.

For some retirees, that goes against the grain. They worry about dipping into their principal and seek safer programs focused on bonds and other income investments. As the years go by, however, and inflation rises, income investing won't keep up. You'll run out of cash unless you also invest for growth. At 55, most planners tell clients: 60 percent stocks, 40 percent bonds. At 65, they lean toward 50-50 stocks and bonds.

But don't go by age alone, says investment adviser Stuart Zimmerman of Buckingham Asset Management in St. Louis. A 50-50 mix might be right for a 65-year-old who needs the assets to live on. But if you have more than you need, you're managing some of the money for the next generation. That calls for a more aggressive 60-40 mix of stocks to bonds.

To Roll or Not?

At retirement, should you leave your 401(k) in your company plan or roll it into an Individual Retirement Account? In big-company plans with low-cost choices and good sources of advice, retirees could leave the money there, says Cindy McGhee of A&F Financial Advisors in Charleston, W. Va. If you die, your spouse can treat the plan as his or her own. But if your kids will inherit, it's smarter to take all the money and switch to an IRA. IRAs let them stretch the payouts over their lifetimes, giving them years of tax-deferred growth.

15—Percentage of retirees forced to quit working for health reasons

Employee Benefit Research Institute

Here's an important tax-saving tip for employees with major capital gains in their company stock. Empty your 401(k), but instead of rolling the stock portion into an IRA, put it into a regular brokerage account. In an IRA, you'll wind up paying income taxes on the capital gain. By taking it out of the plan, you'll owe income taxes only on the original cost. The appreciation will be taxed at the low 15 percent rate on capital gains, says IRA expert Ed Slott, author of "Parlay Your IRA Into a Family Fortune." "I shudder when I hear ads saying, 'Call to roll over your 401(k)'," he says. "Those rollover jocks never ask about company stock, and you wind up paying extra tax."

You can also roll your money into tax-deferred annuities. That's a controversial choice, but not for Dan Breeding, 57, and his wife, Susan, 53. He took early retirement last year, mainly because his firm had been downsizing and he worried about his job. They're pretty new parents, with two adopted children from Kazakhstan, now 4 and 5. They moved from Indianapolis to Lone Jack, Mo., where it costs about 10 percent less to live.

Breeding is well organized and likes guarantees. His planner, Amy Rose Herrick of Topeka, Kans., rolled his savings into six different tax-deferred annuities. These annuities amount to mutual funds in an insurance wrapper. If you die at a time when your funds are worth less than you paid, your beneficiary will get your original investment back. You may also get a minimum-performance guarantee. In return, you pay much higher total fees than you would for straight mutual funds—in Breeding's case, about 1.65 percent a year (to cover expenses and commissions), plus the cost of the funds, so future investment performance won't be so hot. Also, there may be penalties for cashing out too soon.

Most of the planners NEWSWEEK spoke with say they avoid annuities—especially costly bonus annuities. Breeding has three of them. They yield a little more upfront—but, the Securities and Exchange Commission warns, you may pay for that "bonus" in the form of higher fees or surrender costs or longer required holding periods. Herrick says the value of the bonus exceeds its cost after six to eight years. Still, it's an expensive choice.

Tap Your House for Cash

You can't count the value of your house as a retirement asset unless you're prepared to tap the cash. You might buy something smaller or move to a cheaper part of the country. Or like Neil and Nancy Collins, both 60, of Melrose, Mass., you might decide to rent. The Collinses aren't retiring yet (he's a financial planner, she's a teacher). But they're preparing for the change by selling their house, harvesting the equity and buying a condo in Estero, Fla. In Melrose, they'll move to an apartment. Renting "gives us tremendous flexibility," Neil says—"financial, geographic and lifestyle."

57—Percentage of seniors who will eventually need paid assistance

Peter Kemper, Harriet Komisar and Lisa Alecxih "Long-Term Care Over an Uncertain Future: What Can Current Retirees Expect?"

They're right to watch their costs. Planner Ron Rhoades of Joseph Capital Management in Hernando, Fla., sees too many retirees buying dream houses they can't afford. He says that for every extra $100,000 you spend on a home, you'll be out $7,000 in expenses and lost investment revenue.

But for everyone eager to move, there's someone who can't bear the thought. Take Elene Wilburn, 70, of Twinsburg, Ohio, who lives on her public-school pension and Social Security. "I love my house," she says. "I like planting flowers in the yard and don't want to move." Her solution? A reverse mortgage that put a pile of cash in her pocket. It sounded so good, she thought at first it was a scam.

With a reverse mortgage, you get a loan equaling 50 percent or more of the value of your home. But you never make any monthly payments. Instead, the loan gradually builds up—compounding interest costs and fees. You can stay put for as long as you want. The debt doesn't fall due until the house is sold, when you move or die.

Wilburn learned all the details at a sales meeting held by American Reverse Mortgage, and decided to sign up. She borrowed $286,000 on a loan insured by the Federal Housing Administration—some in a lump sum, the rest in a credit line for future use. She'll take a Caribbean cruise—"something I've always wanted to do"—and set up college funds for her grandchildren.

94—Percentage increase in sales of reverse mortgages in two years

U.S. Department of Housing and Urban Development

The drawback to reverse mortgages is their cost. You're charged a variable interest rate—now at 6.3 percent (and rising). The mortgage broker or lender can charge up to 2 percent—that's $5,000 on a $250,000 loan. There are also closing costs, servicing costs and insurance fees. All told, the expenses could reach $25,000 or more, says Ken Scholen, AARP's reverse-mortgage expert. The more your home is worth and the younger you are, the more the loan costs. Ideally, he says, you should consider this mortgage later in life. For a good, free booklet explaining the ins and outs, call AARP at 800-209-8085 and ask for Home Made Money, or read it on the Web at **aarp.org/revmort**.

Cover the Cost of Care

"Don't risk a lot for a little." That's what financial planner Charles Buck, 58, of Woodbury, Minn., tells the students who take his retirement-planning class at the state university's Mankato campus. Taking his own advice, he and his wife, Dianne, 53, bought a joint long-term-care insurance policy. They've both seen dementia in their extended families, and don't want to impoverish each other if one of them becomes ill.

These policies aren't for people with modest incomes (you can't afford them) or the superrich. They're for people in between, says planner Dean Harmon of The Woodlands, Texas, who recommends them to clients with assets ranging from $500,000 to $4 million. Shop when you're 55 to 65. Generally, you shouldn't pay more than 7 percent of your future retirement income (not your working income), says planner Robert Pagliarini of Allied Consulting Group in Los Angeles. You might balk even at that expense—but it sure brings peace of mind.

Most of all, you need to save—and yes, "panic saving" works. Hurl money into a retirement account. It's never too late.

Reporter Associates: **TEMMA EHRENFELD** with **PATRICK CROWLEY** and **RAMIN SETOODEH**.

Secrets of the Centenarians

In certain families, small genetic variations bring good health and long life. Can researchers apply this knowledge to benefit us all?

MAYA PINES

I s there a formula for living to the age of 100 or beyond? HHMI investigator Louis M. Kunkel believes there is, and he's working hard to define it.

Besides a healthy dose of good luck (Kunkel says it helps to not be killed in a war or a traffic accident), one key to longevity is a highly unusual combination of gene variants that protects against the customary diseases of old age. Several research teams are now in the process of uncovering these genes.

Kunkel, director of the Genomics Program at Children's Hospital in Boston, and his associates recently identified a genetic variant that is particularly prominent among sibling pairs in the New England Centenarian Study, perhaps the world's largest pool of centenarians. They are seeking additional genetic variants that might retard—or perhaps even prevent—many of the diseases that debilitate the old. "People with this rare combination of genes clearly age more slowly," Kunkel says. "When they reach 90, they don't look any older than 70."

Hundreds of centenarians around the world are now contributing their blood and medical histories to the search for these precious genes. They have become a key resource for researchers who hope that as these genes are revealed, their good effects may be reproduced in other people with the help of new drugs.

Clustered in Families

Kunkel was drawn to the hunt for longevity genes about six years ago, through a chance encounter with Thomas T. Perls, a Boston University Medical School geriatrician who had enrolled a large group of centenarians for his New England Centenarian Study. Kunkel's own research was focused on a deadly genetic disorder called Duchenne muscular dystrophy, which affects mostly boys. In 1986, he discovered a mutation that causes this muscle-wasting disease, and he is still working on a therapy for it (see Cures for Muscle Diseases?). But he could not resist the opportunity to also apply his knowledge of genetics to what he heard from Perls.

The two men were acquainted through Perls's wife, Leslie Smoot, who happened to be a postdoc in Kunkel's lab. When they met on a street in Cambridge, Massachusetts, in 1997 and started talking about their work, "Tom told me that many of the centenarians whose lineage he was examining were clustered in families," Kunkel recalls. "I realized that's just got to be genetics. We soon started a collaboration."

For his part, Perls remembers that at the beginning of his study he thought the centenarians had little in common except for their age. But he soon realized that many of them had an unusually large number of equally aged relatives. "We had a 108-year-old man who blew out his birthday candles next to his 102-year-old sister," Perls recalls. "They told us they had another sibling who was 103, and yet another who was only 99. Two other siblings—also centenarians—had passed away. Four siblings had died in childhood. So here was an incredible clustering, 5 or maybe 6 siblings out of 10! We've since found about 7 families like that." This implied that all these families carried especially protective genes. Shortly after the two scientists met, a new postdoc arrived in Kunkel's lab—Annibale A. Puca, a young Italian neurologist who wanted to work in genetics—and Kunkel suggested he take on this new project. "I warned him it was going to be a lot of work and high risk, but he said okay," Kunkel says, "and he spearheaded the whole program."

Puca and Perls rapidly expanded the group of centenarians, recruiting them through alumni associations, newspaper clippings, and state census lists. After taking samples of the centenarians' blood, the researchers extracted DNA from it and started looking for genetic markers—specific stretches of DNA that might occur more frequently among these extremely old men and women than among a group of younger people who were the study's controls. Most scientists believed that human longevity is far too complicated a trait to be influenced by only a few genes. There are so many independent mechanisms of aging that "the chance that only a few major genes control longevity in man is highly unlikely," wrote a self-styled "pessimist" on this issue, George M. Martin of the University of Washington in Seattle, in the journal *Mechanisms of Ageing and Development* in 2002. But Kunkel's lab took a different view. "In lower organisms, such as nematodes, fruit flies, and yeast, there are only a few genes that need to be altered to give a longer life span," Kunkel says. "My feeling was that there were only a few genes, perhaps four to six, in humans that would do the same."

Who Are These Centenarians?

"Centenarians tend to be independent, assertive, funny, and gregarious," says Boston University Medical School geriatrician Thomas T. Perls, who at 43 has probably met more people over the age of 100 than anybody else. "They also seem to manage stress very well, which makes sense, since we know that not handling stress predisposes you to cardiovascular disease and high blood pressure."

During a fellowship in geriatrics at Harvard Medical School in the early 1990s, Perls took care of 40 patients at Boston's Hebrew Rehabilitation Center for the Aged. Two of his healthiest patients, who looked as if they were in their seventies, were actually over 100 years old. "They were in really terrific shape," he says. "It was so different from what I expected! This sparked my interest."

As a result, Perls founded the New England Centenarian Study in 1994, becoming one of only a few researchers studying the very old at that time. He started out by looking for people over 100 in eight towns around Boston, using census records, voter registration files, and the media. Later, he expanded the study by adding centenarians from all over the United States. Now it includes 1,600 centenarians and 500 of their children. About 20 percent of the centenarian women in his study had given birth after the age of 40, Perls found, compared to a national average of only 3 percent of mothers. "It showed that these women were aging very slowly," he says.

He also studied the centenarians' siblings and concluded that their chances of living to their early nineties were four times greater than average. More recently, Perls examined the centenarians' children. At the age of 70, he found, they had a 24 percent reduction in mortality compared to the general population, as well as about a 60 percent reduction in the risk of heart disease, hypertension, and diabetes.

More than 90 percent of the centenarians had been in good health and completely independent until their early to mid-90s, Perls says. "They lived the vast majority of their lives with good function," he emphasizes. "So it's not a matter of 'the older you get, the sicker you get' but rather 'the older you get, the healthier you've been.' This is a different way of thinking about aging."

By the time people reach the century mark, however, the healthy ones are in the minority. "We found that 25 percent of the centenarians were doing well, but the remaining 75 percent had mild to severe impairment," Perls reports. "In the end, they die of cardiovascular disease or something that's related to frailty, such as pneumonia."

This fits in well with the theories of Leonard Hayflick, of the University of California, San Francisco, who showed in 1961 that there are limits to the number of times a normal human cell can divide. Even under the most favorable conditions, he said, noncancerous human cells die after about 50 cell divisions (this is now called the "Hayflick limit"). Eliminating the leading causes of death in old age—cardiovascular diseases, stroke, and cancer—"will only result in an increase of about 15 years in human life expectancy," Hayflick declared in the November 9, 2000, issue of *Nature*. Although these 15 years would be a great gift, assuming that people remained healthy during that time, nothing could stop "the inevitable increase in errors and disorders in the cells of vital organs" that results from age, he pointed out. Even the cells' repair processes would become disordered, leading to extreme vulnerability and death.

Then would it be a good thing for more people to live to 100? "Absolutely," says Perls. "Centenarians are sentinels of the health of older people. Our goal is not to get a bunch of individuals to be 120 or 130, but to discover which genes are most protective and then use this information to get a majority of people living almost all their lives in good health, as centenarians generally do."

The team proceeded to examine genetic markers for the entire genomes of 308 people, selected because they belonged to 137 sibships (sets of siblings) in which at least one member was over 98 and the others were over 90. "From early on, we saw a blip of a peak on chromosome 4," says Kunkel. "Eventually, in 2001, we found a linkage between one region of this chromosome and longevity."

Search for a SNP

It was "phenomenal" to get a real linkage from such a slight hint in the original data, Kunkel declares. But that didn't mean further research would be easy. This stretch of DNA was so large—12 million DNA base pairs long—that it seemed it could contain as many as 200 genes. Furthermore, the researchers knew that within these genes they would have to look for variations in single bases of DNA—"single-nucleotide polymorphisms," or SNPs (pronounced "snips"). "SNPs really represent the difference between individuals," Kunkel explains. "Everybody's DNA is 99.9 percent identical—it's the SNPs that make us unique and allow certain people to live longer. Even though

most of our DNA is alike, the 0.1 percent variation means that we have more than 10 million SNPs across the genome. And we're on the verge of being able to map them." For Kunkel, the critical question was "how would we find the one SNP in a single gene that might help a person to live much longer than average?"

The groundbreaking work of the Human Genome Project had not yet been completed at that time, and Kunkel realized that finding this particular SNP would be both expensive and time-consuming. It would also be quite different from zeroing in on a missing or severely garbled gene, as had been done for cystic fibrosis, muscular dystrophy, and other single-gene disorders. The widespread diseases of aging—heart disease, stroke, diabetes, cancer, and Alzheimer's disease—are much more complex and are triggered by subtle gene variations that produce only slightly altered proteins, Kunkel says. These proteins may either work a little better or be less active than those in the normal population, and several of them may work in concert. Searching for a single SNP would require doing thousands of genetic analyses on each of his subjects (now numbering 653) and comparing the results with the control group. "We es-

Cures for Muscle Diseases?

Ever since Louis M. Kunkel discovered the cause of Duchenne muscular dystrophy (DMD) in 1986, he has been laboring to find a cure for this muscle-wasting disease. DMD—the result of an error in a single gene—attacks 1 out of every 4,000 newborn boys, progressively crippling and then killing them at an early age.

Kunkel saw that patients with DMD lacked a protein, dystrophin, which this gene would have produced if it were functioning normally. So he knew he had to replace the protein somehow. He and others tried many methods—gene therapy to deliver a normal gene to the defective muscle cell, drugs to help restore the mission protein, and cell therapy to inject normal cells into muscle or blood—but despite some partial successes in animals, nothing really worked.

Kunkels lab worked mostly with *mdx* mice, a naturally mutant strain that lack dystrophin. When he and his colleagues attempted to cure these crippled mice with injections of muscle stem cells from normal mice, "some of the donor cells did go into the damaged muscles." he recalls, "but we never got more then 1 to 2 percent of the muscles repaired. Part of the problem was that when you inject cells into a mouses tail vein, which is the most accessible part of its circulation, the donor cells to through all the organs—the lungs, liver, heart, and so on—and out through the arterial system. Most of the cells get filtered and lost, and don't contribute to the therapy."

Today, however, Kunkel feels he is on the verge of success. The big breakthrough came last summer when a team of Italian scientists headed by Giulio Cossu of Milan's Stem Cell Research Institute announced it had found a new route for the injection of stem cells into dystrophic mice directly into an artery. The cells seemed to lodge within the capillary system near the injection site. From there, about 30 percent of them migrated to the diseased muscles. Not only did the cells get there, he says, but at later time points, you could see a larger number of donor cells than at the earliest point, as if they were trying to divide.

"Can we improve on this?" asks Kunkel with a glint in his eye. "If we can get the stem cells into 50 percent of the dystrophic muscles, thats basically a cure."

They had trouble at first because "the mouse artery was 10 times smaller than our smallest injection needles—it was like trying to hit it with a hammer!" Kunkel says. Though a tail vein is even smaller than an artery, it can be hit much more easily because it is right under the surface of the skin and can be made to swell up by warming it. In the new system, the mouse had to be anesthetized and opened up to expose its artery, which was lifted out—a complex procedure.

"It wasnt until we started collaborating with some vascular surgeons who had been doing heart transplants in mice that we were able to get the stem cells into the mouse arteries efficiently," he says. In humans, of course, reaching an artery would not be a problem given that human arteries are so much larger.

Getting the stem cells into the muscles was just the first step. Unless these cells supplied enough dystrophin, the diseased muscles would not be repaired. So Kunkel also tried to find different stem cells that could do the job more effectively. In 1999 his lab and that of his colleague Richard Mulligan announced they could restore some of the missing dystrophin in mdx mice with the aid of a new kind of stem cells called "side population" (SP) cells, which seemed to work much better. These SP cells had to be taken from muscle tissue, however. Last year Kunkel's lab succeeded in deriving similar SP cells from adult skin, which is easier to obtain. Since they originate in adult tissue, both kinds of SP cells will be much less controversial then embryonic stem cells.

"Its my belief that you can do a lot of therapeutic intervention with adult-derived cells," says Kunkel. He notes that the new stem cells seem ready to differentiate into every type of muscle tissue, which implies that they have the potential to treat many forms of muscle disease.

The combination of new cell type and a new delivery system "may revolutionize how one does therapy for muscle diseases," Kunkel suggests. "When we get it perfected in mice, we'll go to humans." He thinks this might happen in a couple of years.

timated it would cost at least $5 million," Kunkel said. "It finally cost $8 million and took one-and-a-half years."

Ultimately, all that painstaking work paid off. The paper announcing the discovery of a SNP that contributes to longevity was published in the November 25, 2003, issue of the *Proceedings of the National Academy of Sciences*.

Now for the Others

The long-sought SNP turned out to lie within the gene for microsomal transfer protein, or MTP, which had been known since the mid-1980s to be involved in cholesterol metabolism.

"It's quite clear that to live to be 100, you've got to maintain your cholesterol at a healthy level," says Kunkel. "It makes perfect sense. We know that increased LDL (the 'bad' cholesterol) and lowered HDL (the 'good' cholesterol) raise your cardiovascular risk and that cardiovascular diseases account for a large percentage of human mortality. So variations in the genes involved in cholesterol packaging will influence your life span. It's as if these centenarians had been on Lipitor [a cholesterol-lowering drug] from birth!"

This discovery might lead to drugs that are tailored to intervene in the cholesterol pathway. Because the MTP gene was already in the public domain, however, it could not be patented, much to the disappointment of the former Centagenetix Corporation (founded by Puca, Perls, and Kunkel and now a part of Elixir Pharmaceuticals of Cambridge, Massachusetts), which had bankrolled most of the study.

In any event, this SNP "cannot be the whole story," Kunkel declares. "There must be other gene variations that enable people to avoid age-related diseases. Some of our original families did not show linkages to chromosome 4." Nor did a group of centenarians who were tested in France.

Determined to find some of the other SNPs that produce longevity, Kunkel says he's going back to his sample and will redo the whole study. "We now have 310 sibships," he says. "Our genetic markers are much denser. I believe we can get 10 times the power in our next screen than we had in the first."

Moreover, the work can be done much more rapidly and inexpensively than last time, he notes, given the giant strides that have been made recently in human genetics. Not only has the entire human genome been sequenced, but many of the errors in the original draft have been corrected. Equally important, all the known genes in the genome are now available on a single Affymetrix DNA chip, allowing researchers to promptly identify which genes are activated and which are damped down in any given situation. In addition, as many as 10,000 different human SNPs have been placed on a single chip.

Similar tools have already turned up new gene variants in yeast, worms, and flies. But Kunkel will use the chips to analyze the DNA of humans. Once his lab gets started on the new longevity project, he believes, it will not take very long to get some definitive answers. He hopes these will lead to drugs that could mimic the protective effects of the centenarians' genes.

Gold Standard

In fact, these studies foreshadow a far-reaching attack on all complex diseases—not just those of the aged but others, such as autism and hypertension. None of these ills could be tackled efficiently in the past. "The centenarians are the ideal control group for such research," Kunkel says. "To reach 100, you must have good alleles [versions of the genes] at all points. So if one wants to find the genes that are connected with hypertension, for instance, one can look across the genome for genes that are highly active in the hypertensive population but down-regulated in centenarians. Ultimately, that's what the centenarians' genes will be used for."

He believes that in the future, "every person who comes to our genetic clinic—or goes through any type of care system—with what appears to be a complex disease should be analyzed in detail. I mean that we should gather all the information we can about each patient's symptoms, the family history of these symptoms, any environmental insults the patient suffered, any learning disability—anything that would allow us to categorize the patient and [the patient's] family into subtypes of the disease which could be more related to one another and thus more likely to involve the same gene." To make this happen, Kunkel has just appointed a director of phenotyping (the Greek roots of this word mean "classifying phenomena into specific types") who will collect, categorize, and catalogue such patient information.

"We will also analyze the patients' genes but only in the context of the category of symptoms they exhibit," he says. "The samples we collect—under appropriate protocols—will be available to the national groups of patients and researchers that are organizing to find the underlying genetic bases of specific diseases." Eventually, he hopes, many complex disorders such as heart disease, diabetes, and autism will be broken down into more specific categories, which in turn may lead to more precise treatments or ways of preventing the disorder. Kunkel expects this process to accelerate in the near future as more patients' genes are compared with those of the gold standard for humans—the centenarians.

Lost & Found

Promising therapy for Alzheimer's draws out the person inside the patient

BARBARA BASLER

The woman wore a plain housedress and a big apron, its pockets stuffed with plastic checkers. Head down, eyes blank, she shuffled aimlessly around the activity room. Cameron Camp, a research psychologist who was visiting this assisted living home in Kentucky, watched the 70-year-old woman for a moment. Then, he recalls, "I went up to her and gave her one of our books—the one on Gene Kelly, the dancer—and asked her to please read a page."

He pauses, remembering the woman and the skeptical staff—and the very next moment.

"She took the book and read aloud—clear as a bell," Camp says with a smile. "A shocked staffer turned to me and said, 'I didn't even know she could speak. That's a miracle.'"

Camp heads the Myers Research Institute in Beachwood, Ohio, and his cutting-edge work with patients in all stages of Alzheimer's has left him improbably upbeat—because he sees miracles like this day after day.

His research is part of a sea change in the care of Alzheimer's patients who are in the later stages of the disease: "Ten to 15 years ago these people were institutionalized, and their care involved physical or chemical restraints," says Kathleen O'Brien, vice president of program and community services for the Chicago-based Alzheimer's Association, which, with the National Institutes of Health, has helped fund Camp's work.

Psychologist Cameron Camp says patients live in the moment. "Our job is to give them as many good moments as we can."

"Today," she says, "more than 70 percent of those with Alzheimer's are cared for in the family home, and we talk about controlling the disease and enhancing daily life for those who have it."

Alzheimer's, the most common form of dementia in people over the age of 65, affects 4.5 million Americans. An irreversible brain disorder, the disease robs people of their memory and eventually impairs most of their mental and physical functions.

While research typically focuses on preventing Alzheimer's or delaying its progress in the early stages, some medical specialists and long-term care professionals are investigating activities that will help patients in the later stages.

"We can't stop cell death from Alzheimer's," Camp explains. "But at any stage of dementia there is a range of capability. If you give people a reason to get out of bed, activities that engage them and allow them to feel successful, they will be at the top of their game, whatever it is."

Camp, 53, began his research 10 years ago when he looked at the activities developed for young children by the educator Maria Montessori, whose "method" is followed today in Montessori schools around the world. There, children learn by manipulating everyday objects like balls, seashells and measuring spoons in highly structured activities that engage children but rarely allow them to fail.

Camp adapted these kinds of exercises for older people with dementia, tailoring them to the individual's background and interests, and found he could draw out the person inside the patient.

"Suddenly, they just wake up, come alive for the moment," he says.

That happened to Mary Anne Duffy's husband when they took part in Camp's research. James Duffy, 77, has Parkinson's disease and dementia and is confined to a wheelchair in a nursing home in Mentor, Ohio.

"James loved woodworking," Duffy says, "and he liked fixing things, so the researcher brought him a small box to paint, nuts and bolts to put together, puzzles." Before her husband began the activities, she says, he "just sat there, nodding off."

But when he was working a puzzle or painting a box, "James actually smiled—something I hadn't seen for a long time," Duffy says. "And he would talk. That was amazing."

People with Alzheimer's "live in the moment, and our job is to give them as many good moments as we can," Camp says. "We need to be thinking about these people in a new way. Instead of focusing on their problems and deficits, we need to ask what strengths and abilities remain."

People had assumed, for instance, that the woman with the checkers in her apron pockets was too impaired to read. But studies have found that reading is one of the very last skills to fade away. "It's automatic, almost a reflex," Camp says.

"If the print is right," he says as he flips through one of his specially designed books with big, bold letters, many Alzheimer's patients can read.

One goal of Camp's work has been to turn his research into practical how-to guides for professional and family caregivers. Published by the Myers Research Institute, the guides have been translated into Chinese, Japanese and Spanish.

While long-term care residences may have some activities for dementia patients—like coloring in a picture or listening to a story—often they don't have activities "that are meaningful, that call on an adult's past," Camp says. "And even people with Alzheimer's are bored if an activity isn't challenging or interesting."

Much of Camp's research is with residents at Menorah Park Center for Senior Living in Beachwood, which is affiliated with Myers Research. After Alzheimer's patients were given the large-print books that he and his colleagues developed, many could read aloud and discuss the books.

A brief biography of Leonardo da Vinci, for instance, talks about some of his wildly imaginative inventions, like a machine that would let soldiers breathe underwater so they could march underneath enemy ships, drill holes in their hulls and sink them.

"It's a wonderful, wacky idea," Camp says. "Dementia patients react to it just as we do. They love it. They laugh, they shake their heads. They talk about it."

Education Director Lisa P. Gwyther of the Bryan Alzheimer's Disease Research Center at Duke University Medical Center recalls visiting a facility where she saw Alzheimer's patients themselves teaching some of the simple activities they had learned to preschool children. "I was so impressed with the dignity and the purpose and the fun that was observable between the older person and younger child," she says. Camp's work has been rigorously studied in a number of small pilot projects, she adds, "which means this is a reliable, valid method."

At Menorah Park, Camp and his team look at what basic skills remain in those with dementia: Can the person read, sort, categorize, manipulate objects? Then they customize activities for those skills.

"We had one man who loved baseball," Camp says. "We had him sort pictures of baseball players into American and National leagues. Another man who loved opera sorted titles into operas by Puccini and operas by Verdi."

The activities help patients maintain the motor skills needed to feed themselves or button buttons. They also trigger memories, then conversations that connect the patient and the caregiver.

People with dementia won't consciously remember the activity from one session to the next. But, Camp says, "some part of them does remember, and eventually they will get bored. So you can't have them match the same pictures each time."

It doesn't matter if patients make mistakes, Camp adds. "What's important is that they enjoy the process."

Mike Skrajner, a project manager for Myers Research who monitored an Alzheimer's reading group at Menorah Park, recalls one morning when the group was reading a biography of Gene Kelly and came to the part where Kelly tells his father he is quitting law school—to take ballet lessons. "They stopped right there and had a great conversation about how they would react to that news," he says. "It was a wonderful session, and at the end they all wound up singing 'Singin' in the Rain.'"

Manipulating everyday objects helps patients maintain skills for feeding themselves or brushing their teeth.

Camp's research shows that people who engage in such activities tend to exhibit fewer signs of agitation, depression and anxiety.

George Niederehe, acting chief of the geriatrics research branch of the National Institute of Mental Health, which is funding some of Camp's work, says a large study of patients in long-term care facilities is needed for definitive proof of the effectiveness of Camp's approach. But his method could be as helpful to caregivers as it is to people with Alzheimer's, he says, because it would improve "staff morale, knowing they can do something useful for these patients." And that, he adds, would enhance the overall environment for staff and residents alike.

One vital part of Camp's theory—like Montessori's—is that residents need activities that give them a social role, whether it's contributing at a book club or stirring lemonade for a party.

The Menorah Park staff worked with one patient, a former mailman, who loved folding pieces of paper stamped with "Have a Nice Day!" He stuffed the notes into envelopes and delivered them to other residents.

"What we try to do," Camp says, "is let the person you remember shine through the disease, even if it's only a few moments a day."

To Learn More

- To download samples of Cameron Camp's activities for dementia patients, go to **www.aarp/bulletin/longterm**.
- The caregiver's manual "A Different Visit" costs $39.95 plus shipping, and the special large-print books for Alzheimer's patients cost $5.95 each (or six copies for the price of five) plus shipping. To order, go to **www.myersresearch.org**, or write Myers Research Institute, 27100 Cedar Road, Beachwood, OH 44122.
- For general information, go to the Alzheimer's Association website at **www.alz.org**.

For nine simple habits you can adopt that may delay dementia, see the September-October issue of *AARP The Magazine*.

Navigating Practical Dilemmas in Terminal Care

HELEN SORENSON, MA, RRT, FAARC

Introduction

It has been stated that one-fourth of a person's life is spent growing up and three-fourths growing old. The aging process is universal, progressive, irreversible and eventually decremental.[1] Cellular death is one marker of aging. When cells are not replaced or replicated at a rate constant enough to maintain tissue or organ function, the eventual result is death of the organism.

Although not an unexpected endpoint for any human being, death unfortunately is often fraught with turmoil and dilemmas. Patients, family, friends, caregivers and health care professionals often get caught up in conflicting opinions regarding how terminal care should be approached. For the patient, the result often is suboptimal symptom management, an increased likelihood of being subjected to painful and often futile therapy and the unnecessary prolonging of death. For the family and friends of the patient, the psychosocial consequences can be devastating. Conflict at the bedside of a dying loved one can result in long-lasting and sometimes permanent rifts in family relationships.

There are some complicated issues surrounding terminal care, such as fear, lack of trust, lack of understanding, lack of communication, and stubbornness on the part of both the physician's and family members. There are moral, ethical, economic, cultural and religious issues that must be considered. Some of the dilemmas in terminal care come up more frequently than others. This paper will discuss some of the more commonly encountered ones. And possible interventions and/or alternate ways of coming to concordance regarding end-of-life care will be presented for consideration by the reader.

Fear/Death Anxiety

A degree of fear is the natural response of most individuals to the unknown. Despite many attempts at conceptualization and rationalization, preparing for death involves coming to terms with a condition unknown in past or present experience. Fear of death has been referred to in the literature as death anxiety. Research indicates that younger people have a higher level of death anxiety than older people.[2] The reasons are not difficult to understand. Younger adults in our society are often shielded from death. Many young adults may not have had close contact

with individuals dying from a terminal or chronic disease. When younger people confront death, it is most likely that of a grandparent, a parent, a sibling or a friend. Death is commonly from an acute cause. Grief is intense, with many unanswered questions and psychological ramifications.

Older adults have had more experience with death, from having lost a spouse, colleagues, a friend or relatives over the years. They undoubtedly will have experienced grief and worked through loss at some time in their life. Older adults may be more apt to express the fear of dying alone.

When facing a terminal diagnosis and impending death older adults are more likely to be concerned with "mending fences" and seeking forgiveness for perceived wrongdoing. There is a need on the part of many adults to put their affairs in order and resolve any outstanding financial matters. Some interesting research on death anxiety and religiosity conducted by Thorson & Powell,[3] revealed that persons higher in religiosity were lower in death anxiety.

How can the potential dilemma caused by fear be circumscribed? Possibly allowing patients to discuss the issue may ease death anxiety, but patients may be advised not to talk about funeral arrangements, since "they're not going to die." While well intended, the statement may not be helpful. Instead of preventing the patient from discussing "depressing thoughts," encouraging frank discussions about end-of-life issues may ease death anxiety. Asking the patient to verbalize his or her fears may lead to understanding the fears and alleviate the anxiety they cause.

It is important to guard against treating dying patients as though they are no longer human. For example, asking if a person would like to talk to a minister, priest or rabbi does not impinge the religious belief of the patient—it simply allows another avenue to reduce death anxiety.

Issues of Trust

Patients who have been under the care of a personal physician for an extended period of time generally exhibit a high level of trust in the diagnosis, even when the diagnosis is that of a terminal disease. Good end-of-life care requires a measure of continuity among caregivers. The patient who has had the same physician from the onset of a serious illness to the terminal stages of the disease has a substantial advantage.[4]

Planning, family support and social services, coordinated to meet the patient's needs, can be more easily arranged if there is an atmosphere of trust and confidence.

Health care today however, has become increasingly fragmented. A physician unknown to the family and/or patient may be assigned to a case. It is difficult for very sick patients to develop new relationships and establish trust with an on-going stream of care providers.[5] When circumstances are of an immediate and critical nature, issues of trust become paramount. Lack of trust in the physician and/or the health care system can erode into a lack of confidence in a diagnosis, which often results in a conflict between the patient, the family and the health care system.

Navigating this dilemma can be challenging. Recommending that the services of a hospitalist or a palliative care team be requested may be beneficial. Patients and families that are versed in the standard of care for the specific terminal disease may be in a better position to ask questions and make suggestions. Trust is associated with honesty. Conversely, trust can be eroded by what is perceived as the incompetence of or duplicity by health care providers.

An increased, concerted effort to communicate effectively all pertinent information to a patient and family and members of the health care team caring for the patient may not instantly instill confidence, but it may forestall any further erosion of trust. It is a good feeling to think that everyone on the team is pulling in the same direction.

Issues of Communication

Communication, or lack of adequate communication is problematic. A recent article published in *Critical Care Medicine* stated, "In intensive care settings, suboptimal communication can erode family trust and fuel so called 'futility disputes'."[6] Lack of communication does not imply wrongdoing on the part of the caregivers, nor does it imply lack of comprehension or skills in patients and families. The message is delivered, but not always in language that is readily understandable. While the message may be received, at times it is not comprehended due to the nature of the message or the emotional state of the recipient.

A few years ago, during a conversation about end-of-life care, a nurse shared with the author a situation she had encountered. The patient, an elderly female, had undergone a biopsy of a tumor. The physician, upon receiving the biopsy report, asked the nurse to accompany him to the patient's room to deliver the results. The patient was told "the results of the biopsy indicate that the tumor was not benign, so I am going to refer you to Dr. ***, an oncologist, for further treatment." The physician asked for questions from the patient and, receiving none, left the room. The patient then got on the phone, called her family and stated: "Good news, I don't have cancer." The nurse left the room and called the physician, who expressed surprise that the patient had misunderstood the message. Reluctantly, he returned to the patient's room and in sim-

ple terms told her that she did indeed have cancer and that Dr. *** was a cancer specialist who would discuss treatment options with her and her family. Did the physician, on the first visit, tell the patient she had cancer—of course. Did the patient receive the message—unfortunately, no.

Although anecdotal, the case demonstrates a situation in which there was poor communication. Had the nurse not intervened, how long would it have been before the patient was adequately apprised of her condition?

Because quality communication with patients and families is imperative, the dilemma deserves attention. Many articles have been written, discussing optimal times, situations and environments best suited for end-of-life care discussions. Unfortunately, end-of-life does not always arrive on schedule or as planned.

Because of the severity of some illnesses, intensive care units may be the environment where the futility of further care becomes apparent. Intensive care units are busy places, sometimes crowded, and replete with a variety of alarms and mechanical noises on a continual basis. About 50 percent of patients who die in a hospital are cared for in an intensive care unit within three days of their death. Over thirty percent spend at least ten days of final hospitalization in an intensive care unit.[7] This is a particularly sobering reality for patients with chronic lung disease. Many COPD patients have had serious exacerbations, have been admitted to intensive care units, and many have been on mechanical ventilation. Fortunately, the medications, therapeutic interventions, and disease management skills of physicians and therapists often can turn the exacerbation around. Unfortunately, the airway pathology may not be reversible.

How and when and with whom should communication about the gravity of a situation be handled? Ideally, it should occur prior to any crisis; realistically, when it becomes obvious that a patient is unlikely to survive. Regardless of the answer, effective communication is vitally important.

Because few intensive care unit (ICU) patients (less than 5%) are able to communicate with the health care providers caring for them at the time that withholding/withdrawing life support decisions are made,[8] there is a real need to share information with and seek input from the family.

A recent article published as a supplement to *Critical Care Medicine* reviewed the importance of talking with families about end-of-life care. Although few studies provide hard evidence on how best to initiate end-of-life discussions in an ICU environment, Curtis, et al[9] provides a framework that could serve as a model for clinicians and families alike. The proposed components of the conference would include: preparation prior to the conference, holding the conference, and finishing the conference.[9]

Preparing in Advance of the ICU-Family Conference

It is important for the participating clinician to be informed about the disease process of the patient, including: diagnosis, prognosis, treatment options, and probably outcomes of various treatments. It is important also for the clinician to identify areas of uncertainty or inconsistencies concerning the diagnosis, prognosis, or potential treatments. Any disagreements between sub-specialists involved in the care of the patient should be resolved before the family conference. Additionally, in preparing for the family conference, it is advantageous for the clinician to have some familiarity with the attitudes of the family and the patient toward illness, life-extending therapy, and death. When possible, the determination of who will attend the conference should be done advance of the conference. The location of the conference should also be pre-determined: a quiet private setting, with adequate comfortable seating is ideal. Asking all participants to turn off cell phones and pagers is appropriate and will prevent unwanted distraction. (If the patient is able to participate in the conference but is too ill to leave the ICU, then the conference should take place in the patient's room in the ICU.)

Holding the ICU Family-Conference About End-of-Life Care

Assuring that all participants are introduced and understand the reason for the conference will facilitate the process. It is also helpful to discuss conference goals and determine what the patient and his or her family understand about the prognosis. If the patient is unable to participate in the conference, it may be opportune to pose the question: "What would the patient want?" Explaining during the conference that withholding life-sustaining treatment is not withholding care is an important distinction. Another recommended approach to achieve concord in the conference is to tolerate silence. Giving the family time to absorb any information they have just received, and allowing them to formulate questions, will result in better and more goal-oriented discussions. When families are able to communicate the fears and emotions they may have, they are better able to cope with difficult decisions.

Finishing the Conference

After the patient and/or family have been provided with the facts and have achieved an understanding of the disease and the treatment issues, the clinician should make recommendations regarding treatment options. It is a disservice, for example, to give family members the impression that they are single-handedly making the decision to "pull the plug" on a loved on. Soliciting any follow-up questions, allowing adequate time, and making sure the family knows how to reach you, should end the conference on a positive note.

Understanding Choices

Another commonly encountered dilemma in terminal care is the number of choices involved, as well as the medical terminology that sometimes mystifies the choices. Advanced directives, living wills, health care proxies, durable powers of attorney for health care; what they are, what they mean, how much weight they carry, are they honored, and does everyone who needs them have them? Not long ago during a conversation with a chaplain at a hospital, the advice shared with me—to pass on to

others—was to give family members the gift of knowledge. The final gift you give them may be the most important gift of all. Let them know your wishes.

When advanced directives became available in the late 1980's, it was presumed that the document would solve all the problems and that terminal care would adhere to the patient's wishes. The Study to Understand Prognoses and Preferences for Outcomes and Risks of Treatment (SUPPORT), initiated in 1988, however, showed severe shortcomings in end-of-life care.[10]

Advanced directives, as a legal document, have not necessarily lived up to expectations. A viable option is a Durable Power of Attorney for Health Care, in which a trusted individual is designated to make health care decisions when the patient cannot.

Another option is to have advanced planning sessions with family members. If the patient and his or her family can come to consensus about terminal care in advance, and the doctor is in agreement with any decisions, unnecessary suffering probably can be avoided. (When death becomes imminent and the patient's wishes are not followed, waste no time in seeking a meeting with the hospital ethics committee.)

Adaptive Techniques

There is no "recipe" that, if followed precisely, will allow for the successful navigation of all potential dilemmas. There is no way to prepare for each eventuality that accompanies terminal illness and death. Knowledge remains the safest shield against well-meaning advice-givers. Asking questions of caregivers is the best defense against misunderstanding and mismanagement of the patient.

The University of Iowa Research Center is working on an evidence-based protocol for advanced directives, which outlines in a step-by-step fashion assessment criteria that factor in the patient's age, primary language, and mental capacity for making health care treatment decisions. The protocol also provides a check-list format for health care providers, the documentation thereof is easily accessible and in a prominent position in the patient's chart.[11]

Another alternative health care benefit being proposed is called MediCaring, which emphasizes more home-based and supportive health care and discourages hospitalization and use of aggressive treatment.[12] While not specifically aimed at solving end-of-life care issues, there may be parts of MediCaring that mesh well with terminal care of the oldest old.

Whether in a home setting, a community hospital or an intensive care unit, terminal care can result in moral, ethical, economic, religious, cultural and/or personal/family conflict. Even when death is universally accepted as a normal part of the life cycle, there will be emotional dilemmas to navigate around. Additional education and research initiatives, however, may result in increased awareness that this currently is an unsolved problem, for the patient, the family, and the health care providers. Notwithstanding, however, the medical community should continue to persevere in trying to understand patients' and families' fears and needs, the need for quality communication with questions and answers in lay vocabulary. The clinician's task is to balance communication and understanding with medical delivery.

References

1. Thorson JA. *Aging in a Changing Society*, 2000. 2nd Ed. Taylor & Francis, Philadelphia, PA.

2. Thorson JA & Powell FC. Meaning of death and intrinsic religiosity. *Journal of Clinical Psychology*. 1990;46: 379-391.

3. Thorson JA & Powell FC. Elements of death anxiety and meanings of death. *Journal of Clinical Psychology*. 1998;44: 691-701.

4. Lynn J. Serving patients who may die soon and their families. *JAMA*. 2001;285(7): 925–932.

5. Pantilat SZ, Alpers A, Wachter RM. A new doctor in the house: ethical issues in hospitalist systems. *JAMA*. 1999;282: 171-174.

6. Fins JJ & Soloman MZ. Communication in the intensive care setting: The challenge of futility disputes. *Critical Care Medicine*: 2001;29(2) Supplement.

7. Quill TE & Brody H. Physician recommendations and patient autonomy: Finding a balance between physician power and patient choice. *Ann Internal Med*. 1996;25: 763-769.

8. Prendergast T.J. & Luce JM. Increasing incidence of withholding and withdrawal of life support from the critically ill. *Am J Respir Crit Care Med*. 1997;155: 15-20.

9. Curtis JR et al. The family conference as a focus to improve communication about end-of-life care in the intensive care unit: Opportunities for improvement. *Critical Care Medicine*. 2001;29(2) Supplement. PN26-N33.

10. Pioneer Programs in Palliative Care: Nine Case Studies (2000). The Robert Wood Johnson Foundation in cooperation with the Milbank Memorial Fund, New York, NY.

11. Evidence-based protocol: Advanced Directives. Iowa City, IA: University of Iowa Gerontological Nursing Interventions Research Center. 1999 .
Available; [http://www.guideline.gov/index.asp].

12. Lynn. J. et al. MediCaring: development and test marketing of a supportive care benefit for older people. *Journal of the American Geriatric Society*. 1999;47(9) 1058-1064.

HELEN SORENSON, Assistant Professor, Department of Respiratory Care, University of Texas Health Science Center at San Antonio in San Antonio, Texas. Ms. Sorenson is also Managing Editor of "Emphysema/COPD: The Journal of Patient Centered Care."

Index

Index

Test Your Knowledge Form

We encourage you to photocopy and use this page as a tool to assess how the articles in *Annual Editions* expand on the information in your textbook. By reflecting on the articles you will gain enhanced text information. You can also access this useful form on a product's book support Web site at *http://www.mhcls.com/online/*.

NAME:

DATE:

TITLE AND NUMBER OF ARTICLE:

BRIEFLY STATE THE MAIN IDEA OF THIS ARTICLE:

LIST THREE IMPORTANT FACTS THAT THE AUTHOR USES TO SUPPORT THE MAIN IDEA:

WHAT INFORMATION OR IDEAS DISCUSSED IN THIS ARTICLE ARE ALSO DISCUSSED IN YOUR TEXTBOOK OR OTHER READINGS THAT YOU HAVE DONE? LIST THE TEXTBOOK CHAPTERS AND PAGE NUMBERS:

LIST ANY EXAMPLES OF BIAS OR FAULTY REASONING THAT YOU FOUND IN THE ARTICLE:

LIST ANY NEW TERMS/CONCEPTS THAT WERE DISCUSSED IN THE ARTICLE, AND WRITE A SHORT DEFINITION:

We Want Your Advice

ANNUAL EDITIONS revisions depend on two major opinion sources: one is our Advisory Board, listed in the front of this volume, which works with us in scanning the thousands of articles published in the public press each year; the other is you—the person actually using the book. Please help us and the users of the next edition by completing the prepaid article rating form on this page and returning it to us. Thank you for your help!

ANNUAL EDITIONS: Human Development 07/08

ARTICLE RATING FORM

Here is an opportunity for you to have direct input into the next revision of this volume.
We would like you to rate each of the articles listed below, using the following scale:

1. **Excellent: should definitely be retained**
2. **Above average: should probably be retained**
3. **Below average: should probably be deleted**
4. **Poor: should definitely be deleted**

Your ratings will play a vital part in the next revision.
Please mail this prepaid form to us as soon as possible.
Thanks for your help!

RATING	ARTICLE	RATING	ARTICLE
	1. The Identity Dance		22. The Blank Slate
	2. The Power to Divide		23. The Power of No
	3. The Age of Genetic Technology Arrives		24. Parents Behaving Badly
	4. Brave New Babies		25. Where Personality Goes Awry
	5. Inside the Womb		26. When Cultures Clash
	6. The Mystery of Fetal Life: Secrets of the Womb		27. *Brown v. Board*: A Dream Deferred
	7. The Smallest Patients		28. What Makes Teens Tick
	8. Four Things You Need to Know About Raising Baby		29. A Peaceful Adolescence
	9. Who's Raising Baby?		30. Jail Time Is Learning Time
	10. Reading Your Baby's Mind		31. Hello to College Joys: Keep Stress Off Campus
	11. 20 Ways to Boost Your Baby's Brain Power		32. How Spirit Blooms
	12. Long-Term Studies of Preschool: Lasting Benefits Far Outweigh Costs		33. The Battle for Your Brain
	13. Guilt Free TV		34. Grow Up? Not So Fast
	14. Raising a Moral Child		35. Emotions and the Brain: Laughter
	15. A Time and a Place for Authentic Learning		36. Alcohol's Deadly Triple Threat
	16. The New Science of Dyslexia		37. How AIDS Changed America
	17. The Trouble with Boys		38. The Myth of the Midlife Crisis
	18. Why We Need "The Year of Languages"		39. Aging Naturally
	19. Failing Our Children: No Child Left Behind Undermines Quality and Equity in Education		40. When Your Paycheck Stops
	20. The Power of Teaching Students Using Strengths		41. Secrets of the Centenarians
	21. Raising Happy Achieving Children in the New Millennium		42. Lost & Found
			43. Navigating Practical Dilemmas in Terminal Care

BUSINESS REPLY MAIL
FIRST CLASS MAIL PERMIT NO. 551 DUBUQUE IA

POSTAGE WILL BE PAID BY ADDRESEE

McGraw-Hill Contemporary Learning Series
2460 KERPER BLVD
DUBUQUE, IA 52001-9902

NO POSTAGE
NECESSARY
IF MAILED
IN THE
UNITED STATES

ABOUT YOU

Name   Date
_____   _____

Are you a teacher? ☐   A student? ☐
Your school's name
_____

Department
_____

Address   City   State   Zip
_____

School telephone #
_____

YOUR COMMENTS ARE IMPORTANT TO US!

Please fill in the following information:
For which course did you use this book?
_____

Did you use a text with this ANNUAL EDITION?   ☐ yes ☐ no
What was the title of the text?
_____

What are your general reactions to the *Annual Editions* concept?
_____

Have you read any pertinent articles recently that you think should be included in the next edition? Explain.
_____

Are there any articles that you feel should be replaced in the next edition? Why?
_____

Are there any World Wide Web sites that you feel should be included in the next edition? Please annotate.
_____

May we contact you for editorial input?   ☐ yes ☐ no
May we quote your comments?   ☐ yes ☐ no